KT-153-638

INSIGHT GUIDES

MalaYSIa

Discovery
CHANNEL

APA PUBLICATIONS
Part of the Langenscheidt Publishing Group

![INSIGHT GUIDE]

Malaysia

Editorial
Project Editor
Francis Dorai
Editorial Director
Brian Bell

Distribution
UK & Ireland
GeoCenter International Ltd
The Viables Centre, Harrow Way
Basingstoke, Hants RG22 4BJ
Fax: (44) 1256-817988

United States
Langenscheidt Publishers, Inc.
36–36 33rd Street 4th Floor
Long Island City, NY 11106
Fax: (1 718) 784-0640

Australia
Universal Publishers
1 Waterloo Road
Macquarie Park, NSW 2113
Fax: (61 2) 9888-9074

New Zealand
Hema Maps New Zealand Ltd (HNZ)
Unit D, 24 Ra ORA Drive
East Tamaki, Auckland
Fax: (64 9) 273-6479

Worldwide
Apa Publications GmbH & Co.
Verlag KG (Singapore branch)
38 Joo Koon Road, Singapore 628990
Tel: (65) 6865-1600; Fax: (65) 6861-6438

Printing
Insight Print Services (Pte) Ltd
38 Joo Koon Road, Singapore 628990
Tel: (65) 6865-1600; Fax: (65) 6861-6438

©2006 Apa Publications GmbH & Co.
Verlag KG (Singapore branch)
All Rights Reserved
First Edition 1972
Eighteenth Edition 2000
Updated 2005 (Reprinted 2006)

CONTACTING THE EDITORS
We would appreciate it if readers
would alert us to errors or out-
dated information by writing to:
Insight Guides, P.O. Box 7910,
London SE1 1WE, England.
Fax: (44 20) 7403-0290.
insight@apaguide.co.uk

NO part of this book may be reproduced,
stored in a retrieval system or transmitted
in any form or means electronic, mech-
anical, photocopying, recording or otherwise, without prior written permission of
Apa Publications. Brief text quotations
with use of photographs are exempted
for book review purposes only. Information has been obtained from sources
believed to be reliable, but its accuracy
and completeness, and the opinions
based thereon, are not guaranteed.

www.insightguides.com
in North America:
www.insighttravelguides.com

ABOUT THIS BOOK

The first Insight Guide pioneered the use of creative full-colour photography in travel guides in 1970. Since then, we have expanded our range to cater for our readers' need not only for reliable information about their chosen destination but also for a real understanding of the culture and workings of that destination. Now, when the Internet can supply inexhaustible – but not always reliable – facts, our books marry text and pictures to provide those much more elusive qualities: knowl-edge and discernment. To achieve this, they rely heavily on the authority of locally based writers and photographers.

How to use this book
The book is carefully structured to convey an understanding of Malaysia and its culture, and to guide readers through its diverse range of sights and attractions:

◆ The **Features** section, with a yellow colour bar, covers the country's history and culture in authoritative essays.

◆ The main **Places** section, with a blue bar, is a complete guide to all the sights and areas worth visiting. Places of special interest are cross-referenced by numbers or letters to specially commissioned full-colour maps.

◆ The **Travel Tips** listings, with an orange bar, provides information on travel, hotels, restaurants and other practical aspects of the country. Information can be located using the index printed on the back cover flap.

The contributors

Apart from the usual tourist stomping grounds, this new 18th edition covers exciting new sights in both Peninsular Malaysia and the Borneo states of Sarawak and Sabah. Supervised by Singapore-based managing editor **Francis Dorai**, the book was completely restructured, building on the earlier edition put together by **Jessamym Cheam-Gwynne**.

Updating the history chapters and writing new essays on contemporary politics and religion was **Desmond Tate**, author of several books on Malaysian history. Malaysian Nature Society managing editor **Gail Saari** revised the environment chapter. Practising architect **Puvan J. Selvanathan** wrote the piece on architecture. The Insight On picture stories were largely the work of **Wendy Moore**, who also wrote the arts and crafts essay.

In the Places section, Peninsular Malaysia was updated by Kuala Lumpur-based freelance journalist **Siew-Lyn Wong**, who also wrote the piece on adventure sports and the new Travel Tips section; Sabah and Sarawak were handled by veteran photojournalist **Jill Gocher**.

New photography was provided by **HBL Network**, **Arthur Teng**, **R. Mohd Noh** and **Jill Gocher**.

In 2005, the guide was updated with the help of Kuala Lumpur-based **Fong Peng Khuan** and Sabah-based **Wendy Hutton**.

This edition retains material from previous editions, largely the work of writers **Star Black**, **Harold Stephens**, **Sharifah Hamzah**, **Marcus Brooke**, **Susan Amy**, **Joseph Yogerst** and **Jeremy Cheam**. The copy was edited by **Tim Harrison** and indexed by **Hilary Cooper**.

Map Legend

─ ∙ ─ ∙ ─	International Boundary
─ ─ ─ ─	State Boundary
⊖	Border Crossing
─ ∙ ─ ∙ ─	National Park/Reserve
─ ─ ─ ─	Ferry Route
✈ ✈	Airport: International/Regional
🚌	Bus Station
P	Parking
❶	Tourist Information
✉	Post Office
✝ ✝	Church/Ruins
✝	Monastery
☾	Mosque
✡	Synagogue
⛫	Castle/Ruins
∴	Archaeological Site
∩	Cave
⚊	Statue/Monument
★	Place of Interest

The main places of interest in the Places section are coordinated by number with a full-colour map (e.g. ❶), and a symbol at the top of every right-hand page tells you where to find the map.

INSIGHT GUIDE

Malaysia

CONTENTS

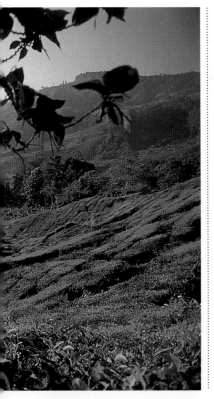

Lush tea plantations of Cameron Highlands in the morning light

Insight on ...

Information panels

Travel Tips

◆ **Full Travel Tips Index is on page 345**

Places

A PALETTE OF IMAGES

Blending millennia-old rainforests with high-tech skyscrapers,
Malaysia will astound the most jaded of travellers

Selamat Datang ke Malaysia – "Welcome to Malaysia" – is perhaps the first sign you'll see walking past the cool steel and glass corridors of the gleaming Kuala Lumpur International Airport (KLIA). It is a sentiment that will be warmly echoed by the smiling Malay, Indian or Chinese taxi driver who takes you from the airport into the booming capital of Kuala Lumpur. Even if you enter Malaysia by road and arrive first at a small Malay *kampung* (village), this same friendly greeting will be warmly offered.

Over the centuries, Malaysia has been open to millions of visitors from all over the globe, and its people have changed, absorbed and adapted customs and traditions from far-flung countries to suit the Malaysian way of life.

What is the most accurate image of the country? Travel brochures depict a romantic land of beaches with coconut palms, lost idyllic islands and amazing coral reefs. Somerset Maugham's short stories paint vivid pictures of colonial bungalows set in rubber plantations, while naturalist Alfred Russel Wallace's *Malay Archipelago* conjures up pictures of ancient jungles, screaming with monkeys and orang-utans, and brimming with butterflies. Yet, given the publicity Malaysia has enjoyed in recent years (thanks partly to the strident proclamations of its former prime minister Dr Mahathir Mohamad), the media would have us believe that the country is grooming itself to become the next Asian metropolis with big-ticket projects like the Petronas Twin Towers, the world's tallest pair of buildings, and the Multimedia Super Corridor IT project. These images are far from contradictory; indeed, Malaysia combines, album-like, every one of these visions – and more.

In Malaysia, you may find yourself in many incongruously different scenarios: from bopping at a ritzy Kuala Lumpur nightclub and visiting Malay *kampung* on the east coast to tramping millennia-old rainforests in Pahang and visiting tribes once known for their headhunting exploits in Borneo. And, there's adventure too, everything from climbing to the clouds on Mount Kinabalu to scuba diving at world-famous Sipadan island.

Some of the country's secrets will be unlocked from the pages of this guide; others are waiting to be discovered. You will find those idyllic beaches and islands, those rubber plantations (with the *punkah wallah* replaced by air-conditioning) and you will, if you venture out, find yourself in age-old jungles. But, no matter how strange the sights are to you, there is an innate sense of being in a land that welcomes you – Malaysia beckons, as it has done for countless centuries. ❑

PRECEDING PAGES: a *gasing*, or top spinner from Kelantan; ancient burial poles of Sarawak; Malaysian boys in their traditional finery; patriotic Malaysians at the opening of the 1998 Commonwealth Games.
LEFT: KL's Petronas Towers lays claim to fame as the world's tallest twin buildings.

Decisive Dates

THE EARLY CENTURIES

c.40,000 BC Earliest known habitation at Niah Caves, Sarawak. Remains of a palaeolithic stone-tool workshop at Kota Tampan, Perak, could be even older.

c.2,500 BC Proto-Malays spread south from Yunnan area in China.

c.300 BC Earliest signs of Bronze and Iron Age cultures in Malaysia.

c.200 BC Start of trade with India and China.

100 BC–AD 200 Emergence of trading kingdoms in the Isthmus of Kra.

AD 500–1000 Development of Hindu-Buddhist trading kingdoms in Kedah's Bujang Valley, northern Perak and Santubong, Sarawak.

1303 Terengganu Stone records introduction of Islam to the Malay Peninsula.

THE RISE OF MELAKA

c.1400 Founding of Melaka by Parameswara.

1409 Chinese Admiral Cheng Ho arrives in Melaka.

1411 Parameswara converts to Islam and meets Ming Emperor of China.

1446 Melaka expands under Sultan Muzaffar Shah.

c.1456–98 Tun Perak serves as prime minister under four sultans and Melaka becomes biggest empire in Southeast Asia.

1511 Melaka falls to the Portuguese.

1512 Melaka's deposed sultan sets up new capital in Riau-Lingga which later becomes Sultanate of Johor.

1528 Sultan Muzaffar Shah starts the Perak Kingdom.

1641 The Dutch take Melaka from the Portuguese; start of Dutch dominance in the area.

1699 Assassination of Sultan Mahmud of Johor.

1699–1819 Empire of Johor, mostly at Riau, under Bendahara line.

1699–1784 Period of Minangkabau-Bugis struggle for domination of the Straits of Melaka.

1726 First sultan of Terengganu Kingdom installed.

1784 Death of Raja Haji at Melaka; Dutch break Bugis power in area.

1786 The British occupy Penang.

1812 Death of Sultan Mahmud Shah, last ruler of united Johor-Riau Kingdom.

COLONIAL MALAYA

1819 British occupy Singapore.

1824 Anglo-Dutch Treaty carves up Malay world into colonial spheres: Dutch cede Melaka to British and keeps Riau.

1826 Singapore, Melaka, Penang and Province Wellesley become Straits Settlements under British control.

1831–32 Melaka Malays rebel against British in Naning War.

1840s The importance of tin increases, bringing an influx of Chinese tin miners to the western coast.

1841 James Brooke established as Rajah of Sarawak.

1846 British annex the island of Labuan.

1858–68 Civil war in Pahang.

1867–74 Selangor civil war.

1874 Pangkor Treaty signals start of British intervention in Perak, Selangor and Negeri Sembilan.

1875–76 Perak War signals uprising against British after introduction of controversial tax and subsequent murder of British Resident.

1881 British North Borneo Chartered Company establishes a centre in North Borneo, now Sabah.

1891–95 Pahang Rebellion.

1895–1905 Mat Salleh Rebellion. The introduction of new taxes had earlier created general discontent, and Mat Salleh gathers many supporters in his revolt against the North Borneo Company.

1896 Federated Malay States (FMS) are created.

1909 Treaty of Bangkok transfers four northern Malay states from Thai sovereignty to British control.

1914 Johor brought under British control.

1914–18 World War I.

1920–41 British adopt decentralisation policy in FMS; early signs of a Malay nationalism against British rule begin to surface.

MALAYA, MERDEKA, MALAYSIA

1941–45 Japanese conquest and occupation.

1945 British reoccupy Malaysia.

1946 Malayan Union scheme introduced but is opposed; formation of United Malay National Organisation (UMNO); Sarawak and British North Borneo become Crown colonies.

1948 Malayan Union scheme abandoned; Federation of Malaya inaugurated.

1948–60 Communist uprising – The Emergency.

1952 Municipal elections in Kuala Lumpur; UMNO and Malayan Chinese Association (MCA) parties cooperate.

1953 Alliance coalition comprising UMNO, MCA and Malayan Indian Congress (MIC) formed.

1955 First general elections in the peninsula; landslide win for the Alliance.

1956 Tunku Abdul Rahman leads Merdeka Mission to London to negotiate for independence.

1957 Malaya becomes independent, and the Union Jack is lowered for the last time.

1960 The state of emergency ends.

POST-INDEPENDENCE

1961 Tunku proposes a political association – called Malaysia – that would include Malaya, Singapore, North Borneo, Sarawak and Brunei.

1963 Creation of Malaysia without Brunei.

1963–66 Confrontation with Indonesia. In 1966, Indonesia's Sukarno is ousted; new Indonesian government led by Suharto ends confrontation. Philippines drops its claim on Sabah and recognises Malaysia.

1965 Singapore leaves Malaysia and becomes an independent nation.

1969 Riots in the wake of the general elections on 13 May are the result of racial tension between Malays and Chinese. Violent outbreaks, mainly in Kuala Lumpur, in which hundreds are killed.

1970 New Economic Policy (NEP) established to encourage fairer distribution of wealth among races.

1981 Malaysia's fourth prime minister, Dato' Seri Dr Mahathir Mohamad, takes office.

1983 Constitutional crisis involving the position of Malaysia's hereditary rulers.

1987 UMNO racked by power struggle between Mahathir Mohamad and Tengku Razaleigh Hamzah; "Operation Lallang" carried out by the Mahathir administration results in detention of prominent opposition politicians, trade unionists, educators and community leaders.

1988 UMNO *Baru* (New UMNO) is formed by Mahathir .

PRECEDING PAGES: Selangor royalty, circa 1874.
LEFT: Sultan Abu Bakar of Johor.
RIGHT: new prime minister, Abdullah Ahmad Badawi.

1989 Semangat '46, led by Tengku Razaleigh Hamzah, registered as a new political party. The Communist Party of Malaysia abandons its 41-year armed struggle to overthrow the Malaysian government.

1990 General elections – the ruling coalition retains its two-third majority in Parliament.

1990s National car project, Proton, leads the move to transform Malaysia into fully-developed nation.

1997 Petronas Towers, the world's tallest twin buildings, open. Economic downturn as ringgit plummets and currency control laws are imposed to stop its free fall.

1998 Kuala Lumpur is first Asian city to host the Commonwealth Games. Dismissal of Deputy Prime Minister Anwar Ibrahim from office and his subsequent

arrest creates a political crisis. *Reformasi* movement begins with mass demonstrations in support of Anwar.

1999 Anwar Ibrahim is given a six-year jail term for corruption and is further tried for sodomy. Snap general elections sees ruling coalition retain two-thirds majority, but Malay-dominated states swing to opposition with PAS (Islamic party) taking Terengganu and Kelantan.

2000 Anwar sentenced to additional six year's jail.

2003 Malaysia's longest-serving prime minister Mahathir Mohamad retires. He is replaced by his deputy Datuk Seri Abdullah Ahmad Badawi.

2004 In a ringing endorsement for the moderate and consensus-seeking Badawi, the ruling Barisan coalition wins the elections by a landslide victory, with PAS-controlled Terengganu returning to the government. ❏

BEGINNINGS

Malaysia's ancient history is shrouded in myth, but its ideal position as a port brought rapid development. And with trade came mighty empires

Gentle, young and growing – Malaysia is all this. But peel away the surface layer of modernity, and the kaleidoscope of Malaysia's history unfolds. The beginnings of human settlement go back at least as far as 40,000 years, with a diverse cast of Malays, Ibans and Bidayuhs, Kadazandusuns and Muruts, Chinese, Indians, Europeans and other races. And the land's rich architectural history has borne an abundance of megaliths, ancient inscriptions, traces of Buddhist temples, abandoned forts, medieval mosques, and neo-classical colonial buildings.

Prehistoric Malaysia

The story of human habitation in Malaysia is enveloped in shadows as deep as those cast by the equatorial rainforest. What we know is pieced together from archaeological discoveries and ancient Indian, Chinese and Arab texts. However, these origins are still rife with unexplained mysteries and are hotly debated.

A *Homo sapiens* skull discovered in Sarawak's Niah Caves, and believed to date from 40,000 BC, provides the earliest evidence of human life in Malaysia. In the Malay Peninsula, the discovery of a stone-tool workshop in Kota Tampan, Perak, dates back to 34,000 years ago or even earlier, while the earliest skeletal remains found are at least 10,000 years old. The evidence indicates that these people were Mesolithic (Middle Stone Age) hunters and shifting cultivators. They lived in rock shelters and caves in the limestone hills of the peninsula and used stone implements for cutting and grinding, as well as for hunting wild animals. These people may have been the ancestors of the Negrito aborigines (Orang Asli) or of their successors, the Senoi.

Around 2,500 BC, the Proto-Malays, spreading south from Yunnan in China, made their way to the Malay Peninsula and the islands beyond. These were the Neolithic people, their

LEFT: ancient megalith at Negeri Sembilan.
RIGHT: Orang Asli family, the original inhabitants.

implements more sophisticated than those of the Negritos or Senoi. As well as hunters, they were also cultivators and sailors and thus lived a more settled life. Eventually they forced the Negritos and Senoi into the hills and jungles of the interior of the peninsula.

Much later, around 300 BC, a new wave of

immigrants, also of Malay stock pushed the Proto-Malays inland. Called Deutero-Malays by anthropologists, these were Iron Age and Bronze Age people, who used metal for their weapons and tools. The Deutero-Malays are in fact the direct ancestors of today's Malays in the peninsula and the archipelago.

Through trade, the early inhabitants of the Malay Peninsula were exposed to older civilisations. The peninsula's location (including the Isthmus of Kra above it) interrupted direct sailing on the main sea route between east and west and the area was affected by nature's arrangement of alternating monsoons – southwesterly followed by northeasterly. These factors made it the natural meeting point for Indian and Chinese traders to exchange their wares. These foreign traders also came to buy the produce of the region itself, such as gold – the Malay Peninsula was known to early geographers as "the Golden Chersonese" – aromatic woods, spices, and as far as the Chinese were concerned, birds' nests, highly prized for making revitalising soups.

The first of these Indian and Chinese trading voyages are believed to have taken place in prehistoric times and by the beginning of the Christian era, the trade routes were already well established. Convenient ports of call soon

The Indian period

Some settlements eventually grew to become kingdoms in which various features of Indian culture were adopted. The local rulers were known as *rajah*, and Brahmin rituals dominated royal courts. Even today, this early Indian influence can still be seen. Many Malay words are derived from Sanskrit, and some Malay social customs, especially wedding rites, reflect Hindu customs. So deep was this impact on local Malay society that the 1,500 years of Malaysian history between the arrival of the first Indians and the coming of Islam is called the Hindu or Indian period.

sprung up, which would later become the nuclei for other minor states.

Trade with China was as valuable as that with India. But the Chinese traders kept to themselves largely and were more interested in trade, thereby making little impression on local Malay culture. But a good number of the Indian traders settled down and integrated with the local inhabitants. As a result, many of the settlements along the straits were influenced by Indian ideas and resulted in many local Malays becoming Hindus or Buddhists. These new converts built temples, traces of which are still visible in the Bujang Valley, Kedah, and Santubong in Sarawak.

The fame and fortunes of the Indianised kingdoms of the region depended entirely on their success in dominating the trade routes passing by their shores. Monopoly was the name of the game, and the port-kingdom which could secure the widest control over international and local trade by attracting foreign traders to its harbour was the winner, and thereby evolved into a maritime empire.

The first of these empires was Funan, based on the Mekong Delta. Next was Sri Vijaya, which from its base at Palembang in Sumatra, dominated the trade of the Straits of Melaka for the best part of a thousand years. In the 14th century, it was the turn of the great Javanese empire of Majapahit to control the trade of the region. Then at the dawn of the 15th century came Melaka, the first maritime power to be based on the Malay Peninsula itself. It is with Melaka that the story of Malaysia truly begins.

The *Sejarah Melayu* or *Malay Annals*, was written in the early 1600s. Part historical fact and part legend, the text traces the transformation of a small coastal village into this famous trading empire. According to the *Malay Annals*, it all began on the island of Tumasek (now Singapore) at the tip of the

RAPID DEVELOPMENT

Parameswara founded Melaka with just a handful of followers; within just two years, the population had reached 2,000.

Taking a cue from this good omen, Parameswara decided to build a settlement on the site. As he happened to be standing near a melaka tree, he decided that the settlement should bear the name of that tree. The great port and kingdom of Melaka (or Malacca) came into being.

Parameswara and his followers cleared the land around it, planted rice and orchards, and exploited the rich tin deposits inland. News of the settlement's wealth spread, which soon began to attract passing traders.

Malay Peninsula, which at the time was ruled by a Palembang prince with the Hindu title of *Parameswara*. When Javanese forces attacked Tumasek, Parameswara and his followers were compelled to flee northward to Muar in Johor on the peninsula.

One day, when Parameswara was out hunting near the coast, one of his hounds was kicked by a white mousedeer. The king, always appreciative of valour, exclaimed, "This is a good place! Even the mousedeer are full of fight!"

LEFT: 9th-century Hindu temple in the Bujang Valley, Kedah, reflects the influence of Indian traders.
ABOVE: Melaka was once a bustling trading port.

Chinese protection

At this time, the Ming Emperor of China was sending out large fleets of ships to expand trade with Southeast Asia and beyond. In 1409, one of his most famous admirals, Cheng Ho, called at Melaka. He recognised Parameswara as its legitimate ruler, and at Parameswara's request, placed the new port under China's protection. In 1411, Cheng Ho took Parameswara back with him to China – a trip which confirmed Parameswara's status as a sovereign ruler owing fealty to China alone. These moves were very important for Melaka's survival, for the new port-state was under constant threat of Siamese attack.

Melaka was ideally placed as a port and emporium. It had an ideal position on the Straits of Melaka, astride the great east-west maritime trade route. It also had a fine harbour free of mangrove swamps and deep enough for the ships of the day, with waters sheltered from storms by the island of Sumatra.

Melaka's harbour soon became crowded with ships of all kinds, the streets of the city alive with merchants from all parts of Asia. Its bazaar was crammed with exotic goods: silks, brocades,

and porcelain from China; cloth, glassware and jewels from India; jade and diamonds from Burma; pepper, sandalwood, ebony and rice from the islands of the Malaysian/Indonesian archipelago, and tin, gold and other produce from Melaka's own hinterland.

An important reason for Melaka's success was its ability to ensure the safety of the traders who called there. Melaka's rulers commanded the allegiance of the Orang Laut, or sea gypsies, who managed to curb the pirate menace in the Straits of Melaka. In Melaka itself, *shahbandars* or harbourmasters, were appointed, each representing a particular community of traders. He watched over the daily affairs as

well as settling disagreements among the sailors and merchants in his group.

The first Muslims in Southeast Asia were Arab traders, who can be traced back as early as the 11th century. Marco Polo, the great Italian traveller, discovered a Muslim kingdom in North Sumatra at the end of the 13th century. From North Sumatra, Islam was introduced into Melaka which by the early 15th century had become a fully-fledged Muslim sultanate. Muslim Indian traders played a major role in this conversion and it was through trade that Islam spread to the other parts of the Malaysian/Indonesian world. At the same time, Islam became established wherever Melaka's own power as a maritime empire expanded. By the end of the 15th century, Melaka's empire included all the states of the Malay Peninsula and those on the east coast of Sumatra.

The other states' conversion to Islam was a total revolution for the Malays. Islam brought with it new ideas about government and encouraged literacy by reading the Koran and other Islamic texts. Being a missionary religion with a message for each individual, Islam gradually had a great impact on the values and outlook of ordinary people. At the same time, however, the Malays managed to retain or merge much of their pre-Islamic customs with the new religion.

Mighty power

Over a period of some 20 years, Melaka rose from obscurity to become one of the most powerful states in Southeast Asia. Its population at the zenith of its might was 40,000 – mainly Malays, but also including a large number of Javanese and other settlers from the region, as well as Indian and Chinese traders.

The city was located at the mouth of a river and was divided into two halves. The sultan's palace and the Malay *kampung* were south of the river, while on the north bank the houses and stores of the merchants provided the cosmopolitan bustle of the city. The two halves were linked by a bridge, on which, like the bridges of many medieval European cities, a number of merchants built their shops.

The palace was the centre of life. Peasants, traders and noblemen had the right to present their petitions to the sultans, in his *balai*, or

---

ARABIC ARRIVAL

Muslim traders brought Arabic script to Melaka – the Malay version is called *Jawi* – which replaced the ancient Indian script Melakans had used before.

audience hall. The sultan would sit on a raised platform, surrounded by richly embroidered cushions and flanked by his ministers, two or three steps below him.

The ruler's power was, in theory, absolute and the biggest crime was *derhaka* or disloyalty to him. This concept is well illustrated by the famous tale of Hang Tuah and Hang Jebat, two of the Sultan's most famous warriors, who were also good friends of one another. In an act of treachery intended to please a capricious sultan, Hang Tuah murdered his old friend Hang Jebat. The killer was regarded at the time to have acted correctly; loyalty to the ruler, right

Shapers of Melaka

Parameswara died in 1414, leaving behind him a prosperous trading port. When his grandson, Sri Maharaja, died in 1444, there was a power struggle in the court between Malay chiefs and their supporters who defended Hindu tradition, and a rival group of Malay chiefs who, with the backing of Indian Muslim merchants, favoured Islam. It centred on two rivals as heirs to the throne. In the end the Muslim party won.

Muzaffar Shah, the new ruler, declared Islam the state religion. An able man remembered for his code of laws, his reign saw the emergence of Tun Perak, who was to become the leading

or wrong, came above all else. The *Sejarah Melayu* is full of tales of Melakans who would sooner have killed their friends or relatives, or suffered in silence, than to have shown disloyalty to the sultan.

In his administration, the ruler was assisted by a *bendahara* (chief minister), a *temenggung* (chief of police), and a *laksamana* (admiral). Below them were the various titled nobles. The royalty, common people and traders abided by this system. Apparently, it worked for Melaka.

LEFT: Indian Muslim traders played a crucial role in the expansion of Islam.
ABOVE: a Dutch-built bridge over the Melaka River.

ROYAL PREROGATIVE

The power of the sultan and the royal family was emphasised by a series of special privileges and prohibitions. No commoner could wear yellow, the colour of royalty. White umbrellas were to be used only by rulers, and yellow umbrellas only by princes. And only royalty was allowed to wear gold anklets.

There were also strict rules on language, with special words reserved for royalty and denied to commoners. For example, the everyday Malay word for "to eat" was *makan*; the act of taking sustenance became *santap* when applied to royalty. And while commoners would merely sleep (*tidor*), a tired royal would regally *beradu*.

figure in Melakan politics for 42 years. He became the new *bendahara* in 1456, and in that year repelled a Siamese invasion.

During the reign of Sultan Mansor Shah, who succeeded Muzaffar Shah, Melaka reached the peak of its glory. Its expansion is largely attributed to Tun Perak's efforts, who built a formidable fighting force. He also honoured brave warriors with the title of *Hang*, or captain, including the bearers of such famous names in Melaka's history as Hang Tuah and Hang Jebat. Tun Perak's expeditions led to the conquest of most of the peninsular states as well as those on the Sumatran shore opposite.

Sultan Mansur Shah was succeeded by Sultan Alauddin Riayat Shah. He was probably the strongest and most efficient of Melaka's rulers and took a direct and active part in the administration, including – so the *Sejarah Melayu* tells us – walking the streets at night to check the enforcement of law and order. But his direct methods upset some of his high officials who felt that their own powers were being undermined, and made him many jealous enemies. After a reign of only 12 years, he died in mysterious circumstances, probably poisoned. Alauddin's successor, Sultan Mahmud, was a man of different mould. He was destined to lose Melaka to the Portuguese.

The invasion of the "Franks"

The 15th century was Portugal's age of discovery. The Portuguese had two basic reasons for their voyages of expansion to the far corners of the world. One was to continue their crusade against Islam, for had they not just liberated their own homeland from the Muslims? The second was to grab a slice of the lucrative trade in spices from Southeast Asia. Since that trade was virtually monopolised by Muslims, their two objectives conveniently merged into one. And there was also the fabled Christian kingdom of Prester John, believed to lie in Abyssinia which, if found, could prove a useful ally.

Spices were the most important commodity in the trade between Europe and Asia. Portugal wanted to divert the trade route via the Red Sea and the Mediterranean, which was monopolised by Muslim traders, to a new route around Africa's Cape of Good Hope. Melaka was one of their targets, as it was the collecting point for spices from the Moluccas (the Spice Islands). As the Portuguese writer, Barbosa, put it, "Whoever is Lord in Melaka has his hand on the throat of Venice", which was the European terminal and mart for spices at the time.

The Portuguese first arrived in Melaka in 1509. They sought permission to establish a trading post, but were rebuffed by Tun Mutahir, the *bendahara*, who – backed by the Indian Muslim traders – attempted to seize the Portuguese and their vessels. Warned by a Melakan woman, the Portuguese – whom the Malays had nicknamed the "Franks" – escaped, leaving 20 of their number behind. These men were taken prisoners, giving the Portuguese a good excuse to return in force. This took place in 1511, when a large Portuguese fleet, led by Alfonso D'Albuquerque, the architect of Portuguese expansion in Asia, attacked Melaka. The Portuguese concentrated their onslaught on the bridge over the river, where the Melakan defenders put up a courageous resistance. Even Sultan Mahmud and his son were in the thick of battle, riding on caparisoned elephants. Most foreign traders, however, were either apathetic or supported the Portuguese.

On 24 August 1511, Melaka fell and the sultan and his followers fled into the country. Melaka had lost its independence, and under a string of foreign rulers, it never regained its former days of glory.

D'Albuquerque set up a Portuguese administration and built a fort, calling it *A Famosa* ("The Famous"). Within its formidable walls, a medieval Portuguese-style city developed, with a town hall, offices and homes for the Portuguese civil servants, while locals and other workers lived outside the walls of the town.

The Portuguese set about restoring Melaka to its former status as the leading emporium in the region, a title it formerly enjoyed under its Malay rulers. They also tried to make Melaka a great centre

FORMIDABLE FORTRESS

The *A Famosa* fort, built by D'Albuquerque in the early 1500s, was so solidly constructed that no enemy managed to breach its walls for over 130 years.

fending off attacks from their Malay neighbours on all sides. In many cases, *A Famosa* proved to be the only saving factor. As for the attempts to proselytise, Catholicism did not appeal to the local population – least of all to the Muslims – and the Europeans' arrogance did not go down particularly well either.

Meanwhile, following his flight from Melaka, Sultan Mahmud had settled in Bintang in the Riau Archipelago. He made two unsuccessful attacks on Melaka, and died in 1528. His elder

for Catholic missionary work among the local population. St Francis Xavier, the well-known Catholic missionary, stayed in Melaka three times whilst spreading the Christian gospel.

But the Portuguese did not succeed in either direction. They attempted to obtain a monopoly of the spice trade by requiring all ships using the straits to obtain passes from them, and by imposing arbitrary duties at the port of Melaka. But such actions aroused strong anti-Portuguese feelings, and they found themselves

LEFT: the Portuguese first arrived in Melaka in 1509.
ABOVE: Alfonso D'Albuquerque led the Portuguese conquest of Melaka in 1511.

son established himself in Perak, while his younger son started a new sultanate in Johor, from where he too continued to harass Melaka periodically. Meanwhile, in North Sumatra, Aceh, with a growing monopoly over pepper, became an important local power. It launched attacks on its main rivals in the area – Melaka, Johor and other Malay states. This three-cornered contest for control over the trade of the Straits of Melaka dragged on throughout most the 16th century.

Later developments in Europe led to the arrival of the Dutch and the English in Southeast Asian waters. In 1594, the port of Lisbon, now the spice mart of Europe, was closed to

Dutch and English merchants, compelling them to go direct to the source of the spices and collect them for themselves. The Dutch trading companies combined to form the United East India Company (VOC) in 1602. The VOC's interests were primarily focused on the Moluccas. However, they considered control of Melaka necessary to complete their own monopoly over the spice and local trade of the region,

In 1640, after blockading the port of Melaka and bombarding *A Famosa*, the Dutch encircled the town. As the siege continued, the Portuguese garrison and the people trapped in the fort began to starve and were forced to eat

whatever came into sight – rats, dogs, cats and snakes. It was reported that a mother even ate her dead child. The acute hunger was aggravated by diseases such as malaria, typhoid and cholera. Finally, in 1641, after a seven-month siege, the Dutch forces stormed into *A Famosa* and fought on to victory.

The Dutch were much more powerful and efficient than the Portuguese and were able to establish a much more effective monopoly over the trade of the region, particularly in spices, which they rigidly enforced. Since they made Batavia (now Jakarta) their headquarters, Melaka declined in importance as a trading centre. But it was useful as a base from which to control the local trade (such as tin and pepper) of the Straits of Melaka.

The Malay world

Meanwhile, Johore and the other Malay states of the peninsula continued very much as they had always done, in spite of the Portuguese and then the Dutch presence in Melaka. The main effect of the European presence was to reduce the scope of their trade. The Dutch capture of Melaka put paid to the triangular contest for control of the straits between the Portuguese, the Acehnese and the Johoreans, because the trade of both Aceh and Johore suffered as a result of the Dutch monopoly. Johore was further weakened by a disastrous war with Jambi, one of its former vassals in Sumatra in the 1670s, and at the end of the century, the last of its rulers directly descended from the sultans of Melaka was assassinated.

The pattern of a triangular contest to control the trade of the Straits of Melaka was repeated during the 18th century, but the players were newcomers – the Bugis, traditional seafarers and mercenary warriors from Celebes; the Minangkabau, based on the Sumatran state of Siak; and the Dutch themselves in Melaka.

By the 1780s the Dutch had come out on top, but by this time Bugis "underkings" were in effective control of the Johor sultanate and had established an independent sultanate of their own in Selangor. The Minangkabau settlers in the hinterland of Melaka had also established an independent state of their own in the form of a federation called Negeri Sembilan (The Nine States). Of the rest of the peninsula states, Perak, Terengganu and Pahang still owed allegiance to the sultans of Johor but in practice ran their own affairs. In the north, Kelantan and Kedah had fallen within the orbit of the Thais of Bangkok.

As for what is today Malaysian Borneo, Sarawak was a province of the sultanate of Brunei, while Sabah was divided between Brunei and the Sultanate of Sulu, which dominated the northeastern part of the domain.

Such was the state of affairs when the British appeared on the scene in the form of Francis Light and founded a settlement on Penang Island in 1786. ❑

LEFT: *A Famosa* fort in Melaka still stands today.
RIGHT: a 17th-century Italian map of the peninsula.

COLONIAL MALAYA

Malaya's position as a trading nation continued to attract the attentions

of Europe's imperial powers, eager to exploit its wealth

The British first arrived in Southeast Asia in the early 17th century. But finding their trading opportunities stymied by their more powerful Dutch trading rivals, the British had concentrated their efforts on India instead.

The English East India Company (EIC) had, by parliamentary charter, been granted monopoly rights over all British trade with India and beyond. In the 200 years since their first unsuccessful forays into the region, the EIC had developed a very profitable trade with China, exchanging Bengal opium for Chinese tea. A base along the way would protect the trade and serve as collecting centre for straits produce.

Doing deals

The first step in the formation of the Straits Settlements occurred in 1785 when the Sultan of Kedah allowed the EIC to establish a base on the island of Penang. The sultan saw this as his chance to obtain protection against Siam, his northern enemy, and was prepared to grant trading rights to the British in exchange.

Francis Light, who had negotiated the agreement on behalf of the EIC, landed in Penang in 1786 and raised the Union Jack on the sparsely populated, jungle-smothered island. But Light's agreement with the Sultan of Kedah was based on false pretences. The sultan wanted British protection against his enemies but it soon became obvious that the EIC had no intention of providing this. The angry sultan assembled his ships to recapture Penang, but Light attacked first and destroyed the fleet. The resulting treaty guaranteed the sultan $6,000 a year, in return for which the EIC got Penang.

Penang was declared a free port, attracting merchant vessels from all over the east-west trade route. The population grew rapidly and Light followed the Malay and Dutch practice of appointing several *kapitan* – community leaders with authority to hear all minor crimes committed by members of their representative

communities. For major crimes, Light himself tried offenders with his rough and ready sense of justice. Penang prospered, but not as greatly as the EIC had hoped, for it proved to be a little too far up the Straits of Melaka to be a focal point of regional trade.

The second of the British settlements in the

straits was Singapore, occupied when the EIC's representative, Stamford Raffles, landed there in 1819. Raffles was a great imperialist and champion of free trade – which suited British commercial interests – and he was alarmed at Dutch attempts to restore their monopoly over regional trade. So Singapore was designed as a regional bastion of free trade, as well as a useful port of call on the China trade route. The territory was fully secured by treaty in 1824.

The last of the three main British settlements in the straits was Melaka itself. The British had already occupied Dutch-controlled Melaka on two occasions during the French Revolutionary and Napoleonic wars. The French had occu-

LEFT: James Brooke, first "White Rajah" of Sarawak.
RIGHT: Francis Light monument in Penang.

pied Holland, and the British were concerned that Melaka too might fall to them. The onset of peace saw the Dutch returning to Melaka in 1816, but only for a few years. In 1824, under the terms of the Anglo-Dutch Treaty of that year, which settled conflicting British and Dutch interests in the region, the British acquired Melaka in exchange for their Sumatran settlement of Bencoolen.

In 1826 Penang, Singapore and Melaka came together under one administration based in Singapore, and given the collective name of the Straits Settlements (SS). Singapore soon emerged as the most important. With its free port status and strategic position, Singapore became the new emporium, its harbour crowded with ships of all nations. By the 1850s, it was the leading port in the region and its trade further increased after the opening of the Suez Canal in 1869. Singapore soon became one of the greatest ports in the world.

Strictly speaking, the SS were concerned only with trade, and the British tried to stay out of the peninsula's other affairs. But this official policy of non-intervention was broken on a few occasions, generally in order to protect British trade from Thai interference in the northern Malay states.

ROGUISH RAFFLES

The way in which Stamford Raffles acquired Singapore was as devious as Light's dealings with the Sultan of Kedah over Penang. He took advantage of a succession dispute to the Johor throne, supporting the claim of Tengku Hussain against his rival in Riau who was actually in power but was unwilling to recognise the British. In the end, Hussain became recognised as Sultan of Johor while his rival became the Sultan of Riau. In return, Hussain, and the ruler of mainland Johor granted the British permission to set up their trading post in Singapore. The British gained full possession of Singapore by another treaty between the same parties in 1824.

British intervention

But there were murmurs of dissent from the merchants of the Straits Settlements. Many were growing restless with the policy of non-intervention. The Chinese had started to plant pepper in the neighbouring Malay states of Johor, and tapioca in Melaka and Negeri Sembilan. Prosperous straits merchants wanted similar opportunities for investment. But the biggest attraction was tin.

The Malay Peninsula had always been rich in tin, its ore mined and traded for centuries. In the mid-19th century, with the rise of the canning industry, demand for the metal shot up. SS merchants with money invested in the new mines of Selangor, Perak and Negeri Sembilan now campaigned for British intervention in these states to safeguard their interests.

The tin rush brought with it widespread unrest. Malay chiefs blessed with rich tin deposits in their domains became rich and powerful magnates whom the sultans could no longer control. Conflicting ambitions led to disputes and civil war. Even the Chinese miners who flocked into the tin districts were themselves divided between rival secret societies that constantly fought one

LOCAL GOVERNMENT?

The Straits Settlements were the responsibility of the British government in India until 1867; from then on they came under direct control from London.

nese miners of Larut on his ship off Pangkor Island. This resulted, in January 1874, in the signing of the Pangkor engagement, which settled a dispute over the throne of Perak, and imposed a British "Resident" on the new sultan whose advice had to "be asked and acted upon on all questions other than those touching Malay religion and custom". By August, Clarke had made a similar agreement with Selangor, and soon after that with Sungai Ujong, the largest of the Negeri Sembilan states.

another. These uncertainties threatened investments, and caused a drop in tin exports just as world demand began to exceed supply. The troubles also threatened to overflow into the SS. Meanwhile, British officials feared that if they did not intervene in these states, investors would seek assistance from a rival imperialist power, such as France or Germany.

A new governor, Andrew Clarke, was sent to sort out the situation. First, he met the Malay chiefs of Perak and the leaders of the rival Chi-

FAR LEFT: Stamford Raffles, founder of Singapore.
LEFT: painting of early 19th-century Penang.
ABOVE: British officials pose for the camera.

The residential system

Under the new system in these states, British residents were appointed only "to advise" the rulers on how to improve the administration of their states. However, control would ultimately rest with the resident, and the success of the system very much depended on how each resident exercised his power.

J. W. W. Birch was the first resident in Perak. Intolerant and tactless, with little regard for local customs and impatient for change, his proposed reforms of taxation and the banning of debt slavery threatened to undermine the social fabric of the state. The reforms were naturally opposed by the Perak chiefs and by the sultan himself. In response, in 1875 the governor ordered the state to be placed under the direct rule of British officials. Birch's attempt to put this new command into effect cost him his life. He was killed at Pasir Salak, a village on the Perak River.

Birch's eventual successor was Hugh Low, who took a different approach and laid the foundations for the effective working of the residential system. One of his innovations was the setting up of a state council. Its members included the

> ### THE BIG PAYBACK
>
> Debt slavery – mortgaging yourself to your creditors in return for financial help – was common practice in 19th-century Malaya. In bad times, it was the only way a peasant could raise finances.

port of the *Yam Tuan Besar* or head of the Negeri Sembilan federation and resorted to arms, but were easily defeated by superior British musketry. In the end the progress brought about by the residential system in Sungai Ujong finally won over the Yam Tuan and the heads of the other states of the Negeri Sembilan Federation. In 1895, they were joined by Sungai Ujong in one reunited state with a British resident and the Yam Tuan as their head.

Exaggerated reports of great mineral wealth

resident, the sultan, major chiefs and one or two Chinese leaders who discussed the government's policies. The council provided a useful sounding board for public opinion, but the resident was the real policy maker. The format of the Perak State Council was adopted by the other states which came under the residential system. Low also succeeded in ending debt slavery in Perak, but by gradual means which avoided hardship.

Residential progress

In Selangor, things went a little more smoothly. In Sungai Ujong, the Malays were divided. Those who opposed British rule got the sup-

in Pahang awakened British interest in the state. In 1887, Pahang's ruler, Sultan Ahmad, was persuaded to accept a British agent, but the first agent, Hugh Clifford, found the sultan and his chiefs unwilling to relinquish their rights. The atmosphere grew tense, and when the following year a British subject was murdered in Pekan, the state capital, the British used this as an excuse to force the sultan to accept a British resident. But many of the Pahang chiefs resented the new regime because of their loss of power and income. In 1891, a number of them rebelled against the British presence, led by Dato' Bahaman of Semantan (Temerloh). Though the British were far too strong to be defeated, the rebellion took four years to quell.

In 1896, Selangor, Perak, Negeri Sembilan and Pahang were brought together as the Federated Malay states (FMS), with its capital at Kuala Lumpur. A British resident-general was appointed with jurisdiction over the four states. The purpose of this move was to ensure uniformity in administration, promote faster economic development, and to help the richer members (i.e. Perak and Selangor) assist the poorer ones, especially Pahang. The creation of the FMS made for more efficient government and served the business and commercial interests of the colonial regime.

and Perlis in the north of the Malay Peninsula recognised the general overlordship of Siam. This was demonstrated by the sending of the *Bunga Mas* (golden flowers) to Bangkok.

British strike deal with Siam

However, Thai power over these states was vague and fluctuating. In 1909, the British made a treaty with Siam. This gave to Britain whatever rights and power Siam possessed in these states, so that they now became British protectorates under British advisors with similar status to the British residents in the FMS.

This change was made without consulting

The rulers agreed to the federation thinking that, by joining together, they would exercise more control over the residents and regain their lost authority. Unfortunately, this did not happen. Instead, the resident-general now exercised real power, which he used without reference to the residents or the rulers. In effect, "federation" centralised power in the hands of British officials, who ran the show almost by themselves.

Meanwhile, Kelantan, Terengganu, Kedah

FAR LEFT: Hugh Low, who laid the foundations of the Residential System. **LEFT:** Sultan Abdullah of Perak. **ABOVE:** Frank Swettenham, the Resident of Selangor. **RIGHT:** *Bunga Mas* tribute to appease the Siamese.

the Malay rulers concerned, which caused a lot of resentment. In fact, these states had run their own affairs quite satisfactorily, and British interference was unpopular. In Kedah, a treaty defining the role of the British advisor was not signed until 1923 because of the hard bargaining to win Malay acceptance of the British presence. In Kelantan (1916) and Trengganu (1928), there were popular anti-British uprisings which were put down by force. Finally, in the south, Johor – the most progressive of all the Malay states – was pressured into accepting a British advisor in 1914. British control was complete, and the Malay Peninsula was divided into three separate parts – the Straits

Settlements (SS), Federated Malay States (FMS) and the Non-Federated Malay States (FMS).

The Malay Peninsula had just undergone rapid change. Meanwhile, the territory of Sabah (called British North Borneo) and the "White Rajah" state of Sarawak, had been enjoying developments of their own.

The first "White Rajah" of Sarawak, James Brooke, was an Englishman born in India. As a young man, he had served with the East India Company's army in Burma and when his father died in 1835, leaving

> ### BUOYANT EXPORT
>
> By 1920, the rubber tree was the mainstay of Malaya's economy – the country provided over 50 percent of the world's rubber.

crushed and in return for Brooke's help, Rajah Muda Hashim awarded him control of the province. In 1841, Brooke, aged 38, was installed as Rajah of Sarawak.

With the help of local chiefs, Brooke set out to establish law and order. This meant overcoming Iban and Malay warriors who lived by piracy. He won, because he had the help of British warships against which Iban and Malay *perahu* (boats) were helpless. Brooke did not introduce new laws, but used existing customs and consulted with the chiefs.

Brooke a sum of money, he used it to buy a schooner and organise an expedition to explore Borneo and the Celebes.

Brooke's lucky break

Stopping off at Singapore on his way, Brooke was asked by the governor to deliver a message to the Malay governor of Sarawak, a province of Brunei confined to the area around Kuching. When Brooke arrived in Kuching in 1839, he found the Rajah Muda Hashim, a relative of the Sultan of Brunei, trying to put down a rebellion against Sarawak's governor. On returning a year later, Brooke decided to help the Rajah Muda Hashim. The rebellion was

Brooke was always short of money, but he refused to introduce foreign capital; he believed that government should be in the interests of the Sarawakians, and not of outside business interests. Under his rule, more territories were brought under Sarawak's control. In 1857, a Chinese revolt nearly overthrew him, but it was quickly suppressed. In 1863, he retired to England where he died five years later.

Brooke's nephew, Charles Brooke, became the second rajah. A better administrator than his uncle, he brought Sarawak out of debt, reduced head-hunting, expanded trade, and brought greater prosperity. He died, at the age of 87, in 1917.

Meanwhile, sovereignty over North Borneo (present-day Sabah) was acquired from the sultans of Brunei and Sulu in 1877 by Overbeck, the Austrian consul-general in Hong Kong, and Alfred and Edward Dent, prominent Hong Kong businessmen. In 1881, Overbeck withdrew and the Dents formed the British North Borneo Company under a royal charter.

The North Borneo Company, like the Brookes in Sarawak, faced considerable opposition to the imposition of its rule. The most serious resistance came from Mat Salleh, a Sulu chief, who rose up in revolt in 1895. The introduction of new taxes had created general discontent, and Mat Salleh gathered many supporters. In 1900, Mat Salleh was killed, but the rebellion was not quelled until five years later.

Material wealth

Throughout the entire colonial period, tin and rubber were Malaysia's main exports. It was these that engendered the development and great social changes that the region enjoyed.

Tin rose in importance in the mid 19th century because of the invention of the tin can, the rise of the canning industry and other new uses for tin plate. This created an ever-increasing demand for Malayan tin on the world market. By 1904, the peninsula was producing more than half the world's tin supply. Besides the political repercussions on the Malay States, this also led to a huge influx of Chinese immigrants.

Until the 1900s, tin mining was mainly in Chinese hands. The introduction of tin-dredging in 1912 enabled Europeans to gain an upper hand in the industry, as they had the technology and capital which the Chinese did not.

Rubber arrived in Malaya as a foreign plant but grew to become the mainstay of its economy. Rubber seeds were transported from Brazil to London's Kew Gardens for experimentation as an Asian crop in the 1870s. Some of the seeds were sent to Malaya where they were planted in Singapore and elsewhere. The millions of rubber trees in Malaysia today all stem from these original seedlings.

However, no one took rubber seriously until H.N. Ridley became director of the Singapore Botanical Gardens in 1888. Ridley had no

doubts about the future of rubber but his attempts to persuade coffee planters to experiment with this strange new crop were initially unsuccessful. However, at the end of the 19th century, the price of coffee collapsed. The birth of the motor-car industry and the consequent demand for rubber tyres triggered the rush to farm the plant. Many fortunes were made in the great rubber-boom which followed.

Migrant Indian labour was brought in to work the rubber estates, while many Malays became smallholders. The industry went through gluts and slumps, but remained the mainstay of the Malaysian economy right up to the 1970s.

Revenue from tin and rubber was used to build up the country's infrastructure and social amenities. Attention was focused on the tin mines and rubber estates at the expense of the less profitable areas, which remained neglected. In particular, development and social change were noticeably slower in Sabah and Sarawak, although rubber was still very important to both their economies. As the tin and rubber industries boomed, Malaysia's plural society developed. By the 1930s, the population of Malaya (excluding Singapore) was about 4 million, comprising 49 percent Malays, 34 percent Chinese and smaller groups of Indians, European expatriates and other races. ❑

LEFT: Sarawak's Ibans with their *perahu*, or small boats, were no match for the British warships.
RIGHT: tapping latex, the raw material of rubber.

ڤشوران كمرديكأن

دڠن نام الله يڠ مأمورة لاݢي مڠاسيهاني، سݢل ڤوجي باݢي الله يڠ مها بركواس
دان صلوات دان سلام كأتس رسولڽ دولوله.

بهاواساڽ اوله كران تله تيب ماساڽ باݢي اومة ڤرسكوتوان تانه ملايو اين منچاڤاي طرف يڠ موليا
برڠ داري كأرف داري كأرف كالڬي بردوا اقسام ستمڤت كدودوقكن دڠن سݢل بڠسا داسلوره دنيا

دان بهاواساڽ اوله كران دڠن ڤرجنجين يڠ دسبوت نام ڤرجنجين ڤرسكوتوان تانه ملايو تاهون 1957
يڠدڤربوات اينتارا دولي يڠ مها ملياابڬندا ملايو دولي، يڠ مها ملياراج، دولي ملايو دان فرستوجوي هوا انكري
ملايو يأيت جوهر، ڤهڠ، نݢري سمبيلن، سلاڠور، قدح، ڤرليس، كلنتن، ترڠݢانو، دان ڤيراق نݢري يڠد هولون
دڠكن نݢري ست يأيت ملاك دان ڤولوفينڠ مولاي درڤد 31 هاريبولن أوݢوس تاهون 1957، هندقله منجادي
سبواه ڤرسكوتوان بهارو باݢي نݢري، يڠبرنام ڤرسكوتوان تانه ملايو

دان بهاواساڽ اوله كران تله برستوجوڤول دانتاراكدواڤيهقدالم ڤرجنجين يڠ ترسبوت دأتس
دان ڤولوفينڠ همندقله منداري درڤد ديأن يڠ ترسبوت دأتس دڠ منجادي سبماكين درڤد جاجهن درڤد تعلوق بكندا آكوين، دان
دولي يڠ مها مليا ابكندا آكوين يدق لاݢي برحق منجالنكن اف جوا كدولتن باݢنداأتس ك دواأتس كدواأتس كدوا بواه نݢري يڠترسبوت دأتس

دان بهاواساڽ اوله كران تله برستوجوڤول دانتاراكدوا ڤيهق يڠ ترسبوت دأتس ڤرجنجين ڤرسكوتوان تانه ملايو تاهون 1948،
دان سݢل ڤرجنجين، لاين يڠدأدكان دانتارا دولي يڠ مها مليا ابكندا آكوين دولي، يڠ مها ملياراج، بݢم مها مليا سالة انتوهوم سالة منسوري درڤد بكندا،
ايت سبلوم تاريخ يڠترسبوت همندقله دبطلكن مولاي درڤد تاريخ ايت، دان سݢلا قواتكواس دان حق، دولي يڠ مها مليا ابكندا آكوين انتو
ڤون ڤرجنجين نݢري يڠ دبريت كيݢدم ملاي نݢري سأكت يأيت، انتوڤون يڠ برهوبوڠ دڠن انتوكراجاءن، ملايو انتوڤون ڤرسكوتوان تانه ملايو سلوروهڽ
اوله ڤيهت دڠن سنديريڽ

دان بهاواساڽ اوله كران دولي يڠ مها مليا ابكندا آكوين دولي، يڠ مها مليا ابكندا آكوين، دولي، يڠ مها ملياراج، ملايو، ڤرلس نݢري يونيت دكيݢدم دان مجلس اوندڠ
ڤرسكوتوان دان نݢري، ملايو تله ماولوسكن ڤرجنجين ڤرسكوتوان تانه ملايو تاهون 1957 ايت برجالن قواتكواس

دان بهاواساڽ اوله كران سبواه ڤرليمباݢا باݢي كرليبانڽ ڤرسكوتوان تانه ملايو تله دتنتوكن منجادي سوات قانون يڠ معتمد باݢيڽ

دان بهاواساڽ اوله كران ڤرليمباݢا ڤرسكوتوان يڠ ترسبوت دأتس ملة لندسكن كأتس دسك درسكم شرط انتوكن مڠيا ككسلامتن حق، دان ڤربأن
دولي يڠ مها ملياراج، سرة حق، اساسي كبياسن سلين رعية دان انتوق مأجودكن ڤرسكوتوان تانه ملايو دڠن اماني دان داميي سرة ترأتور
سباݢاي سبواه كرليبانڽ يڠ معقولي راج برڤر ڤرليبانڽ بݢر اسركن دموقراسي چارا بر ڤرليمن

دان بهاواساڽ اوله كران ڤرليبانڽ ڤرسكوتوان يڠ ترسبوت دأتس تله دلولوسكن اوله سوات اوندڠ، بݢد اداكن اوله مجلس اوندڠ ڤرسكوتوان
سرة دڠن اوندڠ، بݢد اداكن اوله نݢري، ملايودان دڠن كتتاف، دد الم مجلس اوندڠ نݢري ملاك دان ڤولوفينڠ، دڠن دمكين ڤرليبانڽ ايت
تله برجالن قواتكواس ڤد 31 هاريبولن أوݢوس تاهون 1957

مك دڠن نام الله يڠ مأمورة لاݢي مها مڠاسيهاني، ساي تڠكو عبدالرحمن ڤوتراابن الرحوم سلطان عبدالحميد
حاليمشاه، ڤردنا منتري وكل ڤرسكوتوان اومة ملايو دڠن ڤرستوجوان دڠ مها ملايو، يڠ مها ملياراج، نݢري، ملايو دڠن اين
مشهوردان ماشتهاركن باݢي ڤيهم اومة ڤرسكوتوان تانه ملايو، بهاوا ملاي درڤد تيݢ كڤوله سأتو هاريبولن أوݢوس تاهون سريبو سمبيلن
راتوس ليم ڤوله توجوه مك ڤرسكوتوان تانه ملايو يڠ مڠندوڠي نݢري، دولي يأيت نݢري، جوهر، ڤهڠ، نݢري سمبيلن، سلاڠور، قدح، ڤرليس،
كلنتن، ترڠݢانو ڤيراق، ملاك دان ڤولوفينڠ، دڠن لمڤه رحمة الله سبحانه وتعالي آكن ككل منجادي سبواه نݢارا يڠ مرديكا دان
برداولت سرة بردسركن كڤد كبياسن دان كأديلن دان منجاݢا كعدالن دان كمعمرنءن بݢي كسنتوسان رعيةڽ دان مڠككلكن كأمانن
دانتارا سݢل بڠسا.

كوالا لمڤور
31 هاريبولن أوݢوس تاهون 1957

ڤردان منتري

MALAYA, MERDEKA, MALAYSIA

After a period of peace and prosperity, World War II shattered the colonial calm.

For good or bad, Malaysia would never be the same again

Between 1900 and 1941, British rule in Malaya was stable, their subject peoples contented, and the economy basically sound and expanding. In many ways, British Malaya was a showcase of benevolent imperialism. The British referred to Malaya during this period as a land without politics.

This, of course, was not quite true. The British had brought into being a multi-racial society, the contradictions of which were steadily mounting – even if they had not yet reached crisis point. Issues which would one day have to be faced, included the rights of the Malays and other indigenous peoples in their own country, and the position of the Chinese and Indians, the two major immigrant groups, who were beginning to regard Malaya as their permanent home. British policy was to stick to the principle that Malaya was the land of the Malays, and that Sabah and Sarawak were also the lands of their indigenous peoples. This was acceptable when there were no pressures, economic or political. But rising nationalism, the threat of international communism, and the impact of the Great Depression of 1929–33 increasingly threatened the Pax Britannica.

The Japanese Occupation

But what finally ended the deceptive calm was the sudden extension of World War II – raging in Europe since 1939 – to Southeast Asia. In December 1941, Japan launched her attack on the Western colonial powers which she believed were out to strangle her. Within 9 weeks, Japanese forces had overrun the whole of Malaya. Their victory destroyed the comfortable colonial world and ended for ever the unchallenged supremacy of British rule. Things could never be the same again.

The writing on the wall had come in 1931 when the Japanese army unilaterally annexed Manchuria, and became the dominant force in

LEFT: the Malay Proclamation of Independence, 1957.
RIGHT: a Japanese Occupation newspaper reports on Japan's successful invasion,1943.

Tokyo. The next move came in 1937, with the attempt to bring China under Japanese control. But China proved unconquerable, and the growing Japanese need for strategic raw materials such as oil and rubber made Southeast Asia the target, especially the British and Dutch possessions where these materials abounded

but were denied them by the Western powers. In early 1941, the Japanese took advantage of France's defeat to occupy French Indo-China. It was clear that Malaya would be next.

Among the many reasons advanced for Britain's humiliating failure to defend Malaya – poor strategies, untrained troops, guns pointing in the wrong direction, etc. – the most telling is British weakness in the air. Effective airpower would have crippled the Japanese invasion. Instead, it was Japanese airpower that triumphed; by sinking two capital British warships in the first week of the invasion, the British were crippled.

The Japanese Occupation caused great hardship among the peoples of Malaya. The Japanese arrived with persuasive propaganda about a "Co-prosperity Sphere" and "Asia for Asians". But they had won a great battle, not the war, so were unable to put these promises into effect. Instead, they were obliged to rule with an iron fist to control the resentment of a population suffering from shortages of food and essential goods, high inflation and low incomes.

The Japanese were especially wary of the Chinese, most of whom were hostile towards

---

NEW NATIONALISM

The end of World War II saw conspicuous growth in political self-determinism, now summed up by the fashionable slogan: *Malaysia Boleh*! (Malaysia Can Do It!)

---

ority before the white man. Those working in the administration, in public utilities and wherever else assumed the responsibilities once held by their European masters, and gained a new self-confidence and self-respect. This was the beginning of the spirit of *Malaysia Boleh*! (*see page 47*). As a result, when the Japanese were finally defeated by the Western powers, Malayans had a new attitude and new outlook. They were no longer prepared to go back to the way things were before World War II.

them because of "the China incident". The brunt of Japanese brutality was directed against the Chinese, tens of thousands of whom were executed or imprisoned. Europeans (except for nationalities who were neutral or Japanese allies in the war) ended up living under atrocious conditions in detention camps. Some were sent, along with thousands of Indian labourers and a good many Malays, to work on the notorious "Death Railway" – constructed to provide a rail link between Thailand and Burma. Conditions there were even worse, and many died.

Despite the terrible suffering, the Japanese Occupation did have an important plus side. It liberated Malayans from their sense of inferi-

Peace and a fresh start

The Japanese Occupation ended as swiftly as it had begun with the dropping of atomic bombs on the Japanese cities of Hiroshima and Nagasaki in early August 1945. The war finally ended in Malaya in September, when British and Australian forces landed in Malaya and Borneo – in fact the liberation of Borneo had already begun – and re-established British authority. The British received a warm welcome; their return promised relief from the hardships of the Japanese occupation. But everyone agreed, including the British themselves, that the political situation had changed and that British rule could not last for ever.

In fact, the British had already decided to form the FMS, the non-FMS, Penang and Melaka – but not Singapore – into a single state to be called the Malayan Union. The union would have a central government headed by a (British) governor and the former Malay States would cease to exist, their rulers simply remaining as heads of Islam.

At the same time a common citizenship was created, including long-term Chinese and Indian residents as well as the Malays. In short, Malay sovereignty was to be transferred to the British Crown, turning Malaya into a colony and destroying Malay political pre-eminence. A British envoy came to Malaya, and after using a lot of pressure, got all the Malay rulers to accept the scheme.

However, this proposal was strongly opposed, especially by the Malays, who felt that they were being sold down the river. In March 1946, representatives of 41 Malay associations met in Kuala Lumpur to form a national movement to oppose it. This led to the birth of the United Malay National Organisation (UMNO) led by Dato' Onn Jaafar. UMNO demanded the repeal of the union. Although the British inaugurated the union in 1946, Malay opposition was so strong that after negotiations with the Malay rulers and UMNO it was replaced by the Federation of Malaya, which included all the Malay States and Penang and Melaka as members. The new federation came into being on 1 February 1948.

The Malays accepted the federation because it preserved the sovereignty of the rulers and restored state rights. Because the citizenship terms for Chinese and Indian Malaysians were not so generous as before, it was more grudgingly accepted by those communities.

Meanwhile, in 1946, Sarawak and North Borneo became crown colonies. The cost of post-war reconstruction was beyond the resources of the Brooke government and of the British North Borneo Company. In Sabah, the change was accepted without protest, but in Sarawak there was serious opposition, particularly from the Malays who feared they would lose their privileged position without the Brookes. The climax of this opposition came in 1949 when the new British governor was

assassinated in Sibu. This action was too extreme for most Malays, and the movement gradually lost momentum and faded away.

The Emergency

During the Japanese occupation, guerrilla groups which were mainly Chinese, lived in the jungles and organised resistance against the invaders. The most important group was the Malayan Communist Party (MCP) whose guerrillas called themselves the Malayan Peoples' Anti-Japanese Army (MPAJA). Their aim, once the war was over, was to expel the British and set up a communist republic in Malaya.

When the MPAJA was disbanded after the war, the MCP believed that they could overthrow British rule by stirring up mass unrest, particularly through the trade union movement. Communists began infiltrating the unions and succeeded in organising a series of strikes among dockworkers, tin miners and rubber plantation labourers demanding better living conditions. This alarmed the colonial authorities and laws were passed to bring the trade unions under stricter control. This was probably the main reason for the MCP's decision in 1948 to abandon its non-violent strategy and to resort to armed insurrection instead. Under its new leader, Chin Peng, the MCP was reorganised and

LEFT: Japanese leaders surrender their swords in 1945.
RIGHT: a Communist caricature.

all its activities moved underground. After a spate of attacks on European miners and planters, the government proclaimed a national state of emergency in June 1948. "The Emergency" became the official name for the communist insurrection which lasted 12 years, so called, it is said, to escape inconvenient insurance requirements connected with acts of rebellion – a matter of some importance to rubber and tin companies whose property was being attacked and destroyed by the insurgents.

From their secret jungle bases, the communists caused widespread confusion. They would also coerce food and supplies from Chinese

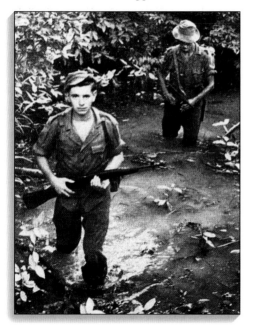

COMMUNIST TACTICS

For a guerrilla army, the Communist Malayan Peoples' Anti-British Army (MPABA) was a well-organised fighting force. They grouped themselves into regiments and lived in jungle camps. These camps, well-screened from the air, with effective escape routes and well-organised living quarters, could often accommodate 300 men. From these bases, the communists would attack rubber estates and tin mines in order to disrupt the colonial economy. High wire fences were put up around tin mines and rubber estates to keep the communists out, but travel was particularly risky because of the danger of ambush lurking at every corner.

squatters in remote areas, and attempt to indoctrinate them. But clamping down on guerrilla activity was made especially hard by the lack of coordination between the various security forces. However, the tide began to turn with the appointment of General Sir Harold Briggs as Director of Operations in 1949. Briggs, a veteran of the World War II Burma campaign against the Japanese, was responsible for the basic strategies which overcame the MCP revolt. He set up war executive committees which coordinated military and civil operations, and created 500 new villages to re-house squatters in less remote areas. This cut off the main source of the communists' food supply. As anticipated, the insurgents attacked the new settlements, but the security forces, now fighting on their own ground, were too strong for them. These forces were soon able to concentrate on jungle operations to destroy the communists and their camps.

In 1953, areas from which the communists had been eliminated were declared "white areas". Food restrictions and curfews in them were relaxed, inducing fuller local co-operation with the government. By 1954, a large number of the communist guerrillas had been eliminated. Many more surrendered later, and the few remaining guerrillas retreated deep into the jungle. The state of emergency officially ended on 31 July 1960.

Malayan nationalism

A major factor that enabled the quelling of the communist revolt was that it was largely a Chinese affair – few Malays or Indians were involved. At the same time, the British saw the need to meet the growing demand for national independence. If they had not done this, many Malayan nationalists might have made common cause with the rebels to oust the British.

Stirrings of a Malayan nationalism were felt throughout the country soon after World War II. The problem was how to unite the three main races in the peninsula in a common struggle for independence from the British. The first step was taken in 1951, when the Malayan Chinese Association (MCA) formed a political partnership with UMNO. The Malayan Indian Congress (MIC) followed suit in 1954, and the political coalition called the Alliance came into being, which played a major role in the struggle for independence.

Elections were held for the Federal Legislative Council for the first time in 1955, and the Alliance won 80 percent of the votes cast. Tunku Abdul Rahman, UMNO's leader, became Malaya's first chief minister. The Tunku was a district officer in Kedah before the war. In the 1950s he took a law degree and soon after entered politics. He took over the leadership of UMNO in 1951.

In 1955, the Alliance government offered an amnesty to the MCP and invited Chin Peng to Baling, Kedah, for talks to end the Emergency.

POLITICAL PEDIGREE

It could be argued that Tunku Abdul Rahman, Malaya's first chief minister, was born to lead – his father was Sultan of Kedah.

based on a memorandum submitted by the Alliance, was accepted by the Malay rulers, and the British and Malayan governments.

Malaya became a constitutional monarchy, with the king selected from among the nine Malay rulers every five years. Parliament consisted of a fully elected lower house and a senate of nominated members. Executive power lay mainly in the hands of the lower house. Each state had its own fully-elected state assembly. Malaya became an independent state at midnight on 30 August 1957.

The talks failed and Chin Peng went back into the jungle. The Alliance now concentrated on bringing about national unity in Malaya's multiracial society. One move was the creation of a national system of education which catered for the needs of Malays, Chinese and Indians alike.

In 1956, Tunku led a delegation to London to negotiate the terms for independence. As a result, a commission of Commonwealth legal experts, headed by Lord Reid, was appointed to draw up a constitution. The draft document,

LEFT: a British jungle patrol to flush out communists.
ABOVE: Tunku Abdul Rahman gives the *Merdeka* salute, declaring Independence in 1957.

The formation of Malaysia

In 1961, Tunku proposed the formation of Malaysia, a wider federation which would include the territories of Malaya, Singapore, British North Borneo (Sabah), Sarawak and Brunei. In Singapore, opinion was sharply divided over the merits of the plan; Brunei decided in the end to stay away. A commission of Malayan and British members investigated the reaction of the inhabitants of Sabah and Sarawak and found that the majority of people there were in favour of the plan. Therefore, the British and Malayan governments set 31 August 1963 as the date on which Malaysia would be established.

But Indonesia condemned the whole scheme as a neo-colonialist plot, and in January 1963 announced a policy of "Confrontation" against Malaysia. Meanwhile, the Philippines also opposed the creation of Malaysia, claiming that North Borneo belonged to them. Confrontation took the form of armed Indonesian incursions across the borders of Sarawak and North Borneo. Indonesia and the Philippines both repudiated a United Nations survey which confirmed that the Borneo territories wanted to be a part of Malaysia.

EARTHY ORIGINS

In local dialect, the Malay people have traditionally been referred to as *Bumiputras*, which translated means "sons of the soil".

Meanwhile, political differences had surfaced between Malaysia and Singapore. On 9 August 1965, Singapore left the Federation and became an independent state.

When Malaysia was formed, its population stood at 10.4 million – Malays forming 47 percent; Chinese 34 percent; Indians, 9 percent; Dayaks, 4 percent; Kadazans, 2 percent; other indigenous groups, 3 percent and foreign immigrants, 2 percent. Turning this medley of peoples into one nation was not an easy feat. Under colonial rule, economic roles tended to

Territorial disputes

When the Federation of Malaysia was officially inaugurated on 16 September 1963, Indonesia and the Philippines severed diplomatic ties with Malaysia; Indonesia intensified its attacks along the borders of Sarawak and British North Borneo (now renamed Sabah) and Indonesian troops made landings in Peninsular Malaysia to carry out acts of sabotage. But they were quickly foiled by the security forces.

In 1966, Sukarno was ousted from power and the new Indonesian regime wanted to end confrontation – negotiations settled the conflict. The Philippines also dropped its claim on Sabah and recognised Malaysia.

be identified with specific ethnic groups. In particular, the Chinese resented the Malays' greater political power, while the Malays feared the greater economic strength of the Chinese. The simmering racial tension erupted on 13 May 1969 in the wake of the general elections. Communal riots broke out, mainly in the capital, Kuala Lumpur, killing hundreds of people and destroying a considerable amount of property. As a result, the constitution was suspended and a Department of National Unity was set up to formulate a national ideology and social programmes. Finally, a statement of ideological principles, the *Rukunegara*, was produced to guide the national polity.

The 13 May incident represented a watershed in Malaysian politics, as the government was forced to formulate new economic and political strategies to restore long-term national stability. The riots would also spawn the New Economic Policy (NEP) and the formation of the Barisan Nasional (BN) or National Front.

The BN was the work of Tun Abdul Razak, successor to Tunku Abdul Rahman who resigned a month after the riots. Tun Razak reorganised the Alliance, incorporating every political party except the Democratic Action Party (DAP) and some smaller parties. In 1974, the BN won a landslide majority, and won again in 1978.

Economic policy

Although the nation's new constitution gave the Malays considerable political power, their participation in the country's trade and commerce was minimal. Despite accounting for over half of the country's population, the Malays owned only 2 percent of corporate equity. The Chinese, on the other hand, practically ran the economy, holding prominent positions as bankers, brokers and businessmen.

In 1970, the New Economic Policy (NEP) was launched to encourage a fairer distribution of wealth among the races. This involved setting up corporations and share-ownership schemes to elicit greater Malay participation in the economy. Racial quotas, scholarships and subsidies were introduced to raise the Malay stake in the economy to 30 percent. However, the plan was to achieve this by increasing the size of the pie, and not at the expense of the non-Malays. Therefore, everybody would benefit.

The NEP was inevitably deemed unfair by many non-Malay critics who felt that the Malays already had too many privileges and that "positive" discrimination on the basis of race and not merit would seriously undermine the economic, political and cultural position of non-Malays in Malaysian society.

In any event, the business acumen of the Chinese has kept them prosperous. Twenty years later, however, the Malay, or *bumiputra* stake has reached only 20 percent, the majority of which is owned by big *bumiputra* investment

companies. In 1991, the old policy was replaced by the New Development Policy (NDP), a more liberal strategy which uses incentives rather than quotas, and sets no deadline for the 30 percent *bumiputra* ownership target.

The boom years

When Malaya became independent in 1957, the economy was almost completely dependent on exports of tin, rubber, palm oil and tea. Therefore, in the early 1970s, the government launched an ambitious crusade to transform Malaysia from its agro-mining foundation to a mixed economy with a strong manufacturing

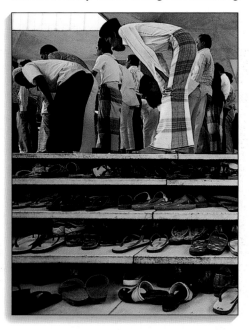

sector. By the end of the 1970s, substantial progress had been made. Light industries had been formed and were now saturating the local market. The country was poised to make an industrial leap to becoming an exporter of manufactured goods and in concentrating on heavier industry. The 1970s also witnessed the harvesting of newly-found offshore oil and natural gas reserves in the South China Sea, giving a spectacular boost to the economy.

This impressive economic performance was brought about by a series of Malaysian Five-Year Plans. However, much of the credit for the country's rapid economic progress since 1981 must go to one man: Dr Mahathir Mohamad. ❑

LEFT: Tun Razak (with cane) succeeded Tengku Abdul Rahman as PM. **RIGHT:** Islam figures strongly in Malaysian politics; prayer time in KL's Jame Mosque.

THE MAHATHIR ERA

*Under the leadership of Dr Mahathir Mohamad, Malaysia became one of
the stronger economies of Asia. But at what price to political freedom?*

The appointment of Mahathir Mohamad as Malaysia's fourth prime minister in 1981 marked the start of a new era in the nation's politics. It was an era that lasted over two decades until his retirement in 2003 – one of the longest terms of political leadership in Southeast Asia – and left behind an indelible stamp; half the country has grown up knowing only Mahathir's tough leadership style.

The Mahathir era marked a break with the past. Unlike his three predecessors, Mahathir was not only a commoner, but also the first Malaysian prime minister to have received all of his education locally and not in Britain. He was also much younger on taking office, a member of the post-World War II generation of students who were actively involved in the struggle for national independence.

Right from the start, Mahathir was a stormy petrel in UMNO politics. Although he was sitting on its Supreme Council by 1965, he was expelled from the party four years later for criticising what he saw as the failure of the then prime minister, Tunku Abdul Rahman, to protect Malay political interests. Mahathir's political comeback began in the 1970s. Re-admitted into UMNO, in 1974 he took his first ministerial post (Education) and the following year was re-elected to the Supreme Council to became the party's vice-president. In 1978, he was appointed Deputy Prime Minister under Hussein Onn.

Radical reforms

Anyone who knew Mahathir also knew that things would change under him. One of his first acts on assuming office in 1981 was to make all government servants clock in for work, – a harbinger of the no-nonsense style of government he aimed to promote. Since that day, there has hardly been a dull moment. Mahathir's initial priorities were to shake the Malaysian, and more particularly, the Malay mindset out of its

---

LEFT: Malaysia's hosting of the 1998 Commonwealth Games was a high point. **RIGHT:** much of its economic success is due to its manufacturing expertise.

colonial mould, to make Malaysians more self-reliant, and to raise their self-esteem. He also wanted to put Malaysia on the world map, to establish the country as a power to be noticed and taken heed of. All this is conveniently summed up by the now fashionable slogan, *Malaysia Boleh!* (Malaysia Can Do It!).

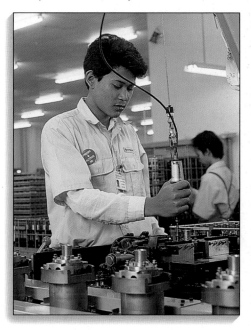

To achieve these aims Mahathir resorted to shock tactics. One of them was to jolt Malaysians out of their reverential attitude towards all things Western, and particularly British, by attacking these icons. In 1982 came his "Buy British Last" campaign. This was ostensibly in retaliation for the British Government's action in raising university fees for foreign students, but in reality it was designed as a slap in the face for Malaysians brought up to believe that "British is Best." He also urged Malaysians to adopt a "Look East" policy, and singled out Japan, the villain of World War II, as a role model of hardwork and efficiency that Malaysians should emulate.

Mahathir also commissioned numerous civil engineering projects, building roads, bridges, and, most spectacularly, skyscrapers. While each has its own merits, these high-profile schemes also served collectively to demonstrate to the world what can be done when a Malaysian puts his mind to something.

In the same vein, Mahathir encouraged Malaysians to make their mark in the world arena as individuals, by going in for world-class exploits. By the turn of the 20th century, Malaysians had climbed Mount Everest, taken part in international safaris and even sailed solo around the world, charting a new course on the way. The successful hosting of the Commonwealth Games in Kuala Lumpur in 1998, a triumph of both individual and collective Malaysian effort, seems to have marked the apogee of Mahathir's grandiose mega-schemes.

Another of Mahathir's efforts on the global stage was to project himself as a world leader, at least in the eyes of his countrymen. He certainly succeeded in making Malaysia heard as a champion of the Third World and as cheerleader for the countries of the undeveloped "South" in their attempts to secure a better deal from the wealthy industrialised "North".

Mahathir's strident criticism of Western val-

ENGINEER OF SUCCESS

Mahathir's almost obsessive love of ambitious mega-projects has seen Malaysia trumping the world in many aspects of civil engineering. The 7-km (4½-mile) long bridge linking Penang Island to the mainland is Asia's longest; Kuala Lumpur Tower was the world's third-highest when built, and the Petronas Twin Towers, completed in 1998, is currently the world's tallest building. Kuala Lumpur also lays claim, bizarrely, to the world's highest flagpole, at Merdeka Square. Most recently, the country saw the construction of one of the most sophisticated airports in the world, Kuala Lumpur International Airport (KLIA).

ues and policies had been good for Malaysian pride throughout his leadership, however much it had irritated people in the West.

Mahathiresque economics

Nevertheless, the most important of Mahathir's initiatives laid in the realm of economic policy and affairs.

After only a couple of years in power, the Mahathir administration was confronted with a major global trade recession; but it proved its mettle and was able to ride the storm. Assimilating the new trend away from government control over national economies towards liberalisation and the free market, Mahathir launched a thoroughgoing privatisation programme of his own, tagging it with another catchy slogan, "Malaysia Inc." – i.e. the entire nation as a commercial enterprise involving everybody.

After its inception early in 1983, when the programme was widely publicized, a whole series of government institutions and agencies were gradually privatised, including power and water supplies, telecommunications, postal services, the railway, the national airline, and the construction of toll highways.

BOUNCING BACK

Among its many economic achievements, Malaysia is the largest producer of condoms and surgical rubber gloves in the world.

creation of a local automobile manufacturing industry which in 1985 produced the Proton Saga, the first locally manufactured car and the first to be made and designed in Southeast Asia (with a little help from Mitsubishi of Japan). Today, the Saga not only dominates the domestic market but is exported to more than a dozen countries. This and ventures into iron and steel manufacture were projects instigated by the government-owned Heavy Industries Corporation of Malaysia (HICOM).

Other giant infrastructural projects included

Boom time

Privatisation proved highly successful; the country was brought out of recession, and the government divested much of its heavy burden of expenditure on basic services. Foreign capital poured in, business boomed, the property market expanded, and the stock market soared.

At the same time, another major thrust with image-building implications has been the fostering of heavy industry along with a massive broadening of the infrastructure. First came the

---

LEFT: KL's National Stadium was erected for the 1998 Commonwealth Games. **ABOVE:** Symbols of success, Malaysian-built Proton car and country flag.

the 848-km long (527 miles) North-South Expressway (NSE); ocean ports at Pasir Gudang, Port Klang and Lumut; the huge natural gas plant at Bintulu, and the controversial Bakun Dam, postponed because of the economic crisis, then restarted at the time of writing.

Most ambitious of all, was the attempt to catch the wave of the future by making Malaysia a frontrunner in information technology through its Multimedia Super Corridor, a new international hub of IT centred in the Klang Valley where the capital sits. Low labour costs have also enabled Malaysia to become a world leader in electronic goods and microchips.

By the early 1990s, locally manufactured

products had become the country's greatest export earner, leaving the traditional export of raw materials far behind. Malaysia had also become one of the fastest growing economies in Asia, with one of the highest GDPs in the region.

Much of the credit for Malaysia's success must go to the innovative thinking and bold entrepreneurial moves that Mahathir promoted. But providence has played its part, not least the discovery in the 1960s of substantial natural gas and oil reserves off Malaysian shores.

The new prosperity has been reflected in the rash of high-rise office blocks and condominiums in Kuala Lumpur and the larger towns.

Vision 2020 and the future

All this material progress found philosophic expression in another typical Mahathir contribution – "Vision 2020" (*Wawasan 2020*), a statement setting out the targets that the nation should achieve by 2020. Though primarily economic – i.e. the achievement of Newly Industralised Country (NIC) status by that date – the "vision" also incorporated the goals of creating a common and unified Malaysian identity to replace the various communal identities – Chinese, Indian, Malay and so on – that stand for "Malaysian" today. Mahathir also hoped to establish an educated society based on spiritual values.

POLITICS IN SABAH AND SARAWAK

In Sarawak, the ruling coalition – led by the Parti Pesaka Bumiputera Bersatu Sarawak (PBB) – has been in power for over a quarter-century. In Sabah, the Malay/Muslim ruling coalition is dominated by UMNO (of Peninsular Malaysia) – a result of political developments in the 1990s.

Politics in Sabah and Sarawak have little relevance to the peninsula, and vice versa. However, Sabah's and Sarawak's support for the Barisan National (BN), the ruling coalition in the federal parliament, is vital. Without it, the BN could lose its majority and its control over constitutional change. So the federal government's policy towards these political parties has been highly flexible, subject to their unquestionable loyalty to the BN. Kuala Lumpur has never tolerated any chief minister in either state showing signs of independence. Hence, the ousting of Kalong Ningkan, Sarawak's first chief minister, in 1966; the eclipse of Dato Mustapha Harun, Sabah's first head of state, in 1976; and the downfall of Pairin Kitingan, the chief minister of Sabah, in 1992. The BN hasn't yet found the need to establish a presence in Sarawak, but the strong opposition to federal influences in Sabah resulted in UMNO making a base there in 1992. With Kuala Lumpur's financial backing and carefully redrawn constituency boundaries, UMNO and its local allies have ruled the roost ever since.

However, the achievements of the Mahathir era were suddenly placed in serious jeopardy by the Asian financial crisis of 1997. Over the next 18 months, the Kuala Lumpur stock market index fell by 80 percent, precipitating a political crisis on top of economic problems, the repercussions of which are still being felt today.

Benevolent dictator?

The political crisis centred on the sudden dismissal in September 1998 of Anwar Ibrahim, the deputy prime minister and his subsequent arrest, trial and imprisonment on charges of corruption and homosexuality. The vicious manner in which this was carried out and the perceived unfairness of the court proceedings evoked an outburst of protest, especially amongst the Malays, on a scale not witnessed since independence. More than anything else, these events put in high relief the most prominent political trend manifest during the Mahathir era – the steady growth of authoritarian government.

Mahathir's long tenure of office showed that he was a shrewd political operator, but his success had been largely achieved by gathering power into his own hands and using it to maintain his own position. During his office, the constitution was amended almost beyond recognition, the fundamental rights which it originally enshrined strangled by various escape clauses and qualifications. The prerogatives of the monarchy was also reduced – in a manner that enhanced the power of the prime minister.

Amendments to parliamentary procedure have robbed the legislature of much of its authority. The independence of the judiciary was emasculated, a process begun in 1988 with the removal of its head. Draconian legislation (the Internal Security Act) today allows detention without trial, muzzles the press and restricts access to official information. And as anyone who has watched Malaysian television or read the national dailies will tell you, these are basically little more than organs for orchestrated official news.

Nevertheless, the Barisan Nasional (BN), the name of the ruling coalition, has romped home in each of the last four general elections. A deep-rooted desire for security and stability, and fear of communal unrest and disorder form the glue

which binds many Malaysians to the present regime – feelings more firmly entrenched amongst the Chinese and Indians in the peninsula than amongst the Malays.

However, the Anwar affair, as well as the perceived corruption of the ruling coalition with its "money politics" has seen the Malay-dominated areas turn to the main opposition party PAS (Islamic party). Having lost Kelantan state to PAS in the 1990 election, the ruling party was dealt a second blow in 1999, when Terengganu too came under the PAS fold. The politics of Sabah and Sarawak, however, is another thing. (*see box opposite*).

Riding on pro-Anwar sentiment, the opposition parties attempted a coalition in order to challenge the ruling party but this fizzled out in 2001. Then a year later, the world's longest-serving prime minister made a shock announcement that he would retire, naming his deputy Abdullah Badawi as successor. Since assuming power in October 2003, Badawi has shown himself as the people's Prime Minister, rehauling the civil service, dealing with corruption in the police force, and halting the expensive mega-projects that marked the Mahathir era. The people responded by voting overwhelmingly for the Barisan coalition in the 2004 elections, a major victory being the return of Terengganu to the Barisan fold. ❏

LEFT: ex-PM Dr Mahathir at a signing ceremony.
RIGHT: On his way to court, ex-DPM Anwar Ibrahim.

THE LIVING WORLD

From lush rainforests to the coral reefs that fringe its shores, Malaysia has some of the most important – and fragile – environments on earth

The Indo-Malayan rainforests are the oldest in the world, making those in Africa and South America seem adolescent in comparison. While creeping icecaps were swelling and shrinking across the northern hemisphere, the Indo-Malayan jungles lay undisturbed – for an estimated 130 million years. As a result many diverse species of animal and plant life evolved, with a large number of these occurring nowhere else in the world.

Amazing biodiversity

Rainforests on the Malaysian peninsula and in the Malaysian states of Sabah and Sarawak on the island of Borneo continue to excite a great deal of scientific interest. But those visiting for only a few days, or even weeks, will miss most of the rare flora and fauna; scientists can spend entire lifetimes at work here. Optimists believe that the plants and animals yet to be investigated may hold cures for many human diseases.

The biodiversity is truly staggering. It is estimated that over 15,000 flowering plant species (9 percent of the world's total) and 185,000 animal species (16 percent of the world's total) are found in Malaysia. The flowering plants include some 2,000 types of trees, including 200 different palms, and 3,000 species of orchids, the most exotic of flowers. The 50-hectare (125-acre) Forest Research Institute of Malaysia (FRIM) contains more tree species than exist in the whole of North America. The world's largest flower, the *Rafflesia*, is unique to the region (*see box right*). Carnivorous pitcher plants can be seen, most abundantly on the slopes of Mount Kinabalu in Sabah but also on the peninsula, waiting for careless insects to drop in and drown. Another record-breaker is the towering *Tualang tree*, tallest of all tropical trees. It can reach up to 80 metres (260 ft) in height and over 3 metres (10 ft) in girth.

The rainforests also hold hundreds of thousands of animal species, many of which are unique to the region. Almost 300 species of mammals live here including tigers, elephants, rhinoceros (though sadly their numbers are greatly diminished), black and white tapirs, civet cats (*musang*), leopards, honey bears, and

RAFFLESIA

The *Rafflesia* sp. is the largest flower in the world, measuring up to 1 metre (3½ ft) in diameter when in full bloom. Rafflesia can be found in forests on the Main Range in Peninsular Malaysia as well as in Sabah and Sarawak. There are seven species altogether, *R. arnoldii* being the largest.

A parasite by nature, the plant lives by infecting the roots of a woody climber, *Tetrastigma* sp. The flower takes many months to develop, and the open bloom – which lasts for only a few days – looks like dead meat, crawling with maggots when it starts to rot. It emits a similar odour, thereby attracting flies for pollination.

PRECEDING PAGES: *Rafflesia*, the world's largest flower. **LEFT:** orang-utan, or "man of the forest" in Malay, hanging onto the jungles of Borneo. **RIGHT:** one of Malaysia's myriad butterflies rests on a hibiscus.

two kinds of deer – the *sambar*, and the barking deer (*kijang*) with its dog-like call. Malaysia is also home to the cat-sized mousedeer (*kancil*), which is technically not a deer at all, the scaly anteater (*pangolin*), the badger-like *binturong* with its prehensile tail, and many kinds of gibbons and monkeys including the quaint loris with its sad eyes and lethargic manner. Borneo is also home to the extraordinary orang-utan ("forest man" in Malay).

Whether you venture into the jungle or not, you are sure to see some of the estimated 736 species of birds (11 of which are endemic) and quite a few of the 150,000 species of invertebrates. Alfred Russel Wallace, the celebrated Victorian naturalist who spent more than ten years in the Malay Archipelago, had a particular fondness for insects of all sorts and often described himself as "trembling with excitement" upon the discovery of a new type. The country is also home to over 1,000 species of butterfly, and an estimated 12,000 different species of moth.

Shades of green

About three-quarters of Malaysia is covered in trees (about 50 percent forest and 25 percent rubber and oil-palm plantations.). The green

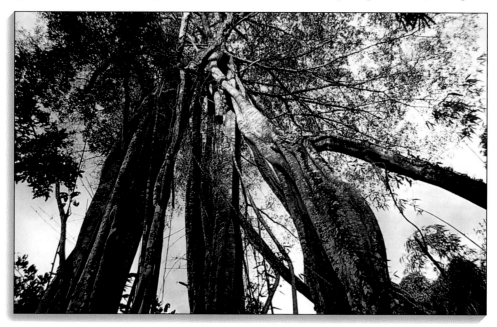

ORANG-UTAN

Orang-utan means "man of the forest" in Malay, a name given to the primate by the indigenous people of Borneo, probably because its appearance and behaviour is similar to that of humans. The orang-utan found in Borneo are a protected species. They prefer to live in swamp forests, and forests near the coast and along the sides of rivers. Though strong, they are peaceful animals.

Orang-utan are normally quiet and difficult to spot in the wild. It's easier to see them at the Lanjak-Entimau Wildlife Sanctuary in Sarawak and the Sepilok Orang-utan Centre in eastern Sabah, which rehabilitates young orphans and re-introduces them into the wild.

cover begins at the edge of the sea and climbs to the highest mountain peaks. Along the coastline, there are extensive areas of mud swamps, peat swamps, and mangroves. Behind the mangroves are lowland dipterocarp forests, which extend to an altitude of 600 metres (2,000 ft) and where some forest giants attain heights of 80 metres (262 ft), with the first branches 20 metres (65 ft) above ground. Much of these forests, particularly on the peninsula, have been logged or replaced by plantations. Timber is one of Malaysia's main exports – comprising 10 percent of its earnings – and efforts are being made to control logging so that the country's fertile jungles will assure the industry a green future.

The next level of forest is mostly oak and chestnut. Above 1,500 metres (5,000 ft) it becomes a kind of never-never land with elfin woodlands of small gnarled trees covered in folds of hanging mosses and lichen.

With growing awareness of the importance of conservation, the government has set aside 12.5 million hectares (30 million acres) as Permanent Forest Estate, to be managed sustainably, and an additional 1.2 million hectares (3 million acres) as National Parks, Game Reserves and Wildlife Sanctuaries. There is room for hope that the Malaysian jungle will be allowed to flourish and retain some of its great biodiversity.

In this regard, the Wildlife Department has evolved from an office that mostly oversaw the issuance of hunting licences, into an organisation that actively enforces preservation of wildlife and habitats, though at present the department remains handicapped by a lack of resources and manpower. Poaching is still a problem, as there are markets both locally and abroad for the parts of wild animals, especially as traditional remedies and aphrodisiacs.

Lush vegetation

A smooth highway unrolls through green hills. Rubber trees flash by in never-ending even rows, and tin mines appear where plantations leave off. Freshly-planted oil palms cover the land in a patchwork of deep green against cleared red earth. In northern and coastal areas, fields are rich with stalks of golden rice.

As far as the eye can see the lush green vegetation of the tropics smothers the landscape. Yet, contrary to its looks, Malaysia is not suited to intensive agriculture. Unlike the Nile River Basin or the Ganges Valley, where seasonal rains flooding the land bring new fertile soil, the torrential downpours in Malaysia wash away the thin but valuable topsoil, leaving only red mud and filling the rivers with silt.

Erosion is one of Malaysia's oldest problems. Geologists believe that the Malay Peninsula and Borneo were once a single rugged landmass running the length of the Indonesian and Malay archipelago. Over millennia the sun, wind and

LEFT: the sculptural form of the strangling fig.
RIGHT: buffaloes working the rice fields.

torrential rains have reduced the mountains to hillocks and outcrops. Precious soils were washed into the sea, and land became cut off by subsidence and erosion.

Despite the shifting landscape and annual monsoon rain, Malaysia's early settlers were basically food growers. As far back as AD 500, crops such as sugar cane, bananas, pepper and coconuts were grown for export, while rice was introduced over 1,000 years ago. Traditionally both men and women were involved in rice cultivation – the staple food and prime

> **MALAYSIAN MAJESTY**
>
> The beautiful Rajah Brooke's Birdwing, with its emerald markings on jet-black wings, is Malaysia's national butterfly.

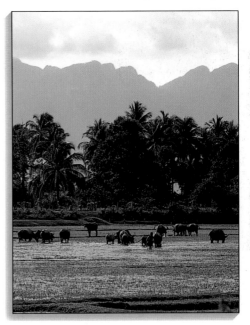

source of income for rural Malaysians. The tempo of kampung life has quickened with the introduction of double cropping, using hybrids which yield a second crop every year. Although it is not as prevalent as it once was, the rubber tree, originally from Brazil, was initially viewed with great scepticism, and even some scorn, by the planters.

The man inspired to bring the rubber tree to Malaysia was H. N. Ridley, director of the botanical gardens in Singapore, where some of the first trees were planted. "Rubber Ridley", as the planters called him, was convinced that his crop had great possibilities and he journeyed around the country with seeds in his pockets, looking for anyone he could convince to plant them. It was a farsighted and lonely crusade until John Dunlop invented the tyre and Henry Ford put the automobile on the assembly line.

Agricultural expansion

To this day the rubber tapper continues to set out before dawn to collect the cups of latex that make up nearly half of the world's rubber supply, but he stops short of the old estate boundaries to view a field planted with oil palms.

The Malaysian government encourages farmers to diversify their crops by growing coconut, coffee, tea, fruits, nuts, spices – and oil palm.

pled with the discovery of large tin deposits in the early 19th century, led to new settlements springing up from a few prospector's shacks and growing into large cities like Kuala Lumpur. The industry gave the British the revenue to build roads and railways through the jungle, and it also introduced Chinese settlers to Malaysian soil.

The all-male mining townships were rough and risky. Malaria and cholera thrived in the intense heat and wiped out thousands. Those who survived did so under a constant threat of tiger attacks, recorded at one time as a daily occurrence. Thousands more perished in

The first commercial planting of oil palm started in Malaysia in 1917, but development was slow until the 1950s, when the government embarked on a massive commodities diversification programme. Many estates replaced rubber with oil palm and opened up new land for its cultivation. The area planted with oil palm increased from 54,000 hectares (130,000 acres) in 1960 to almost 3 million hectares (7.4 million acres) in 2002. Today, Malaysia is easily the world's largest producer of palm oil, accounting for about half of the world's output.

For over a century, tin and rubber were the two main pillars of the Malaysian economy. The growth in industrial demand for tin, cou-

Chinese secret-society feuds. Others made fortunes; for decades, the Chinese held a virtual monopoly on the tin-mining industry.

By 1883, Malaysia had become the largest producer of tin in the world, and by the end of the 19th century, it was supplying about 55 percent of the world's tin supply. Today, it is still a significant player, contributing about 30 percent of the world's output.

Tides upon the sea

For three months of the year, fishing people on Malaysia's east coast store away their nets, dock and repair their boats, move their fishing huts far up the beach and settle down in the shelter of their wooden houses to wait for the winds to change. During the rainy season, time is spent in more leisurely pursuits: repairing fishing nets, making a trip to the city or even embarking on a pilgrimage to Mecca if the year's trade has been prosperous. When the winds drop, they will again venture out to sea in search of the wide variety of fish and other seafood for the nation's markets. This pattern of life has characterised Malaysia's eastern shore for centuries.

TRADING CENTRE

Business in 16th-century Melaka was conducted in 84 languages. Small wonder that Malay contains words adopted from Arabic, Chinese, Sanskrit, Persian, Portuguese, Dutch and English.

Six hundred years ago, spices were literally worth their weight in gold, and it was the Moluccas, with their cherished aromatic produce, that set Asian maritime kingdoms against one another and sparked off the European Age of Discovery in the 15th and 16th centuries. In time, the spice trade to Europe became so lucrative that a vessel loaded with spices from the Far East could make enough profit to pay the cost of the voyage, including the value of the ship, 10 times over. "Melaka is the rich-

Almost entirely surrounded by water, Malaysia has always been where the monsoons meet, where the tides of the Indian Ocean and the South China Sea flow together into the Straits of Melaka. Seafaring merchants, explorers, adventurers and pirates stopped along the coasts to wait for the tradewinds to blow their way and carry them onward on their journey. As Malaysia was midway between China, India and the Moluccas (Spice Islands), some of its ports became major entrepots.

LEFT: the rubber industry was once a significant contributor to the economy. **ABOVE:** cruising around the islands that dot Malaysia's coast.

est seaport in the world with the greatest number of merchants and abundance of shipping that can be found in the whole world," wrote one Portuguese sailor in the 16th century.

Ocean bounty

Piracy was once widespread and for centuries sailors trembled at the thought of passing unarmed through Malaysian waters. The most formidable pirate bands were the Lanun from Mindanao in Philippines who would sometimes recruit Borneo head-hunting warriors. While the captains pillaged the cargoes, the crew collected war trophies. Today, piracy has been largely eradicated, although there are still sporadic episodes, especially in the seas off Sabah.

Above water, a steady stream of oil tankers and cargo vessels ply the Straits of Melaka, transporting crude oil and natural gas instead of silks, spices and porcelain. The recent increase in offshore oil exploration and mining has greatly enhanced the value of sea territory with the result that the nations of the region are involved in a number of sovereignty disputes.

On the other hand, progress has been made among ASEAN nations to address cross-boundary problems, including pollution of the Straits of Melaka and air pollution from forest fires. It is hoped that these efforts and a growing rounded by coral reefs, and Malaysia is known for its great diversity of coral species, and for the marine life that inhabits them.

To protect these unique and biologically important ecosystems, Malaysia has gazetted 38 of its coral islands as protected areas. Some of the more important are Perhentian, Redang, Kapas and Tioman on the east coast of the peninsula, and Langkawi and Pangkor on the west. Consistently voted as one of the world's best dive sites, Pulau Sipadan in Sabah is Malaysia's only oceanic island. Also worth visiting in Sabah is the Tunku Abdul Rahman Park, and the Semporna and Turtle islands.

awareness of its uniquely rich environmental heritage will enable Malaysia and its neighbours to manage their natural resources wisely.

Underwater treasures

Malaysian seas today hold untold riches from ships wrecked by storms or plundered by pirates. Rumours still circulate of hidden treasures buried in caves on islands off the east coast of the peninsula.

Whether or not there are secret treasure troves loaded with gold and precious jewels, there are certainly other underwater treasures – the beautiful and varied marine life of the Malaysian waters. Much of the coast is sur-

Four species of giant sea turtles, including the endangered Leatherback, lay their eggs on Malaysian shores, while offshore the *dugong*, or sea-cow, can occasionally be found.

Until recently, the seas were thought of only as a source of food, but today there is growing interest in underwater discovery. Numerous scuba-diving and marine clubs are springing up as interest in the sport grows. Malaysia is reaping new profits from its long stretches of beach and coral-fringed islands as tourists flock to these places for recreation. ❏

ABOVE: Good visibility and a thriving underwater life make for some excellent diving in Malaysia.

An Environment in Danger

Malaysia is one of the world's 12 mega diversity areas. Many plants and animals are found nowhere else in the world and the majority most likely have yet to be identified and named. Tropical forests, the most biologically diverse ecosystems on earth, cover approximately 46 percent of the land. In addition, Malaysia is blessed with a variety of other ecosystem types, including mangrove and peat swamps, mountain ranges, coral reefs, limestone habitats, and caves.

Whether Malaysia can maintain its unique natural heritage will depend on its ability to balance environmental conservation with economic development and a fast-growing population. Malaysia's population has doubled in the past 30 years and is expected to double again by 2025, with some major urban areas experiencing up to 5 percent growth annually. Squatter settlements have mushroomed and in many cases intruded into forested reserves. As such illegal settlements are not usually serviced by the cities' infrastructure, this leads to open burning or dumping of wastes into rivers.

As the country has progressed, there has been competition for land use for agriculture, mining, industry, timber and development. Decisions about land conversion are based exclusively on economic rates of return on investment. This contributed to massive deforestation for tin mining in the early 1900s, for agriculture and land development schemes in the 1960s and 1970s, and for urban and industrial development in the 1980s and 1990s. Rubber and oil palm are two major cash crops, occupying 15 percent and 12 percent, respectively, of the total land area in Peninsular Malaysia. Oil palm cultivation is the main reason for the loss of lowland forests, and the amount of land under oil palm cultivation was increased by 10 percent annually from 1970 to 1992.

Another major money earner is timber. In response to international consumer pressure, there is a declared objective to implement sustainable-yield harvesting, and Malaysia's furniture-making industry is being promoted so that more money can be made from fewer logs. Nevertheless, the authorities find it difficult to police the vast, densely-forested areas involved, so excessive logging continues.

As Malaysia makes the transition from an economy based on commodities to an industrialised one, future threats to the environment are likely to be from industrial pollution. During the early industrial phase of the 1970s, palm oil and rubber processing resulted in the discharge of large amounts of organic effluents into Malaysia's water. With growing industrialisation, the Department of Environment has identified the chemical, food and beverage, textile, metal finishing, and animal husbandry industries as additional contributors of pollution. Of 119 rivers monitored for water quality

in 1995, 14 were categorised as highly polluted and 53 as slightly polluted. Air pollution has also increased, with the Klang Valley regularly experiencing smog during the annual dry season.

Malaysians have recently suffered a series of environmental disasters, including months-long blankets of smoke from the burning of forests in neighbouring Indonesia, landslides, flooding and contagious-disease epidemics. These have begun to drive home the importance of nature's role in the preserving of the quality of human life. Changes in attitude and policy are clearly perceptible; one can only hope that Malaysians care enough to preserve their land and seas with all their lush beauty. ❑

RIGHT: lorries laden with tropical timber – sometimes illegally gotten – are a familiar sight on interior roads.

THE PEOPLE

Aborigines, Malays, Indians, Europeans, Chinese – these are just some of the many and diverse peoples that have given Malaysia its unique character

The traveller in Malaysia will be fascinated by the obvious multi-culturalism of the country: there are Malays, Chinese, Indians and Eurasians; as well as large tribal communities like the Kadazandusuns of Sabah and the Iban of Sarawak. And given the melting pot of ethnicities, a sizeable number of people of mixed race abound as well.

The population stands at around 25 million today, with 83 percent living in Peninsular Malaysia, 9 percent in Sarawak and the remaining 8 percent in Sabah. The distribution of population is grossly unequal when one considers that most people are found in the peninsula, which at 131,587 sq km (50,800 sq miles) is considerably smaller than Sarawak (124,967 sq km/48,250 sq miles) and Sabah (72,500 sq km/27,900 sq miles) put together.

The original inhabitants of the peninsula, the Orang Asli, were followed by the Malays, who built upon traditions of the soil and ocean, and embraced influences from elsewhere as well. Due to its rich resources and strategic location, Malaysia attracted still others – the culturally-rich Indians, Chinese, and Europeans – resulting in rich yet culturally diverse traditions.

Orang Asli

The Malay term Orang Asli means "original people" and covers three more or less distinct groups and a score or more of separate tribes. Of the estimated 98,000 Orang Asli, 89 percent live in rural areas, many of which are on the fringes of towns, selling forest produce such as bamboo, and wild fruit and vegetables to the townspeople. The British were perhaps the first to group the Orang Asli together, using the term *sakai* or debt-slave to define them. Their origins still remain something of a mystery; what is known is that the main groups vary from one another racially, culturally and linguistically.

Undoubtedly, the oldest inhabitants of the

PRECEDING PAGES: snapshots on a longhouse wall.
LEFT: the new breed of high-tech workers.
RIGHT: inside a makeshift Orang Asli home.

Malaysian Peninsula are the Negritos, arriving in the Malay Peninsula at least 10,000 years ago. Numbering around 2,000, they are mostly dark-skinned and frizzy-haired, their features, though unique, are similar to the peoples of Papua New Guinea or East Africa. The Negritos mostly inhabit the northeast and northwest

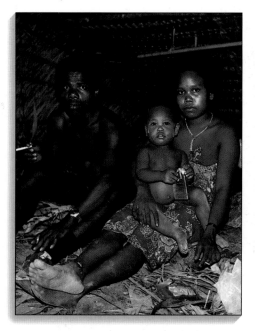

of the peninsula, and are the only truly nomadic of the Orang Asli tribes. Practising little or no cultivation, the Negrito tribes pride themselves on their mobility. However, like other tribes, some Negritos have left the forest and sought education and jobs in the city.

The largest group, numbering around 40,000, is the Senoi – thought to share a common ancestry with the hill peoples of northern Cambodia and Vietnam – arrived in the Malay Peninsula between 6,000 and 8,000 years ago. Most of the tribes are shifting cultivators, moving from a settlement when the land is exhausted. Many Senoi in the Cameron Highlands have become wage-earners, working on the highland tea estates. Others have headed for the bright city lights, getting jobs as varied as civil servants and taxi drivers.

The last group of Orang Asli, the Proto Malays or Aboriginal Malays, were the last to arrive – from the Indonesian island of Sumatra – around 4,000 years ago. Many of this group also have a distinct resemblance to the Malays; indeed modern Malays have a common ancestry with many of them.

Malays

The Malays, long linked to the land as *bumiputra*, or sons of the soil, are known for being

duced to raise the Malay stake in the economy.

Rural Malays today still cherish the simplicity of the uncluttered, outdoor life, nurturing a provincial conformity laid down centuries ago. Malay *kampung* are peaceful enclaves, with wooden houses propped up on stilts above courtyards shaded by coconut palms, banana and papaya trees. The village mosque calls the faithful to prayer several times a day, often interrupting evening television programmes that are now a part of everyday family life.

Kampung youth and children may favour shorts and blue jeans but the daily dress code is still the comfortable cotton *sarung*. Rolled

generous and hospitable with an easy smile and a well-developed sense of humour – traits perhaps of a people who have had the good fortune to live peacefully in a land abundant year-round with food.

As a whole, Malays comprise 52 percent of Malaysia's population. Historically, as *bumiputra* or "sons of the soil", the Malays have always wielded political authority. However, when the status quo of the Malays was threatened in the 1969 elections, culminating in bloody racial riots, the New Economic Policy (NEP) was set in place to protect the interests of the *bumiputra*. Racial quotas, scholarships and business and housing subsidies were intro-

HOME CLEAN HOME

In Malay homes, be it a humble *kampung* dwelling or a high-rise condominium in the suburbs of Kuala Lumpur, traditional customs hold sway.

The most noticeable hallmark of a Malay home is cleanliness, a trait considered next to godliness. It is said that the brighter the house, the more blessings God will bestow upon those who dwell within its walls. In *kampung* homes, a basin of water is always placed at the bottom of the entrance stairs. This is to allow for the washing of feet before entering. As in practically all Asian cultures, to tread into someone's home wearing any form of footwear is absolutely unthinkable…

expertly at the waist, and topped off with either a batik shirt or T-shirt, this airy garment is especially indispensable among older Malays. On special occasions, the traditional and comfortable *baju kurung*, a long-skirted suit usually made of colourful silk, is worn by women, while men don their *baju melayu*, a loose pantsuit worn with a short sarong, topped with a black velvet fez known as a *songkok*.

The inherent talents of the Malays, however, find outlets far from the countryside. Malay businessmen and civil servants in the cities wear Western-style clothes, drive cars, speak English fluently, and carry mobile phones. Urban youths pick up the latest in street fashion from the US and display their new togs in shopping malls. Hard rock and heavy metal is popular, as is the electric guitar. The amplified sounds of the instrument can even be heard blaring from isolated *kampung* houses.

Although the rift between the *kampung* and the city has widened over the years, it does not threaten the strong unity the Malays derive from a common faith. The laws of Islam immediately set a Malay apart from fellow Malaysians. Intermarriage between races is uncommon, though Muslim foreigners are accepted, keeping the Malay-Muslim cultural identity distinctly separate.

Muslim women, especially, stand out from other ethnic Malaysians mainly because of their dress codes. Recently, an increasing number of Malay women have chosen to wear the veil, or *tudung*, a garment of modesty. Despite this seemingly strict dress code and traditional Islamic laws (which, for example, allows polygymy), Muslim women in Malaysia are given an increasing amount of employment and property rights; many run their own businesses and have high-profile jobs.

Indians

Indians began visiting Malaysia 2,000 years ago, following rumours of fortune in a land their ancestors knew as Suvarnadvipa, the fabled "golden peninsula". Tamil blood even flows through the royal lineage dating back to

---

THE BIRTH OF ISLAM

The earliest record of Islam on the Malay Peninsula is an inscription in Terengganu dating from 1303, prescribing penalties for those not observing the faith's moral code.

13th-century Melaka, where the first sultanate was found. But it was not until the 19th century that Indians arrived and stayed in large numbers, employed mainly as rubber tappers or other plantation labourers. Most came from south India, and about 80 percent were Tamil, with small numbers of Sikh, Bengali, Keralan, Telugu and Parsi. Malaysian Indians still maintain strong home ties with their former villages, sometimes even taking wives from there and bringing them to live in Malaysia.

Today, Indians (mostly concentrated in the states of Selangor, Perak and Penang) make up less than 10 percent of the population of Malaysia, yet they own less than one percent of the country's corporate wealth. It has been estimated that four out of five Indians, mostly Tamils, are still manual labourers on plantations, a situation that has been explained as a legacy of colonial Malaysia.

However, as the country gains in economic prosperity, other Indian communities are increasingly well-represented in the various professions. Several programmes have been initiated to raise the Indian share of Malaysia's wealth but the general consensus is that the eco-

---

LEFT: friendly Malays, also known as *bumiputera* or sons of the soil. **RIGHT:** Indians are a minority race.

nomic restructuring plans of the NEP have generally overlooked the Indians.

Indian Muslims are also a significant part of the Indian community. When they arrived in Malaysia, many opened restaurants, textile shops and other successful businesses, and some of them married Malay women.

Southern Indians have brought a rich cultural influence and colour to Malaysian life. Bright silk saris, fiery Indian cuisine, Tamil movies with their song-and-dance scenes, and the indomitable

EARLY ARRIVALS

Chinese Ming admiral, Cheng Ho, first visited Melaka in 1403; many Chinese traders afterwards followed his example and set up warehouses for trade there.

tants:... they are the only people from whom a revenue may be raised without expense and extraordinary effort by the government."

It was for both fortune and adventure that the Chinese first headed for *Nanyang*, the South Seas. From the 13th century onwards, the Chinese were frequent traders in the Indonesian and Malay archipelago. However, the majority of the Chinese arrived in the 19th century during the Manchu dynasty when problems were rife in China. An edict was issued banning Chinese

prevalence of the Hindu faith that continues to absorb change have all become part of Malaysia.

Chinese

The Chinese population makes up 30 percent of the country's total, yet their presence and control of major industries such as rubber and tin and the commercial sector would seem to make their numbers far greater. They can be found in any trading centre, from Kuala Lumpur to the smallest isolated shop far up the Rejang River in Sarawak. In 1794, Francis Light, founder of Georgetown, Penang, was so impressed by the hardy Chinese that he wrote: "The Chinese constitute the most valuable part of our inhabi-

from travelling abroad, but a number risked their lives and escaped. These later Chinese immigrants were organised under clan associations (*kongsi*) and secret societies, which often engaged in rival warfare. The new settlers took on many of the toughest jobs in tin mining, road and railway construction; but they also played as hard as they worked, and opium and gambling were popular pastimes.

Rather than integrating with Malay culture, the Chinese community has put its own traditional stamp on the land. Officially, all Chinese must learn Malay, but at home, Mandarin and local dialects prevail. Younger generations, however, are more caught up in modern Western lifestyles.

There is a strong belief in self-help and industriousness among the Chinese, but close family and clan ties are also priorities. The Chinese in Malaysia are defined by their history of hardship and pioneering, as well as the three important Chinese code of ethics: Confucianism, Taoism and Buddhism. Even if converted to Islam or Christianity, this background is deep-rooted and many of the associated festivals are regularly celebrated.

Even among modern Malaysian Chinese, the belief in symbolism is prevalent. Jade is worn by the majority of Malaysian Chinese for aesthetic reasons as well as for its evil-warding powers. *Feng shui* (literally, "wind, water") is the Chinese belief system based on geomantic omens. The numeral 8 is extremely coveted for house numbers and car licence plates, as it sounds like the Cantonese character for "prosper"; meanwhile, the number 4 is carefully avoided, as it sounds like "death".

Peranakans

The Peranakan culture was first established when Chinese trade missions established a port in Melaka in the early 1400s. Inter-cultural relationships and marriages were forged between traders and local Malay women, as well as between Melaka's sultans and the Chinese Ming emperors. In 1460, Sultan Mansor Shah married Ming Princess Hang Li Poh, who brought with her 500 "youths of noble birth", and many handmaidens and settled around Bukit Cina (Chinese Hill).

Subsequent generations of Chinese-Malays were known as Straits Chinese, or Peranakan, which in Malay means "born here". When the Dutch colonists moved out in the early 1800s, more Chinese immigrants moved in, thus diluting Malay blood in the Peranakans, so that later generations were almost completely Chinese. However, this did not alter the Straits Chinese identity, which combines the best of Malay and Chinese cultures. This colourful balance encompasses Malay dress such as the *sarung kebaya*, a unique bi-cultural cuisine, and a spoken language of mixed Malay, Chinese and some English colloquialisms.

Peranakan culture reached its height in the

19th century, and though Melaka was the Peranakan centre, large communities also flourished in Penang and Singapore. Today's Peranakans are proud of their heritage and consider themselves different from the other Chinese, although they are counted as part of the community.

Eurasians

When the Sultanate of Melaka fell to Portuguese invaders in 1511, the new rulers sought to establish control by encouraging the Portuguese soldiers to marry local Melakan women. As can be expected, a strong Eurasian community grew up with loyalty to Portugal

through its ties of blood and the Catholic faith.

Nearly 500 years after their arrival, there is still widespread evidence of the Portuguese legacy. Eurasians in Melaka, as well as in other towns in Malaysia, bear such Portuguese surnames as Sequiera, Pinto, Dias, D'Silva and D'Souza, and still cherish the traditions of their European lineage. They are proud of their unique Eurasian cuisine, and some still continue to speak *Cristao*, a medieval dialect from southeastern Portugal. The language has long since died out in Europe, but is still used in some parts of Malaysia. Descendants of cross-cultural marriages in the 19th and 20th century are equally proud of their English or Dutch heritage.

LEFT: the Chinese are well known for their business acumen and industriousness. **RIGHT:** a Peranakan bride getting dressed for her big day.

The people of Sabah and Sarawak

The two easternmost states of Sabah and Sarawak, situated in the north of the island of Borneo, have the most diverse racial groups of all Malaysia. Most of them are of Mongoloid extract and moved here from Kalimantan (Indonesian Borneo).

In Sabah, the largest group comprises the Kadazandusun tribes, followed by the Murut, Bajau and Rungus, and Bisaya, Suluk, Lundayeh and Kedayan in smaller numbers.

In Sarawak there is an even greater diversity of peoples and languages: the Dayak include Ibans, who make up the majority of the Sarawak population, and the Bidayuh or land Dayaks. The Melanau are also a large community, and then there are many tribes lumped together under the name of Orang Ulu. This term, meaning "interior people", has become somewhat derogatory in the sense that it denotes a primitive and ignorant people – most tribes prefer to be known by their own names. The Orang Ulu group includes the nomadic Punan and Penan, the highly structured Kayan and Kenyah communities, and the Kajang, Kelabit, Lun Bawang and Bisaya. Even these names house several different tribes who have their own special names. ❏

MYTHS AND TRADITIONS

Borneo has been known as a land of head-hunters, a term which seems to conjure up a cruel and aggressive people. Contrary to this misconception, the people of Sarawak are a gentle, law-abiding people and in the days of head-hunting, taking the heads of one's enemies only occurred when the community suffered some plague. The heads of enemies were thought to bring protection from danger and sickness. Taking a head was also a way of proving one's manhood. Only the heads of warriors were coveted, and the women and children of the enemy eventually became integrated into the victor's community. Today, head-hunting is outlawed, and the skulls seen hanging in longhouses are those that have been inherited by families.

Tattoos are another cultural tradition in Borneo, and both men and women sport elaborate designs on their bodies. Worn both for protection and decoration, each tattoo is designed to suit the wearer. These days, however, tattoos are becoming more of a fashion statement for young urban Iban.

In the past many tribes also placed long weights or simple wooden plugs in the ears of children in order to stretch the earlobe. Women wore the heaviest ones so that their lobes eventually stretched down to their chests. Such lobes are still considered a sign of great beauty by traditional tribespeople, although this practice has now died out.

Festival Fever

Malaysia's multi-cultural population makes for a heady mix of festivals. Not only are all the major religious events celebrated but there are dozens of other secular happenings around the country – from kite-flying to Formula One racing. Most religious festivals are calculated on the lunar calendar and their dates change each year, so check with a tourism office first.

If you don't know any locals, the big religious celebrations can be a non-event for tourists as most of the action happens in the home. If you get an invitation take it up, as it is the only way to really experience these events. Enquire at tourism offices about "homestays" and families who invite tourists to participate in their celebrations.

Here are just a few of the major events:

January–March

● During the Chinese New Year, which culminates in the festival of *Chap Goh Mei*, houses and shops are decorated, lion dances are performed and temples are thronged with worshippers. To immerse yourself in the action, visit Kuala Lumpur's Petaling Street night market before the event.
● Thaipusam, a spectacular Hindu festival where penitents pierce their bodies with hooks and shoulder huge yokes, draws up to a million spectators to Kuala Lumpur's Batu Caves; also held in Penang.
● Le Tour de Langkawi, Malaysia's answer to the classic Tour de France, a gruelling bike race.

April–June

● The International Kite Festival, attracting the world's largest and weirdest kites, is held at Tumpat Beach in Kelantan.
● Sabah Fest is an annual 2-week get-together for the state's 30 colourful ethnic groups, showcasing Borneo's unique cultural heritage.
● Gawai, Sarawak's biggest event, is a celebration of the rice harvest, with dancing, feasting and bountiful toasting with *tuak* (rice wine).

July–September

● The International Towerathon sees marathon racers running up the KL Tower.
● National Day, the commemoration of Indepen-dence, is held every 31 August with pomp and parades, in a different location each year.
● World Rainforest Music Festival, at the Sarawak Cultural Village, Damai, brings together the best of world music and indigenous beats.
● The Moon Cake Festival and the Lantern Festival mark an ancient Chinese peasant victory over Mongolian warlords. Special cakes are eaten and children celebrate with lantern processions.

October–December

● Deepavali, the Hindu Festival of Lights, is a family affair to celebrate the triumph of good over evil. Tiny oil lamps flicker all night long in Hindu homes.

● Mount Kinabalu International Climbathon, the toughest mountain race in the world, attracts the world's best mountain runners.
● Christmas is best enjoyed in Melaka, especially in the Portuguese Settlement, where the Eurasian Catholic minority celebrate in exuberant style.

Variable Dates

● Hari Raya Haji marks the completion of each year's pilgrimage to Mecca.
● Hari Raya celebrations at the end of the month-long Muslim fast of Ramadan include special food, prayers, and a month-long "open house" when families and friends visit each other and enjoy a spectacular array of cakes and snacks. ❑

LEFT: An Iban of Sarawak in traditional dress.
RIGHT: the Lion Dance is a vibrant highlight of the Chinese New Year celebrations.

RELIGION

*Malaysians have long enjoyed a harmonious atmosphere of religious tolerance.
But recent outpourings of Islamic extremism could presage future strife*

For anyone wanting a crash course in comparative religion, Malaysia is the place to come. From animism to the latest revivalist movement, Malaysia is home to all the world's major beliefs and a host of minor ones besides. Religion is found everywhere – in mosques, temples and churches, in the perpetual round of religious festivals, in diverse rites of passage, and in a multitude of everyday sights and sounds.

Each faith tends to identify with a specific ethnic group. Every Malay is a Muslim, but there are also Indian Muslims, Sarawak Muslims (Melanau) and Sabah Muslims (Bajau and Orang Sungai), as well as small but significant groups of Chinese, Kadazandusun, Murut and other converts. Buddhism is allied to the Thais and the Chinese, while most Chinese who are not Buddhists are Confucians, Taoists and/or ancestor-worshippers. Hinduism is the preserve of the Hindus, and Sikhism of the Sikhs. Only Christianity is truly multi-ethnic, embracing small minorities of Indians and Chinese in the peninsula and rather larger groups of Ibans, Bidayuhs, Kedayans, Kadazandusuns and Muruts in Sarawak and Sabah. Folk religion holds sway among many in these Bornean states. In the interior of the peninsula, small clusters of Orang Asli (aborigines) still cling to their ancient animism.

Religious tolerance

This great variety of faiths within the compass of a small nation is hardly surprising, given the rich ethnic mix that Malaysia enjoys. What is more surprising is that the followers of these different creeds – some of whom are at daggers drawn with one another elsewhere – live here in relative peace and harmony.

Although Islam is the official religion and Muslims account for over half the total population, the constitution guarantees the free pursuit of all other beliefs. Religious friction rarely arises. If it does, it is easily controlled by a combination of effective monitoring by government, and of a lively awareness among people at large of its destructive and antisocial consequences. In any case, ethnic interaction, particularly in urban areas – at the workplace,

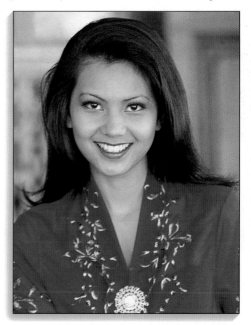

in shops and offices, in the arts, on the sportsfield, and on social occasions – contributes towards mutual understanding and tolerance.

One advantage of a land with many different creeds is a prolificacy of public holidays. All the major religious festivals are treated as national holidays, and a list of minor ones at state level adds to the score.

This happy state of affairs has given rise to the peculiarly Malaysian "open house". Guests don't have to be followers of the particular religion whose sacred feast is being celebrated. Operating at all social levels, at its pinnacle, the homes of royalty and political leaders are thrown open to everybody, including tourists.

PRECEDING PAGES: Kayan girls of Sarawak.
LEFT: Impish schoolgirls sporting *tudung* (Muslim headwrap). **RIGHT:** a more liberal Muslim sister.

Islamic Resurgence

Islamic resurgence in Malaysia forms part of a global Muslim phenomenon which has emerged since the end of World War II. In general, its proponents say that it is a movement to restore Islamic civilisation to its former prominence, and to re-establish an alternative world social order to the existing one dominated by the individualistic and materialistic values of the West. The ultimate goal of this re-ordering of Islamic society is the creation of Islamic polities, whose government and administration are based on the *Koran* and the *Sunnah*

(i.e. the words, deeds and actions of The Prophet).

Since the early 1970s, there has been a conscious attempt to establish an Islamic identity in law, medicine, education, economy, and ultimately to set up an Islamic state. From the purely religious point of view, this is all well and good. But in Malaysia's plural society, Islamic resurgence poses problems both for Muslims (especially the Malays) themselves, and for non-Muslims who make up almost half the country's population.

For the Malays, the growing trend of Islamic resurgence has deepened the rifts already existing between fundamentalists and moderate Muslims, politically expressed in the rivalry between the fundamentalist Pan-Malay(si)an Islamic Party

(PAS) and the United Malays National Organisation or UMNO, the party of the moderates. A foretaste of what life might be like in an Islamic state is provided by Kelantan, where PAS forms the state government and imposes strict regulations regarding the consumption of alcohol, dress codes and forms of entertainment, including traditional ones. However, the rights of non-Muslims in the state have been equally strictly respected.

Tensions caused by stricter interpretations of Islamic rules have been sharpened by UMNO's identification with a rising Malay middle class wed to the inequalities of capitalism and the shortcomings of urban living, as opposed to PAS's stand for a pristine Islam rooted in a rural society. For non-Muslims, the spectre of Islamic rule, with all the implications this holds, has reinforced their support for the ruling coalition, the Barisan Nasional (BN), of which UMNO itself is the leading member.

The successful Iranian Revolution of 1979, as the first successful Islamic revolution in modern times, gave an enormous fillip to Islamic resurgence everywhere and aggravated existing tensions between fundamentalists and moderates. The BN and its antecedents have been in power ever since independence in 1957, and so politically have had the upper hand. However, PAS has managed to collect an average of almost one-fifth of the total votes cast in most general elections and made large gains in the 1999 elections.

Aware of the dangers of extremism in a multiracial society, BN has met mounting Islamic resurgence with a policy of adoption and assimilation. Existing Islamic institutions have been strengthened and new ones added, including Islamic banks, schools and colleges and an international Islamic university, a system of separate *syariah* courts with judicial autonomy, and greater media coverage has been given to Islamic issues.

These strategies proved quite successful in containing Islamic resurgence until very recently. However, the political repercussions of the summary dismissal in late 1998 of Anwar Ibrahim, the deputy prime minister, himself a prominent champion of Islamic values, have alienated many Malaysians, especially Malays, from their traditional support for the BN. The net result has been to give a new complexion to Malaysian politics and a further impetus to the Islamic resurgence movement, with consequences which are difficult to predict. ❑

LEFT: Islamic not just in manner but in dress – Kelantan schoolboys in traditional garb.

The reward for queueing long hours to gain entry is the chance to greet the VIP in person and to partake of the fare always provided.

Another revelation for the visitor from abroad is the devoutness of the adherents of all faiths. Religion is a living force in Malaysia. At prayer times mosques and temples are packed and the large congregations in churches must be the envy of any parish priest in the West. Hindu and Chinese devotees perform their penance in their thousands. The faithful participate in

> ### BEAUTY FATWA
>
> Although Malaysia's Islamic law is generally moderate, in 1997 *ulamas* (muslim theologians) in Selangor placed a *fatwa* banning beauty contests in the state.

not make Malaysia an Islamic state, because government is not based on Islamic law. But it does mean that Islam has the full backing, financial and otherwise, of the state. Left to fend for themselves, other religions are all the more conscious of their dependence on their own efforts to survive and flourish.

As for the administration of Islam itself, each of the 9 Malay rulers is the religious as well as political head of his state, while in states not headed by Malay royalty – such as Sabah and Sarawak – the

religious parades and processions in the tens of thousands. Religious devotions are observed with equal zeal at home.

Of course, not all Malaysians take their religion so seriously. But religious faith is real and palpable and forms an important element in determining public values to a degree rarely found in modern Western society.

The role of Islam

This great religious fervour is probably a consequence, at least in part, of Islam's position as the official religion. Islam's official status does

ABOVE: Islamic calligraphy outside a KL mosque.

King of Malaysia fills the gap. Maintaining the Malay rulers in this traditional role – acting at federal level collectively through the Conference of Rulers, with the king as their chairman – helps solve a major dilemma; reconciling Islam's dogma of the unity of the religious and the secular with modern Western pragmatism, which keeps the two distinctly apart. The arrangement also facilitates the acceptance by the Muslim majority of secular laws for secular affairs, while domestic religious issues (such as property rights, marriage and divorce, etc.) remain under the jurisdiction of the Islamic *syariah* courts. By the same token, the Islamic courts hold no jurisdiction over non-Muslims, so that the system safeguards the interests of other creeds as well.

Despite its obvious pre-eminence today, Islam was a late arrival in Malaysia, long preceded by Hinduism, Buddhism and animism. The Malay conversion to Islam was only effectively completed some 500 years ago, during the days of the Melaka sultanate. Before that, Malays had been Hindus, Buddhists or animists (or all three rolled into one). But unlike the aristocratic forms of Hinduism and Buddhism which it replaced, Islam is a religion of the people, with a message of salvation for everyone. Propagated by generations of Arab and Indian-

sist of Malaysian Thais and smaller Burmese and Sinhalese groups.

The main difference between the two seems to be one of sophistication. The Theravada School is much simpler, more abstract and claims to be much closer to the original teachings and way of life of the Buddha. The Mahayana School, having absorbed other influences in the lands where it flourishes (such as in China itself) acknowledges a number of deities, the most famous in Malaysia being the Goddess Kuan Yin. The Mahayana School also has far more complicated rituals and observances.

Chinese Buddhists have been long established

Muslim missionaries, the new faith gained an unshakeable hold over the Malays. It is probably the single most important factor that saved Malay society from disintegration under the pressures of the industrial imperialism of the West in modern times.

Malaysian Buddhists

Next to Islam, in terms of numbers, comes Buddhism, forming just under a fifth of the total Malaysian population. Buddhists fall into one of two main schools, the Mahayana and Theravada (Hinayana). The Mahayana (Great Path) School is the Buddhism of the Chinese, while Theravada (Little Path) Buddhists con-

in Malaysia, being virtually synonymous with Chinese settlement in the country. Their earliest contact probably goes back to the days of the Sri Vijayan Empire during the 9th century AD, when its capital, Palembang in Sumatra, was a great centre for Buddhist studies. But Chinese Buddhism only achieved a permanent presence when the Chinese began to establish themselves as a community in Melaka. Most Chinese Buddhists today are the descendants of the droves of Chinese immigrants who arrived during the 19th century and the first half of the 20th.

Chinese Buddhists are far more numerous than their Thai counterparts. It has been reckoned – though no one has actually taken a count

– that there are at least 3,000 Chinese Buddhist temples, societies and organisations in Malaysia, all of which run their own affairs, although most are also members of the Malaysian Buddhist Association. Thai Buddhists arrived on the scene much later, namely during the late 18th century when their political influence penetrated deepest into the Malay Peninsula. As a result, they are mostly concentrated in the peninsula's northern states where their legacy lies in some of the most beautiful temples to be found anywhere. Apart from the Thais, there is a community of Burmese Buddhists in Penang, and one of Sinhalese

pounded with traditional ancestor worship into an intricate web of ideas, beliefs and ritual that is best described simply as "Chinese Religion".

Wherever the Chinese went, they took their "religion" with them as an integral part of their culture. Today, Chinese religious traditions reveal themselves in ubiquitous household altars, in little shrines along the roadside, in giant joss sticks smouldering at temple thresholds, and in little prayer slips and red paper banners serving a multiplicity of purposes; keeping evil spirits at bay, seeking a cure for an illness, and paying respect to the dear departed.

As with Buddhist organisations, Chinese

Buddhists, whose impressive headquarters forms a prominent landmark in Kuala Lumpur.

Chinese religion

The line between Chinese philosophy and religion has always been a tenuous one. The thoughts of Confucius and the mysticism of the Taoists have been dominant influences in the evolution of the Chinese world view. Down the centuries, these influences have become com-

temples are run autonomously by local associations, although most of them also are members of the umbrella Buddhist, Confucian and Taoist Association of Malaysia. Altogether, about one tenth of all Malaysians come under the category of Chinese religion.

Hindus and Sikhs

Hinduism goes back to the dawn of history, when it came with the first Indian traders to Malaysian shores. The new religion created a cultural revolution. It transformed Malay headmen into kings who absorbed Hindu beliefs and cosmology and adopted Hindu traditions of government without losing their own identity as

FAR LEFT: a Chinese house altar with offerings.
LEFT: Thai-inspired image of the Buddha.
ABOVE: a Hindu devotee carrying sacrificial *kavadi* during the festival of Thaipusam.

Malays. This Hindu period, which lasted for 1,500 years before it was replaced by Islam, has left its traces in Malay language and literature, in Malay art forms such as the shadow play (*wayang kulit*) and in such traditions as the *bersanding* ceremony, when the bridal couple sit in state during a Malay wedding.

However, the Hinduism of the past has very little to do with today's Malaysian Hindus. Now numbering around one million, they are the descendants of Indian immigrants who over the last 200 years came to work as contract labourers, with a seasoning of English-educated clerks, apothecaries, shopkeepers and mer-

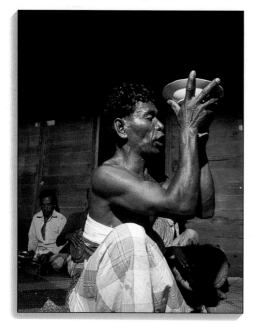

chants who laid the foundations of a modern Indian middle-class. Hindu temples in Malaysia are managed by local committees, following closely the traditions of their place of origin in India. Temples in the towns are more sophisticated affairs, supported by wealthier members of the community.

The 50,000 Sikhs in Malaysia are the representatives of a Hindu sect which became a religion. It was founded in 15th-century India by Guru Nanak who, influenced by Islam, converted his pantheist Hindu followers into monotheists. The Sikh presence in Malaysia is a direct result of British recruitment of members of this famous warrior community to provide the core of the new police forces in the country. Sikhs nowadays are prominent in business and the professions, and despite their small numbers, are found in all the main centres in the land, including Sarawak and Sabah.

Christianity

The first Christians in Malaysia were the Portuguese conquerors of Melaka in 1511, whose descendants from inter-marriage with local women still live there, forming a distinct group of their own. The Dutch, who followed a century later, made no attempt to convert their subjects and so the great period of Christian proselytisation came in the 19th century with the British. Official British policy was not to interfere with other people's beliefs, but Western Christian missionaries were given a free hand to spread their religion, which they did primarily by founding English-medium schools. Christian missionary activity got a second wind after World War II, led by small Christian revivalist churches, many from the USA.

Today, there are about one million Christians in Malaysia, two-thirds of them in Sabah and Sarawak. The three main Christian divisions are all present, but Orthodox Christians constitute only a handful. Roman Catholics, of whom the first were the Portuguese, form the largest group, about two-fifths of the whole. The Protestants are represented by Anglicans – a legacy of British colonialism – Methodists and Presbyterians, largely American-dominated, and smaller groups amongst which the Baptists are the most prominent. ❑

SPIRITS IN THE TREES

In traditional Malay society, the *bomoh* (witch doctor) is a respected spiritual expert, often called upon to use *ilmu* (knowledge) and herbal potions to heal illnesses, especially those caused by *hantu* (spirits). Primitive animism, which peoples every article of creation with resident spirits, is practised by a tiny, dwindling group of Orang Asli (aborigines), living in the remoter areas of the peninsula's interior.

The folk religions of the indigenous peoples of Sarawak and Sabah are more sophisticated, and feature ingenious theories about the origins of life. Their deities are often imbued with very human foibles.

LEFT: a *bomoh* seeking help from the spiritual world.
RIGHT: St. George's Church in Georgetown, Penang.

ARCHITECTURE

From traditional homes to the shining splendour of the world's tallest skyscraper,

Malaysia's buildings reflect both its colourful past and its hopes for the future

It is said that the spirit of a society is embodied in its architecture, and Malaysia, a champion and torch-bearer for developing nations the world over, has taken this sentiment to heart. As a result, the evolution of vernacular and modern architecture on the Malay Peninsula and in the Borneo states of Sabah and Sarawak ably documents not only the history of the land, but also the essence of its various indigenous and immigrant peoples.

The evolution has been guided by historical markers, the colours of which are strong even today: the first ocean-canoeing Polynesians from the Pacific; Indian and Arabic traders from the West; the era of the wealthy sultans; the European influence; imported Chinese and Indian cultures; the elation of Independence; and the path to globalisation.

City of dreams

The architectural journey begins at the US$6 billion-plus Kuala Lumpur International Airport (KLIA). When craning to view the skylights 40 metres (130 ft) above you, the grandeur of the project becomes apparent. As all architects agree, design is in the details, and KLIA bags the prize in every category: from the conical columns-cum-air-conditioning vents and returns; the inspired "forest-canopy" effect lighting and the highly contrived but suprisingly effective "forests" within the satellite building. International flights are usually routed through the satellite, involving a breakneck electric shuttle journey into the main terminal – leaving you suitably shaken for your encounter with Malaysian immigration.

The show continues along the 88-km (55-mile) journey as an autobahn-standard highway snakes its way into the capital. Kuala Lumpur rears into view, as any city sporting the world's tallest buildings might, with as much drama as surprise. The highway links directly with the

---

PRECEDING PAGES: Kuala Lumpur's National Stadium. **LEFT:** Minangkabau-inspired architecture, Negeri Sembilan. **RIGHT:** Kuala Lumpur International Airport.

inner ring-road and the Golden Triangle in the most built-up part of the city. Among a drab offering of 1970s international styles and post-modern aspirants, the elegant Tabung Haji (or Pilgrim's Fund) "hourglass" building draws the eye, but then, out of the concrete forest, rises the Petronas Twin Towers.

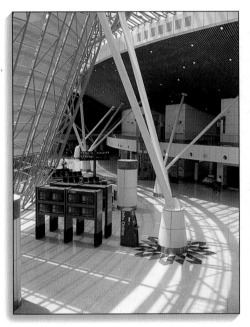

The towers bought Kuala Lumpur the kind of instant charisma once promised to puny boys in the advertisements at the back of comic-books – no more would this former tin-mining outpost have sand kicked in its face! During office hours, visitors can ascend to the Skybridge on the 42nd floor for expansive views of the city. Entrance is free but you'll be encouraged to part with your foreign exchange in the vast shopping mall "podium" from which the monument rises. Also at the towers is the impressive home of the Malaysian Philharmonic Orchestra, the Dewan Filharmonik Petronas concert hall which, on a per-seat basis, is the most expensive ever constructed.

Colonial past

Stepping outside brings you back to the real Kuala Lumpur, with the standard architectural hang-ups of any insecure city. Eagle-eyes will spot many high-rises with pitched-roofs: a contemporary vernacular that captures domestic Malaysian sensibilities, and couples them with the country's reach-for-the-sky aspirations. Lower your view, and head toward the tallest flagpole in the world (it's even in the record books). Located in the *Padang*, upon which cricket is still played, the Malaysian flag flies over the centre of the former British administrative headquarters of Malaya. As with all colonial planning, the adage "God, King and Country" are literally represented by St Mary's Cathedral, the Sultan Abdul Samad Building and the Royal Selangor Club. Of the three, it is the club which has changed the most architecturally: its mock-Tudor facade has undergone numerous face-lifts and extensions over the years. On the other hand, the conspiratorial chattering of the lawyers who frequent its Long Bar has probably altered little since the distant days of Governor Swettenham.

The legacy of Victorian society can be seen along every trunk-road out of the city, in the form of estates of linked-terraced houses. These

THE MALAY KAMPUNG HOUSE

Once out of the urban centres, which are dominated by the ethnic Chinese, the *kampung* (villages) are characterised by a simplistic vernacular architecture representative of the ethnic Malay lifestyle. The basic elements are a single-level wooden structure, raised off the ground with wooden or bamboo walls and a thatched roof; these have evolved to incorporate many decorative influences from Indonesia and Thailand (in the south and north of the peninsula, respectively), and also from Indian and Arab traders.

There are four acknowledged styles of Malay house – Perak, Melaka, Kedah and East Coast. The styles are pri-

marily differentiated by roof shapes, geometric patterning of the wall panels, fenestration and layout. Generally, the climate-friendly design accommodates a verandah, a sleeping area, the main living room and a kitchen at the back. The windows are shuttered and set at a low height to allow occupants to look out when seated. There are several practicalities to the design: the raised floor protects against floods and fauna, and also against heat gain from the ground by circulating air beneath the structure; the steep roofs shed water quickly, their deep eaves shade windows and the thatch dampens the sound of beating rain – while the high interior disperses warm air effectively.

have become the preferred dwelling-type of a burgeoning middle-class. Built to government order, such developments grow in strict regimen; you'll see various stages of completion in sequence on the same site. Sub-contractors move from ground-beams up, until the homes are completed.

An imaginary line joins the Twin Towers to the airport, known as the Multi-media Super-Corridor (MSC). Planned as a "global-gateway" for everything "cyber", the MSC has suffered from an over-liberal planning brief. The result is a mish-mash of architectural styles that spectacularly fails to match the political coherence of Malaysia's policy on new technologies. MEASAT (the Malaysian Satellite Broadcasting company) managed a low-rise brick-motif gesture with a Vegas-esque signboard, while Microsoft and all the others who took advantage of the everything-exempt sweeteners to take up space, are planning sheds that appear to import their aesthetic from Nebraska.

Ancient origins

An hour or so south of Kuala Lumpur sits Melaka, founded around 1400 by fleeing Sumatran Prince Parameswara. He laid the foundations for what was to become a centre of teaching and trade in the thriving Southeast Asia of the 15th century. The Melaka Cultural Museum is housed in an 1895 replica of the timber-framed palace of the third sultan, Mansur Shah, which was originally destroyed by the Portuguese during their 130-year rule. The Portuguese's architectural artefacts in Melaka are the most significant – including the formidable *A Famosa* fort of 1512.

In 1641, control of Melaka was wrested by the Dutch, who set about building a regional trade hub, the administration of which was housed within the Stadhuys. This 1650s town hall, together with the Christ Church of 1753 (the ceiling beams of which are formed from single trees with no joints), represent probably the most complete examples of 17th-century colonial Dutch architecture in the region.

Commerce with the Dutch saw the growth of Johor as an urban centre. However, the architectural character of the city was defined later, in the 17th and 18th century with the influx of

Minangkabau and Bugis immigrants from Sumatra and Sulawesi respectively. The ordered and highly artistic Minangkabau later headed north – their tall, sweeping roof-style is found throughout the state of Negeri Sembilan (adjacent to Melaka). The Bugis, however, a feared warrior race, stayed in Johor, establishing a distinctive vernacular of ornate timberwork and design. Modern Johor has suffered from its proximity to Singapore. Having assumed the role of a black-market border-town, its grandiose "floating-city" schemes have resulted in urban erosion and negligible architectural worth.

THE STRAITS ECLECTIC STYLE

The favoured building-type in the Straits Settlements (from Penang down to Singapore) was the "shophouse", a double-storey unit with a lower level business floor and a verandah to keep pedestrians sheltered from the sun or rain, while upstairs the family maintained a residence. The style evolved from buildings favoured in mainland China, but Malay, Indian, Arab and Peranakan (Straits-born Chinese) flavourings have created lively and colourful variations on every street facade. This building-type has since matured into the most ubiquitous commercial architectural form on the peninsula – new shophouse developments climb six storeys or more.

LEFT: KL skyline with the green expanse of the *padang* as focus. **RIGHT:** Dutch architecture, Melaka

Kampung life

Island-life encounters along the east coast are far more inviting. Although the journey from Johor up to Terengganu takes in a number of vast hotel resorts, you'll also see scattered fishing communities with their beach-huts and stilt-raised shelters nestling in quiet coves and on the shore above the cobalt surf. The traditional thatched roof and walls, however, have given way to utilitarian zinc sheeting and planks.

Although not as dominant as the west coast colonial settlements, the east displays every evolutionary variant of the Malay *kampung* (village) house.

Crossing to the east coast involves a trek over a highland spine featuring architecture both wholly indigenous and imported. Taman Negara National Park occupies tens of thousands of hectares between the coasts and is home to the Orang Asli, or "original people". Their transient settlements are driven by their nomadic lifestyle – simple shelters of bound leaves and flexible supports adjacent to a hearth for cooking and warmth, all built using materials from the jungle.

The cultivated contrast of the colonial Cameron Highlands hill resort offers the peculiar charm of an English country village surrounded by verdant tapestries of lush tea plantations. Die-hard archaeologists could circuitously route themselves via the state of Kedah in the northeast corner and find in the Bujang Valley remnants of the 9–11th-century *candi* (temples) of the Malay Peninsula's Hindu-Buddhist period.

The quiet reflection of such an experience offers a delicate preamble to the bustling urban centre of Penang which attracted the most dynamic influences of British and Chinese architecture. The British contribution is apparent in the urban planning, wide boulevards, sea esplanade and imposing administrative buildings; the East India Company literally ran the island from 1786 onwards, and a great deal of capital was invested in its power base. Building conventions and by-laws took root here which set a precedent for almost every other high-street in Malaya.

Travelling back to Kuala Lumpur via Ipoh reveals another important architectural phase fuelled by wealth (primarily from tin-mining) and independence in the 1960s. Self-determination brought with it an architectural self-actualisation that resulted in forms unmatched ever since in integrity or detail. The cantilevered free-forms of amoebic car-porches were perfectly in tune with the swinging culture that borrowed the very shiniest from the West and cultivated home-grown heroes such as the legendary actor P. Ramlee. In the light of contemporary attempts at seeking a distinct Malaysian architectural identity – the current common approach being to slap a suitably Islamic motif on a pre-packaged curtain wall system – the 1960s remain a beacon of light.

Over in the states of Sabah and Sarawak, 1,000 km (620 miles) over the South China Sea on the island of Borneo, the longhouse (see *pages 294–5*) is the typical indigenous building. The basic construction follows the lines of a *kampung* house, but is extended to provide dwellings for many families – and sometimes an entire village. While the layout remains simple, including a "street" formed either between facing rows of living units or on their perimeter, the social organisation is highly complex; where, when and how units are allocated are based on hierarchy, and define cultural rituals of welcoming visitors, marriage, childbearing and security. ❑

LEFT: a Malay *kampung* house on stilts for ventilation.

Petronas Twin Towers

The Petronas Twin Towers stand 452 metres (1,480 ft) tall and are the focal point of the new Kuala Lumpur City Centre development. Although there was some contention when first commissioned, the towers currently enjoy the status of being the world's tallest twin buildings. However, such records are, inevitably, held only briefly.

A more pertinent attestation would be that a small developing country like Malaysia managed to muster enough global wealth, expertise and local confidence to not only conceptualise but also realise such a feat. Many may quibble on points of political motives, white elephants, Other People's Money and absolute irrelevance – but there is no denying the extraordinary power of such monumental architecture. On par with Gustav Eiffel's tower heralding the advantages of steel-construction, or the dramatic urban planning of Christopher Wren's St Paul's rising goliath-like over a shanty 17th-century London, the spirit of the Twin Towers is historic and "millennial". Considering that the local content (both in terms of expertise and materials) is minimal, the fact that they were built in Malaysia at all is testimony to the power of globalisation and how projects of any nature and size will be developed in years to come the world over.

Architecturally, the towers are practically faultless: the American architects delivered a Gotham-esque vision shinily clad in about 85,000 sq metres (280,000 sq ft) of imported European stainless steel. Executed with the simple, almost fascistic clarity of vision of all great monuments, scores of imported consultants laboured for just under – a remarkably short – four years to deliver the Kuala Lumpur skyline an attention-wrenching silhouette. When pushed into providing a link with local sensibilities, some rather contrived sketches reveal an 8-pointed star superimposed on eight semi-circles which together yield a tenuous Islamic floorplate geometry, giving face to Asian Values.

The path to realisation was fraught with having to achieve as many "world-firsts" as possible – the Malaysian rally-cry that screams "*Malaysia Boleh!*" ("Malaysia can do it!") could permit an attitude of no less. Some of these include the blistering construction schedule of two daily 12-hour shifts util-

ising over 2,000 workers at any given time; the double-level skybridge on the 42nd level, which is one of the highest in the world at 170 metres (560 ft) and took 4 weeks to lift into place; and the highest number of "double-deck" lifts to be contained in a building ever, running at speeds of 5 metres (16 ft) per second – going from the basement to the top floor takes about a minute.

When completed, the record height was disputed by the incumbent Sears Tower in Chicago; the latter wasn't quite ready to step off its podium. However, Malaysians insisted that the towers were the final word on the matter. To cap it all, literally, and somewhat controversially, were the two 75-metre

(246-ft) stainless-steel spikes that sat atop the 88th level, which, arguably, gave the buildings the winning edge over Sears Tower. But such unbecoming squabbling was put to rest when Malaysia declared that it was never the original intention to construct the tallest buildings in the world – it was just a "happy coincidence".

Visitors are allowed to ascend to the Skybridge on the 42nd floor from 9–10.30am and 2.30–4pm daily except Sunday. Access is at the ground floor of Tower Two where there is an information desk. Sean Connery and Catherine Zeta-Jones had access to the top when they filmed the movie *Entrapment*, but if you want to get to the higher floors, you had best ask the Prime Minister. ❏

RIGHT: the stunning Kuala Lumpur City Centre.

CUISINE

Malaysia's many peoples have retained their own culinary traditions. The result is a deliciously diverse national menu – and a playground for the tastebuds

Malaysia has been blessed with reliable weather and a lush landscape: tropical jungles, verdant rice paddies, endless coconut groves and teeming coral reefs submerged in emerald seas. These gifts of nature, and the ethnic complexity of Malaysia's population, combine to provide the country with flavours to thrill the palate.

This hedonistic encounter extends not only to multicultural tastes, aromas, colours and textures, but also to the vast spectrum of dining experiences available in Malaysia. Eating establishments range from dusty roadside stalls and noisy Chinese coffee shops, to smart air-conditioned restaurants and Western-style fast-food joints. The choices are infinite.

Village fare

For centuries, Malays lived in *kampung* (villages) close to rivers and coasts, enjoying the natural abundance of food. Traditional meals consisted of rice, fish, vegetables, and chilli sauces (*sambal*), while fresh herbs and coconut milk added fragrance and richness. However, until the 20th century, travel across the jungle-covered country was limited and regional styles of cooking prevailed. The northern states of Kedah, Kelantan, Perlis and Terengganu, for instance, have incorporated sour tamarind (*asam*), limes and fiery chillies in their cuisine because of the influence of neighbouring Thailand. One of the best known northern dishes is *nasi ulam*, a dish consisting of rice, finely sliced raw herbs and vegetables, a spicy chilli-coconut sauce, grilled fish and other cooked side dishes.

Indonesian influences are evident in various Malaysian states. In Johor in the far south, Javanese food was assimilated into Malay cooking over the past few centuries. In the central state of Negeri Sembilan, Minangkabau settlers from West Sumatra brought with them their rich, spicy dishes cooked in coconut milk. A perfect example is *rendang* – a semi-dry coconut-based curry which needs hours of gentle simmering, melding beef with fresh herbs like lemon grass, turmeric and ginger, and spices such as coriander, nutmeg and cloves. The result is pure ambrosia.

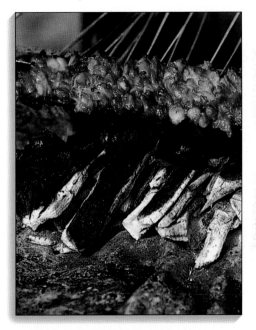

SATAY

SATAY

Satay is possibly the world's most popular Malay food, but whatever else you've tasted in your own country, nothing can prepare you for the real thing. Marinated bite-sized pieces of beef, mutton or chicken (and pork if sold by Chinese) are skewered onto thin, bamboo sticks, and barbecued over a charcoal fire. The sizzling satay is served with thick, spicy peanut gravy, chunks of raw onion and cucumber, and *ketupat* – compressed squares of rice. Leave the remaining bamboo sticks on the table, as the "bill" is settled by counting the total number of sticks left. For the adventurous, there are even satay variations of tripe, intestines, or crispy chicken skin.

PRECEDING PAGES: rice is the focus in this spread of fiery but flavoursome Malay fare.
LEFT: local produce on sale at a Kota Bharu market.
RIGHT: charcoal-grilled *satay*.

Despite differing regional styles, Malay food is, in general, heavily seasoned. Chillies are an everyday pick-me-up, either in dishes or as a blended *sambal* side-dish. The key to almost any Malay dish, however, is the *rempah* – a pounded paste of onions, garlic, chillies, fresh turmeric, and galangal (*langkuas*). The rempah is stir-fried in hot oil in a *kuali* (Chinese wok) and patiently stirred to prevent sticking and to release its tantalising aromas; it is said that this process is the make or break of the whole dish. A subtle seafood flavour is often added in the form of dried shrimps, dried anchovies (*ikan bilis*) or a pungent shrimp paste (*belacan*).

Rice and noodles

Mouthwatering as they may sound, Malay recipes are lost without the simple, indispensable staple: rice (*nasi*). Rice dishes take many forms: *nasi minyak* (flavoured with spices like cardamom and cinnamon), *nasi tomato* (with tomatoes for a hint of sourness), *nasi goreng* (stir-fried with meat, eggs and chillies), and entire meals consisting of rice and side dishes: *nasi padang* (of Indonesian influence), *nasi kandar* (famous in Penang), and *nasi dagang* and *nasi ulam* (in Kelantan and Terengganu). Another popular rice dish is *nasi lemak*. The name means "rich rice" – a savoury rice cooked

MILDER MALAYSIAN

The keynote of any Malaysian dish is chilli – and often lots of it. For milder tastes, the selection at hawker stalls and in Chinese coffee shops presents a mind-boggling selection. Among the more popular fare, **wantan mee** are thin, fresh egg noodles either served in a broth or tossed in a chilli and oil-and-soy-sauce dressing, and topped with roast pork slices and prawn and pork dumplings. Another popular noodle dish is **Ipoh kway teow**. As the name suggests, this soupy dish gained fame in the town of Ipoh, Perak. Smooth, translucent strips of rice noodles are served in a prawn and pork broth and garnished with bean sprouts, shredded chicken and prawns. Ipoh boasts the most

delicate *kway teow* and fattest bean sprouts, supposedly because of the soft water which flows down from the surrounding limestone hills.

Char kway teow is another classic Malaysian-Chinese noodle dish: stir-fried flat rice noodles, garlic, prawns, cockles, bean sprouts, eggs, chilli paste, and lashings of thick, dark soy sauce for a hint of sweetness. Finally there is **chicken rice**, which no gourmand should miss. There are several variations, but the most popular is the Hainanese style, where whole chickens are simmered in chicken stock so that each slice is moist and tender, and served with delicious rice cooked in chicken stock instead of water.

not in water, but gently steamed in coconut milk till every drop of the liquid richness has been absorbed. The rice is then served with a fiery *sambal*, cucumber for coolness, small crispy fried fish, and a fried egg or omelette.

When you tire of rice, try noodles. Chinese immigrants introduced noodles to Malay cuisine and they are now an indispensable part of Malay cuisine: *mee* (a spaghetti-like yellow wheat noodle), *kway teow* (flat strips of smooth rice noodle), and *mee hoon* (thin rice vermicelli) – all can either be stir-fried (*goreng*), served in a light soup, or in speciality dishes such as *mee siam* (mee hoon in a red, spicy, and sour soup), and *mee rebus* (mee in a thick, brown spicy gravy). Chinese immigrants also brought with them the cooking styles of their mainland regions; Cantonese, Hokkien, Teochew, Hakka, and Hainanese predominate.

You are what you eat

Symbolism plays an important part in Chinese cuisine. There is a belief that parts of the animal are supposed to strengthen the corresponding part in the human body. Hence, eating pig's brain soup will increase concentration and alertness, braised beef tendons will boost tired legs, and so on.

Symbolic meaning also comes from the names of foods. For example, a kind of seaweed that looks exactly like black hair is called *fatt choy*, meaning hair vegetable; an unappetising pronunciation, but one phonetically identical to the Chinese characters meaning "to prosper". This weed is often stewed with dried oysters (*hou si*), which sounds like "good business". Not surprisingly, this dish is a standard inclusion on annual Chinese New Year menus, as are prawns (*ha*), which symbolise happiness.

Restaurant Chinese food in Malaysia is considerably more traditional and less novel. Dainty Cantonese *dim sum*, spicy Sechuan food, crispy Peking duck, shark's fin and other Chinese classics are available and cooked to high standards. Although many authentic mainland dishes still remain intact, some so-called Chinese food in Malaysia would baffle any mainland Chinese, just as "chop suey" and "egg rolls" confound many non-American Chinese.

LEFT: *mee rebus*, Malay-style noodles smothered in spicy gravy. RIGHT: for chicken rice, whole chickens are simmered in stock for extra flavour.

Go Indian

Although Indians make up only about 10 percent of the population, Indian stalls and restaurants proliferate. The majority of Indians are Tamils from the south Indian state of Tamil Nadu, whose food is hot and spicy and served with rice. But there are also northern Indian restaurants, dishing up milder fare with delicious breads like *naan* and *poori*. In addition, there are eateries run by Indian Muslims, who observe strict Muslim dietary laws.

Eating at one of the many south Indian "banana leaf curry" restaurants in Malaysia, you will experience one of the heartiest and

most colourful culinary spreads around. The banana leaf itself is not eaten, but acts as a natural, disposable green plate from which spicy dry *mysore* mutton, fried fish, chicken curry, red curried crabs, and a variety of spiced vegetables and pickles are eaten. The meal is often accompanied by fresh yoghurt to cool the palate, and cups of thin, spicy soup (*rasam*) to aid digestion. The meal is strongly seasoned with the dried spices used by Indians for thousands of years: chillies, cardamom, cloves, cumin, fenugreek, cinnamon, fennel and mustard seeds, to name just a few of the aromatics used. Fresh lime juice is almost always available to top it all off.

Malaysians would stand firm on the claim that India's greatest culinary contribution to Malaysia is the multi-layered, feather-light *roti canai* (flattened bread) – a flaky fried bread made of wheat flour, *ghee* (clarified butter) and a touch of milk for lightness. A stretchy dough is kneaded, rolled into balls, then dramatically tossed repeatedly into the air; the resulting dough is paper thin, and is folded and fried on a griddle to yield a crisp, flaky pancake. A popular breakfast item, *canai* can also be eaten at any time of

---

PRECISION CUISINE

Nothing in traditional Peranakan cooking is large or clumsy; every bite has to be equal in size, and measure approximately 2 centimetres (1 inch) in length.

---

the day. When visiting Indian hawker stalls, don't forget to try Indian *mee goreng* (fried yellow noodles), which are similar to the Malay version, but with slightly different spices, and Indian *rojak*, deep-fried fritters dipped in a sweet, hot sauce.

Peranakan cuisine

Peranakan food is a bi-cultural cuisine unique to Malaysia and its island neighbour, Singapore. It is a food of love, conceived by the interracial marriage of early Chinese immigrants and native Malays, resulting in the Peranakan, or Straits-born Chinese culture. These Nyonya women combined the best of both cuisines, pro-

ducing delectable dishes for their Baba men.

Peranakan food subtly merges typical Chinese ingredients such as pork, soy sauce and preserved soya beans with Malay spices, *rempah* ingredients and the ever-present coconut milk and/or tamarind juice. Being non-Muslim, Peranakan pork dishes are everyday fare. Some favourites are *babi asam* (a tamarind-based pork curry), and pork satay, with pineapple-enhanced peanut sauce.

Duck, traditionally not consumed by Malays, is popular in Peranakan kitchens, where it is braised whole, or made into a curry or sour soup (*itek sio*). Chicken is also commonly used, transformed into varied dishes such as chicken *kapitan* (chicken in spicy coconut milk) and *enchee kabin* (fried chicken with a tangy dip).

Much like Malay cuisine, Peranakan food evolved differently in different parts of the peninsula. *Laksa*, a classic Nyonya dish, comes in two varieties: Melakan cooks favour *laksa lemak* (also called curry laksa) which consists of noodles, prawns and other toppings bathed in a *lemak* (rich) spicy coconut soup. Then there is *asam laksa*, a famous speciality of Penang Nyonyas. This variety, with distinct Thai influences comprises noodles in a clear, fish-based soup, topped with raw cucumber and onion rings, pineapple chunks and mint sprigs.

Not only is Peranakan food delicious, it is also painstakingly prepared. Despite the many servants of old-style Peranakan homes, young Nyonya women traditionally spent hours in the kitchen mastering the precise culinary skills that would please their would-be Baba husbands. Under the watchful eye of elder Nonya women, the girls would practice pounding *rempah*, and slicing and chopping everything in the correct manner.

Eurasian and colonial

Malaysia's other ethnically complex cuisine is Eurasian food. The mecca of this type of cooking is undoubtedly Melaka, which fell to Portuguese invaders in 1511. Although Portuguese rule ended in 1641, and Dutch sovereignty some 150 years later, three centuries of mixed marriages resulted in modern-day Catholic descendants of Portuguese, Dutch, Malay, Javanese and Indian ancestry.

Eurasian cuisine is typically multicultural: Malay herbs enliven Chinese cuts of pork, further enhanced by Indian mustard seeds and chillies. A famous dish is devil curry, a fire-and-brimstone name for a spicy dish based on a Goanese vindaloo, further pepped up with vinegar, mustard and chillies. Similarly, English dishes such as stews and roasts are transformed with the simple addition of soy or oyster sauce, green chillies, or sour tamarind juice.

Undoubtedly, though, the highlight of any Eurasian kitchen wafts through the air in the form of warm, buttery, baking aromas. Eurasian cakes are sinfully delectable – rich fruit cakes, and the infamous *sugee* cake: a rich yellow cake made with heaps of only the best churned butter (traditionally imported in a can), sugar, vanilla, and a mixture of wheat flour and gritty *sugee* (semolina). The result is a decadent tea treat favoured highly by most Eurasians.

Related to Eurasian cooking is colonial food – British dishes that were originally cooked by a hired help (almost always Hainanese Chinese). These cooks slipped Chinese seasonings such as soy sauce and oyster sauce into sedate English food, resulting in tastier roasts, and famous chicken and pork chops slathered with peas, onions and a gravy seasoned with garlic and soy sauce. The altered dishes met with little protest and have remained till today, in older hotels and locally-run Western restaurants across Malaysia.

Food from the jungle

Traditional Borneo food is hard to find outside the longhouses and remote villages. Rice is the staple, although some tribes still adhere to diets based on boiled sago palm and tapioca root. Raw meats and fish are preserved by smoking, or curing in salt. Jungle vegetables like bamboo shoots and fern tips are regular accompaniments, as are lashings of lime and chilli.

Nowadays, what is typical food in Sabah and Sarawak is in fact a Chinese- and Malay-influenced cuisine. From the Chinese immigrants this century, Borneo food has adopted ingredients like soy sauce, and stir-frying and other cooking methods; from the Malays, chillies, dried shrimp, and prawn paste (*belacan*). Using these ingredients, vegetables, jungle animals such as wild boar, and seafood from the coast and rivers are deliciously braised and stir-fried.

Stranger jungle fare can be found even on the peninsula. For those with adventurous spirits and strong stomachs, jungle-food restaurants can be found in many states. Johor, for example, boasts popular Chinese restaurants serving bullfrog, wild-boar, snake, flying fox, civet cat and a host of seasonal "chef specials", which should be tasted first before being identified if they are to be enjoyed. Although the meats used may turn Western stomachs, the cooking is imaginative and the dishes usually tasty.   ❏

LEFT: in "banana leaf restaurants", food is served on a natural, disposable green "plate". **RIGHT:** a sampling of spices and herbs used in Peranakan cooking.

LOCAL EATING HABITS

To be completely immersed in the whole Malay culinary experience, it is imperative to try at least once the traditional Malay way of eating, still practised in the average Malay home – with your fingers. It may look simple, but it is a skill to be mastered. Using only the tips of the fingers on the right hand (the left hand is considered unclean and never used), any Malay can pick, tear, and scoop with complete deftness.

Increasingly, however, outside the home many Malays use a spoon in the right hand, which is brought to the mouth, and a fork in the left, used mainly for manoeuvring food onto the spoon.

HAWKER FOOD AND OUTDOOR EATS

The best of Malaysia's food isn't served at fancy restaurants but at stalls set up by the roadside, in hawker centres, or in street-side coffee shops

Patronised by rich and poor alike, hawker stalls are found all over Malaysia, from urban sites beside busy highways, to idyllic seaside locations. Feeding and slaking the thirst of the nation is a round-the-clock affair: Malaysians, as a rule, live to eat and not the other way around. With such low prices who'd be bothered to cook, and as most hawkers specialise in only a few dishes, they have perfected their culinary skills to a degree where most people would prefer to eat out than in. Basic tables and stools are provided on-site. Hawkers will often ask if you want to *makan* – "eat there", or *bungkus* – "take-away".

WHERE TO EAT

Each state has its own famous outdoor eating centre. In Kuala Lumpur (KL), head for Chinatown's famed Petaling Street night market (*above*) for Chinese specialities. For Malay food don't miss the Saturday night market in Kampung Bahru. After dark in Penang, Gurney Drive offers an array of multi-ethnic treats by the sea. In Kota Bharu, have breakfast upstairs in the Central Market, and dinner at the car park, which turns into a night-time eating centre, offering mouth-watering Kelantanese delicacies. Melaka's best-known hawker scene is at the Glutton's Corner overlooking the Mahkota Parade shopping centre.

▽ NASI LEMAK
Malaysia's favourite breakfast consists of rice cooked in coconut milk, served with egg, cucumber, anchovies and a spicy *sambal* sauce.

▽ SNACK TIME
A variety of sweet and savoury snacks, go by the generic name of *kuih*. These stalls proliferate during the Muslim fasting month of *Ramadan*.

▽ MORNING TEA
On KL's Jalan Silang, office workers enjoy mid-morning snacks of banana-leaf-wrapped savouries, cakes, curry puffs and tarts.

△ PENANG TREAT
At Georgetown's Esplanade, hawkers prepare *rojak pasembur*, deep-fried seafood and tofu smothered in peanut sauce.

▷ KL BREAKFAST
KL's Masjid India area is popular for *roti canai* with *dhal* or lentil gravy, and accompanied by *teh tarik*, a sweet strong tea.

ROTI CANAI BREAKFAST

Walk through any Malaysian town mid-morning, and the most crowded eateries will usually be those serving *roti canai*. Its English description, an unleavened pancake served with dhal, just doesn't do it justice. It is deliciously light, flaky and crisp, the perfect vehicle to soak up spicy sauces and curries.

Most cooks show off their skills at the front of their shops; it takes years of practice to swing out the dough until it is paper thin. The theatrical flourishes when tossing the *roti* may appear excessive, but are needed to keep the pancake as light and flaky as possible.

A speciality of Indian-Muslim cooks, the origins of *roti canai* are obscure, and like many Malaysian favourites, it has evolved over generations into a strictly localised dish.

△ CHINESE BREAD

Deep-fried *yu char kway*, a Chinese snack, on sale near Georgetown's Campbell Street market, Penang.

△ SATAY

Marinated morsels of meat are grilled over a charcoal brazier for *satay*, a popular after-dark snack and the unofficial "national" dish.

▷ INDIAN PANCAKE

Roti canai is best eaten with your hands. Just tear off a flaky portion, and dip it into a saucer of *dhal* or lentil curry.

ARTS AND CRAFTS

Malaysia has always been proud of its rich craft tradition. Now a new breed of artists are pushing back the boundaries of contemporary Asian art

From prehistoric cave murals to cutting-edge contemporary oil painting, the story of Malaysian art spans over 2,000 years of creativity; traditional crafts, which still survive on the Malay Peninsula's east coast and in the longhouses of Sarawak, could well have been around for even longer. Located at the heart of Southeast Asia, at the meeting of the ancient trade routes, Malaysian culture has always been heavily influenced by external influences; its arts and crafts a reflection of this cross-cultural interweaving.

Prehistoric art

Over two millennia ago, unknown artists painted abstract designs, human figures and animals on the walls of a cave near Ipoh, Perak. Meanwhile, across the South China Sea in Sarawak, artisans in the Niah Caves were also painting over 100 depictions of human figures and boats, in murals which stretch over 50 linear metres (165 linear ft). Cave paintings are rare in Malaysia and for many years scholars wondered who these artisans were, and what the drawings meant. Later discoveries of contemporary Orang Asli cave drawings in Perak, in Sarawak and in Sabah, suggest that the prehistoric artists were probably the ancestors of the more recent Orang Asli cave painters, and that the murals depicted the cultural and religious aspects of the original prehistoric painters' lives.

Malaysian crafts date back to the earliest human settlement. A Palaeolithic workshop for making crude stone chopping tools, excavated at Kota Tampan, Perak, dates to 38,000 years ago, while sophisticated flaked stone tools from Sabah's Tingkayu region can be traced back some 28,000 years.

Around 2,000 BC, during the Neolithic era, pottery and polished stone tools appeared. Wooden paddles and anvil stones were proba-bly used to produce some of the pottery, including sophisticated three-colour urns from the Niah Caves. This production method is still used today by Sarawak's Iban peoples.

In the remote highlands of Bario in Sarawak, and in the lowland wetlands near Santubong, there are some unusual rock carvings where

figures and spiral designs have been engraved into boulders. The only stone carvings in Peninsular Malaysia are a group of carved megalithic stones at Pengkalan Kempas in Negeri Sembilan. This group of three stones, of unknown origin and age, are one of Malaysia's greatest archaeological mysteries as they depict Hindu-type phallic symbols along with the Islamic script for Allah (God). Scholars are divided as to whether the carvings were done at the same time, or whether the Allah inscription was done later to sanctify a pagan site. Stone foundations of buildings and temples found in Kedah's Bujang Valley apparently supported a wooden infrastructure which has long since perished.

PRECEDING PAGES: an oversized Malaysian kite or *wau*. **LEFT:** fine art of handpainted batik. **RIGHT:** megaliths in Negeri Sembilan testify to early artistic leanings.

Wood-carving is a popular craft in Sarawak, where the Kajang people still carve wooden burial poles, or *klirieng*, to house jars containing ashes of deceased chiefs. The oldest surviving pole is 200 years old, but the tradition is believed to date back many centuries more. Other wood-carving traditions survive with the Mah Meri of Pulau Carey, Selangor, who carve legendary figures believed to be the spirits of their ancestors, and the Jah Hut of Pahang, who also sculpt their legends in wood. The Iban of Sarawak carve spectacular hornbill sculptures, while the upriver Kenyah carve mythical dog-god ancestors.

Examples of his work still exist and show how upper-class houses were constructed using no nails, with beautifully carved panels of floral patterns and verses from the Koran.

Metalwork and jewellery

From the first century AD, Indian and Chinese travellers told of legendary Malay kingdoms like Langkasuka and Chi Tu (Red Earth Land). They would describe ancient courts where rulers wore fabulous gold jewellery and dressed in "rose-coloured cloth" – possibly the first-known reference to Malay handwoven *songket*. It is hard to separate reality from fiction in these

Carving comeback

In the peninsula, wood-carving is undergoing something of a revival. There is a new interest in the old craft, and today Malay wood-carvings not only adorn the walls of museums, but decorate the foyers of banks, businesses and government offices, including that of the prime minister. Some of the finest antique wood-carvings can be seen on the panelling, pillars, windows and doors of the nation's oldest royal palaces, which were all built of wood. Encik Long of Besut, Terengganu, was a celebrated master carver, and during four decades of his century-long life he was the principal builder for the Raja of Besut.

fabled accounts, but by the time of the Melakan Sultanate in the 14th century, artisans and craftspeople were an integral part of the royal court. Many lived and worked in the villages beside the palace. Sultans, chiefs, nobles, and their wives and families were the moneyed class, and silversmiths and goldsmiths, silk-weavers, and wood carvers depended on royal patronage for their existence.

A royal wedding was the ultimate event and every artisan was involved in preparing the trousseau and the ceremonial items needed for such a prestigious affair. However, when the courts became more westernised, rulers started buying imported jewellery, clothing, and artefacts. The habit of betel-nut chewing went out of fashion, for instance, rendering obsolete the silver items used in its preparation, and forcing many artisans to hang up their tools. Similarly, many traditional arts and crafts are in danger of extinction.

Fortunately, however, in the predominantly Malay-populated regions of the peninsula's east coast, craftsmen and women have preserved their age-old practices. Today, silverworking, silk-weaving and wood-carving are all experiencing a huge revival. For example, silversmiths still thrive in Kota Bharu, despite having vanished elsewhere. These days, jewellery and functional pieces like fruit bowls, tea-sets and spoons are popular, and although past fashions called for different artefacts, the designs and techniques employed are the same. In Islam, it is taboo to use anthropomorphic figures, and many of the patterns are therefore inspired by flowers, branches and even clouds.

Early silverware is often of exceptional craftsmanship and some pieces, like the earliest surviving example – a royal Johorean betel-set from the early-18th century – employ a painstaking technique that is seldom seen these days. Probably the most fascinating of all the old pieces are leaf-shaped modesty discs which until the 19th century were the only clothing worn by little Malay girls.

In the 1800s, the Straits Chinese of Melaka and Penang, also known as Peranakan – whose ancestors were early Chinese traders who intermarried with local women – borrowed heavily from Malay silver and gold traditions to create their own craft, which is distinguishable from traditional Malay work by its designs which often feature birds and flowers.

Fabrics and weaving

Silk brocades, known as *kain songket*, have always been the favoured textiles for royal occasions, and these elegant woven cloths are still the preferred wear, not only for courtly occasions but for government functions. They are most often used as traditional bridal wear, when both the bride and groom are dressed in sumptuous brocade outfits. At a Kelantanese

---

FAR LEFT: Sarawakian burial pole. **LEFT:** traditional dress made of rich *songket*. **RIGHT:** a *songket* weaver.

> **MYSTIC CRAFT**
>
> Traditionally, a wood-carver would enter the forest to select his own timber and chant incantations to appease forest spirits.

weaver's showroom, a pale mauve colour is still sold only to royalty, and there are certain designs which are even now the prerogative of the traditional ruler.

Weavers are usually women who have learnt the craft from their mothers and grandmothers. The very best weavers worked for the palace, like the grandmother of one of Terengganu's top weavers, who was picked from two thousand local artisans of her day to become the sultan's head weaver. Like most other time-honoured crafts, *songket* weaving is practised in

Terengganu and Kelantan, and the techniques and looms used are the same as in the old days. Woven on a simple four-posted loom, the brocade consists of a coloured silk background with a floating weft of gold and silver threads. A distinctive part of every length is the *kepala*, a centre panel with a particularly elaborate pattern. The names of the designs echo the Malay fascination with nature and the countryside: one is known as "bamboo shoots", another "the tail feathers of a cock". Traditionally, nobles would design their own *songket* patterns. This legacy lives on today as a Terengganu prince, Tengku Ismail Tengku Su, continues to create new designs at his well-known workshop. Related to the *kain songket* is *tekat*, an ancient craft of gold embroidery on rich, dark velvet. This luxurious material is popular among Malays for home furnishings, wall hangings, cushions and even bedroom slippers.

From Sarawak hails *ikat*, a unique woven fabric with a tie-dyed warp. Iban textiles serve many ritual purposes: newly-born babies are wrapped in them to ward off evil influences and in the past, trophy heads from headhunting expeditions were even draped with *ikat* cloths.

CLASSY CLOTH

Batik derives from the Malay word *tik*, meaning "to drip". It is thought that batik replaced tattooing as a mark of status in Malay culture.

Batik

Batik cloth is often used to symbolise Malaysia. The national airline uses it for its uniforms, batik shirts are *de rigueur* as men's formal attire and are even compulsory dress at the nation's only casino. It is also worn as sarongs and used for the fashionable and traditional women's dress known as *baju kurung*. But batik-making is not a traditional Malay craft: it was introduced from Indonesia in the 1930s. However, although it is of recent origin, there is no denying that batik-making is now the nation's most popular craft.

Using a wax-resistant technique, the patterns are stamped onto lengths of cloth using a printing block made from zinc strips bent into the desired shaped, and dipped in molten wax. However, the biggest success story is of hand-painted batiks, where the designs are drawn on the cloth using a *canting*, a "pen" filled with liquid wax, with the dyes then painted on with brushes. This latter method means that more colours can be used than with the vat-dyeing method, and the freehand designs are only limited by the artisan's imagination. Batik workshops are now opening up all over Malaysia, but the majority of craftspeople are based on the east coast of the peninsula.

Pottery and other crafts

Beside the Perak River, opposite the royal town of Kuala Kangsar, is the village of Sayong, renowned throughout Malaysia for the manufacture of *Labu Sayong*. Literally "Sayong Pumpkins", these gourd-shaped pottery water vessels keep liquids cool in even the hottest weather. The women of Sayong are the potters, and have been for more generations than they can remember. The pots are made in moulds from local clay, and then finished on the wheel where they are incised with freehand designs. After drying in the sun they are fired in small brick kilns. Both terracotta and black-coloured wares are made, with the latter obtaining their distinct colour from being buried in rice husks while they are still hot from the kiln.

In Sabah and Sarawak, the indigenous peoples are renowned for their skill in weaving baskets and hats. The nomadic Penan weave fine black and white baskets from split rattan. To find the best materials they often have to walk a day's journey deep into the forest, then they dry, split, and finally colour the rattan with dye made of forest leaves.

Making mats from *nipah* palm or *pandanus* leaves is a more down-to-earth craft, though one that still requires great skill. Throughout the country, woven mats are an essential part of daily life, used on the floor in *kampung* houses, on beds, on the beach, in mosques, for drying food under the sun, and anywhere else that a convenient, light covering might be needed. Weaving begins at the centre of the mat and moves outwards, using dyes to produce simple criss-cross patterns. More professional weavers (mostly women) fashion hexagonal boxes of nipah palm leaves. In Sabah and Sarawak, floral and even pictorial stories are part of the woven mat's design.

Contemporary art

When the British colonial era introduced industrially-made goods, it was inevitable that traditional arts and crafts would go into decline. At this same time, however, new arts were being introduced like oil painting and watercolours. At first, Malaysian artists emulated Western styles, but after independence a new group of artists came into their own, creating their own brand of abstraction more in line with Islam.

Hoy Cheong's epic series on immigration, Ahmad Zakii Anuar's smoke-blurred portraits and Lee Joo For's bonding of Eastern and Western visual language, to name but a few. Some of the new breed trained overseas, bringing a fresh angle to local traditions. During the 1960s and 1970s, artists were keen to distance themselves from local motifs in order to look "modern". However, after more than four decades of independence, Malaysian artists have come of age, and have rediscovered their roots while continuing the Malaysian tradition of blending both local and foreign influences. The result is a style uniquely their own. ❏

Three of the best known of this group are Latiff Mohidin, who uses indigenous motifs and the environment as inspiration; Syed Amad Jamal, who champions abstract expressionism; and, most famous of all, Ibrahim Hussein, whose linear abstracts can be seen at his gallery/workshop in Langkawi.

In the economic boom of the late 1980s and 1990s, a new breed of artists emerged whose works sold as fast as they were being produced: Rafiee Ghani's colourful "roomscapes", Wong

FAR LEFT: pumpkin-shaped pottery of Sayong, Perak.
ABOVE: an example of Rafiee Ghani's "roomscape".
RIGHT: contemporary Malaysian painter, Rafiee Ghani.

RAFIEE GHANI'S WORLD OF COLOURS

Kedah-born and Kelantanese-raised Rafiee, one of Malaysia's hottest new artists, combines European style with tropical Malaysian colours and patterns. His signature "roomscapes" are of everyday objects infused with extraordinary light and colour, bold and spontaneous in the tradition of Van Gogh and Matisse. While his oils celebrate everyday life, much of his inspiration is derived from his travels in Europe, Asia and Australia. Rafiee's big break came in 1993 with the success of his "Room of Flowers" exhibition, and he has exhibited widely ever since. His work can be seen at Rusli Hashim Gallery of Fine Art in the Crowne Plaza Mutiara Hotel shopping arcade in Kuala Lumpur.

ADVENTURE SPORTS

Forest-clad mountains, giant caves, roaring rivers and deep oceans make
Malaysia a challenging destination for the thrill seeker

Drenched in rain and sweat, too tired to pluck off yet another leech, you make the decision to slide the rest of the way down the almost vertical slope of soft clay. Through the drizzle, the welcome sight of smooth large boulders can be barely made out, beyond which is the source of the roar audible for the last hour: a 30-metre (100-ft) high waterfall, thundering down in fine spray.

This is adventure indeed, a 3-day trek in the rugged interior of a tropical rainforest. Malaysia's highland forests are also the source of swift, bubbling headwaters that run into massive river systems, offering superb rafting and kayaking. Some of these streams seep through the porous limestone massifs, forming huge cave systems waiting to be explored and mapped. Their tiny entrances are often masked by thick foliage – which is also why few cliff faces are available for rock-climbing. Those that are suitable, however, are excellent.

Outdoor pursuits

Malaysia's rainforests offer all manner of challenges to both body and mind; but this is largely ignored by its populace. Trekking is popular among boy-scouts and university students, but Malaysians are generally not fond of the outdoors. Blame it on the rain, blame it on the sun. Blame it on the mosquitos and the leeches, the sweat and the dirt. To the urban Malaysian, leisure means a family picnic in a carefully-landscaped park or at one of the easily-accessible beaches or waterfalls near town. Rural folk spend their free time on traditional art forms such as *wau*-flying (kite-flying) and top-spinning. And for the indigenous people, these challenges *are* part of daily life.

Yet adventure sport is slowly gaining ground among younger, more affluent Malaysians, whose exposure to western trends comes as a

PRECEDING PAGES: windsurfing on the wide open South China Sea, off the peninsula's east coast. **LEFT:** whitewater action at one of several rivers in Sabah. **RIGHT:** the majestic Gunung Kinabalu.

result of time spent abroad, at an overseas university or travelling. Sometimes, the interest is driven by Malaysia's expatriate community. The exception would be scuba diving, which, due to the heavy promotion of Malaysia's underwater attractions for tourism, is enjoying a massive growth in popularity.

For other adventure sports, however, the infrastructure is nascent, expertise is scarce, and sites undeveloped. Taking up these activities is also very expensive, as much of the equipment has to be imported – which is why they are largely limited to middle-income, city-dwelling 30-somethings. Nonetheless, there are clubs for kayaking, a mountaineering association (whose members were the force behind Malaysia's successful 1997 Mount Everest ascent), rock-climbing, as well as jungle-trekking and caving (under the Malaysian Nature Society Selangor branch). These are all, however, based in Kuala Lumpur.

Multi-sport expedition racing is gaining some

interest. In the early 1990s, the punishing Raid Gauloises, the so-called Holy Grail of expedition racing, was held in the spectacular mountain, jungle and cave terrain of Mulu, Sarawak. Each team had to have an obligatory local participant. Then in 1998, a local team became the first Asian team to complete the other big international expedition race, the Eco-Challenge, going on to finish another three in subsequent years. The team leader, Chan Yuen-Li, now organises short adventure races under the Eco-X label.

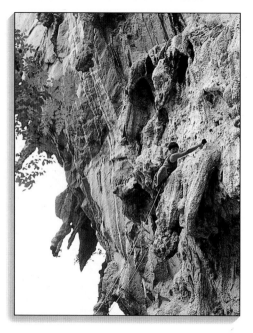

Probably the greatest difficulty faced by rainforest-based adventure sports proponents in Malaysia is the humidity, which can reach close to 100 percent in the forest. Dehydration is another problem because of the heat. Luckily there is always an icy-cold river close at hand. In some areas, fortification is necessary against the threat of tropical diseases such as malaria.

The most challenging jungle-trekking is to be found in the country's mountainous interiors. In the peninsula, these concentrate in the backbone of Banjaran Titiwangsa (Main Range); in Sabah, the Crocker Range; and in Sarawak, the northern Mulu area. Countless routes can be taken, whether in the Livingstonian quest for

> **RAINY DAYS**
>
> Highland rivers can swell to Grade 5 rapids after a downpour. In some areas, "dry season" means that it only rains in the afternoon instead of all day.

waterfalls, or to scale a mountain, or simply to experience the many ecosystems that make up the rainforest. Hundreds of kilometres of trails wind through protected park areas, mainly serving conservation objectives. Other trails have been trammelled for generations by the indigenous people who still travel on foot to their remote villages. In wilder country, it is the animal trails along the steep ridges that form some kind of pathway through the thorny rattan- and liana-strewn undergrowth.

Many of the longer trails involve ascending to mountain tops, such as the 7-day hike to Gunung Tahan (2,200 metres/7,000 ft) in Taman Negara, and the 4-day ascent to Gunung Mulu (2,400 metres/7,900 ft). The popular overnight trail up the country's highest peak, Gunung Kinabalu (4,100 metres/13,400 ft) is relatively civilised, if stamina-sapping. Exciting country lies in the largely unvisited northern tracts of Banjaran Titiwangsa in the peninsula's Belum area, steep hilly terrain full of hidden waterfalls, and in Sabah's Maliau Basin, termed East Malaysia's last frontier.

Trekking is often a wet experience on muddy trails and across numerous rivers, sometimes by boulder-hopping. However, hot-footing it with a backpack is the best way to experience the amazing jungle, and have a chance to encounter the extremely elusive tropical wildlife. And because the Orang Asli and natives make the best jungle guides, it provides a chance to learn about remarkable and fast-disappearing ways of life.

Climbing the walls

Rock-climbing has long been popular among tiny pockets of enthusiasts. But the sport's best shot in the arm came in the early 1990s when, in line with world trends, Malaysia saw the advent of sport-climbing, which is more accessible than traditional climbing. The other factor was that climbing was part of the government's *Rakan Muda* youth programmes, prompting the growth of artificial climbing walls. In 1999, the first indoor climbing gym opened in Kuala Lumpur, the brainchild of Chan of the Eco-Challenge fame, also Malaysia's pioneer and foremost rock-climber.

All of Peninsular Malaysia's rock-climbing

surfaces is limestone, characterised by steep overhanging rock and often stalactites, which make routes tough (at least 6A French grade; climbing grades range from 3 to 9A). The cliffs are also high, usually 100 metres (300 ft), so paths have to be established from the ground up.

The most frequently visited rock-climbing spots around the capital are Batu Caves and Bukit Takun near Templer's Park. The former is easy to access and has moderately challenging routes. Takun is a more traditional rock face,

TOUGH GOING

Malaysia makes for challenging climbs. Rock faces are always steep, cliffs are often high, and dense vegetation makes some faces almost impossible to scale.

water-level fluctuations, depending on rain; dry floors are often thick with guano. There are spectacular traverses, squeezes and stretches of tough ropework. There is plenty of clambering around massive stalagmites and crossing narrow bridges of fretted rock. No one knows how much more of Mulu remains to be discovered, and foreign caving groups come in on surveying expeditions virtually every year.

A brand new area north, called Buda, is also opening up for spelunking. Described by Amer-

which involves a bit of a clamber through thick undergrowth to reach. However, both offer several interesting routes. The highest grade of climb locally is 7C.

Cave adventures

Superlatives abound when it comes to the caving haven of Mulu – largest, longest, most decorated. Mulu's giant caves offer superb adventure and technical caving opportunities. Most of the area's 200 km (124 miles) of surveyed passages are wet, with large and sudden

LEFT: rock-climbing near Batu Caves, Kuala Lumpur.
ABOVE: inside a cavern in Sarawak's Mulu Caves

ican caving expeditionists as "a literal garden of Eden complete with fruits, serpents and an eternity of virgin passage". Truly one of the most spectacular areas for caving in the world, among its wonders is the deepest vertical drop in Southeast Asia (140 metre/460 ft), accessible through challenging ropework amid thundering waterfalls. Another cave houses the region's greatest vertical relief at 465 metres (1,500 ft). Not surprisingly, Buda has been proposed as a state park or an extension of Mulu.

If pre-arranged, equipment and guides can be hired at the Mulu National Park headquarters. There are no caving clubs, but the Malaysian Nature Society has a caving group.

On your bike

While old timber trails in the interior sometimes give hikers access to undisturbed forest, they are more popular with mountain bikers. There are no clubs as such, but various groups comprising mainly friends spend weekends exploring oil palm and rubber plantations, as well as secondary forest near towns. These provide everything from fairly simple trails to challenging hilly terrain, and the vegetation makes for much cooler riding than on the road.

CAPITAL WHEELS

Specialist mountain bike shops are centred in Kuala Lumpur, and sell a range of bikes and accessories. They are also a good place to find out about biking groups.

Wider and flatter jungle trails can actually also make good, if tough, riding – with their root-covered paths, numerous river crossings and breathtaking views. The Headhunters' Trail in Mulu, Sarawak, is one such trail, while another good trail is the dirt road on the border of Taman Negara which leads from Jerantut to the Kuala Tahan *kampung*, opposite the park headquarters.

Aerial sports

Flying microlight or ultralight aircraft is almost prohibitively expensive to take up in Malaysia, but instruction is available. A good start is the 20-minute introductory training lesson, where students are accompanied by licensed pilots.

In Malaysia, microlights are allowed to fly at a maximum height of 150 metres (500 ft), with a 5-km (3-mile) radius from the point of take-off. "Cowboy" operators abound, so check if the outfit is licensed by the Department of Civil Aviation (DCA) Malaysia, whether the instructor has certification and that a logbook is maintained.

Lessons to fly four types of parachute and winged aircraft are offered by the Experimental Aircraft Association of Malaysia (www.ultralight.bizland.com). The outfit operates from the Nusajaya Flight Park in Johor state located just off the Second Link to Singapore.

Introductory lessons cost around RM125, and the flight course takes in mangrove swamps, rivers and rubber plantations, spectacular both in the early morning – when flying is best – and at sunset. Getting a licence for the powered paraglider and powered parachute requires three and six hours respectively, while a student pilot's licence for winged aircraft requires 30 hours of flight training.

Like microlighting, skyjumping is offered by only a handful of operators in Malaysia. One operator uses the Segamat Country Club, a golf course in Johor, for student jumps. The 2-day course includes ground training, and static jumps must be completed before freefalling is allowed. Equipment can be rented and jumps are charged according to height. Tandem skyjumping with an instructor is also available.

Whitewater action

Malaysia's many rivers offer good whitewater experiences. One of the top sites is the spectacular Padas Gorge in Sabah. Tour operators usually offer rafting experiences on 8- to 10-seater inflatable rafts with river guides. Generally, whitewater tour operators are well-organised, experienced and provide safety equipment, a briefing, sometimes insurance, and lunch. In some places, competent paddlers can have a go at one- or two-person kayaks.

Two rivers in Perak, about two hours north of Kuala Lumpur, have become centres for nice-and-easy kayaking and rafting, with up to Grade 3 rapids. Sungai Sungkai near the town of Sungkai and Sungai Kampar near Gopeng are set in rustic, rural landscapes of lush plantations and Malay and indigenous Orang Asli villages. More adventuresome multi-day destinations include Sungai Nenggiri in Kelantan, and Sungai Endau in the Endau-Rompin Park.

The big blue

Scuba-diving is the fastest-growing adventure sport in the country. Malaysia's precious coral islands offer a multitude of stunning possibilities, and with the gazetting of many sites as marine parks, tourists are flocking to them as snorkellers, and, increasingly, divers.

Almost every diveable Malaysian destination has operators offering tours, full equipment rental and dive instruction in PADI, NAUI and/or SSI.

Sabah, off whose coast is the region's premier dive destination, Sipadan. The island also has the country's only dedicated sports-diving hyperbaric chamber; others are in navy bases in Kuantan, Melaka and Lumut. Close to Sipadan is the muck-diving haven at Mabul, popular with underwater photographers for its exotic life unique to the silt, while hammerhead and manta ray enthusiasts head for Layang Layang, situated in the South China Sea, 300 km (186 miles) west of Kota Kinabalu.

Malaysia's reefs and marine life are among the world's richest and most diverse. Each dive destination, and sometimes dive spot, is char-

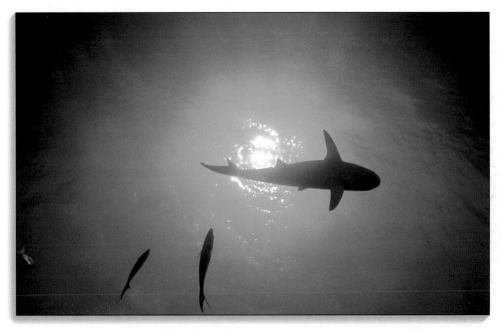

Besides resort-based facilities which accept walk-in trade, scheduled dive trips are offered by operators in Kuala Lumpur, Kuala Terengganu and Kota Kinabalu.

While there are internationally-rated dive centres, at the other end of the scale are operators who are not registered with dive agencies, or are lax about medical and safety equipment such as buoyancy compressors. The Malaysian Sports Diving Association is trying to set local standards and make insurance mandatory. The most developed facilities and services are in

acterised by endemics, from odd macro life in Kapalai to pelagics in Tenggol, coral-wreathed wrecks in Labuan, to the huge diversity of marine life in Redang. Nitrox or technical diving is also becoming popular. Likewise photography, with some operators renting out underwater cameras too.

Other seasports, while popular, do not enjoy such enthusiastic patronage. You'll find windsurfing at beach resorts, while sailing has a small, mainly-expatriate following among members of yacht clubs. Incredibly, there is a surfing group who head regularly to the east coast to take on what must be mere ripples compared to the surf in Bali and Hawaii. ❏

LEFT: paragliding panoramas
ABOVE: be prepared for encounters with sharks.

PLACES

A detailed guide to the entire country, with principal sites clearly cross-referenced by number to the maps

The visitor's first impression of Malaysia when flying into Kuala Lumpur typifies the country. The view from the aircraft window is of a sweeping agrarian landscape, a deep green carpet of oil palm plantations; but then the plane touches down at an avant-garde international airport, one of the most advanced in the world.

Malaysia is a land of surprising contradictions: picturesque fishing villages and opulent hotels share the same sandy beach; cosy colonial resorts nestle on hillsides that host spirit-worshipping tribal ceremonies, while dense tropical forests are penetrated by the strains of karaoke. Throw in the cultural pastiche that is the Malaysian people, and the result is an irresistible combination of charm and adventure that is still just a glimpse of the "real" Malaysia.

Situated right in the middle of Southeast Asia, with a total land area of 342,000 sq. km (132,000 sq. miles), Malaysia is about the size of Japan, and has a population of 21 million. The country's infrastructure is well set-up for tourism and consequently, it is fairly easy and very safe to travel anywhere in the country.

Peninsular Malaysia juts out from the southern-most part of the Asian continent. The most developed part of the country is the west coast, dissected from the more traditional and rural east coast by a chain of mountains. Then, about 640 km (400 miles) of ocean – the South China Sea – separates the peninsula from the east Malaysian states of Sabah and Sarawak on the island of Borneo. With its own diverse ethnic tribes, lifestyles and the rich natural heritage, at times, this part of Malaysia seems almost a different country.

Geography has left an indelible stamp on today's Malaysia. The monsoons were what brought disparate cultures to her shores, bringing the religions that now hold sway, influencing architecture and even the model of government. The changing of the winds still affect the important fisheries industry, but for the tourist, it now signifies merely wet and less wet times to visit the country.

Since independence in 1957, Malaysia has faced a series of economic and political pitfalls. Each time it has emerged with the same clear-eyed determination to succeed. From an almost total dependence on raw commodities like rubber and tin, to a broad manufacturing base, Malaysia is now looking beyond that into 21st century global citizenship with hi-tech industries as its vanguard.

But Malaysia's soul is still very much in its *kampung* (villages) and its small town heartlands; in its rainforest and marine heritage; in its religious foundations; and in its cultural roots. And while the quest continues, all these have found some form in a unique Malaysian identity. ❑

PRECEDING PAGES: the majestic Batang Ai river in Sarawak; Pulau Manukan in Sabah's Tunku Abdul Rahman Park; Sultan Abu Bakar Mosque in Johor Bahru
LEFT: picture-perfect Pulau Tioman, where the musical *South Pacific* was filmed.

Chawang
THAILAND
Ban Pak Phanang
Gulf
of
Thailand
VIETNAM

Thung Song
Ban Hua Sai
Phatthalung
Ranot
Thale Luang
Trang
Songkhla
Ban Hat Yai
Khlong Ngae
Pattani
Satun
Perlis
Yala
Narathiwat
Pulau Langkawi
Kangar
Kuala Nerang
Sungai Kolok
Kota Bharu
Alor Setar
Kedah
Baling
S. Petani
Pulau Perhentian
Georgetown
Butterworth
Pulau Pinang
Kulim
Selama
Kuala Terengganu
P. Pinang
Taiping
Perak
Kelantan
Terengganu
Gua Musang
Dungun
Lumut
Ipoh
Pahang
Kuala Lipis
Cukai
Teluk Intan
Raub
Jerantut
Kuantan
Sabak
Bentung
Maran
Lubukpakam
Selangor
Temerloh
Pahang
Pekan
Tebingtinggi
Kuala Lumpur
Labuhanruku
Tanjungbalai
Shah Alam
Negeri
Prapat
Asahan
Labuhanbilik
Sembilan
Rompin
Bandar Baharu Rompin
Balige 2300
Bedongkong
Seremban
Gemas
Segamat
Pulau Tioman
Tarutung
Rantauprapat
Melaka
Labis
Mersing
Kotapinang
Bagansiapiapi
Muar
Keluang
Padangsidimpuan
Tanahputih
Melaka
Johor
Duri
Dumai
Batu Pahat
Kota Tinggi
Daludalu
Bengkalis
Kudap
Johor Bahru
SINGAPORE
Siapu
Sungaiapit
Kukup
Muarasoma
Pasirpangarayan
Pekanbaru
Singapore
Tanjungpinang
Pelalawan
Kepulauan Riau
Sasak
Lipatkain
Langgam
Kampar
Sekapil
Teluksabah
Bukittinggi
Sungailimau
Telukkuantan
Rengat
Lingga
Daik
Padang
2597
Pulaukijang
Kepulauan Lingga
Siberut
Painan
Kualatungkai
Muarasigep
Muarasabak
Muarasiberut
437
Taileleo
Muaratebo
Ratangan
Muarakumpe
Sigoisooinan
Sipura
Kambang
3805
Belinyu
Kaliet
Indrapura
Bangko
Jambi
Mentok
Pagai Utara
2933
Sarolangun
Bayunglincir
Pangkalpinang
Bahatmonga
Pasarbantal
Surulangun
Grisik
Bangka
Bale
Pagai Selatan
Ipuh
Koba
Ketahun
Muaralakitan
Batubetumbang
Tanjungpandan
Palembang
Dendang
Lubuklinggau
Toboali
Belitung
Bengkulu
Wiralaga
Pasarseluma
Baturaja
Martapura
Manna
Menggala
Muaradua
Bintuhan
2232
Kotabumi
IND
INDIAN OCEAN
Krui
Kotaagung
Tanjungkarang
Telukbetung
Enggano
Bandaragung
Tampang
Kalianda
Belimbing

Peninsular Malaysia

SOUTH

MALAY

Kepulauan Natuna Utara
Kepulauan Anambas
Kepulauan Natuna Selatan
Samb
Pemangkat
Singkawang
Kepulauan Tambelan
Sungaipinyuh
Pontian
Telukpakeda
Pul. Padangtik
P. Pulau Karimata
Selat Karimata

Sumatera
Pegunungan Barisan
Selat Mentawai
Tembesi
Musi

KUALA LUMPUR AND ENVIRONS

*Young, vibrant and bursting with energy, Malaysia's
capital is the epitome of a modern Asian city*

First-timers expecting to see shanty towns, a populace in Oriental dress, and other "quaint" aspects of Asia, are in for a severe
dose of disillusion when they actually reach Kuala Lumpur.
What they get instead are skyscrapers of contemporary design,
gleaming European and Japanese cars, sober-suited executives, and
brand names from Marks & Spencer to Louis Vuitton.

The economic meltdown may have taken away some of its bite, but
this Asian Tiger's capital is still a force to be reckoned with on the
world stage. For Malaysians, Kuala Lumpur is the centre of everything: business, trade, finance, politics, arts, fashion, trends… in
short, it all starts here. You feel it in the air, the mad pace of life, in
the traffic-choked streets, the crowded malls, and the incessant beat
of techno in the discos. And you feel it when at last you reach your
hotel, peel off your dusty shoes and wash the grime from your face.

The capital sits in the Klang River Valley, referred to as the Klang
Valley, an area of townships and large industrial estates linked by a
network of highways. The Klang Valley is the hub of development,
the economic magnet that draws in Malaysians hungry for money,
experience, and a taste of big city life.

In the city, tourists like to head to the pockets of colonialism and
old Asia, but cannot escape the thrust of modernity. They try to frame
a picture of the old Moorish mosque with their camera, but it is
impossible to exclude the metallic light rail tracks in the background.
Even in a Chinatown wet market, a chicken-seller on a stool is consulting his stockbroker on his mobile phone.

The "real" thing does exist, in the *kampung* just outside the Klang
Valley. For while "kampung" translates literally as "village", in city
terms, it also carries connotations of being rural, rustic, almost back-
ward. The Klang Valley is forward-looking, technologically-bonded,
and even Western in outlook. But to many, it is also just a place to
cari makan, to "earn a living". It is certainly not home, for home is
still the *kampung* – where the heart is.

And so, during the major festive occasions of Hari Raya Puasa
and Chinese New Year, hundreds of thousands *balik kampung*, return
home to their villages or towns.

This annual exodus sees the highways deserted, hawker stalls
closed, while the city's parks echo to the *caw caw* of crows. After
the holidays, you can almost hear the machine grinding up again, and
before long, it is throbbing once more with noise, chaos, and life. ❑

PRECEDING PAGES: the glittering Kuala Lumpur city skyline.
LEFT: Jalan Petaling night market all lit up for the Chinese New Year.

City Centre

0 ——— 200 m
0 ——— 200 yds
N

Masjid India
Masjid India 17
Klang
J. Melaka
Jalan Ampang
Lorong Bukit Nanas
Dewan Bandaraya (City Hall)
Gombak
St Mary's Cathedral
Jl. Tangsi
Wisma Kraftangan
Masjid Jamek 18
Masjid Jamek
Jalan Ampang
Jalan Gereja
H.S. Lee
Hang Lekiu
Royal Selangor Club 3
Dataran Merdeka 1
2 Bangunan Sultan Abdul Samad/Sultan Abdul Samad Building
Plaza Putra
Sri Putra
Perpustakaan Peringatan KL (KL Memorial Library)
Sin Seng Nam
Jalan Raja
Jalan Tun Perak
Muzium Sejarah Nasional (National History Museum)
Lebuh Pasar Besar
Jalan Silang
Kompleks Dayabumi
Central Market 12
Lebuh Pudu
Kompleks Kota Raya
Jalan Bukit Aman
Jalan Tugu
Jalan Cenderasari
Jalan Sultan Hishamuddin
13 Hsien Szu Yeh Miao
Kasturi
Jalan Tun Tan Cheng Lock
CHINATOWN
Jalan Benteng
Pejabat Pos Besar (General Post Office)
Pasar Seni
Jalan Hang Lekir
Jalan Hang
Muzium Kesenian Islam Malaysia (Islamic Arts Museum)
16 Sri Mahamariamman Hindu Temple
Jalan Sultan Mohamed
Jalan Sultan
Jalan Petaling
7 Masjid Negara (National Mosque)
Klang
Jalan H.S. Lee
8
J. Lembah Perdana
Victorian Institution
J. Balai Polis
14
Stadium Chinwoo
6 Bangunan KTM
Pusat Islam
5 Stesen Keretapi KL (Railway Station)

Kuala Lumpur

0 ——— 500 m
0 ——— 500 yds
N

Putra World Trade Centre
Putra
Pan Pacific Hotel
The Mall
PWTC
Jalan Ipoh
Chow Kit
L. Raja Laut
Jalan Chow Kit
Lorong Hj. Taib Lima
Jalan Tuanku Abdul Rahman
Jalan Hj. Hussein
Jalan Raja Laut
Jalan Hj. Taib
Lorong Hj. Taib Dua
Lorong Hj. Taib Satu
Jalan Sri Amar
Bangunan U.M.N.O.
Jalan Kuching
Jalan Putra
Jalan Tun Ismail
Jalan Ceylon
Jalan
Sultan Ismail
J. M. T. Satu
CHOW KIT
Sultan Ismail Centre
Jalan Raja Laut
Medan Mara
Medan Tuanku
Wisma Loke
MEDAN
Jalan Medan Tuanku
Jalan Semarang
Kompleks Pertama
Gombak
Jalan Dato Onn
Jalan Dang Wangi
Kompleks Campbell
J. Doraisamy
J. Kemunting
Sogo
Jln Istahan
Jln. Bandaraya
Semua House
Jalan Tuanku Abdul Rahman
Lorong Tuanku Abdul Rahman
Lorong Tuanku Gombak
Jalan Munshi Abdullah
Coliseum Cafe & Hotel 10
Jalan Dato Onn
Jabatan Perdana Menteri
Bgn PKNS
Malayan Mansion
Masjid India
Selangor Mansion
Jalan Ampang
Jabatan Kerjaraya (Ibu Pejabat)
P. Tun Ismail
Jabatan Kerajaan
Jabatan Pelajaran
Jalan Tun Ismail
Jalan Mahameru
Experimental Theatre
Jalan Parlimen
Parliament House
Tugu Kebangsaan (National Monument) 10
ASEAN Sculpture Garden
Jalan Tangsi
St Mary's Cathedral
Dewan Bandaraya (City Hall)
J. Melaka
Jalan Melayu
St John
Muzium Telekom
Bgn. Anglo Oriental
Royal Selangor Club
Wisma Kraftangan
Masjid Jamek
Masjid Jamek
Lorong Ampang
Jalan Ampang
Jalan Tun H. S. Lee
Gereja
Hang Lekiu
Bukit Mahkamah
Jalan Raja Chula
Kinabalu Raja
Jalan Raja
Dataran Merdeka
Bangunan Sultan Abdul Samad (Sultan Abdul Samad Building)
Jalan Silang
Jalan Tun Perak
Menara Maybank & Muzium Numismatik
Jalan Bukit Aman
Perpustakaan Peringatan KL (KL Memorial Library)
Lebuh Pasar Besar
Puduraya
Pudu
Plaza Rakyat
Muzium Sejarah Nasional (National History Museum)
Hsien Szu Yeh Miao
Kompleks Kota Raya
J. Tun Tan Cheng Lock
Gereja Methodist
Kompleks Dayabumi
Central Market
Kasturi
CHINATOWN
Jalan Hang Lekir
Jalan Wesley
Jalan Tugu
Jalan Cenderasari
Pejabat Pos Besar (General Post Office)
Pasar Seni
Sri Mahamariamman Hindu Temple
Jalan Sultan Mohamed
Jalan Sultan
Jalan Tun Tan Cheng Lock
Jalan Sultan Hishamuddin
Muzium Kesenian Islam Malaysia (Islamic Arts Museum)
Masjid Negara (National Mosque)
Klang
Jalan Petaling
Stadium Chinwoo
Jalan Tembusu
Panggung Anniversari
Royal Lake Club
Jalan Kebun Bunga
Hibiscus Garden
Butterfly Park
Cenderawasih
Jalan Lembah Perdana
Victorian Institution
J. Balai Polis
Jalan Sultan
Carcosa Seri Negara
Bird Park
Jalan Perdana
Jalan Kinabalu
Bangunan KTM
TAMAN TASIK PERDANA (LAKE GARDENS)
Deer Park
Memorial Tun Razak
9
Tasik Perdana
Istana Tetamu (Gue Palace)
J. Mahameru
Muzium Polis Diraja Malaysia (Royal Malaysia Police Museum)
Pusat Islam
Bulatan
Bgn. Shell
Merdeka
Chan See Shu Yuen Clanhouse & Temple 15
Stadium Merdeka
Jalan Stadium
Jalan Damansara
Planetarium Negara
Balai Kuala Lumpur
Stesen Keretapi KL (Railway Station)
Jalan Sulaiman
Jalan Maharajalela
25 Istana Negara
Maharaja
26 Tien Hau Temple
Jalan Damansara
11 Muzium Negara (National Museum)
Bgn. Sulaiman
J. Bentara
Sulaiman
J. Kampung Attap

KUALA LUMPUR

From colonial mansions and the bustle of Chinatown to the modern magnificence of the Twin Towers, Kuala Lumpur represents the true essence of today's Malaysia

Map on pages 130–31

A mining outpost 150 years ago, a dynamic Asian city today, Kuala Lumpur is the capital of Malaysia and home to about 1.6 million people. With its constant facelifts and ever-rising skyline, Kuala Lumpur – or KL, as it is popularly known – embodies the aspirations of a nation working hard to carve its niche in an era of globalisation.

It is therefore in KL that the East-West and old-new juxtapositions are most apparent. Stately old mansions of eclectic style, traditional mosques and Hindu temples are squeezed between concrete high-rises and steel and chrome office blocks. Trendy 30-somethings trade pleasantries with traditionally-garbed shop-keepers. *Feng shui* and Islamic values blend in global deal-making, while even in the face of leading-edge technological innovation, a fortune teller is consulted. With its variety of sights, food and shops, cosmopolitan Kuala Lumpur offers something for every visitor.

Bare beginnings

The most popular tale of how KL got its name is the simplest: the miners and traders who first came in search of tin poled up the river to where the Klang and Gombak rivers converge. The Gombak estuary was the highest point upstream that the miners could land their supplies for prospecting for tin in Ampang, a few kilometres further inland. They named the settlement Kuala Lumpur, which means Muddy Estuary in Malay. By the 1860s, the landing place had become a flourishing village.

However, these were turbulent times, and fierce rivalries over mining claims and water rights led to gang clashes and bitter feuds. Finally, the predominantly Chinese settlement was put under the leadership of Yap Ah Loy, the *Kapitan China* or Chinese headman. The *Kapitan* warred against crime, built a prison and quelled revolts. Under his supervision, KL obtained some semblance of a township.

Then Frank Swettenham, the British resident of Selangor, moved his administration to KL. Brick buildings were introduced and street by street, the wooden shanties were pulled down. In 1886, the country's first railway line connected KL to the coastal town of Klang.

As the state capital of Selangor, KL grew to become the centre of administration, business and trade. In 1946, it was established as the headquarters of the Federation of Malaya, with its development intensifying after independence from the British in 1957. But KL truly came of age in 1974, when it became a unit of its own called Wilayah Persekutuan (Federal Territory). Today, it is the business hub and commercial centre for the whole of Malaysia.

LEFT: coloured umbrellas in front of the Dayabumi Complex.
BELOW: Malay cultural show.

Fountain detail from the Dataran Merdeka.

Colonial core

KL's central attractions are close enough together to cover on foot. To reach the sights that are a little further away, hop into a taxi, commuter train or LRT (Light Rapid Transit) – but walking is definitely quicker during the traffic-choked peak hours. Alternatively, there are plenty of city tours that cover the main sights in KL as well as its surroundings. You can book with local tour companies, and major hotels. Or make up your own tour by hiring a taxi for the day (negotiate the price before you set off).

A good starting point for your walking tour is in the city's historic centre at **Dataran Merdeka ❶** (Independence Square). Flanked by graceful cupolas and Moorish minarets, the square first saw life as a *padang* or green. This was the playing field of a club at which the colonial community congregated. Apparently, it was also in the *padang* that the British flag was lowered for the last time on 31 August 1957.

Today, Dataran Merdeka is the venue for cultural events such as the colourful parades held in conjunction with national festivals and other celebrations. Casting a 100-metre (328-ft) high nationalistic shadow on the green is the world's tallest flagpole, which rises from an underground entertainment complex and car park.

The most photographed of Moorish buildings facing the green is the imposing **Sultan Abdul Samad Building ❷** (Bangunan Sultan Abdul Samad). The former colonial administrative centre, it now houses the High Court and Supreme Court. Constructed between 1894–7, it was the first of the Moorish-style buildings introduced to the country by two Public Works Department architects, A.C. Norman and A.B. Hubbock. Both men had spent some time in

BELOW: the Royal Selangor Club faces the green expanse of the *padang*.

India, and deemed that an architectural style featuring Moorish, Indian and Arabic motifs would best suit a predominantly Muslim country, apparently ignoring the fact that the Malays already had a highly developed style of their own.

Sir Charles Mitchell, the governor of the Straits Settlements at the time, thought the building a ridiculous extravagance, and was heard to say: "The tin won't last forever, you know." One wonders what he would have had to say about the multi-million ringgit Petronas Twin Towers.

At one end of the Sultan Abdul Samad Building sit the **Sessions and Magistrates Courts**, with their twin tower-flanked entrances. Take a stroll down the palm tree-lined road to the other end. On Saturday evenings, this whole road is closed off to traffic, to be taken over by hand-holding couples and parents with tots gleefully playing on the road. Nightime also sees the buildings beautifully lit with fairylights.

At the end of the Padang, the **Muzium Sejarah Nasional** (National History Museum) continues the Moorish tradition, while next door, the **KL Memorial Library** (Perpustakaan Peringatan KL) is striking in being the only neo-Rennaisance style building in the lot. Both are open to the public.

Facing the Sultan Abdul Samad Building across Dataran Merdeka is the **Royal Selangor Club ❸**, built in 1884 in mock-Tudor style. The club was sometimes known as the Spotted Dog, a derisive allusion to the club's emblem of a running leopard. Today, senior government administrators and prosperous businessmen prop up the long bar where the British once sat over their *stengah* (literally half, meaning half a peck of liquor). Completing the square is the neo-Gothic **St Mary's Cathedral ❹**, built in 1894 on what was previously the horse stables of the Royal Selangor Club. It is one of the oldest Anglican churches in this region.

Map
on pages
130–31

TIP

The National History Museum (open daily; tel: 03-2694 4590; www.jma.gov.my; free) at 29 Jalan Raja, a repository for museological activities and research, has a library, souvenir shop and book corner. Guided tours are available.

BELOW: the Moorish-inspired Sultan Abdul Samad Building.

TIP

Visitors can enter a mosque outside of prayer times. Decorous clothing and behaviour is recommended, and shoes must be removed before entering. Scarves and robes are available for women.

BELOW: a lasting British legacy – the Victorian KL Railway Station.

Victorian station

The southern end of the Moorish design stretch is capped by the Kuala Lumpur Railway Station and Bangunan KTM. En route to these from Dataran Merdeka on Jalan Sultan Hishamuddin, is the **Kompleks Dayabumi** (Dayabumi Complex) with its filigree-like Islamic-design arches. It is most impressive at night when it is floodlit. At its base is the **Pejabat Pos Besar** (General Post Office).

Beyond this sits the old, magnificent **Stesen Keretapi Kuala Lumpur ❺** (Kuala Lumpur Railway Station). Turrets, spires, minarets and arches greet the eye in every direction. The station was constructed in 1911 to the standards applied to Victorian public buildings all over the empire. So much so, in fact, that construction was once held up because the roof did not meet the specifications stipulating that it support one metre of snow! It was once a wonderful entry to the city but now, only the intra-city KTM commuter and the E&O Express trains stop here. All interstate trains and city trains stop at the ultra-modern Sentral Station in Brickfields, near the National Museum.

Opposite the station is the **Bangunan KTM ❻** (KTM Building), headquarters of Malaysian Railways. This was the last of the Moorish buildings to be erected.

Heading back to Dataran Merdeka, you will see the **Masjid Negara ❼** (National Mosque; open Tues–Sun 9am–6pm; Fri 3–6pm). Its Grand Hall, busiest on Fridays, can accommodate 8,000 worshippers. Completed in 1965, this was one of the country's first post-independence constructions. The jagged 18 points of the star-shaped roof represent the 13 states of Malaysia and the five pillars of Islam. However, it represents national unity as well, for non-Muslim Malaysians also donated generous funds towards its building.

From the mosque, follow Jalan Lembah Perdana to the magnificent **Islamic Arts Museum ❽** (Muzium Kesenian Islam Malaysia; open Tues–Sun 10am–6pm; entrance fee) built at a cost of US$50 million. Uzbekistan craftsmen created the mosaic domes, including the unique inverted dome in the interior. The museum has a spectacular collection of crafts from all over the Islamic world and fine models of the world's best-known mosques.

Behind it is the **Royal Malaysian Police Museum** (Muzium Polis Diraja Malaysia; open Tue–Sun 10am–6pm). In the grounds, kids will enjoy exploring armoured tanks and the Police Force's first aircraft – a single-engined Cessna. Inside, the Weapons section is particularly interesting for its guns confiscated from post-World War II Communist guerillas, and a display of wicked-looking Secret Society weapons.

A garden retreat

Downtown KL is so crowded with buildings that the visitor may begin to wonder if there are any green spaces in the city apart from Dataran Merdeka. However, right in the middle of the city is its largest park, **Taman Tasik Perdana ❾** (Lake Gardens).

The Lake Gardens (open Mon–Sat 9am–6pm; Sun and public holidays 8am–6pm) and their surrounding attractions are actually perched on a number of adjacent hills. The gardens themselves comprise 92 hectares (240 acres) of undulating green with magnificent trees and flowering plants. Popular with locals

Map on pages 130–31

and visitors alike, they are especially crowded at weekends. Early in the morning and in the evening, you'll see joggers puff their way past picnickers, star-crossed lovers and old Chinese folk going through their *tai chi* routines. It is a great place to watch the Kuala Lumpur family at play.

For a taste of wildlife, the **Bird Park** and **Butterfly Park** (open daily 9am–5pm; entrance fee) house local and foreign species in pretty, forested enclosures. The **Planetarium**, which sits in a landscaped garden, has a 36-cm (14-inch) telescope, a theatre and the Arianne IV space engine used to launch Malaysia's first satellite, the Measat I. Other attractions in the gardens include an orchid garden and deer park.

On the fringes of the gardens is the members-only Royal Lake Club, founded by breakaways from the Selangor Club in the early 1900s. Of much greater interest is a pair of colonial mansions that overlook the gardens. The **Carcosa Seri Negara**, built in 1896, was once the official residence of the British governor of Malaya and is now an exclusive luxury hotel. The neighbouring **Istana Tetamu** (Guest Palace) is a reserved for visiting foreign dignitaries. The latter was built in 1913 for the British King, who never visited the country.

Fallen heroes

On another hill opposite the gardens stands the solemn **Tugu Kebangsaan ⑩** (National Monument), which commemorates those who died in the struggle against the communist insurgency in the 1950s. The monument is modelled on Washington DC's famous Iwo Jima Monument, and the galleries at its base record the names of the units who fought, including British, Australian, Fijian, Maori and Malay troops.

Opposite Lake Gardens is the Tugu Kebangsaan, a tribute to those who died in the communist insurgency of the 1950s.

BELOW: Lake Garden's oar-boats.

TIP

The Museum Garden Shop in the National Museum's grounds sells Kelantanese coconut craft and ceramics from Kedah. It also has a range of Asian knick-knacks.

Nearby is the **Cenotaph**, erected by the British to commemorate the soldiers who died in world wars I and II. At the base of the hill is the ASEAN **Sculpture Garden**, a symbol of the solidarity among the 10-member Southeast Asian regional group.

A little down the road is the **Parliament House**, which appears on the back of all Malaysian coins. The 1960s building is usually not open to visitors.

Nearby, history is on display in the Minangkabau-roofed **Muzium Negara ⑪** (National Museum; open daily 9am–6pm; entrance fee) on Jalan Damansara facing Jalan Travers. Its galleries showcase local culture, natural history (including an extensive mounted insect collection), and arts and craft displays. Whilst the museum is not particularly interesting, do look out for its thematic exhibitions; about eight are staged each year. The museum's extensive reference library, with its original manuscripts and charts, is accessible to the public with permission from the curator.

Head back towards Dayabumi Complex and cross the river to get to **Central Market ⑫** (Pasar Seni). A former fruit-and-vegetable market, this Art Deco showpiece was saved from demolition by conservation-minded architects, who eventually won an award for their restoration and renovation efforts. It is currently a favourite hangout for KL's youth.

Central Market has it all, from key-chains and batik scarves, to traditional basketry and woodware from all over the country, as well as preserved foodstuffs. Artists will paint your portrait for you or inscribe a dedication on a pencil-holder. There is often an event or exhibition happening – if you're lucky you could catch a *wayang kulit* (shadow puppet) performance or *bangsawan* (traditional Malay theatre) production in full swing. Outside the building, buskers and medicine men give their own impromptu shows.

BELOW: Central Market shopper.

From Central Market, head down Jalan Hang Kasturi to the oldest temple in Kuala Lumpur, the **Hsien Szu Yeh Miao ⑬** (Temple of Szu Yeh). Make sure you duck your head to avoid the low-hanging awning poles, and walk past the alley's food stalls to arrive at the temple gate.

Built in 1884 by Yap Ah Loy, the first headman of old KL, the temple is rather small and dark, its ceiling blackened by non-stop smoke curling up from the joss-sticks below. Fine examples of wood carvings illustrate scenes from the various Buddhist canons. A framed photograph of Yap Ah Loy sits on a side altar, looking more like a kindly and gracious saint than the tough and exacting leader he was in reality.

Chinatown

Arriving at this point, you're in the vicinity of Chinatown, whose main streets are Jalan Sultan, Jalan Tun H.S. Lee and Jalan Petaling. For the inveterate shopper and connoisseur of exotic oddities, Chinatown is a paradise. Chinese apothecaries display their herbs and medicines in porcelain pots or beneath glass counters amid more familiar international brands. There are jewellers and goldsmiths, casket and basket makers, dry goods stores, pet shops, herbalists, frame makers and haberdashers. Modernisation wields its hand in air-conditioning and contemporary decor, but there is still plenty to experience.

The tourist trade has long realised the area's magnetic draw. Here are any number of backpackers, and at night you'd be hard-pressed to find local patrons at the Jalan Hang Lekir open-air eateries. Still, local bypassers stare as hard at the visitors as the latter do at them.

The term Chinatown is often used interchangeably with **Jalan Petaling ⓮**, site of the famous night market. Better known as Petaling Street, this section of town is as different at night and in the day as, well, night and day. The action begins at dawn, to the delicious aroma of traditional dumplings and breads filled with red-bean paste and chicken curry. The wet market is the place to find Chinese housewives haggling for fresh chicken slaughtered on the spot, greens of all kinds, and chrysanthemums for their altars. Be warned, though – the smells are something else. As the city wakes up, stalls begin to line both sides of the road and pedestrians zig-zag from coffeeshop to fruit stall and back, impervious to the heavy traffic. A respite from the crowd and heat can be found in the interior of the **Chan See Shu Yuen Clanhouse and Temple ⓯**, near Bulatan Merdeka. Built in 1906, it is decorated with elaborate ceramic glazed tiles and ornamentation, and intricate wall paintings.

Street eats

At midday, office executives begin to fill the eateries. Chinatown is reputedly where the best Chinese street food can be found, from all sorts of noodles to pork ribs soup (*bakut teh*) and roasted meat snacks. There is "home-made" *dim sum* (little Chinese dumplings and pastries) from 6am, mooncakes for the autumnal Moon Festival, and bittersweet herbal brews to cure all sorts of ailments at the roadside medicinal drinks stalls.

Map on pages 130–31

Chinese dim sum dumplings are heavenly when freshly steamed. Look out for them in Chinatown.

BELOW: Jalan Petaling by day.

Hindu devotees who
make the annual
pilgrimage from KL's
Sri Mahamariamman
Temple to Batu
Caves, skewer their
bodies with metal
rods and carry great
steel structures as
penance for favours
asked from the gods.

BELOW: Sri
Mahamariamman
Temple

Petaling Street assumes its festive air from 5pm. A section of the street closes to traffic for the *pasar malam* (night market), where the stalls, restrained all day at the kerbs, take over the road, joined soon by twice as many again, are erected at lightning speed. Here you can find all the "genuine" copies of brand name watches and tee-shirts, as well as videos recordings of movies that haven't even made it to the local cinemas yet. Visitors are confronted by a medley of stalls on both sides of the street hawking precious stones, antiques and household goods. First rule of thumb when buying: shop around. Second rule of thumb: bargain.

However, this being Malaysia, Chinatown is not all Chinese. At the end of Jalan Tun H.S. Lee sits the old **Victorian Institution**, built in 1893 in an incongruous English cottage style. This was the city's first boy's school. It has now been turned into a drama hall.

Then, parallel to Petaling Street on Jalan Bandar is one of KL's most famous Hindu temples, the **Sri Mahamariamman Hindu Temple** ⑯. Its towering gate is decorated with an explosion of colourful gods entangled in an arresting design of South Indian origin. Built in 1873, it occupies an important place in Hindu religious life. This is the starting point each January for the annual Thaipusam pilgrimage of penance to the Batu Caves temple, just outside KL. On other days, women and children sell strings of fragrant jasmine in the, as pavements here are called, "five-foot-way" and a man in a traditional *dhoti* sarong keeps watch by a shoe rack for those wishing to enter the temple courtyard. Devotees emerge from prayer, their foreheads smeared with sacred white ash.

Off Petaling Street behind the Traffic Police Headquarters is a little street called **Jalan Balai Polis**, where a new Chinatown is being born. Here, a charming row of pre-war shophouses has found a new lease of life as the centre for the young Mandarin-speaking Chinese of KL. Apart from a string of cafés and pubs, there is the **Old China Café and Gallery**, a Nyonya restaurant-cum-antique shop, where food is served on antique furniture, and virtually everything in the restaurant is for sale. The café was formerly the headquarters of the Selangor and Federal Territory Laundry Association, a trade guild that flourished in the pre-washing-machine days. Photographs of the guild members still hang on the walls and much of the memorabilia dates from those days. There are also several tea houses along the street and in Jalan Panggung. For the uninitiated, these offer a chance to learn about the ancient Chinese art of serving and drinking tea.

Indian and Muslim flavours

On the other side of Dataran Merdeka lies an entirely different experience. This is **Jalan Masjid India** ⑰, where Indian silks, flowery saris and glittering handmade jewellery are the order of the day. After six every evening, portable kitchens with tables and chairs take over the street, offering food which is as spicy as you can stand it.

Eating al fresco is definitely more enjoyable than dining in a large restaurant, where the atmosphere can be contrived, and enthusiastic air conditioning can make you long for winter clothing. Food stalls set up under the stars are common all over the city; those along the riverbank attest to their popularity.

A prominent landmark near Jalan Masjid India is a mosque erected at the site of one of the town's first mosques. Follow the riverbank towards Jalan Tun Perak and you will reach **Masjid Jamek** (Jamek Mosque), standing proudly still at the historic meeting place of the Gombak and Klang rivers. This elegant structure, adapted from a Moghul mosque in North India, is an oasis of serenity once you enter the palm-tree filled grounds through the *sahn* or walled courtyard. At sunset, a mirrored glass skyscraper nearby gives a mystical reflection of the mosque.

From Dataran Merdeka, go along **Jalan Tuanku Abdul Rahman** and explore its interesting shops. Named after the country's first Prime Minister, the area's most written-about restaurant is the **Coliseum Café and Hotel** ⑲. Serving customers for more than 60 years, its bar was once the favourite watering hole for planters, miners, government officials and soldiers. The decor has changed little since those days, and the service by grumpy Chinese waiters certainly harks back to a bygone era. Today, its steaks continue to attract attention for their quality and price. Next door to this establishment is one of the country's first cinemas, the **Coliseum Cinema**, built in the 1920s.

For six days a week, Jalan Tuanku Abdul Rahman is crowded with traffic, but every Saturday night it becomes a pedestrian mall, with stalls offering goods to be had from the bigger shops by day for half-price (or even less).

There are more street markets at **Chow Kit**, where Jalan Tuanku Abdul Rahman crosses Jalan Sultan Ismail. Despite efforts to clean it up, the area retains its shady character, with stalls selling cheap items and Malay eats, while above

Map on pages 130–31

BELOW: a rare sight in the city – a carefully-groomed Triumph.

TIP

Tourism Malaysia has a good collection of travel industry material in its library on the 24th floor of the Putra World Trade Centre. Use of the library is free (open Monday–Friday 7.30am–4.30pm, Saturday 7.30am–1pm, closed lunchtime).

BELOW: Malaysian pottery.
RIGHT: a downtown flowershop.

the roar of the traffic, the air is rent with raucous pop music. Look out for a small crowd gathered in one spot and you may find a snake charmer, or a medicine man proclaiming the miracle attributes of his wares.

On the right, off Jalan Tuanku Abdul Rahman on the way to Chow Kit, **Wisma Loke** poses as another reminder of KL's past. This charming Chinese townhouse was built by Chinese mine owner Cheow Ah Yeok, a contemporary of Yap Ah Loy. Sporting classical Greco-Roman arches and pillars, it also has balustrades of glazed jade-coloured porcelain from China, Melakan tiles and a "moongate" within. Bought later by another self-made millionaire, Loke Yew, this was the first house in KL to be lit by electricity.

At the other end of Chow Kit stands a structure very much of this century: the 40 storey-high **Putra World Trade Centre** (PWTC), which was built at infamous cost, and houses government offices as well as the head office for Tourism Malaysia, the massive Putra Concert Hall and a convention complex.

Next door is the Pan Pacific Hotel with elevators riding on the outside of the building, affording an interesting view of the area. Across the road is a modern shopping centre, **The Mall**, and **The Legend Hotel**.

Saturday's Sunday Market

For yet more *pasar malam* (street market) head for **Kampung Bahru** off Jalan Raja Abdullah near Jalan Ampang. Literally meaning "new village", Kampung Bahru came into being in 1889, and has stubbornly remained a Malay *kampung* while Malaysia's most progressive city grew around it. Even though brick has replaced many of the original wooden houses, to enter the "village" is to leave behind the sounds and smells of a city.

Sheltered by the blocks of flats here, the **Pasar Minggu ⓴** (Sunday Market) springs to life, not on Sunday, but on Saturday night – although it does last into the early hours of Sunday morning. The *pasar* is well worth a visit for its exclusively Malay offerings. *Songkok* (fez), prayer books, Islamic calligraphy, batik *sarungs*, and all kinds of handicrafts are on sale at the stalls, including vases, traditional earthenware pots (*labu*), Kelantan silverware and the richly embroidered *songket* from Terengganu. Besides the ubiquitous *satay*, here is where you find a large choice of Malay cooking, from *nasi lemak* (coconut rice with various condiments) to *bubur* (rice porridge) and spicy regional delights.

Golden Triangle

Further up from Kampung Bahru, historic **Jalan Ampang** presents a very different aspect of urban architecture. Forming a boundary of KL's Golden Triangle business district, its row of old tin miner's mansions is gradually being dwarfed by steel and concrete giants of contemporary design. However, many are being conserved, particularly at the upper end of Jalan Ampang past Jalan Tun Razak, which now houses embassies and consulates.

One of the best preserved of these mansions is the **Malaysia Tourism Centre ㉑** (MTC; open daily 7am–midnight), a tourism and theatre complex at the Jalan Sultan Ismail junction. Built in 1935 by a wealthy Chinese tin mogul and rubber planter, Eu Tong Sen, the chateau served as the war office for the British Army, and later, the Japanese Army. When Malaysia gained its independence from British rule in 1957, it saw the first sitting of the new nation's Parliament. It was also the scene for installation ceremonies for Malaysia's kings, and over the years it continued to play various prominent roles in the

Map on pages 130–31

Look out for bargain-priced batik at the Central Market.

BELOW: The MTC is housed in what was once a tin millionaire's mansion.

Galeri Petronas (open Sat–Thurs 10am–8pm), level 3 of the Suria Mall, KLCC, is a cutting-edge art gallery exhibiting works by both international artists and well-known Malaysians like Latif Mohidin.

BELOW: Suria Mall at the KLCC.

nation's history. In the late 1980s, it was refurbished and commissioned for its present use. A one-stop visitor centre with booking desks and information counters, the MTC is also a centre for Malaysian culture.

The stipulations of a 100-year-old will are preserving the grandeur of another 19th-century Jalan Ampang mansion. The former **Bok House**, which was once a restaurant called **Le Coq d'Or**, has retained much of its original flavour because its owner decreed that it never be sold, nor its design or decor changed. Behind its porticoed verandahs, Italian marble floors and 18th-century paintings, is a charming tale of love and revenge. Bok House was built by a poor young man, Chua Cheng Bok, who fell desperately in love with the daughter of a wealthy mine owner whose house stood on Jalan Ampang. However, the old man forbade the couple to marry. Bitterly disappointed, the young suitor put all his energies into his work, determined to prove that he could make it in the world. Eventually, he was able to build his own mansion – right next door to his enemy's, overshadowing it in size and magnificence. Bok's house still stands, while the arrogant miner's house has long since disappeared.

Tall Towers

The city's newest landmark is on Jalan Ampang and currently holds the record for the world's tallest pair of buildings – the **Petronas Twin Towers** ㉒. Soaring some 451.9 metres (c.1,500 ft) above the traffic-congested streets, its identical towers – linked midway up by a skybridge on the 42nd floor – reach an auspicious 88 storeys. Designed by Cesar Pelli, these glass and stainless steel buildings combine Islamic patterns with state-of-the-art engineering techniques (see *page 89*).

The Twin Towers are actually office blocks, and make up a section of a larger development called the **Kuala Lumpur City Centre** (KLCC). Sitting on what used to be KL's racecourse, the development includes a cinema complex, one of the largest shopping centres in KL (the ultra-modern Suria KLCC) and an oil and gas museum. There is also an art gallery and a small but magnificent concert hall, the first dedicated classical music venue in Malaysia. The development also has a pretty landscaped park, hotels and a big convention centre.

Visitors can ascend to the Skybridge on the 42nd floor of the Petronas Towers (open daily 10.45am–12.45pm and 2.30–4.45pm) but for a higher view head down the road to **Menara Kuala Lumpur** ㉓ (open 10am–10pm; entrance fee). Also known as the KL Tower, this 421-metre (1,380-ft) structure is of impressive height. The public observation platform reveals in one glance KL, its surrounding hills, and as far away as the casino playground of Genting Highlands in the peninsula's mountainous backbone, the Main Range. The Islamic-influenced tower also has a souvenir shop, revolving restaurant and private banquet facilities.

Map on pages 130–31

Along Jalan Ampang is the Khoon Yam Buddhist Temple. This oldest Chinese temple in Kuala Lumpur has been extensively renovated.

High life

The fulcrum of modern consumerism in Malaysia is the intersection of Jalan Sultan Ismail and Jalan Bukit Bintang, an area of expensive shops, high-class restaurants, international hotels and party-till-you-drop nightlife. You will find a number of large shopping malls in this area: Sungei Wang Plaza and the adjacent Bukit Bintang Plaza offer more than 500 shops, including the best bookstores in KL; Imbi Plaza concentrates on computers and software; the upmarket Starhill Plaza is the place for branded designer wear and fashionable eateries; and flashy Lot 10 has its European designer boutiques.

BELOW: the soaring Menara Kuala Lumpur at dusk.

MULTIMEDIA SUPERCORRIDOR

Cult techno-mag *Wired* once called it "the planet's most seductive technopark", a quote later seized upon by the *International Herald Tribune*. They were referring to Malaysia's MSC, the Multimedia Super Corridor, which is anchored in KL by the Petronas Twin Towers. At the other end of the 50 by 15 kilometre (31 by 9 mile) corridor is the Kuala Lumpur International Airport (KLIA) in Selangor.

Though effectively still an experiment, the MSC is meant to leapfrog the country into the knowledge-based world economy of the new millennium. The idea is to invite international participation to explore new ways of doing things in tomorrow's information-driven environment. The Malaysia node would physically be on the corridor of an "intelligent" state-of-the-art infrastructure, linked to an international collaboration of companies, regions and communities via a high-bandwidth fibre-optic backbone. Among its components is Putrajaya, the "cyber" seat of government which will eventually take over Kuala Lumpur's administrative role.

Advising the government on the ambitious project – slated to reach its objectives in 2020 – is an international panel comprising the likes of Microsoft's Bill Gates, Netscape's James Barksdale and NTT's Jun-Ichiro Miyazu.

Map on pages 130–31

TIP

The Golden Triangle is also where you'll find KL's great night life. The hot spots are along Jalan Sultan Ismail near Concorde Hotel and behind it in the bungalows along Jalan Kia Peng.

BELOW: pottery in the Artists' Colony, Komplexs Budaya Kraf.
RIGHT: the glittering Petronas Twin Towers.

On Jalan Conlay, off Jalan Raja Chulan, is the arts and craft centre of **Kompleks Budaya Kraf** ㉔ (Craft Cultural Complex; open daily 10am–6pm). A larger, quieter and more upmarket version of Central Market, it comprises a collection of shops offering traditional and contemporary designs for anything a souvenir-hunter could want, including handwoven textiles, woodwork, batik, basketwork, silver and pewter, native products and pottery. There are also demonstrations of *songket* cloth weaving, batik printing and silver and copper tooling. The building at the back houses a small museum (entrance fee) and cafétaria.

Arts and crafts

In one corner of the sprawling complex is the Artists' Colony, a conglomerate of nine open-air wooden work spaces in the shape of *wakaf* (traditional Malay gazebo). Here, 18 resident artists ply their trade to the sound of Malay rock songs on their radios. The colony presents an excellent opportunity to talk to newly-established and up-and-coming artists, watch them at work, and even buy paintings directly from them.

Indeed, for art lovers, KL has many galleries, some of which are works of art in themselves, such as the minimalist Petronas Art Galley (KLCC) and the charming Gallery Taksu off Jalan Dato' Keramat. A sampling of the broad spectrum of local art can be found in the **Balai Seni Lukis Negara** (National Art Gallery) (open daily 10am–6pm) in Jalan Temerloh. The modern building has three galleries showcasing experimental, permanent, and temporary works.

Down the road from the Golden Triangle is the **Istana Negara** ㉕ (National Palace), the official residence of the *Yang Di-Pertuan Agung* (king). The country has a new *agung* every five years as the position is rotated among its sultans. The palace began life as the town house of a wealthy Chinese businessman and was sold and converted into a palace in 1926. Typical of colonial mansions, it has large balconies and gardens; not so typical are its golden domes. Yellow is the colour for royalty, and only kings may walk on the welcoming yellow carpet while politicians and visiting dignitaries use red. Royal garden parties, investitures and receptions are held here, but the *agung* normally lives in his own palace, every sultan having his own "mini" palace in the capital.

Beyond the National Palace and further south along Jalan Syed Putra is a small road which climbs a steep hill (Jalan Kerayong). Follow it and you will find yourself at another commanding view of the city. On this hill stands the massive **Tien Hau Temple** ㉖. Built in 1985 with the contributions of several Chinese multi-millionaires, each purportedly donated large sums of money to build one pillar of the temple. Although it is known that the cost of building the temple was phenomenal, the exact figure remains a secret.

A much-utilised community centre, the temple complex has a large conference hall for meetings, performances and weddings, a restaurant, youth and women's clubs and offices. The temple itself sits right at the top of the hill. There is even a small garden inside, which can be viewed perfectly from any angle. The building itself is an incongruous mixture, gaudy yet impressive, mystical yet decidedly worldly. ❑

SELANGOR

The area of Selangor around Kuala Lumpur is the developed hub of Malaysia's industrial economy. But beyond the hinterland, the landscape yields to limestone cliffs, caverns and jungle trails

Map on page 150

Heading west from **Kuala Lumpur ❶** on the Federal Highway, massive Moorish arches announce that you are departing the Federal Territory and entering the state of Selangor. According to the Tourism Malaysia brochure, this marble *pintu gerbang*, flanked by ancient Selangor canons, was erected in 1974 "to mark the sacrifice" made by the Sultan of Selangor in ceding Kuala Lumpur to the Federal Government as the national capital.

More than two decades later, more land has been ceded for the new national capital, Putrajaya, the intended heart of the ambitious information technology-driven Multimedia Super Corridor (MSC), which runs through Selangor. At the southern end is the 100-sq. km (36-sq. mile) **Kuala Lumpur International Airport** (KLIA), one of Asia's largest airports: so large, in fact, that it has a Formula One racing circuit running within its perimeter. Near Putrajaya is Cyberjaya, the MSC's dedicated "intelligent" city for multimedia companies. Besides the Putrajaya Mosque, some government offices, the controversial Prime Minister's palatial residence and shopping malls much of the MSC – slated for completion in 2020 – is still under construction at the moment.

LEFT: limestone interior of Batu Caves.
BELOW: the Blue Mosque.

Mining roots

Like Kuala Lumpur and Perak, Selangor grew rich on tin, prompting power struggles and civil wars in the 19th century. Selangor's original Minangkabau settlers were displaced by the Bugis, who established the present sultanate at Kuala Selangor. In 1894, Selangor was among the first four states in the British Federated Malay States (FMS) which later became Malaya and then Malaysia.

Before reaching the state capital, **Shah Alam ❷**, the busy Federal Highway goes through the huge residential town of Petaling Jaya (PJ), whose population commutes daily into KL. Shah Alam was built in 1963 and is more of a quiet suburb than administrative centre, with large houses, tree-lined boulevards, and numerous roundabouts. It is also a centre for heavy industry, including Proton, the national car project developed with Mitsubishi of Japan. You'll see a lot of Protons on Malaysia's roads; the company commands about two-thirds of the local car market, due mainly to high duties imposed on foreign models.

The Sultan of Selangor resides on a hilltop in the lavish Istana Bukit Kayangan. But the jewel in the city's crown is the state mosque, the **Masjid Sultan Salahuddin Abdul Aziz Shah**. Known also as the Blue Mosque, it features some of the Islamic world's tallest minarets and largest domes. Its worship hall is bigger than London's St Paul's Cathedral, and can accommodate 16,000 worshippers.

TIP

Near Putrajaya on the old highway to Kuala Lumpur is a small town called Kajang, which claims to offer the best satay in Malaysia. And many KL-ites agree.

Seafood capital

At the western end of the Federal Highway, **Klang ❸**, the former state capital, conceals a colourful and violent past. Given its commanding position near the mouth of the Klang River, it was obvious that whoever possessed the town controlled the lucrative tin trade. Klang became a centre of fighting during the Selangor Civil War of the 1870s. Raja Mahdi, one of the chief protagonists, built his fort on the hill where the neo-classical municipal offices now stand.

Across the bridge in the old town is a former warehouse called the **Gedong Raja Abdullah**, built in 1857 by Raja Abdullah, one of Mahdi's principal opponents in the civil war. The warehouse exemplifies traditional Malay workmanship and has been converted into a tin museum, bringing Klang's exciting past to life. Klang is linked to KL by the KTM Komuter train system, which ends in Port Klang.

Port Klang ❹ (Pelabuhan Klang), 8 km (5 miles) by road from Klang, is best known for its wonderful seafood restaurants at Pandamaran. The major seaport for Kuala Lumpur and the Klang Valley, it is one of the fastest growing container ports in Southeast Asia. This is also the base for local cruise ship companies, as well as port-of-call for ships from Singapore and other foreign lines. Packages from a 3 day/2 night duration cover destinations such as Singapore, Melaka, Penang and Langkawi, as well as Phuket, which is known for its beaches, and southern ports in Thailand.

For shorter trips, boats and ferries from the port go out to the various islands in the Klang River delta, a favourite spot with weekend anglers. Two hours away through monotonous mangrove scenery is **Pulau Ketam** (Crab Island), probably the last Chinese fishing village on stilts in the state. Unfortunately,

BELOW:
Pulau Ketam's seafood bonanza.

cleanliness is not its strong point, although it offers cheap and excellent seafood.

Head south for about 17 km (11 miles) to get to **Pulau Carey** ❺, home to the most famous of indigenous craftsmen, the Mah Meri Orang Asli traditional wood-carvers. The Sungai Bumbun Mah Meri tribe is best-known for its dream-inspired spirit masks and unique *Moyang Tenong Jerat Harimau* tiger sculpture. Turn right at Teluk Panglima Garang, then right again to enter the Golden Hope estate road, and finally left at the fork. There is a tiny shop opposite the house of the leading woodcarver, Pion Anak Bumbon, which also happens to be the woodcarving centre. Unfortunately, demand for the work isn't high enough to make it worthwhile for many to be full-time artists. Fortunately, the designs are documented in a voluminous research text which doubles as both a "bible" of authenticity and a sort of sales catalogue for potential buyers of the unique craft. Large carvings can take as long as three months to complete and cost upwards of RM300.

Historic Selangor

The road south from Pulau Carey leads via Jenjarom to yet another old Selangor capital, **Jugra** ❻, which, unlike Klang, is completely out of the development limelight. On the hill overlooking the village and estuary are the graves of Selangor royalty and noblemen. The ruins of some old government buildings can be seen below. Standing amid the paddy fields are the abandoned palace, built in the 1800s, and the equally elaborate mosque where the sultan used to pray. Both are fine examples of late 19th/early 20th-century architecture.

The nearby **Morib** is not one of Malaysia's most beautiful beaches, but is nevertheless a popular weekend getaway for Klang Valley residents. It is also his-

Map on page 150

TIP

If not venturing to Pulau Carey, you may like to know that Mah Meri craft can also be bought in Cameron Highlands (*see Hill Stations, page 160*).

BELOW: Mah Meri woodcarving, Pulau Carey.

torically significant for being the landing place of the Allied forces in 1945, ending the Japanese occupation of the peninsula.

Bird sanctuary

About 45 km (28 miles) north of Klang is the pretty, peaceful town of **Kuala Selangor** ❼ on the Sungai Selangor estuary. This was the 18th-century base of the state's Bugis rulers whose mausoleums are now a tourist attraction. The fort was built by the Dutch in the futile attempt to control the tin trade, and it still stands at **Bukit Melawati**, complete with cannons that point out to sea. Today, however, they are merely iron sentinels to the **Kuala Selangor Nature Park** ❽ (entrance fee; tel: 03-32892294), which they overlook.

Protecting the area's coastal mangroves, and therefore its fisheries industry, the park is a joint project between the Malaysian Nature Society (MNS) and the state government. Over 160 species of birds have been recorded here, and an estimated 100,000 birds pass through during their annual migrations south. Artificial ponds that blend in beautifully with the surroundings attract the birds, surrounded by nature trails and observation hides – don't forget your binoculars. A pioneering attempt to breed endangered milky storks is undertaken here in a large aviary. The park has accommodation as well.

There are several interesting Chinese fishing villages around Kuala Selangor, where salted fish and fishballs are prepared, and some great seafood restaurants. Further along the riverbank at **Kampung Kuantan**, hundreds of *kelip-kelip* (fireflies) alight on the branches of the overhanging trees; for a truly other-worldly experience, book yourself on a river trip at the jetty (tel: 03-32892403), which starts at nightfall in good weather.

BELOW: Hindu devotees at Batu Caves during the Thaipusam festival.

A limestone shrine

One of the most amazing sights in Malaysia is Thaipusam, the Hindu festival of penance, which occurs at the end of January. As a sign of repentance for past sins and to demonstrate their vows of reformation, devotees often carry *kavadi* (offerings) to a temple, from a simple milk jug on the head to wooden frames decorated with flowers and fruit and supported by long thin spikes pinned into the body.

The most sacred temple for this festival is the cave shrine at **Batu Caves** ❾ (open daily 7am–7pm). A bold limestone outcrop about 13 km (8 miles) north of Kuala Lumpur, this is the final destination for the rippling sea of devotees who follow the procession from the Sri Mahamariamman temple in Kuala Lumpur and painstakingly climb the 272 concrete steps that lead up to the cave. The pigeons and monkeys that generally rule the area disappear in the face of this massive human onslaught. On normal days, the temple is peaceful. The massif's main cavern, known as the Cathedral Cave, is a huge vault pierced by stalactites that point downwards for 6 metres (20 ft). Eerie shafts of light streak down from gaps in the ceiling high above. Another cave at its base is decorated with colourful and intricate drawings depicting Hindu legends. A row of Indian vegetarian shops at the base of the temple serves cool, refreshing coconut juice.

Map on page 150

Batu Caves is also popular with adventure sports enthusiasts. There are about another 20 caves within the massif, and the **Dark Caves**, open only to MNS tours (tel: 03-22879422) has narrow passages where you could encounter bats and creepy-crawlies. The other side of the cliff is popular with rock-climbers, as is **Bukit Takun** located further north along the old trunk road (Route 1).

Tamed jungles

The Takun area is also home to several parks, offering easy tracks, and pools and waterfalls for swimming. Among them is the popular Templer Park (Taman Templer), and scenic Hutan Lipur Kancing (Kancing Forest Reserve). But better trails wind through the 1,528 hectares (3,776 acres) of the **Forest Research Institute and Museum (FRIM)** ❿ at Kepong, a few kilometres west of Batu Caves. The country's top forest research facility, FRIM has experimental plantations, arboreta, and a traditional medicinal plant plot, as well as an excellent forestry museum and library. The MNS runs nature education courses here.

Malaysia's wildlife is on show at the **Zoo Negara dan Akuarium** (National Zoo and Aquarium; open daily 9am–5pm, entrance fee), 13 km (8 miles) from central KL by way of Jalan Genting Klang. Its collection includes a nice display of birds, reptiles such as pythons, *seladang* (the world's largest wild buffalo), tapir, crocodiles, tigers, and of course, the orang-utan.

On Jalan Pahang, in a suburb called Setapak Jaya, is the headquarters of the famous **Royal Selangor Complex**, the prime mover of the home-grown pewter industry, whose designs are sold the world over. Pewter is made from a combination of antimony, copper and refined tin. The factory holds tours and has a host of quality souvenir items for sale. ❑

Royal Selangor pewterware, a uniquely Malaysian craft.

BELOW: a canopy of Kapur trees at FRIM.

THE NORTHWESTERN PENINSULA

This is an area of immense variety, spliced in the middle by a mountainous jungled backbone, Banjaran Titiwangsa

Heading north out of Kuala Lumpur is like heading through the country's so-called first wave of development – this is the land of tin and rubber, and, nearer the Thai border, rice. Global demand and phenomenally high prices for the first two natural resources were behind the peninsula's rapid growth from the late 19th century till the middle of the 20th century.

Perak's Kinta River Valley was once the tin capital of the world. Now, a daisy-chain of huge mining ponds sit in silence amid deserts of stark, bleached sand and the odd tin dredge made of wood; but life is returning to this seeming desolation. The lakes are slowly evolving into a wetland habitat, attracting many species of both native and migrant bird, some never seen here before. Elsewhere, the concrete and metal of industrial parks are testament to the new manufacturing industries, so vital to the state's continued economic progress.

Some former mining towns remain frozen in time – Papan, Batu Gajah, Pusing. Others retain their charming old-world core but have continued to build on that early prosperity, and are thriving – Ipoh, Kuala Kangsar, Taiping.

However, while many rubber plantations have been supplanted by the more lucrative oil palm, visitors will still pass through acres of this early fortune-maker, thanks to a new rubberwood furniture industry utilising fast-growing, high-yield strains. In the irrigated plains of Kedah and Perlis, paddy covers much of the land in this, the country's largest rice-growing area.

Limestone is another feature of the north. Large outcrops dripping with vegetation dot Perak and Perlis, and make up the entire islands of the Langkawi archipelago. Swathed in mist at dawn, the limestone hills are inspiration for any number of Chinese brush paintings, while the earliest evidence of prehistoric human civilisation in the country can be found among the caves.

On the isles, it is always holiday time. Penang continues to bewitch with its plethora of Buddhist temples, cluttered lively city streets, and golden beaches. More long sandy beaches beckon at Langkawi, still sleepily enwrapped in legend; likewise Pangkor, still following the rhythms of the sea, as it has throughout the ages. ❏

PRECEDING PAGES: rows of terraced vegetable plots in the highland resort of Cameron Highlands.
LEFT: palms reign supreme on Langkawi's beaches.

Northwestern Peninsular Malaysia

0   50 km

0   50 miles

N

HILL STATIONS

With their temperate climates and tranquil gardens, the high hill stations of central Malaysia are as popular with tourists today as they were with the British colonialists before them

Map on page 158

The insufferable heat drove them to the hills. Once there, they pushed back the jungle and created little pockets of England with rose gardens and mock Tudor bungalows; from that point on, life in the colonies assumed a more bearable aspect for the British. Today for much the same reason – cooler climes, those little snapshots of Englishness – tourists flock to the former hill stations of Maxwell Hill, Cameron Highlands and Fraser's Hill. Some of the buildings have been taken over by multinationals as hillside retreats, others are now hotels, while yet more new high-rise developments attempt to emulate their colonial predecessors – with varying degrees of success.

Restful retreat

The oldest hill station, and the one least touched by time, is **Bukit Larut ❶** (Maxwell Hill) in Perak. Rising above the serene Lake Gardens of Taiping, it is largely responsible for Taiping being the wettest place in the peninsula. Bukit Larut has no golf courses, fancy restaurants or swimming pools, only a few jungle walks and a badminton court. However, the attraction for visitors is the cool air and the vistas: thick mist-laden jungles below and clouds that wash off the Straits of Melaka (Selat Melaka) from Penang to Pangkor.

Large bungalows, complete with fireplaces, sit at different elevations of this 1,000-metre (3,300-ft) high hill. The road that climbs up it was constructed after World War II with the "help" of Japanese prisoners-of-war, but before that, anyone who wished to reach the top but did not fancy hiking had the choice of going by pony or sedan chair. At one time, the trail was used by porters carrying heavy loads of fragrant tea downhill. Now the tea plantations are no more, leaving only the **Tea Garden House**, midway up, with its view of Taiping and the Lake Gardens. A handful of labourers keep the jungle at bay and the gardens neatly manicured.

Access to the hill is denied to private vehicles. Instead, government-owned Land Rovers serve as mountain taxis departing every hour between 8am–6pm. They take eight seated, and two standing at the back, hanging grimly on to the top bar. The one-lane road is steep and narrow; at sharp bends the jungle suddenly parts to reveal the green land below divided into a pattern of roads and fields.

The air becomes brisk, and the sun is lost in mist and clouds. The 12-km (7½-mile) journey takes 40 minutes, and you are deposited at the front step of your bungalow. At the foot of the hill sits a war cemetery of Commonwealth soldiers who died in the Japanese invasion. Nearby is a large freshwater swimming pool fed by a waterfall.

BELOW: mist-shrouded Cameron Highlands.

TIP

Try Boh's flavoured teas at their teashop. These are blended with local fruit such as lychee, and spices such as cinnamon and ginger. They have a wide range of beautifully-packaged products including instant mix iced teas.

BELOW:

harvesting tea in Cameron Highlands.

The tea highlands

Crewcut tea bush rows lend the rolling hills of **Cameron Highlands ❷** a soft green glow in the dewy early light. Suddenly the eye catches sight of a tiny figure in a bright scarf, basket on back, moving meticulously among the rows – it's a tea-picker! You raise your zoom lens, and suddenly realise that "she" has a moustache. The tea industry, like all other labour-intensive industries in Malaysia, now employ Bangladeshi workers – male ones at that. The vast tea plantations are the distinguishing characteristic of this most developed of Malaysia's hill stations, which peaks at 1,800 metres (5,900 ft) above sea level. Some of them offer tours, except on Mondays, and no tea is plucked on Sunday.

The prettiest estate is at Sungai Palas in the highest town of Brinchang; the oldest tea-processing factory is the one built in 1929 in the Farlie estate near Habu, in which original processing technology is still used; and the most accessible plantation to photograph is the Bharat Tea Estate near Tanah Rata, which has a teahouse but no tours. The first two estates belong to local giant Boh Tea, who also have a chain of "tea cafés" in big cities as well as at both their highland tea estates.

Incidentally, the South Indians brought in by the British to work in the plantations are into their second generation. Well-educated youngsters now run the factory tours or work in shops in town and behind hotel reception desks.

Although Camerons, as it is called, is actually part of Pahang, it can only be reached through Tapah in Perak. Buses run every hour and taxis can be chartered from here. Tapah is also on the train route, and there are express buses from Kuala Lumpur and Penang that go all the way to Brinchang.

For those with their own transport, there is a turning off the old trunk road just north of Tapah that leads via Chenderiang to the gorgeous **Lata Kinjang**, a towering multi-step waterfall visible from the North-South Highway. Concrete steps lead up to a spray-misted suspension bridge. Orang Asli guides who live at the foot of the falls can guide you to other cascades and to their *durian* fruit orchards in the forest for a fee, but you need to get permission from the Forestry Department in Tapah to enter the area, which is a forest reserve.

From Tapah, the Camerons road twists its way uphill for 90 km (60 miles) through a dense forest of coniferous trees, thick ferns, and clusters of bamboo that add the touch of a Chinese scroll painting. Camerons is particularly well-known for its tree ferns and wild orchids. While you're travelling up, you will pass Orang Asli on motorbikes, or on foot carrying butterfly nets, on their way to their villages which dot the hills.

Ringlet is the first and rather ugly little settlement at the 45 km (30 miles) marker. Push on, and 4 km (2½ miles) later you will reach the **Sultan Abu Bakar Lake** (Tasik Sultan Abu Bakar), an artificial body of water formed by the damming of Sungai Bertam for Camerons' hydroelectric scheme, which is one of the country's oldest. Perched on a bluff above the lake is the first Tudor-style hotel, which has sweeping views of the valley.

Vegetables and inns

Farmlands begin after passing the lake, the cultivated terraces that have earned Camerons the nickname of vegetable capital of the peninsula. Here also, the Chinese farmers have employed Bangladeshi workers. An interesting trend among these growers is the move towards organic farming, thanks to pressure against pesticide use. About 15 km (9 miles) further on lies **Tanah Rata**, the principal township, a bustling tourist centre with hotels, shops, and restaurants.

This development must be a far cry from the sight that caused such excitement to William Cameron, a government surveyor on a mapping expedition in 1885, who reported "a fine plateau with gentle slopes shut in by the mountains". This area was unknown even to the locals in the lowlands. Shortly afterwards, tea planters, then farmers, claimed the plateau, and built a road to carry their produce to market.

Today, Tanah Rata is popular with Malaysian families, college students and diplomats alike Boy scouts with knapsacks on their backs thumb rides up the winding hills, while Singaporean tourists from the south lounge on colonial-style verandahs, munching fresh strawberries and cream. To some, arriving from the tropical lowlands, it seems somewhat incongruous to arrive at Tanah Rata and find logfires lit every night, and Devonshire tea and English breakfast on menus. But the local steamboat soup dish is also popular, and among the Chinese hotels are several very good Indian restaurants, serving simple snacks and meals that agree well with the climate here.

Check out the excellent Yung Seng souvenir shop at No. 23 on the main road, which has beautiful native craft, including the wonderful Mah Meri masks of Selangor, and Temiar fishing traps, as well as craft from other Southeast Asian countries.

Map on page 158

Cameron Highlands is home to many rare species of butterfly.

BELOW: a temperate haven in the tropics.

Cameron's Trails and Tours

O ne day in 1967, while on holiday in the region, the American Thai-silk entre-preneur Jim Thompson went out for an evening stroll along one of the highlands' many trails. He was never seen again.

Even today, spirit-world, wild-animal and conspiracy theories surround the disappear-ance of the highlands' most famous missing person. Somehow this has added weight to the otherwise standard precautions requir-ing visitors to tell someone which trail they are taking and to stick to the paths.

All Cameron's maps include walking trails but some are not as well-maintained as the maps may indicate. The roads themselves make good walks, and there is a paved walk-way all the way from Tanah Rata to Brinchang. A fairly easy and popular trek at Tanah Rata is the 1-hour **Robinson Descent** (Path 9) which starts at the falls and goes downhill to the

power station – the last stretch is fairly steep though. The longer and flatter **Boh Road** trail (Path 9A) branches off to the left at the top of Path 9 and leads to the Farlie Boh Tea Estate road near Habu. Another easy route is **Parit Falls** (Path 4), a flat 20-minute stroll from the Garden Inn hotel to Taman Sedia.

All these trails join up with the circular **Gunung Beremban** track (Path 8 from Robin-son Falls and Path 3 from Parit Falls). The trek is steep and you need to cross some streams. It takes about 3 hours to reach the 1,800-metre (5,900-ft) peak, but the sunsets and sunrises are great – bring a tent and warm clothes if you intend to camp out. Path 3 actually ends in Brinchang at the golf course, or joins Path 2, to go past the hill-top Sam Po Buddhist temple into town. The Beremban track splinters at various parts, so ensure you take the path you really want to take, or you could end up somewhere else.

There is actually a trail that leads from Brinchang just north of the town, up to **Gunung Brinchang** (Path 1). It is a long 4-hour trek, though a fairly easy one, but can be wet and slippery after rain. Keep your eyes open for pitcher plants in this damp and fern-rich mossy forest.

There are several interesting tours out of Brinchang and Tanah Rata that go off the beaten track but require minimum numbers. Camping Holidays (tel: 05-491 4269; e-mail: ecotour@tm.net.my or enquire at the tour desk of the Heritage Hotel at Tanah Rata) specialise in nature interpretation. Their pro-grammes include treks to the highland cloud or mossy forests at Gunung Brinchang (half-day) and Gunung Irau (2 day/1 night), tours to Semai Orang Asli villages, and the jewel in the crown, a Rafflesia Tour, which is run only when guides encounter a patch where this rare parasite, the world's largest flower is, or is close to, blooming. Trekking packages start at RM45 for a half-day tour.

Other tour companies offer a half-day jun-gle trekking tour that takes in a waterfall, and an all-day tour that covers a tea plantation, a visit to an Orang Asli village, and picturesque cave waterfalls. Contact Jade Holidays at Brinchang (tel/fax: 05-491 4984). Tours start at RM25 and do pick-ups from your hotel. ❏

LEFT: the carnivorous pitcher plant.

En route to Brinchang is an authentic replica of an English Inn, **The Smoke-house Hotel**, with a well-kept garden and ivy-covered walls of stone. Inside the cosy living rooms are stuffed chintz settees and old photographs, clocks, kettles, and other characterful remnants of the British colonial era. The bedrooms are gorgeous but expensive. Behind the inn is one of the country's oldest golf courses, which survived tigers, vegetable-farmers, and World War II to become the 18-hole course it is today, overlooked by a cosy pavilion equipped with a bar and a restaurant.

There is lots of accommodation available along this stretch of road, before you hit **Brinchang** and the Kea Farm area, the heartland of the farms and nurseries growing Camerons' other big product: flowers. This once pretty area has become a mess of exposed and eroded hillslopes and unsightly high-rise development, a scene compounded further by tacky attractions such as Cactus Valley, the Rose Centre and Butterfly Farm. The peak is also at the tail-end of the new Lojing road that links to Ipoh. According to environmental reports liberally quoted in newspapers, the development has raised temperatures around the main towns by a couple of degrees; wearing a sweater during the day is now a thing of the past.

The only worthwhile sight here is the **Sungai Palas Tea Estate**, whose steep road winds 6 km (4 miles) up to Camerons' highest peak at 2,031 metres (6,663 ft), Gunung Brinchang and panoramic views of the forested valley. This also makes quite a nice – if long – early morning walk that takes in the colourful periwinkles growing freely among the tea bushes, a couple of vegetable farms, and bird-filled forest near the top.

You'll find maps, tourist information and tours in Tanah Rata and Brinchang.

Map on page 158

TIP

Bicycles are available for hire at the goldsmiths, Kedai Emas Loon Hing, on the main road.

BELOW: the mock-Tudor Smokehouse Hotel in the Cameron hills.

Tea in the garden

Much quieter is **Fraser's Hill** ❸ (Bukit Fraser) in Selangor, although its past is rather more colourful. The hill resort is named after Louis James Fraser, an elusive English adventurer, who had long disappeared when the hill station was built in 1910. He apparently ran a notorious gambling and opium den here for local miners and planters, as well as a mule train, and later, a transport service in the lowlands.

The 1,500-metre (5,000-ft) high resort is scattered over seven hills on which sit a series of English greystone bungalows, surrounded by neat English gardens blooming with roses and hollyhocks. The tiny town centre around the clock tower has some rather disastrous newer additions, and there are also high-rise hotels which fail to blend with the landscape.

A better bet is to go with the economical if run-down bungalows, now state-run. The prettiest and most expensive accommodation is **The Smokehouse Hotel**, a replica of the Camerons outlet, where you can also enjoy Devonshire tea or apple pie in the lovely garden. The road to the inn leads on to Jeriau Waterfall, once a pretty picnic spot, but now permanently silted, the result of resort development years ago.

Because of its proximity to Kuala Lumpur, Fraser's is crowded at weekends, but there are enough walks and trails to take you away from the madding crowd. The ring road around the 9-hole golf course makes a pleasant two-hour walk, and brings you past the old bungalows and newer resorts. Like the one in Camerons, the picturesque golf course is very old. It was carved out of an old tin mine, and is one of the few public courses in the country.

There are also eight jungle trails of varying lengths, all named after pioneers who built up the resort. The trails are well-marked and easy to follow. The newest is the steep 6-km (4-mile) **Pine Hill Trail** which leads to breathtaking views. The trails run through hilly dipterocarp forests which boasts some of the richest birdlife in the peninsula, hence the high chance of bumping into groups standing rock-still and peering intently through binoculars. There are an estimated 270 local and migratory species in the forest.

If you have your own transport, there are good drives around the area, such as the second loop that goes past the holiday bungalows of multinational corporations. In fact, having your own transport is really the only way to get to the resort. Otherwise, it is a one-hour bus journey from Kuala Lumpur (100 km/60 miles) to Kuala Kubu Baharu, from where you have to board a second bus which takes another one and a half hours to get to the top. The last 8 km (5 miles) is a narrow winding road, on which a one-way traffic system is in place between 7am–7pm; odd hours for going up, even for coming down. It was along the winding road from Kuala Kubu Bahru that British High Commissioner Sir Henry Gurney was ambushed and killed by communist guerillas in 1951.

If you arrive at the gate too early, you could have tea at the Gap Resthouse, or else drive down to a small but scenic waterfall along the main road that leads to the town of Raub.

BELOW: tee off in Fraser's Hill, Selangor.

Gamblers' paradise

Newer hill resorts are popular, but lack the charm of the three "oldies". A definite study in contrast is **Genting Highlands** ❹, 2,000 metres (6,600 ft) above sea level. Just one convenient hour from Kuala Lumpur, it is actually visible from the capital, a mystical palace of pleasure shrouded in mist, on top of Banjaran Titiwangsa (Main Range), the mountain range that runs down the centre of the peninsula.

However, at close quarters, nothing could be more prosaic. For Gentings as the locals call it, is the Las Vegas of Malaysia, a rambling complex of hotels, theme parks and a casino, the country's sole gambling den. And it is something people either love or loathe. Ignoring the originally lush surroundings through which it took such effort and cost to cut, the complex is entirely artificial, giant boulders included, and it is possible to not surface for sunshine the whole time you are there. Gentings just never goes to sleep.

The whole development comes under Genting Highlands Resorts, owned by businessman Lim Goh Tong, who mooted the idea for the resort, spending seven years alone to build the steep road. Gentings has just kept growing in every way, although there is talk that its large revenues are being dented by the increasingly popular cruise liners which operate casinos in international waters.

Gentings' casino is one of the largest in the world and offers the gamut of games, both Western and traditional Chinese like *tai sai*. There are also rows of slot machines and computerised racing. Suits are compulsory for men, or you can opt for a batik shirt, Malaysian formal wear, which can be rented at the door. In accordance with Islamic law, a sign over the casino entrance warns that Muslims are forbidden to try their luck here.

Map on page 158

Batik shirts are considered formal wear and will allow men entry into the Gentings' casino.

BELOW:
Genting Highlands theme park.

Map on page 158

Accommodation is plentiful and cheap, because the real money is raked in at the casino. A range of food is available, yet sharing tables is not unusual at weekends and public holidays. The outdoor theme park, set around an artificial lake, has rollercoasters, boat rides, and a monorail. The indoor theme park houses the largest video/virtual reality arcade in Malaysia. There are also two theatres which feature international magic acts or cabaret dinner shows, and famous singers are occasionally flown in from Hong Kong. Tip: Save your jungle shoes for the other hill stations.

Things are a little less manic 10 km (6 miles) down the hill at the Awana Golf and Country Club, which has an 18-hole golf course and panoramic views. However, driving up the winding road to the casino at night through thick mist can be harrowing.

Express buses from Kuala Lumpur's Puduraya Bus Station run daily to the cable car complex at the foot of the hill. The ticket cost covers the cable car ride. Buses are not allowed up the steep road. There is a special taxi stand at Puduraya servicing Gentings. If you drive, make sure you don't lose your way in the huge maze of featureless carparks.

Aboriginal treasures

Gentings can be accessed from the capital via the Karak Highway or the considerably more pleasant old Pahang Road through Gombak. At Gombak, you might want to pop into **Pak Ali's House** (Rumah Pak Ali) for a quick look at the interior of a traditional Sumatran-style house, which is open to visitors.

About 15 km (9 miles) down the old Pahang road is an excellent **Orang Asli Museum** (Muzium Orang Asli, open daily 9am–5.30pm). Sitting on a hill at an Orang Asli settlement, it provides a fascinating insight on the Malaysian peninsula's aboriginal peoples. A good range of exhibits such as old photographs, artefacts, handicraft, and tools and implements used in daily life, make this museum well worth a visit.

A new highlands road has been in the pipeline for over 10 years to link Gentings to Frasers and Camerons. However, it continues to receive public opposition because of fears it will affect the water catchment and biodiversity of the highlands.

Another (relatively) new resort is **Gunung Jerai ❺**, Kedah's highest peak. The 1,217-metre (3,993-ft) high limestone massif has commanding views of the surrounding rice plains and the Main Range. On the other side, you can see across the Straits of Melaka into Penang, and even as far as Langkawi island. Part of the **Sungai Teroi Forest Recreation Park** (Hutan Rekreasi Sungai Teroi), which has some forest trails, the hill is also home to a forestry museum. At its peak sits a pretty resort. A Hindu shrine was discovered in this area in the late 1880s, but no further excavations have been done.

Jerai is accessed from Sungai Petani or Gurun from the North-South Highway. Turn off Guar Chempedak. If you don't have your own transport, jeeps can ferry you up the 13-km (8-mile) winding road between 9am–5pm. Alternatively, if you are energetic enough, a mountain track goes right up to the peak. ❏

BELOW: Orang Asli child.
RIGHT: jungles of Sungai Teroi.

PERAK

It was once the wealthy tin-mining centre of Malaysia. Now the home of the country's longest-surviving sultanate, Perak woos the tourist dollar to its beaches

Map on page 158

It started with tin in the 19th century, and, like the claws of an excavator, mining has held Perak in its grip ever since. But while tin built Perak all those years ago, it is the state's limestone hills that have today become the building blocks of the nation.

In Bahasa Malaysia, *perak* actually means "silver". But it was the "silver" of the tin revolution that lined Perak's coffers, making it one of the wealthiest states in the land. The accompanying feuds and power struggles prompted greater British intervention in the whole country, eventually shifting the centre of power from the old capitals along the Perak River to the tin-rich areas of Larut and Kinta.

When the bottom fell out of the industry in the 1980s, entire towns shut down. However, thanks to industrialisation and the rapid pace of development in the country, the state's limestone hills are now feeding huge cement factories.

The town that tin built

The Kinta Valley remains Perak's leading district, and its main city, **Ipoh ❻**, the most prosperous of its settlements. Like Kuala Lumpur, Ipoh started as a landing stage at the point at which the river became unnavigable, springing up as a messy shanty-town almost overnight on the ancestral land of Dato' Panglima Kinta, the local Malay territorial chief. However, when Ipoh took over as state capital from Taiping in 1937, it was the best-planned town in the peninsula, with broad, regularly laid-out streets. It is now Malaysia's second-largest city, with a population of half a million.

Nestled in the craggy bosom of limestone outcrops and the more distant hills of the Main Range, Ipoh boasts excellent amenities and quality accommodation. **Old Town** on the west side is where you'll find the *Padang* (Town Green), the epitome of every Malaysian town with a colonial past. Surrounded by the Royal Ipoh Club, court houses, municipal library and the stately **St Michael's Institution**, today, it is the scene of important matches, school athletic meets, and parades. Also in Old Town, near the **Masjid Negeri** (State Mosque) and the Clock Tower, is the Moorish **Stesen Keretapi Ipoh** (Ipoh Railway Station), whose silver dome, graceful arches, and interminable colonnades, bear a striking resemblance to the Kuala Lumpur Railway Station.

East of the river lies the **D.R. Seenivasagam Park** (Taman D.R. Seenivasagam) which, typical of most public parks in Ipoh, hosts large dawn gatherings of *tai chi* practitioners. Here, groups faithfully go through all forms of the martial art, some using swords and fans too.

LEFT: the stately Ubudiah Mosque. **BELOW:** one of many temples embedded in the rockface around Ipoh.

Succulent pomelo, very similar in taste and texture to the grapefruit, is found everywhere in Ipoh.

Down the road on Jalan Panglima Bukit Gantang is the **Muzium Darul Ridzuan** (Darul Ridzuan Museum; open daily 9am–5pm, closed from 12–3pm on Fridays). The century-old mansion used to be the residence of Malay chieftains and British officials, but now showcases the state's history, including of course, the story of tin.

Grand mansions in huge grounds still sit along the prestigious **Jalan Sultan Azlan Shah**, commonly referred to by its old name, Tiger Lane. Along this road is also the **Geology Museum** (Muzium Geologi; open Mon–Fri 8am–4.30pm; Sat 8am–12.50pm). It has over 600 examples of minerals, an exhibition on tin ore, including one of the best examples of cassiterite in the world, and a fine collection of precious stones.

About 15 minutes' drive east of town is **Tambun**. Among its attractions are the Tambun Hot Springs, rather ugly public baths, the National Stud Farm, where thoroughbred race horses are raised, and the Tanjung Rambutan Waterfall. Tambun is also home to an Ipoh speciality, the *pomelo*, a luscious grapefruit.

Temples in the rock

However, Ipoh's undisputed top attractions are its cave temples. The naturally hollowed insides of the Kinta Valley's limestone formations, so reminiscent of southern China, have served as homes for ancient peoples as well as hideouts for bandits.

BELOW: colourful paintings from the cave walls of Perak Tong temple.

They are also spiritually significant for both Buddhists and Hindus. Devotees have built entrances to these temples that range from the simple to the ostentatious; sometimes entire buildings complete with red-tiled pagoda roofs "grow" out from the rock. Walking into the dimly-lit interiors, with their altars, the smell of incense and the occasional echoes of bats and swallows, can make for a heady experience for the uninitiated.

The largest of the rock temples is south of Ipoh on the old trunk road, near a line of stalls selling pomelos and local biscuits. The ornate **Sam Poh Tong** (open daily 8am–4.30pm) dates back to the 1890s when a passing monk found the cave and made it his home and meditation base for 20 years until his death. Today, a group of monks and nuns follows in his footsteps.

Statues of Buddha are dotted everywhere, even among the stalagmites and stalactites. A stiff climb up 264 steps leads to a panorama of Ipoh and its surroundings. Of renown is the temple's pond of small turtles; visitors can buy spinach to feed them. Turtles are Chinese symbols of longevity.

Close by is the **Gua Kek Lok Tong**, known also as the Brass Temple after its gleaming statues. You can walk through the cave to the back where its dog's teeth of limestone formations frame a peaceful green valley of ponds and hills.

Another famous cave shrine is the **Perak Tong** (open daily 8am–6pm), 6 km (4 miles) north of town on Jalan Kuala Kangsar, the old trunk road. Traditional Chinese paintings adorn the walls and relate traditional folk tales and legends. Built in 1926 by a Buddhist priest from China, the temple has more than 40 statues of Buddha, the central figure rising 13 metres (40 ft) high.

Caves and castles

The prettiest view of Ipoh's limestone hills is just past the city as you head south on the North-South Highway. Unfortunately, this gives way briefly to blasted rock, precious material for the country's development, before coming to the imposing Gunung Tempurung limestone massif. One of the show caves,

Map on page 158

On the same limestone massif as Sam Poh Tong is a giant Mercedes Benz logo, presented to the city by the German manufacturer in thanks for the huge purchases by rich miners.

BELOW: Buddhist statues (left) crowd a shrine in Sam Poh Tong, and (right) the temple exterior.

Look hard enough in the countryside of Perak and you may spot abandoned wooden tin dredges, a sight from yesteryear when tin was king in Perak.

BELOW:
Kellie's Castle has a fairy-tale air.

Gua Tempurung (open 9am–5pm) can be accessed from the Gopeng interchange and 2 km (1 mile) down the old trunk road south. The turnoff is at the pretty Kampung Gunung Mesah.

Used variously by tin miners and communists on the run, the 1.9-km (1-mile) long river passageway is now accessible via an illuminated walkway. The concrete pathway climbs up to the 180 metre by 120 metre (540 ft by 360 ft) Alam Cavern, the biggest of the five chambers, and also passes through interesting formations such as gigantic stalagmites and flowstones.

Tours run from a 40-minute basic trip to the 4-hour grand tour, which involves a river stint. There are morning and afternoon sessions for the longer tours, and guides will bring in a minimum of two. Weekends and public holidays can be crowded with tour buses, after which graffiti appears on the walls, to be painstakingly cleaned off by management. Camping is allowed on site.

The old trunk road in Perak goes through mainly flat and open land, offering vistas of deserted mining pools over the bleached scars of tin tailings and glimpses of the wooden *palong* (tin dredges).

An incongruity among these ruins is that of a Scottish Castle, about 5 km (3 miles) from Batu Gajah, half an hour from Ipoh. **Kellie's Castle** (open daily 7am–6.30pm; entrance fee) was built by a William Kellie-Smith, a rubber plantation owner who made his fortune in Malaya. Smith brought in Tamil workers from southern India to build the house in 1915, which was meant to be a reminder of home. Today, although there is a fairy-tale air about the castle, recent shoddy 'rehabilitation' work has stripped away much of its original magic. What is more interesting is a Hindu temple just down the road where Smith is commemorated amid a cluster of rooftop statues.

Historic river valley

For centuries before the tin boom, Sungai Perak provided the only access to the state's interior. The river valley stretches from the royal town of Kuala Kangsar, to the coastal village of Beting Beras Basah, near the town of Bagan Datoh. The main area of Malay settlement, this was also the scene of some of the most dramatic events in Perak's history. Now good roads run along either side of the banana tree-lined banks, through villages which were once the homes of the state's greatest heroes.

Perak is the only state whose royal house can claim direct descent from the sultans of Melaka. Throughout the valley, there are about 20 tombs of Perak's sultans, all carefully marked and cared for by the villagers. Some of the graves have become *keramat* (shrines) visited by humble folk in search of blessings or favours. It is also a tradition that a newly-installed Sultan of Perak must pay his respects at every shrine, travelling by boat, before he can truly be accepted as ruler.

Some of these graves can be found in one of the country's most important sites, which saw the first local uprising against British colonialists. Now a well-organised tourism complex, **Pasir Salak** ❼ was where the state's first British resident, James Birch, was assassinated in 1875 while bathing in the river. The local ringleaders, Dato' Sagor and Dato' Maharaja Lela were executed. Today, there are memorials at the complex to both the British and local heroes.

The complex (open Mon–Fri 10am–5pm; weekends 10am–6pm) is a beautiful collection of original and reconstructed buildings of historic value blended into a peaceful kampung. Of particular note is the architecture, which has elements of Perak's *rumah kutai* (old houses) – two originals sit in the compound. The historical tunnel (entrance fee), which is also the information centre, features a diorama giving a good overview of the country's history. A resort to the left of the complex offers a Malay kampung homestay experience, with riverview chalets and, for large groups, a traditional welcoming ceremony performed by the kampung folk.

To get to Pasir Salak, which is 70 km (40 miles) from Ipoh, head south from the city on the old trunk road towards Kampung Gajah through Bota or Batu Gajah. The journey there passes Bota Kanan which has a hatchery for river terrapins, the *labu* (traditional pottery) area of Pulau Tiga, and fruit orchards, particularly of the pungent *durian*. There are also many delightful kampongs in the area where traditional Perak-style houses are still found.

Island in the sun

If you can't make it to the beaches of the peninsula's east coast, **Pulau Pangkor** ❽, off the coast of Perak, is pleasant. The well-signposted road there from Ipoh goes through Sitiawan to Lumut, the principal base for the Royal Malaysian Navy.

Pangkor is a smaller, less developed version of Langkawi, and is popular with locals, Taiwanese and Germans. Public holidays find it packed, and prices double, but off-peak, the taxi drivers play draughts, and the isle is enveloped in a lovely lazy atmosphere.

There are many versions to the origin of the island's name; one is that Pangkor derived from the Thai

Map on page 158

A Hindu shrine near Kellie's Castle, erected for the plantation workers has, among the figures of animals and gods, a man in a green suit and topee hat – could this be an image of the castle's architect, Kellie Smith?

BELOW: rock inscribed with the coat-of-arms of the Dutch East India Company in Pangkor.

TIP

Teluk Intan, the chief
town of Lower Perak,
has an unusual claim
to fame. The
century-old clock
tower has its own
Tower of Pisa-style tilt.

BELOW: salted fish
being sun-dried
in Pangkor.

"pang koh", meaning "beautiful island". Like so much of Malaysia, the isle's place names are legend-inspired. For instance, the northern Pantai Puteri Dewi (The Beach of the Fairy Princess) is named after a princess who flung herself off a cliff when she learned of the death of her suitor during battle. However, for the Malaysian schoolchild, Pangkor is better known for the historic treaty signed there in 1874, granting the British entry into the Malay states for the first time. From Lumut, ferries run to the Pangkor jetty every 15 minutes from 6.30am–7pm. The fast ferry takes about 20 minutes, while the slower ones take twice as long.

The beach resort stretch is on the western side of the island, and has great sunset views. The only means there from the jetty is by taxi-vans at government-fixed rates. However, the closest beach, **Pasir Bogak**, is only 20 minutes' walk away. The most established of the beaches, Pasir Bogak is by no means the prettiest, but it does make a good base from which to explore the island by rented bicycle or motorcycle. Cyclists should note, though, that the island is pretty hilly. Pasir Bogak has plenty of accommodation and places to eat.

North of Pasir Bogak is the prettier **Teluk Nipah**, packed with virtually identical backpacker accommodation. There are a couple of souvenir shops and a good Chinese seafood restaurant here. Don't be surprised to see a hornbill or two sitting on an electricity pole outside your resort. In the adjacent beach, **Coral Bay**, is a hawker centre. As with Teluk Nipah, the waters here are lovely, and great for snorkelling. Just before Teluk Nipah is **Teluk Ketapang**, where turtles sometimes come ashore to lay eggs.

Heading north again through rainforest, the road cuts inland at a narrow point of the island. The left branch goes to the upmarket Pangkor Island Beach Resort on the lovely Beach of the Beautiful Princess, more popularly called Golden Sands. There is a nine-hole golf course in the hotel's grounds. The beach and hotel facilities are open to day visitors for a fee.

Head out through more rainforest, and the lovely kampung-style Teluk Dalam Resort spreads out before you. Just before the road reaches the fishing villages on the east coast, there is a jungle trek to Pasir Bogak that climbs **Bukit Pangkor**, offering good views.

Tourists and traditions

Little has changed in the eastern villages of **Kampung Sungai Pinang Kecil** (better known as SPK, also a ferry stop) and **Kampung Telok Kechil**, with their quaint tiny wooden houses on stilts over the water. Despite tourism being well-established, the island's economy is dependent mainly on the sea. The villages are therefore alive with activity when the bright yellow boats leave and return from their night stints. To reach any of the jetties, just head right through the courtyard and what looks like someone's living room – ingeniously-converted warehouses! At SPK, drop in at the famous **Hai Sap Hei satay fish factory**, where sea produce is dried, packed and sold.

South of the island in the middle of a *kampung* sit the remains of a Dutch fort, **Kota Belanda**, built over 300 years ago in an attempt to control Perak's tin trade and to fight the tyranny of piracy in the Straits of

Map on page 158

Melaka. Reconstructed by the National Museum in 1973, features of the original building still survive such as the Dutch East India coat-of-arms chiselled on a boulder close to the fort. Later adventurers have added their own "messages". A fisherman who is immune to snake bites used to demonstrate his affinity with the creatures close by, but has since retired. On a large rock opposite the fort is the remains of a drawing of a tiger mauling a boy. The drawing has been crudely etched in and the child is believed to be the son of a Dutch dignitary who disappeared mysteriously in the forest.

Smart resorts

Off the coast of Pasir Bogak is the exclusive patrons-only **Pangkor Laut Resort** on a small island of the same name. The resort was one of the first in Malaysia to build chalets on stilts that extend into the sea. The island's most famous feature is Emerald Bay, a gorgeous beach with powdery, white sand and clear, blue waters. The resort has its own ferry from Lumut.

Lumut is a well-developed jump-off point for Pangkor, with tourist information, money-changers, car-parks, and food. It is busiest during Pesta Laut (Sea Festival) in August, a popular local attraction. Pangkor can also be crowded at this time and during the Malaysian school and public holidays. Because Lumut sits on the Dinding River, it has no beach, but it does have some good accommodation, and is a quiet, pleasant getaway.

Often, locals don't even cross to Pangkor, but head for **Teluk Batik**, a public beach 5 km (3 miles) from Lumut packed with food stalls, seafront A-frame accommodation for backpackers, and classier hotels on the headland and inland. At **Teluk Rubiah**, several kilometres south is another stretch of sandy beach.

BELOW: gorgeous Emerald Bay, Pangkor Laut

Golden dome, royal town

Perak's royal capital, **Kuala Kangsar** , is a lovely garden town about 35 km (20 miles) north of Ipoh across the Perak River. Within walking distance of the town's attractions is the quiet Government Rest House on Jalan Istana, which overlooks the river. It also has a charming little museum.

Follow Jalan Istana past the Old Residency to reach Bukit Chandan, where the huge golden dome of the century-old **Masjid Ubudiah** (Ubudiah Mosque) gleams. Its striking and symmetrical domes and minarets make it one of the most photographed Muslim buildings in the country; if it is reminiscent of Kuala Lumpur's Moorish architecture, it is because it had the same architect.

Beyond the mosque, the road circles the Sultan of Perak's palace, the modern **Istana Iskandariah**, with its rather watered-down Moorish architectural elements. Next to it is the smaller but more dignified and charming **Istana Kenangan** (open daily 9.30am–5pm). Its name translates as the Palace of Memories and it served as a temporary residence while the Istana Iskandariah was being built. The original construction was in accordance with Malay tradition, without a single nail or architectural plans. Subsequent preservation attempts have not remained faithful to this requirement, however, but the building is still a beautiful example of Perak architecture. It is now a royal museum and contains an interesting collection of mementos and photographs of the Perak royal family. All displays are in Bahasa Malaysia, however, although a guide is sometimes available to bring tourists around.

Kuala Kangsar is also home to one of the pioneer batch of rubber trees that arrived here in the 1870s as seeds from Brazil and eventually took over the country. One of these first trees is found near the agricultural office in town.

BELOW:
Istana Kenangan
in Kuala Kangsar.

Though some plantation owners have switched to oil palm because of higher revenues, others are cashing in on rubberwood, an important new commodity for Malaysia's booming furniture industry.

Close by is the Malay College Kuala Kangsar (MCKK). Founded in 1904 as a residential school for the sons of the Malay aristocracy, it is now the seedbed for a good cross-section of Malaysia's political establishment.

On the outskirts of Kuala Kangsar, about 20 km (30 miles) along the Ipoh–Enggor road, is the pottery district of Sayong, also once the home of sultans. Turn off at the bridge and turn left again to get to Kampung Kepala Bendang, the original potter's village, and you will be greeted by scores of vases, ashtrays and ornaments drying in the sun all along this dirt road. The most famous of the traditional designs is the black *labu*, gourd-shaped water pitchers with broad bases and tall narrow spouts that keep cold water really cold.

Sayong is well known as a centre for these characteristic gourd-shaped pottery.

Waterfall haven

From the highlands of the Main Range spring the waters of Sungai Perak, the second-largest river in the peninsula. The river's flow is controlled by Malaysia's largest dam, 150 km (95 miles) upstream from Kuala Kangsar on the Temenggor River tributary. Once a "black area", where armed forces fought the communists, the region is still largely covered by thick mountainous jungle, and forms the northernmost part of the wildlife corridor stretching through Taman Negara and Endau-Rompin. It has one of the best remaining populations of large mammals in the country, including endangered species such as the tiger, Sumatran rhino and Malayan bear.

BELOW: Temenggor is dotted with pretty waterfalls like this.

Cutting through the area is the spectacular East-West Highway to Kota Bharu. This is probably the only public place you'd see a road sign warning of elephants crossing. The road bypasses the picturesque **Empangan Temenggor** ❿ (Temenggor Dam), where there is a resort and floating chalets for fishermen.

The jungles of Temenggor south of the highway are slowly opening up to nature enthusiasts due to the attention brought to it by the Malaysian Nature Society. North of Temenggor across the highway is the lush, mountainous **Belum**, earmarked to be gazetted as a state park. Access to Belum is still restricted, but tour agencies market Temenggor as Belum, after the MNS scientific expeditions.

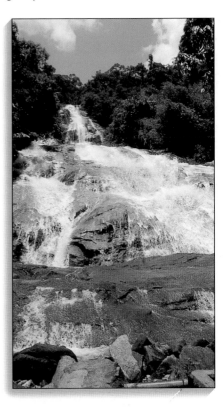

Temenggor is dotted with numerous beautiful towering waterfalls accessible through steep, rugged terrain across swift rivers, on ridges used by the Orang Asli to collect rattan, that follow trails left by animals such as deer or elephants. Among the area's popular sites are the seven-step thundering **Kerteh Waterfall**, where the lucky could catch sight of the giant Rafflesia bloom, and the eight-step **Kelaweh Waterfall**, with a lovely campsite at its spray-misted base.

Animals are difficult to spot, but there are plenty of fresh hoof-prints and droppings on the ground and claw-marks on trees. Trails are flanked by tall hill dipterocarp trees, medicinal plants and shrubs underfoot, and of course, the thorny rattan that grabs at sleeves and flesh. The leech-phobic would do well to stay away. The dryer months are traditionally in the first half of the year, but "dry" is a relative term here.

Tour guides arrange entry permits but the District Office might sometimes require a meeting with foreigners. All groups are guided by the Orang Asli, who comprise the peaceable and friendly Temiar and Jahai peoples, and a tour usually includes a night at their thatched hut villages and a little *bersewang* (traditional dance) performance.

The jump-off point to Temenggor is **Grik**, one and a half hour's drive from Kuala Kangsar on a scenic and winding road. Serenely shrouded in mist in the early morning, the town has basic accommodation, including a government resthouse, and lots of eateries, though serving local food only. During the communist warfare years, Grik was the compulsory check-in point for the daytime-use only East-West Highway.

Town of everlasting peace

South of Grik is **Taiping** , the former state capital. The town with the heaviest rainfall in the peninsula has one of its loveliest names: "everlasting peace" in Chinese. The name derives from the ending of the bloody struggles between rival Chinese mining factions in Larut after the Treaty of Pangkor was signed.

The town's atmosphere is epitomised by the beautiful **Lake Gardens** (Taman Tasik), whose serene lakes and old raintrees were established at an abandoned tin mine on the edge of the town in the 1890s, long before the word ecology was in use. In the grounds is a nine-hole golf course and the rustic 50-hectare (120-acre) **Taiping Zoo** (open daily 10am–6pm) A road leads to Bukit Larut (Maxwell Hill), Malaysia's oldest hill station (*see Hill Stations, page 159*).

There is so much rain in Taiping that its residents place bets on what time it will fall. The bookie's office is a downtown hawker centre with a zinc roof and a digital clock put in by the punters.

BELOW: the Lake Gardens of Taiping.

Map on page 158

The entrance to the gardens is marked by a number of architectural gems including the colonial town hall and the government offices. The **Perak Museum** (Muzium Perak; open daily 9.30am–5pm, entrance fee), housed in a venerable Victorian building, is the oldest in the country. Its collections include some excellent natural history and ethnology displays. The **Ling Nam Temple** is the oldest Chinese temple in Perak, and within it there is a model of a boat dedicated to the Chinese emperor who built the first canal in China.

Mangrove magic

Taiping was also the terminus for the country's first railway line, – now disused – which ended in Kuala Sepetang (Port Weld) on the coast. The road there passes the old fort of **Kota Ngah Ibrahim**, named after the Malay territorial chief of Larut who grew rich through the tin trade, but was unable to control the turbulent Chinese factions producing the wealth.

The road also leads to the **Matang Mangrove Forest** (Hutan Baleau Matang), which has a park with boardwalk going through a sustainably-managed mangrove forest, which has been harvested for charcoal for nearly 100 years. The traditional charcoal kilns make an interesting visit as do the fishing villages, but you might need to find a guide for this. Enquire at Taiping.

A portion of the mangrove swamp further north near Bagan Serai is the **Kuala Gula Bird Sanctuary**. Hundreds of birds, including rare species, feed and nest here. Between August and December, thousands of migrant birds make this their pit-stop en route south to Australia. The sanctuary is also home to otters, monkeys, and the ridge-back dolphin. There is limited and basic accommodation here. For information and bookings, contact the Wildlife Department. ❏

Despite its name, Kuala Gula Bird Sanctuary is also home to monkeys and other small animals.

BELOW: gnarled buttress roots of the fig tree.

THE PERAK MAN

He was about 40–45 years old, they believe. And he was given a proper burial, complete with stone tools, and meat offerings from five different animals as well as shellfish from the river; the shells covered the floor. When they found him 11,000 years later, he was remarkably well-preserved, and still in his original foetal position.

The "Perak Man" is the peninsula's oldest skeleton. He was discovered in a cave in the Lenggong vicinity near Grik by prominent archaeologist Dr Zuraina Majid, who had also uncovered the country's oldest stone tools nearby, potentially dating back 100,000 years. The "Perak Man" is thought to be an ancestor of the Negrito Orang Asli people, a small hunter-gatherer tribe regarded as the oldest inhabitants in the peninsula.

The Lenggong stone tools in Kota Tampan were also discovered intact. Anvils, stone hammers and tools in various stages of being made – complete with flakes and chips – suggest that the site was a tool factory. It was abandoned all those years ago when a volcanic eruption spewed clouds of ash that buried everything – the same eruption that created Lake Toba in Sumatra. Stone tool factories have also been excavated in Tingkayu, Sabah, and Kubang Pasu, Kedah.

CHICK BLINDS: OLD FASHIONED URBAN ART

Malaysian streets are always vivid and colourful, but when shopkeepers lower their chick blinds, the street fronts take on a whole new look

Made of split bamboo or thin wooden rods laced with twine, these sun blinds, known as *bidai* in Malay, serve a dual purpose.

Not only do they shade the colonnaded verandah in front of the shop, known as the "five-foot-way"; they also provide the shopkeeper with the perfect canvas to advertise his goods and services, giving every street a distinct and vibrant character.

With the advent of modern, Western-style shopping malls, some pundits have predicted the demise of the shophouse, and with it the chick blind. This may be true in some Malaysian cities, but in most smaller towns, rows of traditional shophouses prevail and their useful and colourful awnings are still prolific, and as popular as ever.

SIX CENTURIES OF HISTORY

Chick blinds have a long and colourful history. When the notorious Mongol leader Tamerlane and his "Golden Horde" sacked the Indian city of Delhi in 1398, it was noted that the tent openings of the much-feared conquerors were covered with blinds made of thin wands lined with rose-coloured silk. Indeed, the name is thought to derive from the Mongol word *tchik*.

Malaysia's chick blinds first appeared on the front of colonial bungalows in the 19th century, and were most probably introduced as a tropical architectural element from British India. Traditionally, the blinds were painted in black and white stripes, and lined with navy-blue muslin, which is the preferred backing fabric on urban chick blinds even today.

△ **SARONGS FOR SALE**
In Kuala Terengganu, a Malay woman and child leave a shop through the "door" of its chick blind, which advertises "Rajah Brand" men's sarongs.

△ **FUNKY ROLEX**
The world's best-known watches honour a jewellery shop's blind in Taiping, Perak, a town where streets of traditional shophouses still survive.

△ **NOON GLARE**
Hawkers sell tropical *duku* fruit in front of a wall of chick blinds in the main street of Bagan Serai, Perak.

◁ **SPIDER SARONGS**
Men's *pelikat* sarongs come in a variety of brands, including *Chop Laba Laba*, or "Spider Brand".

"FIVE-FOOT-WAY" SHOPS

The long colonnaded space, known as the "five-foot-way", or *kaki lima* in Malay, which fronts all traditional rows of shophouses is said to have originated in a directive by Sir Stamford Raffles, founder of Singapore.

Raffles decreed that all urban buildings should have "a verandah of a certain depth, open to all sides as a continuous and open passage on each side of the street", so people could walk comfortably along, sheltered from the fierce heat of an equatorial sun or a monsoon downpour. However, it wasn't long before hawkers began exploiting these shaded spaces and the "five-foot-way" shop came into being.

Some are merely extensions of the shops behind, or additional display spaces for already crammed premises, but others are individual, cupboard-sized establishments often known as Mamak shops, because they are run by Indian-Muslim Malaysians, colloquially known as Mamak. These miniature shops still survive in many of Malaysia's rural towns.

▷ **STOMACH PILLS**
"Chi-Kit" pills, a Chinese remedy for stomach ailments, are advertised on this chick blind at a Taiping Chinese pharmacy.

▽ **ANONYMOUS ART**
In Taiping, songbirds in bamboo cages share hanging space with a chick blind advertising a popular brand of milk powder.

▷ **BRIDAL TAILOR**
In Kuala Kangsar, Perak, a tailor advertises his speciality – Western-style wedding attire. Some artworks, like this one here, are painted to the client's specification; others, like those advertising brand-name goods, recur in many towns.

Penang

Selat Utara

Selat Malaka

Selat Selatan

Kuah (Langkawi)

Butterworth

Tanjung Kecil

Tanjung Puchat Muka

Tanjung Duyung

Tanjung Besar

Pantai Acheh Forest Reserve

Teluk Bahang

Batu Feringghi

Kampung Tanjung Huma

Tanjung Batu

Tanjung Huma

Teluk Nangka

Teluk Tikus

Tanjung Bungah

Tanjung Bungah

Tanjung Tokong

Teluk Ketapang

Kampung Nelayan

Teluk Bahang

Teluk Bahang

Penang Butterfly Farm

Teluk Bahang Forest Reserve

Waterfall Gardens

Bagan Jermal

Tanjung Keriang

Kampung Tengah

Forest Recreation Park

Bukit Kerajaan Forest Reserve

Nattukotai Chettiar

Wat Chayamangkalaram

Tanjung Kalok

Laksamana Forest Reserve

Bukit Western 833

Highlands Forest Reserve

Pulau Tikus

Tanjung Gemuroh

Bukit Bendera (Penang Hill) 830

Taman Belia Perbandaran (Youth Park)

Penang Buddhist Association

Georgetown

Kampung Pantai Aceh

Datuk Keramat

Bagan Kuala Sungai Pinang

Pinang

Sungai Pinang

Air Hitam

Kek Lok Si

Kampung Baharu

Masjid Negeri (State Mosque)

Kampung Chantek

Kampung Sungai Rusa

Pulau Pinang (Penang)

Air Hitam Dam

Kepala Pancu

Bukit Elvira 695

Jelutong

Kampung Permatang Pasir

Kampung Kastam

Bagan Ayer Hitam

Titi Perupok

Gelugur

Kampung Sungai Gelugur

Balik Pulau Forest Reserve

Kampung Jalan Baharu

Kampung Titi Serong

Bukit Relau Forest Reserve

Universiti Sains Malaysia

Jambatan Pulau Pinang (Penang Bridge)

Kuala Jalan Baharu

Balik Pulau

Kampung Sungai Dua

Kampung Batu Uban

Kampung Kuala Muda

Kebun Besar

Kampung Sungai Dua Laut

Pekan Genting

Kampung Shee Tan

Kampung Kafri

Kampung Batak

Kampung Manggi

Relau

Kampung Sungai Nibung

Kampung Terang

Penara

Kampung Sungai Ara

Snake Temple

Kampung Jawa

Kampung Sungai Nibung Besar

Bukit Jerejak 211

Pulau Jerejak

Pulau Betong

Kampung Genting Dalam

Bukit Genting Forest Reserve

Kampung Sepuluh

Kampung Gedong

Kampung Pengkalan

Kampung Sungai Keluang

Teluk Tengkorak

Kampung Bakar Kapor

Kampung Tengah

Bukit Ayun

Teluk Nahu Ayer Bagi

Pasir Panjang

Pulau Betong

Kampung Long Tambang

Kampung Masjid

Kampung Tengah

Bayan Lepas

Kampung Parlis

Kampung Nipah

Bukit Gemuruh Forest Reserve

Kampung Nelayan

Kampung Utan Nibong

Bayan Lepas

Gertak Sanggul

Bagan Teluk Kumbar

Kampung Teluk Kumbar

Teluk Kumbar

Batu Maung

Teluk Dwalin

Tanjung Bongkok

Kampung Sungai Batu

Kampung Masjid

Kampung Teluk Tempoyak Kecil

Tanjung Gertak Sanggul

Tanjung Chut

Kg. Permatang Bakar Kapor

Kampung Teluk Tempoyak Besar

Tanjung Teluk Tempoyak

Teluk Ikan Mati

Pulau Rimau

0 2 km

0 2 miles

PENANG

A rich heritage and a mystic, spiritual core – as well as fine beaches and wonderful food – make the island state of Penang a perennial favourite among visitors to Malaysia

Map on page 184

Temples shrouded in incense smoke and palm-fringed beaches have been attracting curious visitors to **Penang** for several hundred years. One of the most famous islands in Asia, Penang is also perhaps the best-known tourist destination in Malaysia.

Throughout history, Penang has changed names like the seasons. Early Malays called it Pulau Ka Satu, or Single Island. Later it appeared on sailing charts as Pulau Pinang, or Island of the Betel Nut Tree. The British renamed it Prince of Wales' Island, and finally, with Malaysia's independence, it became Pulau Pinang once again. But romance, sustained by tourist brochure copywriters, is hard to dispel: Penang is also the Pearl of the Orient, Gateway to the East, and the Isle of Temples.

The trade

From the mainland, the 7-km (4-mile) **Penang Bridge** (Jambatan Pulau Pinang) offers exhilarating views of the harbour and the jagged skyline of condominiums and office blocks set against the hilly centre.

A very different aspect would have greeted English trader and adventurer Sir Francis Light in the 18th century, but he saw the advantages of having the island – then under Kedah – as a station for Britain's East India Company. Light saw Penang as a base to replenish company ships on their long haul to China in the flourishing tea and opium trade, and serve as a headquarters to further British interests in Southeast Asia.

Light, fluent in Thai and Malay, and a familiar figure in the Kedah court, persuaded the sultan to trade Penang for British protection against threatening Thai and Bugis enemies. But the British did not honour the agreement, and going to war only saw Kedah lose more land to the Empire – this time on the mainland, named Seberang Prai by the Malays.

To encourage trade and commerce, the British made the island state a free port; no taxes were levied on either imports or exports. This strategy worked and in eight years, the population increased to 8,000, comprising many immigrant races – Chinese, Indians and Bugis, among others.

Today, the state of Pulau Pinang or Penang as everyone calls it, comprises Seberang Prai (or Butterworth as it was formerly known) on the mainland and Penang island, linked by both the bridge and ferry services. The ferries carry both passengers and vehicles; ferrying your car over costs the same as the bridge toll and you pay at the Seberang Prai side. The ferry terminus at the Seberang Prai is linked to bus, taxi and railway stations – the transport goes all the way to Thailand.

BELOW: travelling salesman in Georgetown.

The clock tower opposite Fort Cornwallis in George Town was a gift from a Chinese millionaire to celebrate Queen Victoria's Diamond Jubilee in 1897.

Different faces

Like most cities of Asia that juxtapose the glass and concrete of the new with the tile and teak of the old, Penang has several dimensions. A newcomer can arrive by ferry, be transported by trishaw to a Chinese hotel on Lebuh Chulia in the heart of Chinatown, eat at the outdoor food stalls, visit the waterfront villages, and after two weeks, leave Penang having never stepped into anything built after World War II. On the other hand, another visitor may have cocktails at the poolside overlooking the sea while getting a golden tan, dine in a gourmet restaurant, and never brush shoulders with a Chowrasta Market butcher in town.

But vibrant **Georgetown** ⓬ is the heart of Penang. Named by the British after King George III, it is unmistakably Chinese, its narrow streets congested with pedestrians, vehicles, signboards and temples. The best way to experience it is on foot, or you could hire a trishaw for the day – but bargain first. By trishaw, the city passes by in a kaleidoscope of changing colours, and even in the rain, the driver zips you into a plastic covering, and pedals slowly through the wet streets. At night, there is a special romance about riding in the glow of neon signs and blinking lights.

An excellent route that takes in the main sights is the signposted Heritage Trail – ask for a map from any of the travel agencies near the **Clock Tower Ⓐ**. The trail starts at **Fort Cornwallis Ⓑ** (Kota Cornwallis), the place from which probably the most costly cannon ball in history was shot. When Francis Light was clearing land for his settlement, the thick undergrowth proved arduous work for the sepoys, Indians employed as soldiers by the British and other European powers. The disgruntled sepoys had no compunction in complaining, so Light loaded a cannon with silver dollars and fired it into the jungle. This

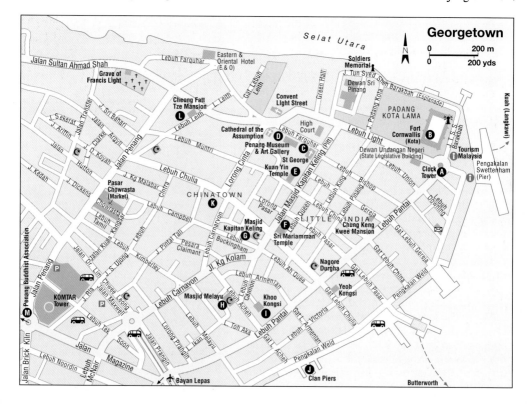

was enough to get them all to work to retrieve the coins; and before long the land was cleared and the first camp established.

Maps:
Area 184
City 186

Magical cannon

Originally a wooden structure, Fort Cornwallis was rebuilt with convict labour in the early 1800s. Today, the old fort's precincts have been converted into a public park and playground. Its ramparts are still guarded by old cannon, the most venerable and famous of which is Seri Rambai, presented by the Dutch to the Sultan of Johor in 1606. Seven years later, it was captured by the Achehnese and taken to Acheh, where it remained for almost 200 years. The cannon was then sent to Kuala Selangor in the quest of a Bugis alliance. After the British bombarded Kuala Selangor in 1871, the cannon was brought to Penang. Like most ancient cannon, Seri Rambai is attributed with magical powers; it is believed that women desiring children will have their wish fulfilled if they place flowers in the cannon's barrel and offer prayers.

Next to Fort Cornwallis lies the *padang* (town green) and the Esplanade (Jalan Tun Syed Sheh Barakbah). The handsome 19th-century colonial **State Legislative Building** (Dewan Undangan Negeri) stands at one end of the Padang; at the other, near the entrance to Fort Cornwallis, traffic circles the Clock Tower, which was presented to Penang by a rich Chinese *towkay* (businessman), Cheah Chin Gok, in commemoration of Queen Victoria's Diamond Jubilee. The dignified **St George's Church** , built in 1818 on nearby Lebuh Farquhar, is the oldest Anglican church in Southeast Asia. Sir Francis Light lies buried in the frangipani-shaded cemetery down the road, along with other notables of old Penang, many of whom succumbed early in life to the rigours of the tropics.

TIP

Public buses cover the whole the island but follow no timetable. Bus terminals are at Lebuh Victoria and Jalan Dr Lim Chwee Leong. Fares are low and you can go around the island in one day with an early start.

BELOW: colonial State Legislative Building.

Dragon figurine at Penang's Kuan Yin Temple, dedicated to the Buddhist Goddess of Mercy.

At the **Penang Museum** (open Sat–Thurs 9am–5pm; entrance fee) on the same side of the street as St George's Church, visitors can peer into a Chinese bridal chamber created in the lavish style of the 19th century, or see a bejewelled *keris*, the dagger Malays used for protection. The **Penang Art Gallery** at Dawan Sri Pinang displays work by local artists, including batik, oils, graphics and Chinese ink drawings. Also along Lebuh Farquhar is Georgetown's oldest hotel, the **E&O Hotel**, which once played host to luminaries such as Rita Hayworth and Somerset Maugham. Established in the late 19th century by the Armenian Sarkies brothers, the property was closed in 1996 for renovations. It reopened in 2001 and once again looks set to claim its place as one of Asia's grand hotels.

Houses of worship

Three of the state's oldest worship houses are in the Jalan Masjid Kapitan Keling area. Along that road is Penang's oldest Buddhist temple, the **Kuan Yin Temple** , which is also the most humble and crowded. The temple belongs to the people in the street – the noodle hawkers, trishaw riders, and the workers building cupboards, repairing bicycles or selling sundry goods. A Buddhist deity who refused to enter Nirvana so long as there was injustice on earth, Kuan Yin typically personifies mercy. She is ever-present on Chinese altars, whether Taoist, Buddhist or Confucian, and is perhaps the most beloved divinity.

BELOW: giant joss stick at the Kuan Yin Temple.

Jalan Masjid Kapitan Keling leads into the tiny "**Little India**" where saris, garlands, and jewellery deck the stores, and the spicy scent of curry wafts through the air. Indian merchants arrived in Penang with the British, as did Indian convicts, who built the first roads and filled in the swamps on which the town now stands. Assimilated into local society, it is not surprising to find their descendants fluent in Tamil as well as in Bahasa Malaysia, English and some Hokkien.

In Lebuh Queen sits the state's oldest place of worship for Hindus, the **Sri Mariamman Temple** , which was built in the 1830s, and boasts an ornate South Indian gateway. However, many Indians who came to Penang were Muslim, and the state has a large Indian-Muslim population, whose delicious *nasi kandar* rice and scorching-hot curry dishes are relished by all Malaysians. Their oldest place of worship, and the state's oldest mosque is on Jalan Masjid Kapitan Keling. The Moorish **Masjid Kapitan Keling** (Kapitan Keling Mosque), erected in 1800, is named after the Indian-Muslim merchant headman, or *Kapitan Keling*, Caudeer Mohudeen, who was responsible for its construction. Head into Lebuh Armenian, which is flanked by early 19th-century shophouses originally belonging to Malays and Sumatrans. An octagonal minaret at the end of the road marks the entrance to the **Masjid Melayu** (Acheen Street Mosque), which is a mixture of Egyptian and Javanese styles.

Narrow alleyways off the bustling roads lead to quiet rows of Chinese homes, with carved lintels and elaborate doorways. The small family temple erected on Gat Lebuh Gereja (Church Street) by millionaire Chung Keng Kwee is a good example. Inside the temple, a lifelike bronze statue of Chung in the robes of a Chinese mandarin stands resplendent. Chung made his fortune from the tin mines in Larut, Perak, and was one of the leaders of the Chinese factions in the Larut Wars of the 1860s.

As you walk around Georgetown, you will keep coming across clan houses, Chinese guild halls that honour both ancestors and outstanding members. Sitting in compounds surrounded by houses, they are reached through narrow entrances. Among these are the Yap Kongsi on Lebuh Armenian and the Cheah Kongsi on Gat Lebuh Armenian.

Map on page 186

King of the clanhouses

The most elaborate of these, however, is the **Khoo Kongsi ❶** (open daily 9am–5pm) at the junction of Jalan Masjid Kapitan Keling and Lebuh Acheh. Designed to capture the splendour of an imperial palace, it has a seven-tiered pavilion, "dragon" pillars and hand-painted walls engraved with the Khoo rose emblem. The original design was so ambitious that conservative Khoo clansmen cautioned against it, lest the emperor of China be offended. After eight years, the building was completed in 1902; but on the first night after it was finished, the roof mysteriously caught fire. Clan members interpreted this as a sign that even the deities considered the Khoo Kongsi too palatial for a clan house. The Khoos rebuilt it on a more modest scale. A recent 15-month renovation process costing RM3 million and painstakingly put together by 16 Chinese artisans using traditional Chinese materials has restored the house to its former splendour.

At Georgetown's waterfront near the ferry terminus, entire villages belong to clans. These are the **Clan Piers ❷**, comprising wooden houses perched on stilts over the sea, which in the pre-condominium era, were the most outstanding feature to greet visitors who travelled to the island by ferry. Each of the six

BELOW: the ornate entrance of a Georgetown clanhouse.

THE CHINESE CLANHOUSES

Chinese immigrants arriving in Malaysia in the 19th century fell under the protection and control of clan associations, whose functions were not unlike those of medieval European guilds: to promote the interests of their members and provide help to those in distress. You'll find the ancestral halls or *kongsi* of associations such as the Khoo, Ong, Tan and Chung clans scattered all over Georgetown.

Many of these clan houses are beautiful pieces of traditional Chinese architecture and house important antiques and artwork. But there is concern about their future, as well as the shophouses in their vicinity, due to the abolition of the Rent Control Act in 2000. The Act limits the rent that owners can charge tenants, but it is feared that its abolition will see owners looking to maximise profits by re-developing the land, or selling it off for money-raking high-rises. The Penang Heritage Council is lobbying hard to save these important buildings. The Khoos, for instance, owners of the Khoo Kongsi clan house (*see above*) are also planning to turn the buildings around their *kongsi* into a cultural and heritage village, with souvenir and retail shops and budget accommodation. It is hoped that this will spur similar projects in George Town.

Wooden clogs like these are more charming as wall hangings than foot wear. Find them in Penang's Chinatown.

villages has its own temple, and houses just one clan, except for one "mixed" village. Therefore, on Lim's Pier, you'll find only members of the Lim family, while Tan's Pier is the sole property of the Tan clan. Nearly all but the Chews have abandoned the fishing trade, but all the houses are occupied, and no one minds if a visitor strolls along the plankwalks.

Backpacker alley

Life in the hotch-potch of streets and alleys of **Chinatown** looks like it has been lived the same way since the immigrants got off the boat. At dawn, goods are unloaded at century-old shophouses, the lorries blocking half the already-narrow road. In the coffeeshops, old men exchange daily news over cracked cups of coffee with bread and *kaya* (coconut jam). For shopaholics, there are antiques and curios galore, as well as more contemporary items such as leather goods and batik. Second-hand bookstores are treasure-troves of old tomes, as well as the latest John Grisham left behind by backpackers in Lebuh Chulia.

The desire to soak-up this atmosphere has ensured that Lebuh Chulia's tiny old Chinese hotels have held out against time (and in some cases, badly-needed renovation). From a cracked window here, you can catch sight of a funeral procession through the streets, complete with drums and gongs and mourners. In the afternoon, a lion dance might be staged to bring luck to a new sundry goods shop – a noisy affair with more drums and gongs. Come evening and it could be a Chinese opera that draws an audience on plastic stools to watch heavily painted faces pantomime classical tales of old. In Chinatown, you can never tell where and when you might find a bargain or a baritone.

The hotels are "supported" by cafés offering "Western food", tours, bicycles

BELOW: rooftop patterns of Chinatown.
RIGHT: Chinese opera in action.

for hire and money-changers. The backpacker row extends to Lebuh Leith, on which enterprising entrepreneurs have turned a row of heritage buildings into trendy restaurants and pubs. Here also is the carefully-restored late 19th-century **Cheong Fatt Tze Mansion ❶**, which has a unique blend of Eastern and Western architectural styles (guided tours 11am Mon, Wed, Fri and Sat; entrance fee). It was built by craftsmen from China's Guandong province.

Georgetown has lots of small and friendly pubs, some of which keep a "family album" of snapshots showing just about every traveller who has ever walked in and bought a drink. They provide jukeboxes for dancing, games machines for entertainment and barmaids for conversation.

Jalan Penang (better known as Penang Road) is the main shopping bazaar, and it ends in the towering air-conditioned KOMTAR shopping complex at the top of a bus station, which also houses a tourist information centre and the Tourism Malaysia office. Take a ride up its probing circular tower for a bird's eye view of the city (entrance fee).

Take a walk through **Pasar Chowrasta** (Chowrasta Market), between Jalan Chowrasta and Lebuh Tamil. A wet market with the customary wet market pong, it has a section facing Penang Road that offers the Penang specialities of local biscuits and preserved nutmeg and mango prepared in a wide variety of styles. On Lebuh Tamil is the row of *nasi kandar* (mixed curry rice) stalls whose food is reputed to be the best in the country.

Food is Penang's favourite export to the rest of the country. Here, hawker centres commandeer every corner, the most famous of which (and you pay the price for it) is on the seaside **Gurney Drive** stretch, open in the evenings. However, wander into the **Pulau Tikus** area behind Jalan Burma, and you pay far less

Map on page 186

BELOW: *kacang puteh* or nuts vendor in Pulau Tikus market.

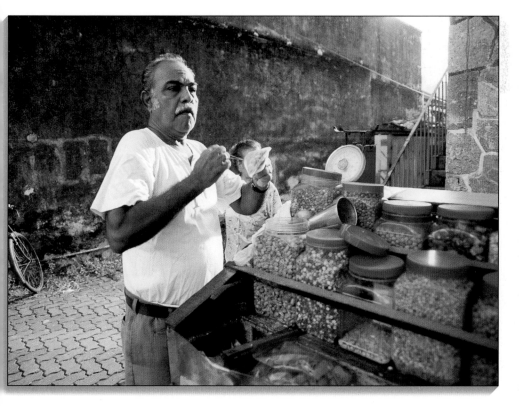

for food that is perhaps twice as good. Pulau Tikus is also the heartland of the *Baba-Nyonya*, descendants of Chinese immigrants who married into and absorbed Malay culture, including wearing batik *sarungs* and the adoption of local spices and coconut milk in their unique style of cooking. Also known as *Peranakan* (locally-born) and Straits Chinese, these communities are predominant in the British Straits Settlements states of Penang, Melaka and Singapore.

Temples of incense

Be prepared to get soaking wet if you visit Wat Chayamangkalaram in April, during the Thai Songkran festival. Mischief-makers hurl water-filled plastic bags on passers-by on the pretext of "purifying" them.

BELOW: The Thai inspired Wat Chayamangkalaram.

The eve of Chinese New Year at the **Penang Buddhist Association** on Jalan Anson is a more formal affair compared to the mad rush of devotees at other temples. Association members busily arrange bright flowers, fruits and coloured cakes on a large, shiny table of blackwood imported from Canton. Enthroned on the high altars are six white marble statues of Lord Buddha and his disciples. Crystal chandeliers from Czechoslovakia hang overhead, and the walls are decorated with paintings depicting Buddha's path to enlightenment. A teenage girl patiently leads her dignified grandfather across the wide marble floor, where a seated congregation chants praises to Lord Buddha.

As temple bells tinkle, the chanting rises to usher in the new year. Outside the front door, beggars sit quietly chatting amongst themselves. They know benevolence is a precept of the Chinese New Year and they receive it passively.

Ordinarily, the large, luminous hallway that dominates the Chinese Buddhist Association is the most serene sanctuary in Penang. The building, completed in 1929, reflects the desire of a Buddhist priest who wanted to indoctrinate his followers with orthodox rites and ceremonies. Joss-stick hawkers or paper-money burners are not found here. Prayers are considered the essence of Buddhist worship, and the association cherishes the simplicity inherent in its Buddhist faith.

The variety of Buddhist worship in Penang is so striking it makes every temple a new experience. One can enter the gigantic meditation hall at **Wat Chaya-mangkalaram** ⓭ and find a workman polishing the left cheek of 32-metre (100-ft) long Reclining Buddha. The *wat*, on Jalan Burma, is a Thai Buddhist monastery. Gigantic *naga* serpents, mystical creatures that link earth to heaven, form the balustrades at the entrance, while fierce-visaged giants tower over the doorways in the role of otherworldly bodyguards.

Another form of Buddhist worship can be seen in the **Burmese Temple** on the other side of the road. A Buddha with a haughty, yet serene expression is worshipped here. Another shrine is surrounded with a moat over which "heavenly" bridges fly. On either side are Buddha images. Little shops in the shaded walkways sell little pink and green lotus flower-shaped candles to worshippers, who leave the lighted candles reverentially in front of the shrines.

Inspired by a vision

Penang's loftiest temple sits on a hilltop at Air Itam, 6 km (4 miles) from the Buddhist Association. **Kek Lok Si** ⓮, the largest Buddhist temple in Malaysia and one of the largest in the region, owes its existence to Beow Lean, a Chinese Buddhist priest from Fujian province in China who arrived in Penang in 1887. As the resident priest of the Kuan Yin Temple in Lebuh Pitt, so impressed was he by the religious fervour of Penang's Buddhists, that he decided to found a monastery. This hilly site at Air Itam is supposedly reminiscent of Fujian.

The main buildings were completed in 1904, and the great Pagoda of a

Maps:
Area 184
City 186

Naga, or serpent guardian at Wat Chayamangkalaram.

BELOW: joss stick offerings at Kek Lok Si temple.

Million Buddhas, erected in 1930, is dedicated to all manifestations of the Buddha, hence its name. It is renowned for the three architectural styles it contains: a Chinese base, a Thai middle section and a Burmese top.

When completed, in addition to being a centre for Buddhist devotion, Kek Lok Si became an instant tourist attraction. The stone walkway from the base to the top is flanked by arcades of souvenir stalls, and you pay "voluntary" contributions for the privilege of ascending the pagoda.

Kek Lok Si is split into three tiers spread over a rocky incline. The three "Halls of the Great" honour Kuan Yin, goddess of mercy; Bee Lay Hood, the Laughing Buddha; and Gautama Buddha, founder of the faith. It is here that the monks pass their hour in prayer. The Tower of Sacred Books on the topmost tier houses a library of Buddhist scriptures and Sutra, many of which were presented by Emperor Kuang Hsu of China. An edict from the same emperor, cemented into a wall of this block, grants imperial approval to the establishment of the temple.

A 3-km (2-mile) road from Kek Lok Si winds its way up to the **Air Itam Dam**, with an 18-hectare (45-acre) lake reflecting the lush green foliage of the surrounding jungle. The cool air and steep road is popular with walkers and joggers in the early morning and late evening.

Hill with a view

Jalan Air Itam also leads to **Bukit Bendera** ⓯ (Penang Hill), established as a quiet getaway in 1897, and saved about 80 years later from large-scale commercialisation by public petition, a rare people-power victory. However, there is little of interest at the top. The best part of the experience is the ride in the

BELOW: the funicular railway at Penang Hill.
RIGHT: the Kek Lok Si Temple.

Map on page 184

Swiss-modelled funicular railway (open daily 6am–9pm; entrance fee); and a 15-minute Canopy Walkway (open daily 8.30am–5pm).

You can also hike up Penang Hill on a trail that starts from the **Waterfall Gardens** ⓰, also known as the Penang Botanic Gardens; if you aren't so keen on the idea of a hot, sweaty trek, you'll enjoy strolling through the gardens. This mature and beautifully-cultivated showcase of tropical plants is about 2 km (1 mile) from Pulau Tikus, with waterfalls that start over a hundred metres above the gardens and cascade through the greenery. On holidays, families round up relatives for a picnic lunch by the stream, while barefoot children romp on the rocks or play follow-the-tourist. Benches are scattered throughout the gardens and provide pleasant resting spots in the shade.

Atop a hill and reached only by a long flight of steps is the Hindu shrine of **Nattukotai Chettiar** ⓱. Every January, this becomes the centre for the Hindu festival of penance, Thaipusam. After a period of fasting, devotees carry devotional *kavadi* structures made of steel, and pierce their flesh with skewers. Many consider the processions here more dramatic and interesting than the one in Kuala Lumpur's Batu Caves. Certainly, more coconuts are smashed in Georgetown's streets, including by non-Hindus, who see no harm in amassing some good luck too.

Watch out for pesky monkeys in Penang's Waterfall Gardens, some of which can be aggressive. Feeding them is discouraged but the notice is often disregarded.

Ferringhi beach

But for many visitors, it is the beach that beckons. Penang's holiday beaches are in the north, from Tanjung Bungah to Batu Ferringhi and Teluk Bahang. The road up from Jalan Tanjung Tokong follows the curve of the land, twisting up and around a hill, or skirting the fringe of the sea. Rocky headlands divide the shoreline into small bays and coves, each with a different character and charm. Although the waters are not as clear as on the east coast, the beaches are still popular for swimming and sunbathing.

BELOW: Batu Ferringhi beach.

The northern beaches are self-contained, with no need for visitors to venture down to town. There is the full range of accommodation, from apartments for longer-stay guests, to beachside places for backpackers, and a bus station, post office, clinic, grocery shops and a host of souvenir outlets. At night, the naked bulbs and blaring music of a *pasar malam* (night market) add to the bustle. Car and bicycle hire is available, and most hotels have a free shuttle service to Georgetown; there are plenty of taxis too.

Activities are centred around **Batu Ferringhi** ⓲, one of the most popular beach resorts in Southeast Asia. This is where the famous luxury hotels are clustered, including the Minangkabau-roofed **Rasa Sayang Hotel** at the start of the stretch. However, small inns and motels are plentiful too, as well as accommodation offered by villagers. Likewise, the whole range of eateries can be found here, from airconditioned steak and seafood restaurants to hawker stalls under winking fairy lights.

Yahong Art Gallery opposite the clinic is a storehouse of some of the finest arts, crafts and antiques of Malaysia and China. It is also the home of Chuah Thean Teng, the internationally-acclaimed Father of

Cocoa pods are cultivated in Penang. Look out for the bright orange papaya-like fruits.

Malaysian batik art. His sons are all talented artists too, and their work is on display and for sale in the gallery.

If Batu Ferringhi is too busy for you, 6 km (4 miles) further down the coast is the fine **Teluk Bahang** beach, dominated by the luxury Mutiara Hotel. En route you'll find the **Tropical Spice Garden**, a quiet haven of flora and foliage set on a hill slope with a tea house and souvenirs galore.

Teluk Bahang has little save a batik factory and other souvenir shops. Further down the road is the **Penang Butterfly Farm** (open daily 9am–5pm; entrance fee), where large varieties of butterflies and unusual insects are bred. A couple of minutes down the road is a **Forest Recreation Park**, good for a picnic. For more trekking and resort-free beaches, head towards the **Pantai Aceh Forest Reserve ⓳** where there are trails to Muka Head, a favourite boy-scout camping-spot. At the fishing village at the entrance of the forest reserve, you can arrange for a boat to pick you up. The sea can be choppy though. The road to Batu Maung, known for its seafood restaurants built over water, goes down the west coast and around the island. Here, a different Penang begins: an agrarian world, quiet, peaceful and thinly populated.

Round the island

As much as the port is Chinese, so is the countryside Malay. The winding and sometimes mountainous round-island road runs for 74 km (46 miles), a journey you can cover in air-conditioned buses with guides, (book through hotels and tour agencies) or rented chauffeured cars with or without guides.

The road through the rolling hills offers striking views of the island dropping to the sea far below. Dense, damp jungles are interspersed with the plan-

BELOW:
Giant moth, Penang
Butterfly Farm.

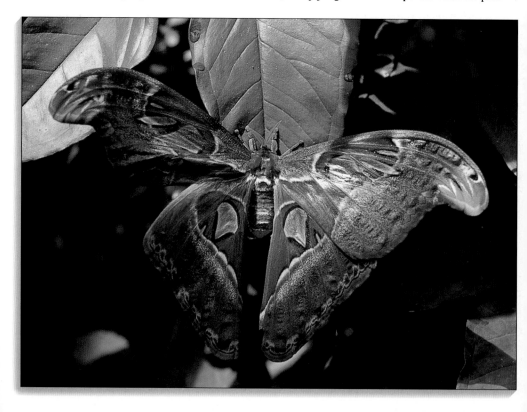

tations of pepper, clove and nutmeg that lured Arab, Spanish, Portuguese and other Western traders to this part of the world long ago. When in season, nets are spread out below the *durian* trees in the orchards, to prevent damage to the fruit, which drops when ripe. Visitors throng the temporary roadside stalls, savouring the pungent flesh or haggling over prices.

At Titi Kerawang, there are waterfalls and a serene view of the Indian Ocean. The natural freshwater pool is filled from the waterfalls, and is suitable for bathing, although a big water pipeline mars the scenery.

Kampungs and footprints

As you head south, the scenery gives way to paddy fields. Several small roads branch off to the coast, usually the commercial link between a fishing village and the trunk road. It was in small villages such as these that the few Malays lived when Francis Light established the first settlement.

Although updated with brick, the *kampung* houses look much the same today as they did 100 years ago. If you have your own transport, it is worthwhile turning off into the coconut tree-lined paths to explore a village. Malays are proud of their homes, and many have pretty courtyards planted with flowers and fruit trees. The smiles are inevitably warm, with locals always ready to make your acquaintance.

As you head to the east coast, bustling urbanity starts to rear its head. Turn off to **Batu Maung** ⑳, about 3 km (2 miles) from the Bayan Lepas Airport, and you will reach a shrine built around a footprint in stone, believed to be that of Admiral Cheng Ho, the Chinese Columbus. The well-kept shrine sits in a beautiful Chinese garden that overlooks the jetty and fishing boats of the village.

Map on page 184

BELOW: Malay *kampung* house.

Map on page 184

At the Snake Temple, pit vipers are venerated by the Chinese because of their kinship to the mythical dragons of Chinese folklore.

BELOW: Cheng Ho's footprint, Batu Maung.
RIGHT: sunset at Batu Ferringhi.

Villagers believe that Cheng Ho called at this spot on one of his seven voyages to Southeast Asia. On Pulau Langkawi, 96 km (60 miles) further north, is a similar footprint. The two are believed to be a pair, and anyone who lights incense sticks and places them in the urns at the shrine will enjoy good luck and great fortune.

There are a couple of large restaurants here which are famous for their seafood. Walk down from the shrine past the eatery next door, and you'll come to a garden of incongruous statues, ranging from mythical Indian and Chinese gods, to Snow White and the Seven Dwarfs, and the Statue of Liberty. The garden is neglected, which is sad, for the choice and juxtapositioning of these figures is an ironically accurate summary of Malaysian life.

Silicon and sleepy snakes

If you take the right fork from Batu Maung to go north, you will pass behind the airport and cut through the **Bayan Lepas Free Trade Zone**, the Silicon Valley of Malaysia. The huge area of sanitised, unimaginative blocks is the home of high-technology industries, ranging from microchip-manufacturing multinationals such as Intel, to success-hungry export-orientated local giants.

These factories have now completely hemmed in the Temple of Azure Cloud, more popularly known as the **Snake Temple**. Here, venomous pit vipers, doped perhaps by the incense, lie coiled around everything: altars, shrines, incense burners, candlesticks, vases, tables, underfoot and overhead. However, the air of mystery surrounding the temple, and the reason why the reptiles would congregate here has vanished, together with the lush jungle behind it; today the temple is now just another commercial attraction.

A highway runs the length of the east coast from here to Georgetown. This is built on reclaimed land, and Penangites joke about how this has changed the shape of the island; before it resembled a tortoise, whereas now it looks more like a rather pregnant one.

More microchips

The mainland section of Penang state is nearly twice as large as the island, a thriving industrial area built around Seberang Prai (Butterworth) that has become one of the world's leading producers of microchips, disk drives and other computer parts. Both sides of the North-South Highway and the approach to the Penang Bridge are covered with sprawling high-tech factories. Amid the factories, in Seberang Jaya, east of Seberang Prai, is the **Penang Bird Park** (open daily 9am–7pm; entrance fee), a lush garden with over 200 species of tropical birds from around the world. The birds are all housed in specially designed homes, including a huge walk-in aviary and geodesic domes.

Another patch of green is the 37-hectare (92-acre) **Bukit Mertajam Recreational Park**, about 18 km (11 miles) from the Penang Bridge. It has numerous walking trails for trekkers and rest huts when you tire. Near its entrance is the stark white **St Anne's Church**, a well-preserved 19th-century colonial relic. It is the site of a candlelight procession each year on the Feast of St Anne's in late July. ❑

KEDAH AND PERLIS

Map on page 158

The most traditionally Malay of the northern states, Kedah and Perlis offer the modern traveller ancient Hindu settlements, lush mountain parks and the carefree resort isle of Langkawi

I t beckoned, a bluish-grey mass which towered in the distance, and so civilisation took root in the land. At 1,200 metres (3,900 ft), Gunung Jerai in the state of Kedah served as a lodestar to early merchant voyagers; it was at its foot that one of the peninsula's first known kingdoms established itself.

But Kedah's position at the crossroads of Southeast Asian trade also exposed it to constant danger. Initially controlled by the great trading empires of Funan in Vietnam, and then Sri Vijaya in Sumatra, Kedah later became part of the Melaka sultanate. Until the beginning of the 19th century, Kedah's rulers were remarkably successful in preserving their independence. However, despite having put their faith in British power (and losing Penang in the process), Kedah fell to the Thais, and Perlis had to be given up as well. Both states were transferred to British suzerainty in 1909, but the mainly Malay population somehow managed to maintain their way of life, unlike other peninsula states.

Ancient temples

Unlike the sailors of old from across the Bay of Bengal, modern-day travellers approach **Gunung Jerai** on the North-South Highway through **Sungai Petani**, Kedah's second-largest town and the country's fastest-growing. Close by, at a slower but no less intense pace, one of the largest archaeological sites in the country, dating back to the 5th century, is being uncovered.

LEFT: Langkawi fishermen heading home.
BELOW: neolithic stone tool from Bujang.

After over a century of digging, archaeological finds from the edges of villages, riverbanks and the foot of jungled hills point to many more treasures in the whole area between the **Lembah Bujang** ㉑ (Bujang Valley) and **Sungai Muda**. This is the site not only of one of the earliest Hindu settlements in Southeast Asia, but also an earlier Buddhist phase, and there is even the possibility of a prehistoric Malay settlement before that. About 10 ancient *candi* (temples) have been excavated and restored, the largest and best-preserved being the **Candi Bukit Batu Pahat** (Temple of the Hill of Chiselled Stone). Inscriptions in Sanskrit, porcelain pieces from China, Indian beads, and glassware from the Middle East point to the site's importance as an international entrepot.

The area now comes under the administration of the **Muzium dan Taman Arkeologi Lembah Bujang** (Lembah Bujang Archaeological Park and Museum), whose museum (open daily 9am–5pm) showcases important finds, and has a display of photographs and models. Pretty landscaped paths lead to the four closest restored temples. Guided tours of the site must be pre-arranged (tel: 04-457 2005). To get there, exit the North-South Highway at Sungai Petani and head towards Bedong, turning left to Merbok and the

In the predominantly Malay-Muslim states of Kedah and Perlis, men wearing the songkok (fez) on Friday prayer days are a common sight.

museum. Taxis can be chartered from Sungai Petani, but there are no buses.

Beyond Merbok, the road winds prettily on and eventually turns south to **Tanjung Dawai**, a postcard-perfect fishing village on the Muda Estuary. A ferry (but not for cars) crosses the estuary to Pantai Merdeka, a popular beach which can also be reached from Penang by road.

Sungai Petani is also the jump-off point on the spectacular East-West Highway to the peninsula's east coast. The road goes via Baling, overlooked by a spectacular limestone massif, and Grik in Perak, an important post during the communist threat of the 1960s.

The rice capital

To get to the state capital of Alor Setar, head north from Sungai Petani on the highway. Here the country flattens out, and depending on the season, oceans of rippling green or gold or brown fallow ground merge with the distant cloud-flecked hills of the Main Range. This is the country's Rice Bowl, producing half the locally-grown rice. There are biannual harvests, thanks to the massive Muda Irrigation Project, which covers 127,000 hectares (300,000 acres). This is one of the few schemes financed by the World Bank which has fulfilled the aims of its sponsors and provided adequate returns. A much older irrigation canal actually runs alongside the old main road from Gunung Jerai to Alor Setar. Built in the 19th century by Wan Mat Saman, the then *menteri besar* (chief minister), the canal is perfectly straight throughout its long length, a feat achieved by aligning kerosene-fuelled flares.

BELOW: sun-ripened rice paddy fields in Kedah state.

Alor Setar ㉒ generally serves as a springboard to the holiday isle of Langkawi, but it does have some fine architecture along the main road, Jalan

Pekan. The large **Zahir Mosque** (Masjid Zahir), built in 1912, has the graceful colonnades and domes of Moorish tradition. Opposite it is the **Muzium Di-Raja** (Royal Museum), a former palace interesting for its layout as well as its royal family displays, including Sultan Abdul Halim's African animal trophies.

Map on page 158

Sacred orchestra

Next to the museum is the charming Thai-style **Balai Besar** (Great Hall), built in 1898. Used as an audience hall by Kedah's sultans of old to receive public petitions and hear grievances, today it is the site of ceremonial and state functions. The **Balai Nobat** down the road plays a unique function: it houses the instruments (*nobat*) of Kedah's royal orchestra. Comprising a horn, three drums and a gong, only four such orchestras exist in Malaysia today, the others being in Terengganu, Selangor and Johor.

Kedah's is reputedly the oldest, a gift from Melaka's last sultan. The *nobat* is considered sacred and an important part of the regalia of state: no Kedah sultan is considered a legitimate ruler if he has not been installed to the accompaniment of the nobat. The Kedah *nobat* is also played on other state occasions when the sultan is present, and may be heard daily during the Muslim fasting month, when it is played for five minutes before the end of the day's fast from the tower-like Balai Nobat. Permission to see the *nobat* may be obtained through the state secretariat opposite.

Further down Lebuhraya Darul Aman, near the stadium, is the **Muzium Negeri** (State Museum; open Sat–Thurs 10am–6pm, Fri 9am–12pm and 3–6pm). This is another Thai-style building, with collections that include Chinese ceramics as well as exhibits from the Bujang Valley.

BELOW: Crown of Kedah monument in the capital, Alor Setar.

Outside the capital

The highway north of Alor Setar ends in **Bukit Kayu Hitam**, the exit point to Thailand. There is an uninteresting duty-free emporium there, and a market that is popular with locals. About one-and-a-half hours' drive east of the capital is **Pedu Lake** (Tasik Pedu), a dammed lake retreat in peaceful surroundings that attracts anglers and golfers. The road there goes through tiny wooden settlements among rolling oil palm and rubber plantations.

Seafood *a la* spicy Malay style is best at the small fishing village of **Kuala Kedah**, 12 km (7 miles) west of Alor Setar. The local *ikan panggang* (barbecued fish) and chilli crab are favourites, as is the Thai-influenced noodle dish, *laksa*.

On the other side of the river is the well-preserved fort, **Kota Kuala Kedah**, the state's last defence against the invading Thais in 1821. Although Kedah's aristocracy was either killed or taken prisoner within the hour, the fort held out for another six days before it, too, fell. This disaster marked the beginning of 20 years of subjugation to Siamese rule. In the midst of Kuala Kedah's wooden warehouses and fish market is a modern jetty, serving Langkawi's holiday-makers. The Perlis jump-off point to the island, Kuala Perlis, is a busy but not particularly attractive fishing village; it does, however, have some excellent seafood restaurants.

Kuala Perlis is about an hours' drive from **Kangar**, the capital of Malaysia's smallest state. **Perlis** is really an extension of the Kedah plain, but the scenery is even more rustic, the peaceful atmosphere more lulling. Unlike Kedah, stark, limestone outcrops stand like sentinels over the flat rice fields. Spectacular and mysterious, many contain subterranean caves, with flora and fauna unique to limestone habitats. The vegetation here is also more similar to Thailand's, with the canopy turning a golden autumnal brown during the marked dry season.

While the North-South Highway ignores Perlis completely, the railway line goes through **Arau**, the royal town. The Malaysian railway system meets its Thai counterpart 50 km (30 miles) north at **Padang Besar**, which has a market that comes alive at weekends. You can also cross into Thailand by road via Padang Besar, but a more spectacular drive is west through the hills to **Kaki Bukit** (literally "the foot of the hill"), a former tin-mining outpost comprising a charming wooden Chinese village. **Gua Kelam**, a tunnel used for mining, is worth a visit, and a must-see is the **Perlis State Park**, close to the Thai border, a peaceful nature retreat with good trails. The road from here goes to Satun in Thailand.

Legendary isle

Once upon a time, **Pulau Langkawi** ㉓ was a sleepy island believed to be under a spell cast by a legendary princess, Mahsuri, who lived in the 14th century and was unfairly executed for adultery. It is largely through the efforts of Kedah-born former Prime Minister Mahathir that it has been elevated to the status of a major tourist destination. Malaysia's Father of Independence, Tunku Abdul Rahman, was of the Kedah royal family and many political leaders are northerners, including current Prime Minister Abdullah Badawi.

Ikan bawal or pomfret from Kedah's coastal waters

BELOW: Kuala Perlis is the jumping-off point for Langkawi.

A beautiful limestone cliff and forest archipelago of over 100 islands, some of which are mere rocks that vanish at high tide, Langkawi is being marketed as a modern-day legend. Ferries service the main island between 8am–6pm from Kuala Perlis at hourly intervals (40 minutes), Kuala Kedah every 90 minutes (1 hour), and once a day from Penang (2½ hours). Boats also go to Satun in Thailand four times a day. During the monsoon months of July to September, seas can be choppy, and services may be cancelled. Malaysia Airlines operates daily flights from Alor Setar, Penang, Kuala Lumpur, as well as from London twice a week.

**Maps:
Area 158
Island 206**

Tax-free shopping

Langkawi's duty-free status has succeeded in injecting life into the island. From the jetty to the main town, **Kuah Ⓐ**, nearly every shop is crammed with chocolates, electronic items and household goods. Not all items are a bargain, but alcohol and cigarettes are exempt from Malaysia's heavy "sin" taxes on Langkawi; however, visitors are only allowed to bring out 1 litre of alcohol and a carton of cigarettes after a minimum stay of 72 hours. The old market is a good place to buy Indonesian batik and Chinese-made towels. Trendy craft shops are moving in with hand-painted fabrics and Asian curios.

Perlis is the only Malaysian state whose royal leader is known as Rajah rather than Sultan.

Yet more shops sit on the reclaimed land which starts right next to the jetty. Here you'll see an enormous statue of an eagle; among the many interpretations of its name, Langkawi is thought to derive from the word *helang*, Bahasa Malaysia for "eagle". The statue of the majestic creature about to soar is a powerful allegory, one might say, for the tremendous success of the island resort.

There is a range of hotels and good seafood restaurants at Kuah, but the more

LEFT: a Langkawi resort at sunset.
BELOW: a fisherman waits for a bite.

TIP

There are convenient ferry services (3 hours) between Kuah in Langkawi and the jetty in Georgetown, Penang. Alternatively, organised day tours are offered by travel agents in Penang.

enjoyable option is to find accommodation at one of the island's many beaches, and head into town for a spot of shopping.

Coves, coral and caves

Langkawi has good roads that go round the island. Cars and motorbikes can be hired at the jetty, in town or Pantai Cenang, the most popular beach. Alternatively, book yourself into a half-day guided tour with any tour agency at Kuah. Most visitors head for **Pantai Cenang B** in the southwest, an hour from Kuah by bus and less by taxi. The beach here is lined with places to stay, while opposite are restaurants, souvenir shops, and yet more accommodation. There is something for every budget, from the luxury Pelangi Beach Resort, to rooms in well-tended gardens and A-frame huts.

The road leads south to **Pantai Tengah C**, which is quieter and more upmarket, but doesn't have such a nice beach. The road ends at a new marina resort and an awful bowling and cinema complex at **Teluk Baru** (literally New Bay), built

Langkawi

on, yes, reclaimed land. En route to Pantai Tengah is **Underwater World Langkawi** (open daily 10am–8pm; entrance fee) which showcases over 5,000 sea and freshwater species. One highlight is a 15-metre (50-ft) glass tunnel within a giant saltwater tank with larger species such as sharks, stingrays and turtles.

At the upper end of Cenang is the **Muzium Padi** (Rice Museum), which celebrates the staple of the Langkawi folk. Further past the airport, the road winds through lush forest, passing **Pantai Kok** ❺, formerly one of the island's most beautiful beaches but now the subject of a misguided reclaimation project. Further on is the pretty beach of **Burau Bay** with two luxury resorts at either end. Behind, the jagged peaks of Gunung Mat Cincang provide a dramatic backdrop to the rather tacky **Oriental Village**, worth visiting only to get on the **Langkawi Cable Car** (tel: 04-959 4225; open daily 10am–7pm; entrance fee). A 20-minute journey along the 2.2 km (1.4 mile) route brings you to two platforms with 360 degree views of the Andaman Sea from 708 metres (2,320 ft) above sea level.

Telaga Tujuh ❻ (Seven Wells) is located further down the road from the Oriental Village; legend has it that mountain fairies come to these pools to bathe but vanish at the sight of humans. Note, however, that the pools evaporate in the dry season.

Rocks and resorts

The Mat Cincang formation is the oldest rock in the peninsula, and a good look at the sedimentary structure can be had at the end of the road at **Teluk Datai** ❼ in the north. Datai is the location of the exclusive resort called **The Datai**, an award-winning Balinese-influenced resort with a golf course and private beach as well as the multi-award winning luxury resort, **The Andaman**. Two exclu-

Langkawi villager weaving nipah palms for roof thatching.

BELOW: the pool at The Andaman resort sits in the middle of lush rainforest.

sive properties, **The Tanjung Rhu** and **The Four Seasons Resort**, are found on the secluded northern beach nestled among mangrove forests at scenic **Tanjung Rhu** . They both have well-known spas, gracious service and a full range of facilities and amenities. Their white sandy beaches on Langkawi's northern cape offer scenic sunsets against a backdrop of mountains rainforest. Gua Cerita across the straits is a cave attraction along with 24 caves that dot the islands, including **Gua Kelawar** (Bat Cave) in the southeast, set among mangroves and **Gua Tanjung Dendang** on Pulau Dayang Bunting.

Outside the glitzy tourist beaches, Langkawi's predominantly Malay population of 43,000 maintain their peaceful agrarian lifestyle in much the same way they did before their home was catapulted into the limelight. The older *kampung* folk do not participate in the tourism industry – hotel staff are overwhelmingly from the mainland – and visitors are generally ignored, particularly in December during the Lima maritime and aerial exhibition when there is not a single free room to be found on the island.

From Tanjung Rhu, continue along the road to Kuah for about 5 km (3 miles) to reach **Durian Perangin Waterfalls** (Air Terjun Durian Perangin), which, unlike Telaga Tujuh, never runs dry. Back on the main road, another turning to the left goes to Barn Thai, a unique Thai restaurant in the middle of a mangrove swamp that features live acts.

Langkawi's islands

From Kuah, head west to go inland for 12 km (7 miles) to reach the tomb of **Makam Mahsuri** ❶ (Mahsuri's Tomb; open daily 8am–6pm, entrance fee), which honours this local heroine. The tomb and the surrounds are constructed

TIP

Tanjung Rhu is probably the last place you can get *mee gulung*, a Langkawi speciality dish on the verge of extinction due to the high cost of *udang galah* (tiger prawns).

BELOW: Durian Perangin waterfalls.

LEGENDARY PLACE NAMES

Langkawi's legends are legion and often more interesting than the places they celebrate. The "main" tale concerns Mahsuri, accused of adultery by the jealous chief's wife. At her execution, white blood spurted out, confirming her innocence. Before she died, Mahsuri laid a curse upon the island's next seven generations.

Immediately after, the Thais attacked Langkawi, and the villagers at **Padang Mat Sirat** burned their rice fields rather than let it fall into Siamese hands – few grains remain at **Beras Terbakar** (Field of Burnt Rice).

A Romeo and Juliet-type legend is behind several other place names. A union between a couple was refused by the girl's parents, and in a family feud, pots and pans were thrown at **Belanga Pecah** (broken pots). The gravy jug landed at **Kuah** (gravy), while jugs of boiling water formed the **Telaga Air Hangat** hot springs. The fighting ended when the two fathers were transformed into mountains – **Gunung Raya** and **Gunung Mat Cincang**.

Tasik Dayang Bunting got its name after a Kedah princess, forbidden to marry her lover, fell pregnant after drinking from the lake. The angry king banished her to the island where she drowned herself in the lake and became a rock.

from Langkawi marble. At the quarry outside Kuah is a showroom with marble crafts for sale. When you return to Cenang, take the southern coastal road, Jalan Bukit Malut, to enjoy some spectacular views.

Langkawi's maze of islands is full of secret channels, narrows, inlets and bays. Shadowed cliffs, topped by dense virgin jungle, reach up to 600 metres (2,000 ft) and drop abruptly into the sea. Three are inhabited by fishermen, the sea gypsies, and it is also obvious why pirates who preyed upon the trading ships in the Straits of Melaka sought refuge here.

Pulau Dayang Bunting ❶, the second-largest island of the group, has a unique deep fresh- and salt-water lake, whose ice-cold waters are believed to aid conception. (Its name translates as 'Island of the Pregnant Maiden'). Next to it is **Pulau Singa Besar** ❷, which is a bird and animal sanctuary located on an interesting hilly island; there is a boardwalk that meanders through mangrove, sandy and rocky coastline. Sun-soakers can enjoy the gorgeous beaches on some of the other islands, including **Pulau Bras Basah**. Boats from Tanjung Rhu, Pantai Cenang and Kuah tour these islands in about 4 hours, but you have to book the whole eight-seater speedboat. The Langkawi Yacht Club at Kuah also organises sunset tours.

Marine life is richest at **Pulau Payar** ❸, a marine park, one bumpy hour by boat from the main island. While underwater visibility is rarely more than 3 metres (10 ft), it has lots of life, including sharks that come right up to shore, encouraged by hand-feeding visitors, and colourful soft coral blooms on wrecks in deeper waters. Book with dive operators on the main island, or if you're interested in snorkelling and a picnic, any boat operator. There are also dive sites at the neighbouring islets of Segantang, Kaca and Lembu. ❏

Map on page 206

In Mawat village is the tomb of Princess Mahsuri, who was falsely accused of adultery, and executed.

BELOW: legendary lake in Pulau Dayang Bunting.

THE SOUTHERN PENINSULA

Village and city, ancient and modern – the contradictions are more obvious in the south than elsewhere

Standing as it does today at the silted rivermouth, it is barely conceivable that tiny Melaka (Malacca) once ruled world trade, and was responsible for the spread of Islam throughout the Malay Peninsula. Although the world still congregates at Melaka, these days it is to gawp at its ruins and relics, and to ride in its riverboats, while the main trade with local merchants is in cheap souvenirs and T-shirts.

Melaka is the undisputed top tourist draw of the southern stretch of the peninsula's west coast. To keep the tourists coming, and coming back, the state takes great pains to keep its artefacts dusted, and monuments spruced up. The authorities have also "developed" newer attractions in other parts of the states, particularly in Ayer Keroh.

It was under the benign rule of Melaka that the people of the neighbouring Negeri Sembilan were able to remain true to the traditions and customs of their native Sumatra; this is most visible today in their architecture, notably the large sweeping roofs reminiscent of buffalo horns. Like Melaka and Johor, the rural parts of the state comprise clusters of charming *kampung* with neat front yards, orchards bursting with local fruit, and a lovely lazy air.

But Negeri Sembilan is no backwater. The state is setting itself up to tap the land and labour needs of the fast-developing Klang Valley. The imminent arrival of the new national nucleus of government and IT industries, and the new aviation hub of Sepang, right on the Selangor-Negeri Sembilan border, offers further opportunities for the state.

Johor has reaped the economic benefits of its prime location next to Singapore. Besides road, rail and shipping links, a pipeline carries precious water to the island nation, a point of contention which crops up whenever there are differences between the two countries. Vast tracts of Johor are made over to rubber, oil palm and pineapple plantations; the state is a prime producer of these goods.

Johor's towns are relatively uninteresting, except perhaps for Muar, which bears a striking resemblance to Melaka – it was to this rivermouth port that the last Sultan of Melaka fled from the Portuguese. Inland, however, is the Endau-Rompin National Park (Johor), a magnificent swathe of primeval rainforest set aside for conservation and nature-based tourism. ❑

PRECEDING PAGES: Melaka village tykes.
LEFT: harvesting oil palm at one of numerous plantations that dot Johor state.

MELAKA

*The site of both the first settlement on the peninsula in
the 1400s, and of the declaration of Independence in 1957,
Melaka can truly be called the birthplace of Malaysia*

Map
on page
216

History is everywhere in **Melaka ❶** (Malacca); peeping out from odd corners, hinting truths from epitaphs, outlined in the weathered face of a fisherman. Melaka is a town with a glorious past; almost five centuries ago, a Portuguese chronicler and frequent visitor said, "Whosoever holds Malacca has Venice by the throat". However, that golden grip lasted a mere 100 years. Today Melaka is in a grip of another kind. Every weekend, you'd be hard pressed to find local car licence plates among the Singaporean vehicles that jam the narrow streets. And in recent years, certain traditional areas have fallen victim to urban mismanagement: in the quest for tourist dollars, traditional craftsmen have been evicted and several historic shophouses have been demolished or else subject to sham restoration projects – diluting somewhat Melaka's cultural and historical environment.

Glory days

In the late 1300s, Melaka was a small settlement of sea gypsies, scraping a living as fishermen and farmers. Then Parameswara arrived, a Malay prince fleeing from his own invaded domain of Palembang, Sumatra. While out hunting in the area, he encountered a tiny *kancil* (mousedeer) which managed to intimidate his dogs; he took this as a sign that this should be the site of his new capital. By the end of the 15th century, Melaka had become the centre of a great trading empire and held an undisputed claim over the southern Malay Peninsula, as well as East Sumatra opposite. From every seafaring nation they came – Persians, Arabs, Tamils, and Bengalis from the west; Javanese, Sundanese and Sulus from the archipelago; Chinese, Thais, Burmese, and Khmers – in search of profit through trade, piracy or plunder. Each in turn left something of their culture behind.

The small colony of Chinese merchants, in particular, stayed behind to found the Peranakan community, which has become one of the most striking and colourful Chinese fraternities in Malaysia today. The Baba men and Nyonya women (or Straits-born Chinese) are descendants of the Chinese pioneers who accepted the practical realities of living in a Malay community, but upheld the social and religious norms of their forefathers in Fujian.

It was also through Melaka that the Islamic faith came to Malaysia. Malays have been Muslims since the early 15th century, when rich Moorish merchants from Pasai in Sumatra settled in Melaka. From here Islam spread throughout the peninsula, and eventually to its neighbouring islands. Geography was responsible for Melaka's multicultural history. Located at the mouth of the Melaka River, astride the maritime route

LEFT: Melaka's crimson Christ Church.
BELOW: a Melakan Baba merchant.

TIP

Trishaw drivers
actually make fine
guides, as they know
the sights and speak
English. Not only
might you learn that
the Portuguese came
"a much much long
time ago" but also that
along the seafront
there is a great stall
that sells some of the
best fried *mee hoon*
(vermicelli) in
Malaysia.

linking the Indian Ocean with the South China Sea, it was at Melaka that the monsoon winds met. Sturdy junks from China and Japan, loaded with silk, porcelain and silver, were driven up the Straits of Melaka by the northeast monsoon. Likewise, the traders from the Indonesian archipelago, with their crafts, spices and sandalwood. At the port, their cargo was exchanged for Indian and Middle Eastern cloth, carpets, glassware, iron and jewellery. When the winds changed, the southwest monsoon assisted the same vessels to return to their homes.

Taking note of this, the West decided that they should assume control of the hub of this lucrative trading operation, and Melaka's golden age came to an end when it fell in 1511 to the Portuguese. The port was theirs for more than 100 years, before they were ousted by the Dutch. After 150 years of occupation, the Dutch in turn ceded the land to the British.

Reflections of a river

Melaka's past is contained within its 1-km (½ mile) historic centre, easily covered on foot or by a leisurely trishaw ride through the narrow streets. The best place to begin your tour is right in the town centre, near the bridge built on the site the Portuguese made their final successful assault on the town. There you will find the helpful **Tourist Information Centre** (open daily 9am–4.30pm, tel: 06-281 4803), where you can get maps, brochures and also book the 45-minute river cruise up **Sungai Melaka**. At high tide, the boats depart hourly from 10am from the jetty behind the centre or the Heeren Street jetty on the opposite bank.

At the jetty are battered junks whose high bows and raised poop decks stir thoughts of their distant cousins who once brought Admiral Cheng Ho's dragon court entourage from China to Melaka centuries ago. These days, the labourers

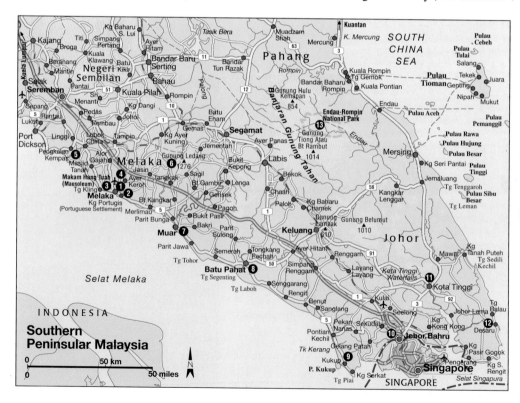

crossing the narrow gangplanks carry no exotic spices or silks, but instead lug the bulky sacks of charcoal that fire the aroma-filled kitchens of Melaka. The river cruise is quite enjoyable – if you ignore its now polluted waters – as it travels past century-old townhouses and warehouses, and ends in a traditional Malay village.

Maps:
Area 216
City 218

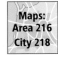

Dutch shapes

If you're hot-footing it, try and get hold of a map of the Heritage Trail, which takes you through the main sights. On the east riverbank is a neat little square with a clock tower, surrounded by terracotta-red buildings and a church. They are distinctly Dutch; you almost expect to see tulips rather than tropical blooms in the flower pots.

Facing what is sometimes known as the Red Square, is the **Stadthuys** Ⓐ (Town Hall). This building, constructed of incredibly thick walls and massive hardwood doors supported by studded, wrought-iron hinges, served as government offices for more than 300 years. Today, it houses the **History, Ethnography & Literature Museum** (open 9am–6pm daily except Mon; entrance fee) which tells the story of the city from the time it was an ancient Malay kingdom to the present. The museum's collections include old coins and stamps, Portuguese costumes from the 16th century, and old sepia photographs of Melaka life. The Stadthuys itself is an antiquity. Erected between 1641 and 1660, it is the oldest known Dutch building still standing in Asia. The handsome General Post Office on Jalan Laksamana is also of Dutch origin, and is now the **Youth Museum**.

On the embankment near the entrance to the Stadthuys is an ancient memorial whose significance has been lost in time. The stone fish with an elephant's head is believed to be a Hindu legacy predating even the Melakan sultanate.

Dutch-built Stadthuys or Town Hall dates back to 1660.

LEFT:
European-inspired architecture.
BELOW: Melaka River.

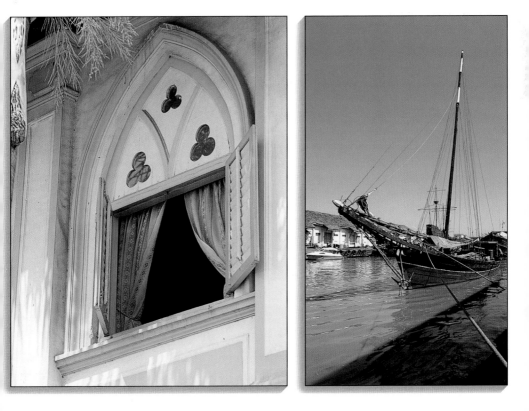

Perpendicular to the Stadthuys is the fabled **Christ Church B** whose bricks were shipped all the way from Holland. Melaka's masons then faced them with local red laterite. The church is full of old, engraved tombstones, many telling a grim tale about the hardships the early European settlers faced. The immense rafters within the nave were each carved from a single tree and above the altar a wooden crucifix hangs from the iron hoops fastened to the wall. When the church was first in use, it had no pulpit. The pastor would sit in a chair that had ropes running to the hoops. When the time came for him to deliver his sermon, his sextons would winch him halfway up the wall.

Outside the church is the century-old **Tan Beng Swee Clock Tower**, presented to the town by the wealthy Tan family. The small water fountain nearby was built to commemorate the Diamond Jubilee of Queen Victoria. Four white *kancil* (mousedeer) surround the fountain – a reminder of Melaka's origins.

Formidable fortress

The only remnants of original Portuguese architecture are on the slopes of St Paul's Hill, behind the square. When the Portuguese conquered Melaka, they were determined to make it one of the mightiest strongholds in the Orient. Hundreds of slaves and captives hauled stones from demolished mosques and elaborate tombs to build the **A Famosa** fortress.

The fortress eventually enclosed the entire hill, and withstood attacks for 150 years, until it was finally breached in 1641 by the Dutch after an 8-month siege. However, the Dutch did not find a rich and prosperous port of the fabulous East, as they had expected. The city they had struggled so hard to conquer lay in near-total ruins. The Dutch lost no time putting things in order, rebuilding the city with a Dutch flavour, and repairing the fortress and renaming the bastions. Melaka was soon a well-defended port once again.

Unfortunately, when the British occupied Melaka at the beginning of the 19th century, they decided to blow up the fortifications to prevent the Dutch from reclaiming it. The walls and gates were badly damaged and all that was left is what stands today: the **Porta de Santiago** ⓒ – a gate without a wall.

At the top of St Paul's Hill are more ruins. In 1521, a chapel, later renamed **St Paul's Church** ⓓ, was built by a Portuguese *fidalgo* to fulfil a vow he made on escaping death in the South China Sea. It was later taken over by the Jesuits, who completed the building and painted it white, so that it could serve as a guidepost for ships out on the Straits. The famous Jesuit missionary St Francis Xavier conducted mass in the church during his several visits to Melaka. After his death near Canton, his body was interred there for some months before being taken to Goa in India.

The Dutch discontinued services in St Paul's Church when their own Christ Church was built. However, the engraved tombstones that line the inside walls are testament to its continued use as a place of burial thereafter.

Mahmud's palace

At the bottom of the hill is an elaborate reconstruction of Sultan Mahmud's 15th-century wooden palace as described in the *Sejarah Melayu* (Malay Annals). This is the **Muzium Budaya** ⓔ (Melaka Cultural Museum; open daily 9am–6pm; entrance fee), which displays aspects of Melaka's royal culture, including clothing, weapons and furniture, as well as a diorama of the court . More museums lie around the west side of St Paul's Hill.

Map on page 218

The remains of Jesuit missionary St Francis Xavier were temporarily interred in Melaka's St Paul's Church after his death in 1552.

BELOW: what is left of the Portuguese A Famosa fort.

A Peranakan Townhouse

The front of the house is so decorative, it is like a heady visual perfume: brightly-coloured tiles, wooden shutters, large gold Chinese characters on the black signboard, and those elaborate doors. It is distinctly Oriental, but the floral plaster motifs look Western. And yet the whole is unified. This is the Peranakan townhouse.

Described as Chinese Palladian, the architectural style of these buildings of the Malaysian Straits Chinese is a unique meld of Victorian, Chinese and Malay. Lining the streets of Melaka's old town, they are also found in Penang's back streets and in selected nooks of Singapore. But the Melaka buildings are among the oldest townhouses in the country, dating back to the 17th century. Those along Jalan Tan Cheng Lock are particularly elaborate because they were status symbols for their affluent owners.

The houses have two sets of doors. The main wooden doors, with their intricately carved panels, are left open during the day to let air in. The second outer set, are swinging half-doors based on the Malay *pintu pagar* (literally, fence door). On either side are large square windows with vertical bars and sometimes shutters. Above the windows are air vents, which are sometimes decorated.

A Peranakan townhouse is much longer than its entrance suggests. In fact, it can be seven times longer than it is wide. The centrepiece of the main or reception hall is usually an altar, large and beautifully carved. More likely than not, the deity among the candles and burning joss-sticks would be the white-robed Kwan Yin, goddess of mercy, flanked by tall vases of fresh chrysanthemums which are replenished daily.

Twin arched entrances lead to the sitting room. The main furniture would usually be imported blackwood furniture inlaid with mother-of-pearl and marble. These are usually set against the walls, from where portraits of ancestors in gilded frames peer down.

Behind the sitting room is the dining room and, right at the back, the huge kitchen. In between would be one or more courtyards or air wells to let light into the otherwise dark house. The courtyards serve as indoor gardens with potted plants, a fountain, and a well or large ornate jar filled with water.

The bedrooms sit upstairs at the top of a wooden staircase with balusters. The rooms and bathrooms are capacious and carry through the elements of carved lacquered wood, embroidery, and porcelain. Sometimes, the bedrooms have windows that open into the landing, complete with shutters.

Many of these houses are being restored for commercial purposes. In the process, however, many traditional tradesmen have been evicted, and the quality of the restoration work has sometimes been compromised in the pursuit of making a fast buck. The best preserved is probably the Baba-Nyonya Heritage Museum on Jalan Tun Tan Cheng Lock. Others have been converted into hotels or restaurants, dishing up Nyonya food with varying degrees of success or else selling tourist trinkets. ❑

LEFT: the ancestral altar is often the focal point of a traditional Peranakan home.

The **Proclamation of Independence Memorial** ⑥ (open daily 9am–6pm; closed Monday) is housed in the former Malacca Club House, a 1911 Dutch building which was the centre of British colonial social life. Its displays chart Malaysia's campaign for independence, including historic documents, films and artefacts. An obelisk outside commemorates British soldiers killed in the Naning War, a farcical affair in the early 1830s, which took two military expeditions over two years to subdue Penghulu Dol Said, the defiant chief of the principality of Naning. The local hero is commemorated at his birthplace (*see page 226*).

The museums face the **Padang** (town green) where Tunku Abdul Rahman first announced Malaya's independence from British rule. Today, it is the scene of a nightly sound-and-light show that recounts the history of Melaka. It also serves as the "walking track" for traditional Melaka bullock carts (RM1 per person). Beside the *padang*, a lane flanked by handicraft stalls leads to a row of foodstalls across from the huge Mahkota Parade shopping mall. Between the park and the river is the disappointing **Melaka Maritime Museum** (open daily 9am–9pm). Its contents are mainly artefacts gleaned from shipwrecks in the Melaka Strait.

Antique streets

Head back to the bridge near the Red Square, and cross over to a completely different experience. The west bank has always been the main centre of Melaka's shopping and business activities; a maze of ancient and narrow streets. **Jalan Tun Tan Cheng Lock** – called Heeren Street by the Dutch – is named after a leading Baba politician and architect. His family house and the palatial townhouses of several other prominent Chinese families line the street, flaunting Peranakan tiles and carved wooden doors. The street is extremely narrow so watch out for traffic; for safety, walk towards rather than against the flow of traffic. At No. 48–50 is the fascinating **Baba Nyonya Heritage Museum** ⑥ (open daily 10am–12.30pm and 2–4pm; entrance fee), where you can explore the unique interior of a typical Peranakan house. The family which owns the house gives guided tours and can tell fascinating stories about some of the architecture and curios, including blackwood tables and chairs from China and the sumptuous traditional wedding costumes.

Parallel to this road is Jalan Hang Jebat, better-known as **Jonker Street**, Melaka's main tourist drag. This once-elegant street filled with quaint Peranakan homes, age-old crafts and trades like acupuncturists, herbalists and wooden clog makers, and Chinese clan associations has lost some of its charm in recent years – thanks to the proliferation of tacky souvenir shops, karaoke lounges and restaurants.

Still, if you search hard enough, you will find what Jonker Street is most famous for – antiques. There are heavy brass irons with receptacles for hot coals, wooden bullock carts, ornate oil lamps, Peranakan-style furniture inlaid with mother of pearl, opium beds and altar stands, Victorian clocks and early gramophones, brass urns and marble statues, silver trinkets and Chinese wedding beds, as well as rare stamps and coins, and Malay *keris* (daggers).

On yet another parallel road, **Jalan Tokong**, are three

Map on page 218

Detail from an ornate wall tile of a typical Peranakan house. Antique tiles such as these are on sale at Melaka's Jonker Street.

BELOW: frontage of a Peranakan-style house.

Kuih lapis, a multi-coloured Peranakan dessert made of rice flour, coconut cream and sugar.

of the oldest places of worship in Malaysia. **Cheng Hoon Teng Temple** , or Temple of Bright Clouds was founded in 1645 and is the oldest Chinese temple in Malaysia. It was originally built by a fugitive from the Manchu conquest, and was later restored by local Chinese leaders. The temple is dedicated to three deities: the main altar to Kuan Yin, the goddess of mercy, and the others to Kwan Ti (also known as Kwan Kung), the god of war who "triples" up as the patron saint of wealth and tradesmen; and Ma Choe Poh, the Queen of Heaven. Look up and you will see the carved roof, ridges and eaves elegantly decorated with Chinese mythical figures – animals, birds and flowers, of coloured glass and porcelain. Step through the massive hardwood gates, and you feel you are stepping back several centuries. Among the wood carvings and lacquerwork within is a stone inscription commemorating Admiral Cheng Ho's visit to Melaka in 1406.

Mosques and temples

Along the same road, now called Jalan Tukang Emas, is the **Masjid Kampung Kling** (Kampung Kling Mosque), the town's oldest mosque, built in 1748. It sports a typical Sumatran design, with a three-tiered roof and rather Chinese-like minaret. This style is characteristic of Melakan mosques. (Another good example is the mosque in Tranquerah, 2 km (1 mile) away.) The cemetery encloses the tomb of Sultan Husain of Johor, who ceded Singapore to Sir Stamford Raffles in 1819.

Nearby is the **Sri Poyyatha Vinayagar Moorthi Temple**, built in the 1780s by the Hindu community of Melaka. The country's oldest Hindu temple, it is dedicated to Vinayagar or Ganesh, the Elephant God, one of the most popular deities among Malaysian devotees.

BELOW: Antique Peranakan silver belt.

Map on page 218

A princess's legacy

There is another historical hill, a little away from the historic centre – which houses 12,000 graves. Hills are auspicious burial grounds, according to the principles of *feng shui* (Chinese geomancy), for they block evil winds and offer the spirits of the ancestors a good view over their descendants. But while most names and dates on the tombstones on **Bukit Cina** Ⓚ (China Hill) have been eroded, what remains eternal is the legacy of a Ming princess.

When Sultan Mansur Shah was in power, he carried on a diplomatic war of wits with the Emperor of China, which grew to be legendary. Around 1460, a Chinese ship sailed into Melaka's port. The entire interior of the vessel was delicately pinned with gold needles, and the message to the sultan read: "For every gold needle, I have a subject; if you could count their number, then you would know my power."

The sultan was impressed. He sent back a ship stuffed with bags of sago and the message: "If you can count the grains of sago on this ship you will have guessed the number of my subjects correctly, and you will know my power." This so moved the Chinese emperor that he sent his daughter Hang Li Poh, to marry the sultan. She arrived with no less than 500 ladies-in-waiting. The sultan gave them "the hill without the town" as a private residence and promised that the land they occupied would never be taken away from them. To this day, Bukit Cina belongs to Melaka's Chinese community. Several of the graves on Bukit Cina date back to the Ming dynasty and are among the oldest Chinese relics in Malaysia.

The princess's followers built a well at the foot of the hill, whose waters soon became as legendary as her marriage contract. After Admiral Cheng Ho drank from the well, its water attained an extraordinary purity. It never dried up, even during the most severe drought, and many believed that if a visitor drank from it he would return to Melaka before he died. Now the **Perigi Rajah** (Sultan's Well) is protected by wire mesh. It has still not dried up and is as pure as ever. Many young Chinese still come to see the landmark and snap some pictures.

Head northwest from here to get to Jalan Bendahara and **St Peter's Church** Ⓛ. The church was built in 1710 by the descendants of Portuguese soldiers given amnesty by the Dutch when the Portuguese garrison was forced into submission.

Today, except for the occasional wedding or funeral, not much goes on at the church. However, on Easter weekends, Melaka-born Catholics try to return to their hometown to attend the mass at St Peter's. On Good Friday itself, thousands of people – Chinese, Eurasian and Indian – take part in a candlelit procession. A life-sized statue of Christ, crowned with thorns and draped in deep purple robes with gold embroidery, is solemnly borne above the devout Catholic congregation. The churchyard becomes a sea of flames from the lighted candles, accompanied by the mournful sound of hymns. After the solemnity of the mass, the crowds gather outside the church to catch up with friends, and children in their Sunday best romp around the lawns.

BELOW: painted temple door, Melaka.

The Portuguese today

The legacy the Portuguese left behind is of far greater significance than mere ruins like the A Famosa fort. "I gave to each man his horse, a house, and land," wrote Alfonso d'Albuquerque in 1604, when he reported with pride to Portugal that 200 mixed marriages had taken place.

On direct orders from the king, d'Albuquerque encouraged the garrison's men to marry local women. Such intermarriages flourished and soon women were even sent out from Portugal to marry local men. The Portuguese were instructed to treat local people as equals; d'Albuquerque himself would courteously escort local women to their seats in church, as though they were members of the nobility.

Therefore, the descendants of Sequiera, Aranjo, Dias, d'Silva and d'Souza remained loyal to Portugal through blood ties and religion. After 400 years, a number of Portuguese Eurasians in Melaka still continue to speak Cristao, a medieval southeastern Portuguese dialect spoken nowhere else now.

At the **Portuguese Settlement** ❷ (Kampung Portugis), 3 km (2 miles) from Melaka's centre, near the beach, there's a community of about 500 Eurasians, mostly fishermen. Their unpretentious dwellings resemble Malay kampung houses with wooden walls and tin roofs, in soft hues of blue and green.

There is little of commercial tourist value here, except for restaurants that serve Portuguese food and cultural performances on Saturdays. But linger and you just might meet young boys who sing beautiful ballads in Portuguese; their sisters could well show you a dance which their grandmother was taught by her grandmother; and an old man at a fruit stall might tell tales about a secluded tunnel from St John's Fort to St Paul's Hill, in which the Portuguese hid all their treasures before the Dutch overran Melaka.

Some of the best places to meet local people are in the open-air cafés around **Portuguese Square** (Medan Portugis), which serve spicy seafood dishes and ice-cold beer.

Local customs

Each year in June, at the Festa de San Pedro, the fishermen decorate their boats with bunting and sacred texts. An open-air mass is conducted and after the boats have been blessed, the evening is spent in merrymaking. Another unusual custom called Intrudu (Introductions) is celebrated on the Sunday preceding Ash Wednesday, when the residents wear fancy costumes and throw water over one another. Even those at home are not spared. The merrymakers make a point of visiting their friends at home, and drenching them with water as soon as they open their doors. To show there are no hard feelings, they are then invited in for refreshments. Later in the day, men dress up as ladies and the ladies dress as men, and go around selling cakes and fruits.

Beyond Melaka town, paddy fields stretch into the low hills and numerous side roads cut through groves of rubber and fruit trees, and past peaceful villages and compact market towns. Traditional Malay houses, with curving gables, carved eaves, wide-fronted verandahs and tiled entrance steps are commonplace

BELOW: Dutch relic from Melaka's early days.

all the way from Tanjung Kling in the north to Merlimau in the south. The house of the Penghulu (chief) of **Kampung Merlimau** is particularly fine specimen of this architecture, boasting delicate wood carvings and art nouveau tiles. It is sometimes open to visitors if the owners are in the mood.

Tanjung Kling, about 10 km (6 miles) from Melaka, has a resort but beach-lovers are not advised to flock to it. You'll find some luxury, resort-style condominiums here, but the sea is not very clean and is sometimes infested with jellyfish. The northern beach of Tanjung Bidara suffers similar problems. However, the seafood is generally good, particularly at Klebang Besar and further north at Pantai Kundor.

Between Tanjung Kling and Pantai Kundor is **Hang Tuah's Mausoleum ❸** (Makam Hang Tuah). Hang Tuah was a local Malay hero of legendary stature who, even till today, epitomises a subject's absolute loyalty to the ruler. He led a band of brave and noble warriors – who were also childhood friends – in the court of Sultan Mansur Shah. However, Tuah was unfairly disgraced over the sultan's consort by a jealous rival and banished from the court. His most loyal friend, Hang Jebat, went amok at this injustice and created havoc throughout the sultanate. Tuah returned, and, though torn apart by the dilemma, killed Jebat on the sultan's command. Jebat's mausoleum lies in Jalan Tukang Kuli.

This classic tale, known to every child, is at the heart of the Malay psyche. The warriors have also been immortalised in books, drama, and in 1998, Malaysia's first home-grown animated movie. Tuah's soul – some say in the form of a crocodile – is believed to reside in a well in Kampung Duyong. The waters of the well are reputed to have medicinal value, and bring good luck to those who drink at it.

Map on page 216

A Eurasian couple decked out in Portuguese costume for a cultural event.

BELOW: Portuguese descendants still speak Cristao, an antiquated dialect.

Map on page 216

Zoos and clubs

Visitors entering Melaka town from the North-South Highway may choose to come in through **Ayer Keroh ❹**, about 12 km (8 miles) from the city. At the Air Keroh Recreational Forest, 70 hectares (170 acres) of jungle have been tamed to provide walks, deer reserves, picnicking spots and camping sites.

Numerous "tourist attractions" are spread along the road, some typical, others not so typical: a butterfly park, a crocodile farm, a fish world, a tennis centre, a *feng shui* (geomancy) garden, and a huge water theme park with rides. There is also a **Taman Mini Malaysia** (Mini-Malaysia Complex), which features model houses representing the traditional architecture of the various states, along with cultural and entertainment programmes. Next door is a mini-ASEAN, a similar park showcasing the architecture of the countries in this 10-nation Association of Southeast Asia Nations grouping. Nearby are the Melaka Zoo and A'Famosa Resort, with recreational and leisure facilities. Several good golf courses dot the area, a result of the huge growth in interest in the sport in recent years.

The old road to Seremban and Kuala Lumpur goes through the district of Alor Gajah and passes **Naning**, the principality whose chieftain defied the British in the 19th century. Dato' Dol Said now rests in his tomb by the roadside. Near his grave and around this area are some 90 mysterious stone megaliths called *batu hidup*, translated as "living stones" because of the belief that they grow. In fact, stones like these can be found scattered throughout the neighbouring state of Negeri Sembilan as well, with a famous cluster at **Pengkalan Kempas ❺** just across the Sungai Linggi border. Some carry Islamic inscriptions, while others act as gravestones, yet others simply offer no explanation as to their origin or purpose.   ❑

BELOW: a Melakan bullock cart with a creative touch.

Minangkabau of Negeri Sembilan

The sweeping, peaked-roofed "buffalo horn" architecture is the most distinguishing feature of the Minangkabau culture of **Negeri Sembilan**, Melaka's northern neighbour. It appears everywhere; in the National Museum in Kuala Lumpur, at luxury hotels fringed by swaying palms, even at a petrol station at a highway lay-by. The roofs have come to signify not just Minangkabau, but Malay and Malaysian.

It is indeed a proud tribute to the heritage of a group of Malay settlers from west Sumatra who first made their new home in the fertile valleys and hills behind Melaka, attracted, as was the world, by the port's remarkable success. They brought with them their style of architecture and, protected by the Malay sultans, continued adhering to the *adat pepatih* customs which govern laws, political organisation, traditions, and social systems.

The small principalities founded by the original settlers formed the nine *luak* or states that became the federation of Negeri Sembilan. Today, although the modern state is divided into districts, the *luak* remain. However, the violent clashes over tin that resulted in British intervention in the 1800s reduced the number of *luak* to five.

Negeri Sembilan's ruler is not a sultan but a Yam Tuan Besar or Yang Di Pertuan Besar (translated as "He Who is Greatest"), who resides in Sri Menanti, 30 km (18 miles) from the administrative capital, Seremban.

Minangkabau culture and history is housed at the **Teratak Perpatih** (State Museum) within the grounds of the **Taman Seni Budaya** (Cultural Handicraft Complex) at the Seremban/Labu exit off the Kuala Lumpur-Seremban Highway. The museum's main building is a 19th-century palace from Kampung Ampang Tinggi that has been carefully reconstructed here. The museum showcases a fine display of ceremonial *keris* (daggers), Bugis and Minangkabau swords, and royal ornaments. Next door is the **Rumah Minang-kabau**, another fine piece of Minangkabau architecture. Unlike the palace's attap roof, the Rumah Minangkabau has a cover of wooden shingles. The main building has handicraft displays and weekly cultural performances such as the *tarian piring* (plate dance) and *dikir rebana* (drumming).

Green hills and landscaped gardens provide the setting for the beautiful **Museum Diraja Sri Menanti** (Royal Museum of Sri Menanti) in the royal capital. A former palace, it was built in 1903 without a single nail. The timber structure sits on 99 pillars, representing the warriors of the various *luak*. It ceased to be a royal residence in 1931, when a new palace was completed in the shape of the blue-tiled **Istana Besar** nearby.

The great, sweeping roofs of the Istana prove to be the crowning glory of the otherwise featureless state capital of Seremban. A fine contemporary use of that traditional style, the **State Legislative Assembly Building** houses various government departments. Opposite it is a gem of neo-classical architecture, the **State Library**. ❑

RIGHT: great sweeping roofs typify traditional Minangkabau architecture.

JOHOR

Its proximity to Singapore makes the state's capital and resorts a favourite with visitors from the island nation; but leave the bustle behind, and you'll find some of the most beautiful habitats on earth

Map on page 216

Beware the Causeway Clog that heads daily south from Johor Bahru, the capital of Malaysia's southernmost state, into Singapore. On weekdays, the 1-km (⅔-mile) road and rail link between the two countries is filled with thousands of Johoreans commuting to their jobs in the Lion City by bus, car, motorbike and on foot. The bottleneck is reversed on weekends, when Singaporeans flock to Johor to take advantage of the lower ringgit to shop, party, and relax in its waterfall, beach and island resorts. Thankfully, the building of a second bridge to the west of Johor Bahru to Singapore, called Second Link, has alleviated some of the weekend traffic jams at the causeway.

It is a symbiotic relationship extended to investments as well, fuelling Johor's development and making prices in its capital and in the Singaporeans' favourite haunts among the highest in the peninsula. Still, Johor has not lost its agricultural roots, with its hinterland almost completely covered with oil palm, rubber and pineapple plantations amid virgin rainforest .

Johor evolved its own identity after the fall of the Melaka sultanate to the Portuguese in the 16th century. The last ruler, Sultan Mahmud, fled to Johor and turned it into a powerful trading empire. Its old capitals along the protected reaches of the Johor River were moved to the Riau archipelago, making them more accessible to trade – and attacks. Johor not only had to fend off the Portuguese, and the Dutch, but also the Acehnese in Sumatra, and later, the Bugis, losing Singapore to the British in 1819.

A turning point

At the end of the 1800s, Johor was the fiefdom of a *temenggung*, an official of the sultan. Abu Bakar, who became *temenggung* in 1862, elevated himself to maharaja, and in 1885 was acknowledged by Britain as Sultan of Johor. Sultan Abu Bakar was educated in Singapore by English clergy. He spoke fluent English and cultivated ties with influential Europeans in the business world. Under his rule, the foundations of modern Johor were laid. In 1866, he moved his capital to Johor Bahru, transforming it into a thriving new town.

The sultan used western methods of policy-making and administration, introduced a modern bureaucracy and gave Johor the first constitution written for a Malay state. Thus he was able to defer the appointment of a British "advisor" to help him rule his state. He maintained good relations with Englishmen in Singapore and London, and was the first Malay ruler to visit England, becoming a personal friend of Queen Victoria. Johor was therefore the last Malay state in the peninsula to come under direct British control.

Johor Malays are of mainly Javanese descent, and known for *kuda kepang*, a dance set to gamelan music.

LEFT: Johor Bahru skyline across the causeway from Singapore.
BELOW: waiting for the school bus.

Waterfalls and tombs

The North-South Highway stretch from Kuala Lumpur to Singapore is a boring, flat, ruler-straight road which encourages the tendency to speed or doze. Entering the state from Melaka on the highway, a turnoff at Tangkak towards Segamat leads to **Gunung Ledang** ❻ (Mount Ophir). While popular with hikers, they unfortunately often leave the mountain litter-strewn. Here, Sagil Falls tumbles off the 1,276-metre (4,186-ft) peak into clear pools below. Ledang has a legend attached to it of a magical princess who finally thwarted the attention of a persistent Sultan Mansur by demanding a cup of his son's blood.

The right turnoff from Tangkak goes to **Muar** ❼, considered a cultural centre for *ghazal* music and *kuda kepang* dances. Sited at a river mouth, Muar is a pretty town with neo-classical government buildings, traditional Malay houses and a pleasant tree-lined walk along the river at Tanjung.

Back on the North-South Highway, a left turnoff further south leads to **Pagoh**, home to the tombs of two Melaka sultans, and **Kampung Parit Pecah** in which stand the 99 graves of an entire village, wiped out – according to legend – by a single spear about 500 years ago. The spear was supposedly tossed by a jealous lover into the chest of a bridegroom at his wedding, removed and tossed again, eventually killing everyone, including the bride.

The highway leads on to **Ayer Hitam**, a popular stopover with coffee shops and rows of street stalls heavily laden with souvenirs, *durian* cakes, peanut nougat and other local produce as well as fresh and preserved fruits.

BELOW:
colourful Aw pottery
in Ayer Hitam.

Half hidden by the stalls is the Claycraft Coffee House, where patrons sit on stoneware stools and drink out of dainty ceramic tea cups; the other half of the tables is crowded with arty relics. There is more pottery south in a village called Machap, including the famous **Aw Potteries** behind whose Minangkabau-style showroom is the studio where you can watch craftsmen at work.

From Ayer Hitam the road to the coast ends at **Batu Pahat** ❽. This is Johor's other Malay cultural heartland, not that this is reflected in its faceless urbanity. However, Batu Pahat is home to one of the last few genuine *kuda kepang* troupes. The town is more notorious for its floods at high tide, but is also known for its cheap and good Chinese food.

A more scenic way to get to Batu Pahat is via the coastal road from Muar. The road goes through little *kampung* and orchards whose goodies are heaped upon roadside stalls during the fruiting season. This road meanders past vast pineapple plantations, and finally ends in a Chinese village raised on stilts above the water. This is **Kukup** ❾, which prides itself as being the southernmost town of the Malay Peninsula, and indeed the Asian continent. Late afternoon is the ideal time to arrive in Kukup, when the sun is low over the sea and the evening breezes begin. However, it is not to watch the sunset that the hordes descend on Kukup, especially from Singapore. It is to eat chilli crabs, for which Kukup is justifiably famous. The restaurants do not have fancy decor – and some do not even have walls – but they do have atmosphere and great food, if you care to look past the unsanitary toilets. There is a golf resort here and hotels in town.

Abu Bakar's legacy

The best-known place in **Johor Bahru** ❿ is probably its immigration point leading to Singapore. Johor also has a less crowded 2-km (1-mile) second link to the island nation at Tanjung Kupang and ferry connections at Tanjung Belungkor and Kukup.

Downtown JB (as the city is known) seems unaffected by the economic downturn, with new air-conditioned shopping malls and high-rise buildings taking shape by the day. Remnants of old Johor can be found behind **Jalan Ibrahim** in old shophouses where Chinese and Indian traders sell everything from spices and joss sticks to tailored suits and the latest colour TVs. Scattered among the shops are cheap Chinese restaurants and Indian cafés specialising in the popular South Indian banana leaf rice and *roti canai* (Indian bread).

Nearby, along Jalan Terus, are the elaborate Rajamariamman Kovil Hindu temple and a Chinese Taoist shrine. At the crest of the nearby hill is the gleaming white spire of St Joseph's Catholic Church. The old colonial train station is in this neighbourhood too.

The State Secretariat Building, **Bangunan Sultan Ibrahim** crowns the top of Bukit Timbalan. A huge Saracen-style building with arches, columns and enclosed stone balconies, it bears a gold seal of the State of Johor on its massive front doors.

The impressive building further down the waterfront and overlooking the Johor Straits is the **Istana Besar** (Grand Palace). Formerly the residence of Sultan Abu Bakar, the stark, white structure with sweeping lawns was commissioned in 1864. It has, over the last century, hosted royalty such as the Duke of Edinburgh (Queen Victoria's son), Archduke Franz Ferdinand of Austria

Ice-cold lime juice is the perfect accompaniment to spicy South Indian fare served on banana leaves.

BELOW:
a spice merchant
in Johor Bahru.

TIP

If travelling to Kukup
from Singapore, avoid
the traffic jam on the
causeway by taking
the ferry from Tuas to
the Kukup pier.

(whose assassination sparked World War I) and the future King Edward VIII of England (who abdicated to marry Wallis Simpson).

Although it remains in royal hands, the palace was opened to the public in 1991 as a museum dedicated to the golden age of Johor. The **Royal Abu Bakar Museum** (open daily 9am–6pm; entrance fee) is rather reminiscent of visiting the aristocratic homes of rural England, and there is no other museum in Southeast Asia quite like it.

The *dewan* (audience hall) is now a gallery detailing the history of the Johor sultanate, while the Grand Palace itself is crammed with antiques and strange knickknacks. The four-poster teak beds in the state bedrooms have British-made Corinthian-style columns dating to the 1860s. The bedrooms are still used for the lying-in-state of deceased members of the royal family. Down the hall is the opulent Reception Room, with a Baccarat crystal table and chairs. The Throne Room, with its matching gilt thrones, is used each year for investiture ceremonies on the sultan's birthday. The opulence of the Banqueting Room has to be seen to be believed.

The surrounding **Istana Gardens** has rolling parkland, immaculate lawns and several flower gardens, while just uphill from the Dewan is a Japanese garden and tea house presented by Crown Prince Hirohito on his state visit to Malaysia in 1936. Within the grounds' handicraft centre sits Mawar House, a carefully restored traditional Johor Malay house.

The next landmark along the waterfront is the **Masjid Sultan Abu Bakar** (Sultan Abu Bakar Mosque), completed in 1900. A bizarre blend of Italian rococo, classical Greek and traditional Muslim styles, the interior is decorated with Corinthian columns, crystal chandeliers and Oriental carpets. At the front

BELOW:
modern mosque
architecture, Johor.

Map on page 216

of the main hall are a fabulously ornate gilt *minbar* (pulpit) and an ancient grandfather clock. Hawkers frequent the mosque grounds selling prayer rugs, velour wall hangings and other souvenirs.

Much further along the waterfront is **Istana Bukit Serene**, home of the present ruler. The huge Art Deco-style complex is off limits to the public, but you can get a good view of the palace from Jalan Sekudai along the waterfront or Jalan Straits View. Its expansive grounds contain a private air strip, a huge satellite dish, an orchid garden and a menagerie.

Nightlife draws many customers from Singapore, attracted by cheaper drinks and a relatively more "liberal" atmosphere, although the JB town council attempts to crack down on less salubrious spots from time to time. Still, the city has numerous nightclubs, discos, hostess clubs and karaoke lounges.

Golf and thundering falls

Back in the early 1990s, at the start of the golf boom, Johor took to developing resorts by the dozen. It therefore boasts the largest number of courses in the country. The best known include the 18-hole Royal Johor Country Club, Desaru Country Club and Palm Resort Country Club, not far from Senai Airport.

Many of these golf and country resorts are in the **Kota Tinggi ⑪** area. Kota Tinggi is a small, quiet town with a loud splash. About 15 km (9 miles) north-east of the town are its famous waterfalls (entrance fee), the bottom-most section of which thunders down 36 metres (118 ft) to the polished rocks below. The entire area is cemented and steps lead up to the third and highest tier. Weekends find the large natural pools and surrounding tree-rooted slopes commandeered by the locals. Chalet-type accommodation and Malay hawker food is available.

From Kota Tinggi, a trunk road goes south through fruit stalls and golf resorts to the golden beaches of **Desaru ⑫**, which is practically a Singapore resort. Many Singaporean visitors travel via the ferry between Tanjung Belungkor, 60 km (37 miles) from Desaru, and Changi Point in Singapore. There is a service four times a day between 9am–6pm, and the ferries carry vehicles too. The big hotels at Desaru provide transfers to the ferry terminal for a fee.

Thanks to free-spending Singaporeans, accommodation in Desaru is expensive – even the no-frills chalets. However, there is a good variety, from a theme park-type 700-roomer to a golf resort and camping grounds, all sandwiched between the beach and forest. Because there is little more than a go-kart circuit at Desaru – not least the absence of the normally ubiquitous *warung* (food stalls) – resorts provide the gamut of activities from watersports to mountain bikes and racquet games.

However, there are interesting side trips from Desaru. About half-an-hour away on the Kota Tinggi road is a turnoff that goes through an oil palm plantation to **Johor Lama** (old Johor) on Sungai Johor. This was once a great trading centre and royal capital, boasting one of the most powerful forts in the area, and probably the peninsula's largest. Today, however, Johor Lama is a sleepy village, and only grassed-over massive ramparts remain of the old fort.

BELOW:
golf is a favourite activity in Desaru.

Tanjung Balau, 5 km (3 miles) from Desaru, has an excellent fishing museum (open 9am–5pm; entrance fee) which charts the industry's history, traditions and methods, and includes displays of traditional boats. The museum fronts a firm, white sandy beach, and the *kampung* has new chalet-type accommodation. Seafood buffs should not miss out on the excellent Chinese-style delicacies at **Sungai Rengit**, 25 km (16 miles) south.

Endau-Rompin National Park in Johor is home to 71 palm species, which comprises 18 percent of Malaysia's palms – all indigenous – and more than 50 percent of its rattan varieties.

Land of palms

The road from Ayer Hitam to Mersing cuts across the state's rainforest heart, 20,000 hectares (49,000 acres) of which are the Johor section of the **Endau-Rompin National Park** ⓭. Named after the Endau and Rompin rivers, the park forms the southern end of the peninsula's wildlife corridor that stretches through Taman Negara up to Belum on the Thai border.

A fine example of ancient virgin lowland forest, the park's gems are its extensive palm forests, pebbly beaches and large rivers of amazing clarity whose headwaters plunge into cascades and waterfalls. A conservation area, it is being developed by the Johor Park Corporation in consultation with the Malaysian Nature Society (MNS). There are chalets and dormitories at the Staging Point (open 8am–5pm), and four campsites within the park.

The **Johor Tourism Centre** (JOTIC; tel: 07-222 3591) has comprehensive information on the park, and travel agencies run tours from there, Kuantan, Kuala Lumpur and Johor Bahru. Johor Parks can arrange boat transfers from the Felda Nita jetty, 25 km (16 miles) from Mersing, as well as accommodation at the Staging Point and Orang Asli guides into the park. They also rent out camping equipment, but food has to be bought outside.

BELOW: gigantic umbrella palm at Endau Rompin.

The boat ride from Felda Nita takes about 2 hours; at the Staging Point, you need to register, get your entry permit and pay park fees (including camera fees and insurance). The largest base camp is **Kuala Jasin**, 7 km (4 miles) away, accessible on foot or by boat. Sited at the Jasin-Endau river confluence, it has great swimming areas, including a 8,000-sq. metre (78,000-sq. ft) pool. There are hornbills at dawn, and you can observe deer and monkeys from a hide.

The **Janing Ridge** trek can be accessed from here: a steep climb to an amazing palm forest. The trail from Kuala Jasin goes all the way to the park's star attraction, the Buaya Sangkut waterfalls, and is a 6-hour, 8 km (5 mile) trek. The first bit is fairly flat, going through riparian (river) vegetation, with some waist-deep rope-aided river-crossings, but the later stages involve some steep stretches. Most people camp at the end of the flat section at Batu Hampar, tackling Buaya Sangkut the next morning.

En route to Batu Hampar are two base camps. **Kuala Marong** overlooks the still, clear Sungai Marong, whose waters were at one time the purest of any river studied in Malaysia. A side trail goes to **Tasik Air Biru**, better known as Blue Lagoon, a deep shady pool that makes for a refreshing swim.

The falls at the **Upeh Guling** base camp has remarkable "bath-tub" formations at the top of rocks, probably formed when pebbles lodged in crevices

Map on page 216

were spun round by flowing water. There is also a tiny island here, Pulau Jasin, which enjoys a remarkable diversity of plants, including wild orchids and four species of the carnivorous pitcher plant.

Batu Hampar also has playful cascades and huge sun-baked boulders. From here, a steep ascent kicks off the section to Buaya Sangkut, and the undulating trail goes through changing vegetation, including the peaty *kerangas* forest, usually found only in lowlands. The umbrella palms, whose leaves reach 4 metres (12 ft) in length, just get bigger and bigger. The leaves function as roofs for the huts at Batu Hampar, fashioned using Orang Asli techniques. Incidentally, the umbrella palm leaf really does work as an umbrella in a downpour!

There is an alternative trail that climbs the final hill – this is actually part of Janing Ridge, and therefore covered by thick palm forest, mainly the indigenous *Livistona endauensis* fan palms.

White crocodile

At the 40-metre (130-ft) **Buaya Sangkut Falls**, seemingly static pools of water tumble down into rugged boulders, the most spectacular being the lowest of the three-step falls. The falls, first sighted on a helicopter reconnaissance of the park, has a charming Orang Asli legend to it, as do many of the sights. Translating as "stuck crocodile", the reptile in question was a mythical albino that had died in battle with a snake, and whose carcass got caught in the falls. The battle was over the hand of a lass of immense beauty, whose father made a drum of the croc's skin. Unfortunately, he hung it over his daughter's bed, and one night, it fell and killed her. Some say the rocks at a certain point at the waterfall's top-most level bear a striking resemblance to a crocodile. ❑

Come nighfall, look out for fluorescent forest mushrooms in Endau Rompin National Park.

BELOW: Wagler's pit viper, Endau Rompin reserve.

THE PENINSULA'S EAST COAST

A world away from its brash western brother, the rural east coast is picture-postcard Malaysia: traditional and unhurried

If ever a mountain divided a land, the peninsula's Banjaran Titiwangsa (Main Range) has, isolating the peninsula's east coast from the progressive west coast. As such, it has retained its rich cultural identity through the ages, despite the ravages of satellite TV. And while it remains economically less advanced, it is also relatively buffered from west coast financial and environmental woes.

Embracing the states of Kelantan, Terengganu and Pahang and the eastern half of Johor, the east coast is as indisputably Malay as it is proudly rural – particularly in the staunchly Muslim north. Local dress dominates, especially among the women who are like colourful butterflies in their batik *tudung* (head-scarfs) and *baju kurung* (Malay dress). Local dialects reign, so that even west coast speakers of Bahasa Malaysia find it difficult to follow a conversation.

The economy remains rooted in fishing and rice cultivation, as it has been for generations. Traditional implements have been replaced by newer, larger, faster models, but the boats of Kelantan, for one, are still splendidly decorated. The fishing industry is celebrated in various museums, themselves fine examples of Malay architecture.

The coastline is a continuous broad beach that invites you to jump into the sea at virtually any point. Here sit peaceful, timeless villages, palms bending out over a bright blue sea, while islands beckon from the hazy horizon. The most pristine beaches of tropical paradise ilk are found on the islands. Here, the shallow waters are the clearest in the peninsula, lapping gently on white sand or crashing against giant boulders.

Underwater, the colourful landscapes are fascinating, and the diversity of life staggering. The east coast islands make up the majority of Malaysia's 38 marine parks, which protect fragile and important habitats.

As noisy as any big city is the cacophony of insect noises, bird calls and animal cries in the rainforest interiors of the east coast. Among the world's oldest ecosystems, the million-year-old forests make up conservation and tourism sites such as Taman Negara, the oldest national park in the peninsula, and the freshwater wetland of Bera, where the indigenous Orang Asli maintain their lifestyles, so closely intertwined with the ways of the land. ❑

PRECEDING PAGES: river tributary just metres away from the sun-drenched shores of Malaysia's east coast.
LEFT: teeing off at Tioman island.

Eastern Peninsular Malaysia

SOUTH CHINA

SEA

Peninsular
Malaysia

MERSING AND ISLES

With long sandy beaches, unpretentious resorts, crystal-clear waters and beautiful coral reefs, these South China Sea islands achieve the difficult feat of being both popular and unspoilt

Map on page 240

Whoever planned **Mersing** ❶ knew how to make the most of her views. Seen from the coast-hugging roads of this bustling fishing and jump-off port, its postcard vistas of the offshore island silhouettes have brought it considerable fame. Despite lost-looking beach-seekers at the jetty, Mersing itself retains its peaceful small-town character.

You need a car to enjoy the winding evening drives to **Kampung Sri Lalang** en route to Endau north of town (turn right just after the bridge), and through **Teluk Iskandar** on the Sekakap road (turn right at Jalan Nong Yahya opposite the hospital). There are no beaches for swimming, but lookout points and hotel rooms overlooking the sea almost make up for it.

On public holidays, Mersing's mini stadium sometimes plays host to the *kuda kepang* performance, a Javanese trance dance set to *gamelan* music and seldom seen outside Johor. Call the **Johor Tourism Centre** (JOTIC; open Mon–Fri 8am–4.30pm, Sat 8am–2.30pm; tel: 07-222 3591) for details.

Because of its proximity to the area, Mersing is becoming a reference point for tours to the Endau-Rompin National Park (*see Johor chapter, page 229*). More accessible, and popular with locals are the recreational forests of **Gunung Belumut** and **Gunung Lambak**, inland from Mersing along Route 50. The former rises up to 1,004 metres (3,290 ft) and it takes about four hours along dense jungle tracks to reach the peak. At the base are some small waterfalls, which are easily accessible by families. Gunung Lambak is an easier climb up to 510 metres (1,670 ft) using trails of footpaths and wooden bridges. It also has pretty cascades.

However, the South China Sea islands are the prime objective of the madding crowd. Over 60 volcanic isles in crystal-clear waters make up the Johor group, six of which have tourist facilities. The Mersing jetty is also an established springboard to the popular Pahang island of Tioman. These islands are protected by their marine park status and are home to prolific and diverse marine life, much of which is endemic to the area. Some of these islands are closed during the monsoon months of November–Feburary.

BELOW: winging it on a microlight off Mersing.

Mythical Tioman

The largest of these islands, **Pulau Tioman** ❷, is popularly believed to be named after the *burung tiong* or mynah bird, said at one time to proliferate the isle. In legend, it is said that the island was created when a dragon, which emerged from Lake Cini inland, froze into rock while waiting interminably for its mate. There is a mention of Tioman before AD 1,000, in what was perhaps the first guide to Malaysia. Arab traders of the time noted in their "sailing directions" that Tioman offered good anchorage and freshwater

TIP

The best diving sea-son along the east coast is from March to May when visibility is at its best. It is possible to dive right until October but from November to February all diving stops because of the monsoon. In fact many resorts close during this period.

BELOW: white-sand beaches are plentiful on Tioman.

springs. Much later, the island's twin southern peaks at Mukut (called "Ass's Ears"), were a guide to Chinese traders between the 12th and 17th century, as evidenced by shards of Ming and other pottery found on the beaches and in nearby caves. Some of the pottery now sits in a lovely little museum at Tioman's Tekek beach. Despite the treasures so far unearthed, it is widely believed that the waters around this crucial trading pitstop harbour many more sunken treasures in the forgotten holds of unknown wrecks.

Beach life

Tioman has been awarded duty-free status in an effort to attract Langkawi-like success, particularly with Singaporeans. At the moment, this translates mainly to the availability of cheap beer. Today, Tioman's beaches continue to attract tropical isle fans, and divers and snorkellers who have come to revel in the marine park's underwater life. The main beaches fringe the west coast, and all are lined with small chalet-type accommodation run by local Malay families. A sea-bus (speedboat) services the beaches between 8am–6pm.

The tiny town "centre" is at **Tekek**, where you'll also find the jetty, airstrip and shops. The long beach, shaded by casuarina and coconut trees, is fronted with chalets and restaurants. Further inland on the other side of the road are *kampung*-style chalets. Despite the development, during the low season Tekek feels pretty much like the *kampung* it always was. The island's only road goes south from here to the island's one large resort, the Berjaya Tioman Island Resort, which also has a golf course. North of Tekek are the smaller beaches of **Air Batang** (better known as ABC after the original chalet operation there) and **Salang**, which also have some interesting mangrove areas.

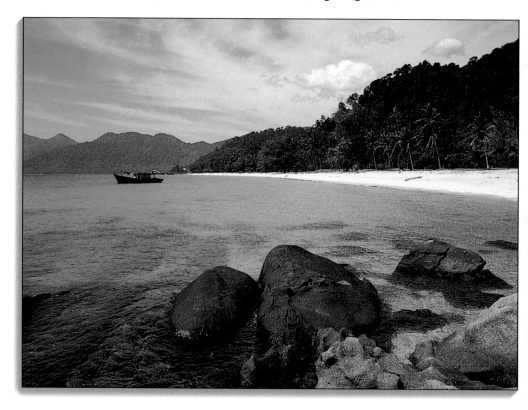

South of Tekek are **Nipah**, a quiet chalet-only stretch, and **Mukut**, way down south at the base of the Twin Peaks, whose view of the wide expanse of blue ocean is obscured by neither islands nor passing ships. Mukut also has lots of fresh springs and a couple of waterfalls, the precious water for which the ancient mariners must have been thankful. Two other stretches on the west coast are not so pretty: Genting which sits on rocks and Paya, which has no beach to speak of, although both have plenty of accommodation.

Juara is the sole beach on the east coast, a long white stretch with relatively little tree cover, great for sun-seekers but it has no coral reefs at all. This is more of a backpackers' stretch, and can be reached from the west coast by sea-bus (2-hour journey) or by a jungle trail which starts at the jetty.

The 2- to 3-hour jungle trek across the island emerges next to the airport at Tekek, from which point you can take a sea bus back. The trail is paved in some stretches, steep in others, and climbs into thick lush forest. Another trail goes from Tekek to Batang Air and Salang.

Giant reefs

Tioman has large coral reefs on the west coast, most of which are close to shore. A feature of its marine life is its giant seafans, particularly at the top dive spot of **Pulau Tulai** or Coral Island, whose shallow waters are also popular with snorkellers. **Pulau Cebeh** provides for some fine swim-throughs, and there is cave diving just off the island while at the cliff-like rocks of Golden Reef are pretty, submerged coral gardens. **Pulau Rengis**, opposite the resort, is an accessible site with an occasional slight drift. **Pulau Jahat** is a good site south of Mukut. It is common to spot hawksbill turtles in the waters too, as well as

Map on page 240

TIP

Be careful of sandflies on Pulau Besar's beaches; the bugs are particularly nasty in the cool evenings.

BELOW: all set to dive on Tulai.

TRICKY ISLAND LOGISTICS

Getting to the isles from Mersing can be a bit messy. First of all, there are three types of boats – the speedboat is twice as fast as the slow boat, while the fast boats refer to the ferries. Secondly there are no schedules, except for Tioman (at least three times a day from 7.30am) and Rawa (once a day at noon). Generally, what boat you take and when you leave depends on the size of the group, and your choice of resort and island. Try to book both accommodation and boat ticket beforehand, especially if your dates coincide with Malaysian and Singaporean public and school holidays. If you can rustle up enough passengers, you can charter the entire boat.

Nine big boat operators servicing all islands belong to the Persatuan Bot-bot Sewa Pelancong Daerah Mersing (Tourist Boat Rental Association of Mersing; open 8am–4.30pm; tel: 07-799 1222), who are at the Plaza R&R near the jetty. Like tour agencies, they can also arrange accommodation at all the islands. Seagull is the other big operator with three ferries that depart in the morning, but only to Tioman. Then there are various small operators, some connected to the resorts, and all congregated at the Plaza and jetty area. You can also check out pictures of their boats before you get on.

The blue parrot fish makes an audible crunching sound when it feeds on coral polyps.

BELOW: snorkelling off Pulau Rawa.

groups of spiny lionfish. Walk-ins and packages are available at the seven dive shops on the west coast beaches, as is full equipment rental. Instruction is offered too, and technical diving is gaining impetus here.

The 55 km (35 miles) to Tioman can be covered in an hour by scheduled ferry from Mersing (try to get there in the morning), or Tanjung Gemok near Kuala Rompin in Pahang. Boats service Genting, Tekek, ABC and Salang. All boats back to the mainland depart Tioman at 7.30am. A high-speed ferry also services Singapore. An even quicker way to get to Tioman – with some spectacular scenery thrown in – is on board Berjaya Air (tel: 03-2145 2828) from Kuala Lumpur.

Island cluster

Johor's islands south of Tioman are also covered in jungle and have some good reefs; the islands are particularly popular with Singaporeans. All tour agencies offer the same 3-day/2-night package regardless of destination island: this comprises transfers, accommodation, tours (including snorkelling), and all meals including a barbeque. An all-day island-hopping trip in a 10–12 seater boat can also be arranged. This covers a few of the nearest islands and hire of snorkelling gear, but you usually have to bring your own lunch.

The closest isle to the mainland, and the largest, is **Pulau Besar ❸**, one hour away. Pulau Besar is one of a trio of islands, including **Pulau Tengah** (which was once used as a refugee camp for Vietnamese boat people) and **Pulau Hujung**, which are popular with day-trippers. However, Pulau Besar is the only one with accommodation, which comprises mainly basic chalet operations, and one two-star hotel. There is also a dive facility here. Trails from the sandy beaches lead to small plantations and wooden *kampung*.

About the same distance from Mersing is the tiny **Pulau Rawa ❹**. The island was once one of the top destinations, but it has declined in popularity somewhat in recent years. Rawa has only one resort, in which Johor royalty have a share, and it has dive facilities but no divemaster. The marine life is nothing to shout about, but most visitors don't mind. They go there simply to enjoy its lovely beach – also on the island-hopping tour list – and do nothing. For the energetic, there is windsurfing, snorkelling, canoeing and fishing available.

Pulau Tinggi ❺, a 40-minute trip from the mainland, has a towering jungled peak, hence its name (*tinggi* means "high"). Like Tioman's mountains, this 650-metre (2,100-ft) giant was used as a navigational marker by Chinese mariners, and is mentioned in their literature as the "general's hat island". There is lots of accommodation here, mainly budget chalets. Two islets nearby have some marine reefs.

Much further away are **Pulau Aur ❻** (3–4 hours) and **Pulau Pemanggil ❼** (4–5 hours). Transport here is by chartered boat only, and is arranged through the respective resorts. Despite the distance, the islands are very popular, particularly for fishing and diving. Accommodation is plentiful but basic, and takes the form of longhouses and dormitories with common bathrooms. The best beach at Aur is actually on a neighbouring islet, Pulau Dayang, which has a dramatic granite rock face looming over its sole resort. Sea fans characterise its reefs, and experienced divers can explore a World War II Japanese wreck another 1½ hours east. The main island is hilly and good for trekking. Secluded Pemanggil has turquoise lagoons and offshore pools, and great shallow waters for snorkelling.

Map on page 240

Deep south

Johor's southern-most pair of holiday islands is accessible from Tanjung Leman, a staging point on reclaimed land about 2 hours south of Mersing. The ferry takes half-an-hour to reach Pulau Sibu Besar and Pulau Sibu Tengah; speedboats do the journey in 20 minutes, but it's a bumpier trip.

Pulau Sibu Besar ❽ has a longer history of tourism, and therefore has more accommodation, although the bulk of it is basic. A large island, it also offers some good walks that weave through its small, forested hills. In the *kampung*, modern solar panels stand out among the traditional wooden houses – they are part of a government-subsidised power programme.

The smaller **Pulau Sibu Tengah** ❾ is being promoted as a one-island, one-resort destination, the same sales pitch as Rawa. A huge three-star resort sprawls over 8 hectares (20 acres) of beachfront, offering a gamut of activities including snorkelling and DIY batik.

One option is to do an all-day island-hopping tour covering these islands from Tanjung Leman. Perched near the islands are also some *kelong*, traditional fishing huts on stilts sunk deep into the ocean floor, which are open to visitors. Popular among anglers, you'd need to bring sleeping bags; food can be arranged. Enquire at the Tanjung Leman staging point. ❏

BELOW: Pulau Tinggi's peaks are among the highest in the island group.

Map on page 240

PAHANG, TERENGGANU AND KELANTAN

On the beaches of the peninsula's beautiful east coast, sun-soakers and coral-lovers mingle happily with the local folk whose families have fished its waters for generations

The Malays say the *pokok rhu* or casuarina only grows near the sound of surf. So it is these trees that flourish along the peninsula's east coast, virtually one long surf-lapping beach running through four states. Between November and February however, the *rhu* are lashed about mercilessly by angry winds which also whip up the seas – this is the monsoon season, where entire villages and even towns are inundated with water.

But this is the reality of life for generations of fishing folk who live on these beaches, their difficult but quiet existence untouched by MTV and stock market fluctuations. Even the towns seem laid back, and hold fast to age-old traditions both culturally – mainly Malay – and religiously – predominantly Islamic.

Old settlements

There is a long history of human settlement in the east coast region. Neolithic finds have been made in Sungai Pahang, while Kelantan's prehistoric finds were in interior caves. Pahang was also mentioned in Chinese texts as being a vassal of the 13th-century trading empire of Sri Vijaya, and Kelantan is thought to have been under its wing too.

Terengganu, meanwhile, was established as a cornerstone of Malay settlement. A 14th-century Islamic inscription discovered there dates. Terengganu as one of the earliest places in the peninsula to embrace Islam, before even Melaka, whose colonisation of the east coast states only happened in the 15th century. Islam has retained its strongest hold here. The Thais, who ruled Kelantan and Terengganu before British intervention, have also left their mark in the local architecture, dialect and art forms.

The east coast is linked to the west by several main routes through the spectacular Main Range: the Karak Highway (Kuala Lumpur–Kuantan), the Gua Musang road (Kuala Lumpur–Kota Bharu), and the East–West Highway (Penang–Kota Bharu). Along the coast, Route 3 hugs the shore from Mersing all the way to Kota Bharu. It is a lovely drive, interrupted occasionally by livestock – and their droppings – and grinning children on bicycles. Go off the beaten track to a small fishing village, and a friendly gesture will be returned with a smile, or perhaps an invitation to tour the village where the soothing rhythms of Malay life have endured for centuries.

Kuala Rompin, near the Pahang-Johor state border, is a new tour destination, mainly as a jump-off point to the relatively undeveloped Pahang section of the Endau-Rompin Park (enquire at the Forestry Depart-

LEFT: colourful motif of a Kelantan fishing boat.
BELOW: kite maker in Kota Bharu.

TIP

If pressed for time, the inland Route 14 is the quicker link between Kuantan in Pahang state and Kuala Terengganu further north – but be forewarned that the drive is much less picturesque.

ment), and to Pulau Tioman from the Tanjung Gemok jetty down south. It is also being promoted as the *udang galah* (tiger prawn) city, in particular the Leban Condong area near the Lanjut Golden Beach Resort. Some travel agencies offer a four-wheel-drive tour to Jakun (Orang Asli) settlements inland at Iban (10 km/6 miles) and Kampung Aur (25 km/15 miles).

Islam, royalty and polo

At the mouth of the massive Sungai Pahang is the Pahang royal town of **Pekan ❿**, the former state capital. The sultan's palace, the **Istana Abu Bakar**, has an enormous polo ground which doubles as what must be the flattest golf course in the world. On 24 October each year, the town is injected with festivities for the sultan's birthday celebrations.

The **Muzium Sultan Abu Bakar** (Sultan Abu Bakar Museum; open Tues–Thurs 9.30am–5pm, Fri 3–5pm and Sat–Sun 9am–12.30pm; entrance fee) has excellent displays on old Pahang, royal family memorabilia, and ancient Chinese glassware and ceramics. Nearby are a mausoleum and two handsome, white-marble mosques with a riot of golden domes. About 5 km (3 miles) from town is a silk-weaving centre at Kampung Pulau Keladi.

Kuantan, the Pahang state capital, 44 km (27 miles) north of Pekan, is not very interesting but it does have an excellent Tourist Information Centre opposite the Kompleks Teruntum on Jalan Mahkota (open Mon–Sat 9am–5pm; tel: 09-516 1007).

The town serves more as a springboard to inland attractions such as **Gua Charah** (30 km/19 miles away), **Sungai Lembing** (45 km/28 miles away), and the seven-step **Berkelah Waterfall** (70 km/44 miles away). Most visitors pre-

BELOW: Muslim schoolgirls in *tudung* (headscarf).

Map on page 240

fer to stay at the pleasant **Teluk Chempedak** beach, 1 km (½ mile) out of town, featuring the usual eateries, pubs and both upmarket (the Hyatt Kuantan) and budget accommodation.

An alternative is to opt for one of the many beach resorts just north of Kuantan in **Beserah**. Known for its dried salted fish, a handful of Beserah's denizens still employ tough lumbering water buffaloes to transport fish from their boats on the beach to the processing areas.

Fun in the sun

From here, it's one long beach resort stretch all the way up to Kota Bharu. About 35 km (22 miles) from Beserah at the Terengganu border is the resort area of **Cherating** ⓫, a *kampung* squeezed out of its gorgeous crescent-shaped golden beach by tourism.

Originally a backpackers' haunt, the accommodation has gone upmarket and even includes a Club Med resort – Asia's first – on a private beach north. There are restaurants galore, souvenir shops (including DIY batik) and pubs; weekends can be one long party starting from Thursday, with the arrival of big city folk. Somehow, though, the area has avoided the claustrophobic feel of some other resort beaches, and maintains its friendly, relaxed air. A huge map at one of the two turnoffs to Cherating from the main road gives more information.

Local buses linking Kuantan and Kuala Terengganu stop on the main road, close to beach where most of the resorts are located. Some resorts organise river trips and tours, and there are also several travel agencies who can also arrange transport to nearby islands as well as onward legs of your journey. Popular tours are to Gua Charah in Sungai Lembing (5-hour trip with a stopover in

Salted fish being sun dried is a common sight along the east coast.

BELOW: the upscale Hyatt Kuantan.

TIP

Cukai town in Terengannu boasts some of the best baked stuffed crab in the east coast – the restaurants are clustered on the main road facing the river.

Kuantan) and Tasik Cini (7-hour trip, including a boat ride and visit to the Orang Asli village). However, minimum numbers are required, so you could end up losing out playing the waiting game.

Near Club Med at Pantai Chendor, sea turtles lay their eggs at night from May through to September. The Fisheries Department is experimenting on-site hatching here and the tiny **Sea Turtle Information Centre** next to the club is well worth a visit, particularly to see its two live turtles in a pool.

Terengganu treasures

Cross into Terengganu and you hit oil country. When black gold was struck in Terengganu in the 1970s, the first buildings to come up in Cukai were the banks, so the story goes. The multi-million ringgit oil and natural gas industry has changed the face of Terengganu's oil stretch beyond recognition. Villages now wear whitewashed brick faces, former fishermen and farmers sport imported overalls and hard hats, and grocery shops stock German beer, Edam cheese, and Japanese seaweed for the cosmopolitan mix who now call Terengganu home. Terengganu contributes about 60 percent of Malaysia's total oil production, but 95 percent of revenues go to federal coffers. As such, fisheries remain the state's main income-earner.

The huge drilling rigs are 200 km (125 miles) offshore in the South China Sea, but giant steel structures, snaking pipelines and bullying tankers dominate the scene from Kemaman to Paka. Before and after office hours, the traffic slows to a crawl in this stretch.

Yet there are some pretty beaches, notably at Kijal. However, it is only at Dungun that the messy industrial scenery falls away and dignified fishing villages and paddy fields reclaim the landscape. Dungun, a dreamy little seaside town and port is a jump-off point to **Pulau Tenggol** ⑫, 13 km (8 miles) offshore. Actually a group of islands, it is a diving destination that features underwater cliffs and boulders. Its deep dive profile attracts a good selection of pelagic (deep water) marine life.

BELOW: mending fish nets for the next workday.

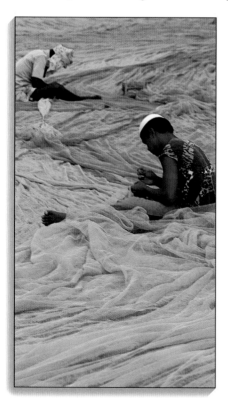

Inland from Kampung Pasir Raja is the majestic **Cemeruh Waterfalls**, 300 metres (1,000 ft) of white water thundering down a sheer rock face. To get there, you need three days through pitcher plant and palm country, across cascades and rapids. Guided tours can be arranged at Kuala Terengganu.

Ancient mariners

North of Dungun, a desperate battle is being waged on a 13-km (8-mile) stretch of golden beach. This is the **Rantau Abang Turtle Sanctuary** ⑬, and the fight is against extinction for Malaysia's oldest marine creature – the sea turtle. This is an important nesting ground for four species of turtle, including the 500-kg (1,000-lb) leatherback, which lays eggs at only six beaches in the world.

Between May and September, females struggle up the beach to lay their eggs at night, shedding "tears" in the process. What is rarer is the sight of the tiny hatchlings running to sea before dawn. Turtle-watching has long been popular entertainment on the east coast, but is itself under threat due to diminishing populations. With the leatherback almost extinct, tour operators now market sightings of the smaller green and hawksbill turtles, but these are also at risk. A wealth of information on turtles, including some depressing statistics, is displayed at the Fisheries Department's small information centre at Rantau Abang (open May– August, 9am–11pm; September–April, Saturday–Wednesday 8am–4pm, Thursday 8am–12.45pm).

Do take note of the do's and don'ts of watching turtles. Lights and noise can scare off the females. Picking up hatchlings could tamper with the imprinting process which registers the nesting location; imprinting takes effect when they run from the beach to the sea. Shining lights at the hatchlings also distracts them – they are guided by the white breakers in the ocean. Distracting them also causes them to use up energy from the tiny yolk sack that they survive on for the 3 or 4 days it takes them to get to driftlines, out of reach of predators. The Fisheries Department employs boys to scour the beaches nightly for landings, and eggs are relocated to hatcheries, away from predators, both four- and two-legged. Sightings are shared with chalet operators around the centre, so they can wake up guests for a sleepy, but worthwhile trek. Flash photography is a strict no-no; souvenir shops have plenty of postcards.

Kampung living

Just south of Kuala Terengganu is the district of Marang, dotted with picturesque villages. **Marang** ⑭ beach is an old favourite of backpackers, although fancier establishments are muscling in. The inland villages, however, are just waking up to tourism. *Gula melaka*, screwpine palm sugar, is still baked in bamboo

Map on page 240

Extensive research to help turn the tide against sea turtle extinction is being conducted at the Sea Turtle Research Unit at University Pertanian Malaysia. Pledge your support in cash and kind. Visit their website at www.kustem.edu.my/ seatru

BELOW: leatherback turtle heading back to sea.

TURTLE WATCH

Nobody knows what happens between the time sea turtle hatchlings swim out into the moonlit sea and are spotted years later as juveniles, perhaps hundreds of kilometres away. Indeed, question marks surround this marine reptile: why does it swim so far away? Why does it return to the same beach to lay eggs? Why do more come up to nest some years than others?

Malaysia's Fisheries Department has been collecting data on the giant leatherback since the 1960s, artificially hatching eggs, and carrying out awareness programmes. Yet, the largest of the four species is almost extinct: there were 1,800 landings in 1956, just 210 in 1994 and by the turn of the 20th century there were less than half a dozen sightings a season. The tiny olive ridley is endangered, while the green and hawksbills have also dwindled in numbers.

The most obvious human threat to turtles is the eating of eggs. Fisheries officers are fighting this by paying collectors for eggs which they then hatch artificially. Turtle mortality due to fishing nets and propellers is also high. Uncontrolled tourist activities can be another killer. But the pollution that affects their habitat is the hardest to monitor – plastic bags that strangle them, or pollution that kills the coral reefs and marine life on which they feed.

Chillies are central to Malay cuisine. Ask before you dig into a dish. If the food proves too fiery, downing a glass of milk instead of water will usually do the trick.

over traditional stoves, while old ladies sit in the shade of *nipah* huts, stitching away at a new "roof" for a beach resort. Tree-climbing monkeys deftly pluck young coconuts whose sweet cool juice makes a refreshing drink. A cruise up the Marang River offers views of mangrove forest from whose banks peep monkeys, iguana and sometimes, otter.

Marang is also only half-an-hour by boat from **Pulau Kapas ⓯** and **Pulau Gemia**, which are good for snorkelling and easy diving. Just before hitting Kuala Terengganu, you will pass the **Masjid Tengku Tengah Zaharah**, also known as the floating mosque. Combining the modern and traditional, its serene white reflection gives an illusion of being afloat in the water.

Setting its own pace

Despite its affluence born of the state's plentiful sources of oil, enough of **Kuala Terengganu's ⓰** old charms remain to save it from facelessness. Possibly the east coast's oldest port, the pulse of the state capital is felt most keenly in the waterfront **Pasar Besar** (Central Market) in the early morning. This is when fresh produce pours in: glistening fish by the lorry-load (the main fishing port is now in Chendering), while coconuts and *pandan* (screwpine) leaves arrive by boat from Pulau Duyung. Though less publicised than the much-photographed Central Market in Kota Bharu, this wet market is just as lively and colourful. Housed also in a concrete building, produce is sold downstairs and in the courtyard while the handicraft shops fill the first floor.

This bustle spills out into Jalan Kampong Cina, a narrow and congested crescent-shaped street lined with Chinese shophouses. This is **Chinatown**, Kuala Terengganu's original thoroughfare, where the architecture dates back to when

BELOW: basket and mat weaver in Terengannu.

Terengganu was an independent sultanate. Stroll down this street, or take a trishaw, still the most popular means of transport in downtown Kuala Terengganu. Peek into the narrow doorways – the houses seem to stretch back forever – and you might see an old lady sipping tea. The young and the trendy are moving in, though, mainly to open art and handicraft shops; this is also where many of **Pulau Redang's** resort operators are located.

Just beyond the market in the direction of the river mouth is a broad esplanade which faces the **Istana Maziah**, the official residence of the sultan, who actually lives in another palace a few kilometres away. The Istana resembles a French country house and was built at the beginning of the century to replace an older palace destroyed by fire.

Across from the Central Market is an island, **Pulau Duyung**, whose master craftsmen were, once upon a time, responsible for the unique fishing boats with decorated fore- and main-masts, and bowsprits called *bedor*. The tradition carries as till today. The island is famous for its wooden yacht builders, notably Haji Abdullah, whose boats are produced out of local *cengal* wood for an international clientele.

Terengganu's heritage

Little remains of Terengganu's beautiful traditional Malay architecture, but the best is preserved in the grounds of the **Terengganu State Museum Complex** (open Wed–Mon 9am–5pm; entrance fee). Malaysia's largest museum sits on the site of the town's first settlement, but its main buildings are obscenely outsized replicas of the real thing, four well-preserved wooden houses with Islamic motifs and shades of Chinese and European architectural influence.

Map on page 240

BELOW: kite-flying is popular in the east coast.

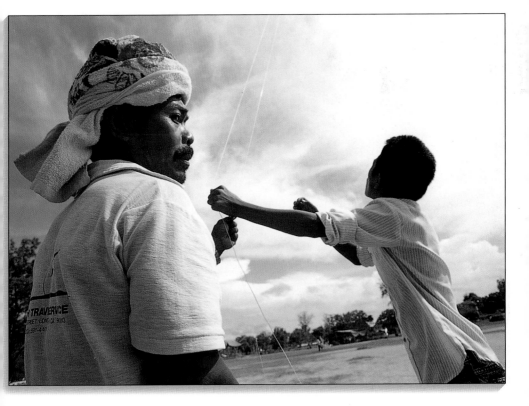

Terengganu batik is generally more expensive than that of the northern-most state of Kelantan. The designs in the former state are finer, and involve more skilled workmanship.

The excellent fisheries and seafaring open-air galleries showcase the gamut of boats, including two original hand-built wooden galleys used for trade in the 19th century. The museum is in Losong, which has charming kampung houses and is home to the famous Terengganu *keropok lekor*, a fishy cracker found only here and Kelantan. On the other side of the Terengganu River, at Kampung Tanjung Sabtu, is **Pura Tanjung Sabtu**, a complex of reconstructed traditional Terengganu houses. The owner, Terengganu prince, Tengku Ismail Tengku Su, is famous for his woven silk songket, and also hosts guests on package deals at the complex.

Like Kuantan, Kuala Terengganu has its own beach. **Pantai Batu Buruk** is a coconut tree-fringed sandy stretch with lots of eateries – try out the local *nasi dagang* breakfast if you can stomach rice and fish curry in the morning. There is also a three-star hotel and budget accommodation here.

Arts and crafts

Though village life in Terengganu has been urbanised, many of the traditional arts it fostered are as alive as ever. Seasonal fishing and farming brought village folk leisure, and from leisure came time to devote to their arts. Folk dances, shadow plays and traditional games such as kite-flying and top-spinning were celebrated during festivals after a harvest. Many processions and rituals were related to the spirit of the rice paddy, a carry-over from ancient animistic beliefs. Today, village festivals are rarer since farmers are busy planting rice twice a year instead of once, and the Islamic doctrine discourages customs connected with spirit worship.

Chendering, 8 km (5 miles) south of town, houses some commercial hand-

BELOW: batik being sun dried in Terengannu.

icraft centres, including the government-sponsored **Pusat Pengeluaran Kraf Terengganu** (Craft Product Centre), which has an apprentice programme for weaving, stitching and brassware. Their showroom also shows off products from the surrounding villages, but you would need a guide to locate them. Here also is the headquarters of the **Noor Arfa Batek House**, the country's largest hand-drawn batik producer, where you can watch batik being made and try your hand at it too.

Jewels in the sea

Like jade in an ocean of clear blue, Terengganu's islands are the most beautiful in the peninsula, and worshipped by sun-soakers and coral-lovers.

Merang, 28 km (17 miles) north of Kuala Terengganu, is the jump-off point to **Pulau Redang** ⑰ and the smaller **Pulau Lang Tengah**. A range of accommodation is available, virtually every one with dive facilities. However, there are no scheduled boats, so visitors have to book beforehand for packages with travel agents in any of the east coast capitals or Kuala Lumpur.

Lang Tengah is less crowded and is good for easy diving and excellent snorkelling close to shore. Redang, two hours from shore, is famous for its great visibility and diverse dive sites, but has become very crowded. Comprising nine islands, it is also probably the peninsula's most researched island. A pleasant cross-island track through rainforest connects the pristine wide beaches of fine white sand at Pasir Panjang and Teluk Dalam. There is also a small traditional Malay fishing village on stilts where you can stop for *teh tarik* (tea) and local *kuih* (cakes).

However, diving is what has carved the island's fame. The Marine Park jetty alone has prolific marine life, including a resident Moray eel. Night dives at the

Map on page 240

Crown of thorns starfish are extremely destructive to reefs as they feed off the coral beds.

BELOW: Redang's talcum powder beaches are divine.

TIP

It doesn't matter what you wear (or don't) on the islands, but spare a thought for a vastly different culture by making sure you are decently clad when you visit a *kampung*.

BELOW: two for the pot – a grinning lobster fisherman.

submerged reefs are particularly fascinating. There is also a high chance of bumping into a member or two of the large green turtle population. In situ hatching is being carried out here, as well as a research programme involving volunteers (*see Margin Note on the Sea Turtle Research Unit on page 251*).

Legend has it that two birds turned to stone and became the gorgeous **Pulau Perhentian Kecil** ⑱ and **Pulau Perhentian Besar** isles, 27 km (17 miles) from shore. *Kecil* and *besar* mean "small" and "large" respectively. The jetty is at Kuala Besut, an unspoilt fishing village where fishing boats make a dramatic show at dawn and dusk. Slow boats reach the isles in 1½ hours and operate between 9am–2pm. Speedboats take 30 minutes, but it's a bumpy ride.

Accommodation at Kuala Besut is limited, but the jetty is well serviced by buses and taxis from any major town. Boats and accommodation can be booked at the jetty complex. Try the Persatuan Pengusaha Pelancongan Pulau Perhentian (Association of Perhentian Island Tour Operators). Walk-ins are common, but book beforehand during public holidays.

Perhentian Besar has a wider range of accommodation spread along the bay facing the smaller island, including the three-star Perhentian Island Resort. Rock-bottom accommodation can still be found at Pasir Panjang on Perhentian Kechil, site of the first backpacker invasion. It has become really crowded here; the island's body-lined beach attests to its popularity. However, water remains a problem in the dry July/August period.

The traditional fishing village on Perhentian Kecil is interesting, particularly at the day's end when the villagers converge on the waterfront for a gossip, surrounded by squealing children at play. The village also sells groceries and other necessities.

The diving here is more leisurely compared to Redang, and the shallower waters are good for snorkelling. There are nine dive facilities in all, each offering instruction. Gardens of soft coral – which grow to huge sizes – lots of shells, and large boulders make for an attractive underwater playground.

Malay enclave

A few kilometres from the Thai border lies **Kota Bharu** ⑲, the cradle of Malay culture. Although it is ruled by the opposition fundamentalist Muslim Parti Islam or PAS, as is Terengganu, Kelantan's capital is not corseted by the party's stringent policies but is, instead, vibrant with life and colour.

Kota Bharu has one of the best-known wet markets in Malaysia. The **Pasar Besar** (Central Market) on Jalan Tengku Chik is where traders – traditionally women – sit in their colourful headscarfs and traditional *baju kurung* on raised dais among vegetables and *keropok lekor*. Upstairs is a shopping haven for east coast crafts, particularly batik and silverwork.

Just beyond the market is a cluster of museums around the old palace, **Istana Balai Besar**, which was built in 1884. Next to it is the pretty **Istana Jahar** another palace that is now the museum of royal traditions and customs. Its displays are a good introduction to traditional Kelantan life and culture; it also has an excellent weapons section. The **Pusat Kraftangan** (Handicraft Village) is notable more for its traditional architecture than its contents. Nearby are the **Muzium Islam** (Islamic Museum), another attractive traditional wooden building, and the more modern **Istana Batu** (Royal Museum) which houses memorabilia of the current sultan.

Kota Bharu's cultural pastimes are showcased at **Gelanggang Seni** (Court of

Map on page 240

TIP

All museums in Kota Bharu are open 10.30am–5.45pm, but are closed on Friday as it's a Muslim prayer day; all charge an entrance fee.

BELOW:
the Central Market at Kota Bharu.

Map on page 240

All in a day's work – monkeys trained to pluck coconuts.

Arts) on Jalan Mahmood. Check the latest schedules at Tourism Malaysia at Jalan Sultan Ibrahim (tel: 09-747 7554; open daily 8am–4.15pm except Fri). Unless you are lucky enough to chance upon festivals in Kota Bharu or its surrounding villages, this is the best place to view these artforms. In a small *wakaf* (rest hut) outside the main hall, old men tune their instruments, and exponents of traditional Malay self defence, *silat*, take to the stage. On the green, the *gasing* (top) spinners are ready to spin down their prized tops onto a concrete square. From here, the tops are removed with a wooden pallet onto dowels. The trick is to keep your top spinning longer than anyone else's. The drummers then beat out rhythms on the rows of colourful *rebana*, huge drums fashioned out of logs.

Wayang kulit (shadow puppet plays) and the Thai-influenced dance-theatre *mak yong*, two of the loveliest Malay artforms, are banned from performance in the state, because they are considered anti-Islam. Luckily, the *wayang kulit* troupes in Terengganu, Kedah and Perlis are alive and thriving. *Mak yong* and its sister artform *manohra*, however, look set for a steady decline into obscurity.

Surprising surroundings

Kota Bharu is surrounded by a patchwork of villages among rice paddy fields and orchards. What might seem surprising in a predominantly Muslim state is the number of Thai *wat* (temples) between Tumpat and Pasir Mas. Among them is the **Wat Photivihan**, which houses the country's largest statue of the reclining Buddha. Some villages even celebrate Thai festivals, like the Songkran water festival.

BELOW: reclining Buddha of Wat Photivihan.

Tumpat is the terminus for the eastern railway line from Segamat. Across the border in Thailand, the line whisks travellers all the way to Bangkok. Head out of Kota Bharu on Route 3 to reach what is reputed to be the oldest surviving mosque in Malaysia (although the Melakans might dispute that). The 18th-century **Masjid Kampung Laut** (Kampung Laut Mosque) was originally on the banks of Sungai Kelantan but was moved out of flood's harm to Kampung Nilam Puri 10 km (6 miles) south of Kota Bharu. Built of stout chengal wood and without nails, it has a pyramidal two-tiered roof, typical of a Javanese mosque.

A great place to watch Kelantan's colourful fishing boats is at the picturesque estuary at **Pantai Dasar Sabak 20**, 13 km (8 miles) north of the town. The boats leave at dawn and return at about 3pm, when it is all bustle with the unloading of the catch and the washing of boats. The beach also has a 20th-century claim to fame: it was here, on 8 December 1941, that the Japanese began their brutal march south to Singapore. (The attack on Pearl Harbor was not to take place until 95 minutes later – 7 December on the other side of the dateline.)

Weekenders head for the city's most famous beach, **PCB** or **Pantai Cahaya Bulan** (Moonlight Beach); the acronym actually used to stand for Pantai Cinta Berahi – The Beach of Passionate Love – in pre-PAS days. Still, PCB remains a handicraft haven. The gold-threaded *songket*, *wau* (kites) large and small, and rows of batik hanging in the sun beckon souvenir-hunters on the 5-km (3-mile) road to the beach. ❑

Kampung Games

Every Malaysian is a *kampung* kid at heart; so says Lat, Malaysia's favourite cartoonist who has a series of books contrasting the easy, down-to-earth *kampung* lifestyle with the mobile-phone and pager-punctuated life of the modern yuppie.

Despite the city-dweller's groomed image and array of gadgets, every holiday in Malaysia results in airports and highways jammed with city residents returning to their villages – *balek kampung*. Their *kampung* are their roots, and bound up in this are the traditional pastimes enjoyed there.

Throughout most of the country, **top-spinning** is a teenage game, but in the Malay *kampung* of the northeast coast, a champion spinner is the village hero. Requiring great strength to spin, tops vary from a simple wooden cylinder to fantastic streamlined discs with spindles trimmed with inlaid gold; large ones can be as big as dinner plates. With the harvest completed and all the rice stored, farmers traditionally settled down to watch and bet on the top local team. Contests feature either the endurance spinners – record times for spinning are about two hours – or the strikers who spin down 7 kg (15 lb) fighting tops faster than a speeding bullet.

Another traditional entertainment most popular in Malaysia's northeastern states, **kite-flying** was enjoyed in the 15th century. Today, great pride is still taken in the design and the hand-crafting of each aerodynamic piece of art. The paper *wau* (kite) comes in unique shapes, and bamboo pieces are often attached underneath a kite to produce a melodic humming sound (*degung*). Contests are still held for serious kite-flyers, and today, international kite festivals are held in Malaysia, drawing participants from both European and Asian countries.

Sepak takraw, a traditional *kampung* game, uses a ball about the size of a large grapefruit, made of woven rattan strips, and weighing 170 grammes (less than ½ pound). The aim of the game is to keep the ball in the air as long as possible by passing it from one player to another, using all parts of the body except for the forearms and the hands. The game requires acrobatic flexibility and practised skills, and is exhilarating to watch.

Congkak is a game requiring more wits than physical skill. Comparable to backgammon, *congkak* features a wooden boat-shaped "board" and marbles or seeds. The *congkak* board has two rows of holes in which the marbles are placed, and the object of the game is to have the most marbles to finish.

The best childhood memories come from games provided by nature. The pea-sized, red saga seeds from the large saga tree, for example, are used in a game of accuracy much like marbles. The game of pick-up-sticks is played with coconut twigs or satay skewers; chicken feathers are stuck into a flat rubber disc, and this *catek*, resembling a shuttlecock, is kept in the air while being nimbly kicked using only the instep of one's foot. Even conker-like rubber seeds are the centre of numerous, imaginative kampung games, all still fresh in the minds of almost every Malaysian. Just go ahead and ask. ❑

RIGHT: top-spinning is taken very seriously in the northeastern states of Malaysia.

THE BANGAU MARITIME FIGUREHEADS

Carved spar holders, or bangau, adorn these colourful fishing boats, and are found only on the Malaysian peninsula's east coast

When engines began replacing sails from the 1950s onwards, it was thought that the *bangau* would become extinct. But, defying all predictions, these colourful objects have been retained, because the spars are still used as gaffs for landing fish and for poling into shore.

In ancient times they were more than utilitarian objects – the *bangau* also served as a repository for the spirit of the boat, and its presence was believed to help keep the boat safe from storms and sea demons.

Bangau are found from the northern shores of Kelantan – notably adorning the boats known as *perahu bauatan barat* – to Terengganu in the south, where they act as figureheads on the curved bows of *kolek* boats.

FIGUREHEAD FASHIONS

Bangau take on various forms. Some are shaped like birds, others of the *naga*, a legendary sea serpent, while a few are even fashioned after figures in traditional shadow-puppet plays. Some prows are even shaped and painted to resemble the *garuda,* a demonic birdman from Kelantanese mythology. Were they originally made to ward off the *naga umbang*, a marine dragon that according to legend lurked in the depths of the sea? Another legendary tale has the *garuda* residing in the top of a huge coconut palm – a symbolic represention of heaven – which rises out of the centre of the ocean.

Although the spiritual significance of the *bangau* has been long forgotten, the tradition of keeping them and the boats they adorn still decorated, survives.

△ **PAINTED PROWS**
A naga "dragon" adorns a prow at Pantai Dasar Sabak, Kelantan.

◁ **THE "ONGKAK"**
Sitting opposite the bangau, the *ongkak* often resembles figures from the shadow-puppet plays.

BIRD-LIKE BOAT SPIRITS

Bangau means "cattle egret" in Malay. It is thought that originally the boat fittings resembled these birds, who, while rarely seen flying over the sea, were perhaps chosen for their symbolic value due to their well-known liking for fish.

Most *bangau*, however, bear no resemblance to this bird, although bird shapes are sometimes used. Their fanciful designs probably have something to do with the strict Islamic edicts banning the portrayal of anthropomorphic figures.

At Kelantan's Pantai Baru near Bachok, a *bangau* takes on a parrot-like look (*above*), but the colours are highly imaginative.

Further south, at Penarik, Terengganu (*below*), a *bangau* keeps the long neck of its namesake but its garish blue colouring is merely for ornamentation.

△ **BEACHED BANGAUS**
One of the east coast's most enduring scenes are fleets of rainbow-coloured fishing boats lined up under the shade of coconut palms.

◁ **BOAT FIXER**
When rough monsoon seas keep boats in port, fishermen repair their craft for the next season.

△ **DEMON DESIGN**
Trident-wielding demons were perhaps originally painted on boat hulls to scare off "sea devils".

◁ **BOAT BEACHING**
Each day at the Bachok district of Kelantan, the fishing fleet is physically hauled up onto the beach.

▷ **BLUE BANGAU**
The tuft of feathers on the head of this *bangau* could have originally mimicked the bright orange feathers which the male egret sprouts during mating season.

EASTERN INTERIOR

Inland from the east coast lies the dark green heart of Malaysia, a land of lakes and forest, of wild animals, ancient myths and the sublime beauty of Taman Negara

Kuala Lumpur

In the still of morning, before the first breath of wind, surreal sculptures of dead wood stand perfectly reflected in the mirror of **Tasik Kenyir ㉑**, Southeast Asia's largest artificial lake. Nineteen hills were inundated to feed the 37,000 hectares (90,000 acres) of water needed to run the hydroelectric power station that supplies about 8 percent of the nation's electricity.

However, the statuesque tree trunks that used to be the lake's outstanding characteristic have been removed, except in its northern fingers. Nonetheless, Kenyir's numerous tributaries continue to be an anglers' favourite, with numerous freshwater species including the *kelah* and carnivorous *toman* (snakehead).

About 14 waterfalls dot the area's 340 thickly-forested islands. The multi-tier 152-metre (500-ft) **Lasir Waterfall** is 45 minutes south of the jetty by boat; and **Tembat Waterfall**, a series of five furious rapids and gorgeous giant sun-baked boulders, is an hour north. You'll find campsites on the pebble-beached **Petuang** and **Saok** rivers, which are also popular fishing spots. Otters, eagles and amphibians are common; if you are lucky, you might even spot elephants or the elusive black panther.

The road to Kenyir

The main gateway to Kenyir is the **Pengkalan Gawi** jetty, an hour from Kuala Terengganu. Buses from the latter go to Kuala Berang, 15 km (9 miles) from Kenyir; take a taxi for the rest of the journey. There are also overnight buses that go direct from Kuala Lumpur (Hentian Putra) to Pengkalan Gawi.

The visitor's centre has a pleasant view, but little else beyond that. Day-trippers can hire boats at the landing near the dam, where the tour operators have eight- to 10-person fibreglass boats. They also have dubious-looking double-decker houseboats that cruise the lake and can sleep 15 people on mattresses. The operators can arrange stays at the resorts too, but contact numbers of the resorts are also published in the Tourism Malaysia Tasik Kenyir brochures and tours can also be arranged from Kuala Terengganu. All resorts offer the same deal: accommodation, all meals, boat transfers, jungle-trekking, a visit to a waterfall and unlimited use of facilities.

En route to Kenyir is the picturesque seven-step **Sekayu Waterfall** (entrance fee) near Kuala Berang. A 25-minute walk up a flight of steps takes you to the top, the least slippery spot for a swim. Kuala Berang was the site of the first Malay settlement in Terengganu, but nothing remains of the original dwellings. Also discovered here was Malaysia's oldest Koranic inscription. The 14th-century *Batu Bersurat* is now in the state museum.

Map on page 240

LEFT: Orang Asli tribesman and his blowpipe.
BELOW: thundering Sekayu waterfall during the rainy season.

En route to Pahang's hinterlands from Kuantan, the turnoff to **Sungai Lembing** ㉒ leads to a towering limestone cliff, **Gua Charah**, whose inner cave houses a 9-metre (30-ft) long limestone statue of a reclining Buddha built by a Thai Buddhist monk. The taxing climb up to the ledge is rewarded by a great view. The cathedral-sized outer cave has thin shafts of light filtering down through cracks hundreds of metres above. There are other caves to explore but a guide is needed. On the same road is the world's second-largest and deepest tin mine, open to tours if prior arrangements are made with Pahang Consolidated Ltd. For details, enquire at Sungai Lembing.

About 16 km (10 miles) inland from Sungai Lembing is **Gunung Tapis**, a mountainous nature park with rapids, fishing and trekking. It takes a 1½-day climb to reach the peak. Contact Pesona Adventure Camp (tel: 09-573 2191), which arranges transport, tours and accommodation.

Mountain skyscapes

Fantastic skyscapes over islands of *pandanus* (screwpines) at sunset; boat-wide "paths" through long submerged grass; and from June to September, fragile pink waterlilies and white lotuses on immense velvet leaf carpets. This is **Tasik Cini** ㉓ (Lake Cini), a rare river-floodplain of 12 interlocking lakes about 100 km (62 miles) inland from Kuantan.

Cini is fascinating for its two main forest types – the riverine forest of massive trees and lianas overhanging the narrow Sungai Cini; and the swamp vegetation, the most prominent of which are the *pandanus*. This is also home to monkeys and birds, including large flocks of hornbills, and kingfishers and broadbills that flash a brilliant blue across the water.

BELOW:
Tasik Cini, Pahang.

Myths and monsters

Legend has it that a lost city, probably Khmer, is believed to lie 12 metres (40 ft) below the lake's surface but Cini is probably best known for its mythical *naga*, a Loch Ness-type monster whose origins are a spiritual dragon-creature of local Orang Asli folklore. Another version tells of how two of these mythical creatures evolved to become the islands of Tioman and Daik.

The Jakun maintain some elements of their traditional lifestyle, planting rice paddy and fishing; they also make fine handicrafts, now predominantly targeting tourists. Try your hand at the blowpipe at Tanjung Puput and Kampung Gumum. There is also basic accommodation and tours at the latter.

By road, Cini is off the Kuantan-Segamat Highway (Route 12), then 32 km (20 miles) from the Pahang bridge turnoff. This road goes to Kampung Gumum and the Kijang Mas Gumum Resort, which has a range of accommodation, a restaurant, as well as public toilets. A jetty here with an association of 19 boatmen (tel: 09-456 7160), offers the lake tour at a more reasonable rate than the association of 15 boaters at the Tourism Complex at the Kuala Sungai Cini rivermouth (tel: 09-420 1196) which lies further down that road. Use the latter's services if you plan to access Cini by boat from Kampung Belimbing off the Karak Highway on the other side of the massive Sungai Pahang; the rate is RM70 per four-passenger boat. If you want to be dropped off at your accommodation, the fare is double. All boatmen can ferry you to the campsites that dot the place.

A worthwhile day trip would cover the dank, winding Sungai Cini, half the lakes, and a short jungle trek from the resort to Kampung Gumum, one of three trails in the area. A longer day trip brings you to the **Mentenang Waterfall**,

Map
on page
240

TIP

The best storehouse of tales from the rich Jakun oral tradition, is probably Tok Batin, the headman at Kampung Gumum – although the local boatmen are good sources too. You would need a translator though.

LEFT: waterlily at Cini.
BELOW: Orang Asli blowpipes.

TIP

Club Med Cherating usually sends busloads of tourists to Lake Cini on Mondays, and weekends are usually busy for boat operators.

while an overnight option is **Gunung Cini**. Tours can be arranged from Kuantan and Cherating. Public transport runs from Kuantan and Pekan to Cini town; call the resort and they will pick you up. An express bus also goes to Cini from Kuala Lumpur's Mara Bus Station.

Unfortunately, all is not well at Cini. The leafless trees at the waters' edge are the result of a bungle by authorities on a dam built in the early 1990s to regulate water fluctuations; it let in too much, and was knocked down too late, killing off large numbers of the huge *tembusu* trees. The current, British-designed dyke is the third attempt to get it right. Behind the beauty of the increasingly abundant water lilies is also the ominous sign that the lake is getting shallower; the ecosystem has not found its balance yet.

Ancient lifestyles

A similar lake experience is to be had at **Tasik Bera** ❷ (Lake Bera), 1½ hours from Cini. Though the largest freshwater lake in Southeast Asia, its waters are contained in narrower "fingers" rather than the open lakes of Cini, thanks to the greater abundance of screwpine.

Bera's 26,000 hectares (64,000 acres) of wetland and swamp ecosystems are protected under the Ramsar Convention as a wetland of international importance. Like Cini, the water rises up to 3 metres (9 ft) in the wet months of September to January, blessing the rivers with fish, and making the post-monsoon months the best angling period. As the boat snakes through the narrow channels, a splash of colour in the orchids amid ferns and epiphytes catches the eye. Less obvious are the pitcher plants among the tall reed fields. Above, a hawk wings its solitary way, keeping a keen eye out for supper.

BELOW:
view from the
East-West highway.

Map on page 240

The Ramsar Convention, instituted by the Malaysian authorities to protect traditional human use of the area, allows the Orang Asli of the Semelai tribe to maintain their traditional lifestyles. The indigenous people here live in bamboo and bark huts, using traditional implements to trap fish for the lucrative aquarium fish industry, and fashioning handicrafts from forest products. An interesting tradition is the collection of *minyak keruing* resin from the *keruing* tree, used for making torches, boats and perfume. Homestay packages are also available for those who wish to spend time here.

Tasik Bera's Pesona Lake Resort (tel: 09-276 2505) has rooms, dorms, campsites and covered platforms overlooking the serene waters. Packages include a 3-day/2-night lake tour, trekking and Semelai experience, birdwatching tours, and a homestay programme with the Semelai. Three trails run around the area and there are also canoes and mountain bikes. Tasik Bera is difficult to access, but the resort does pick-ups for a fee from Temerloh and the Triang train station.

Rainforest thrills

There is shuffling and grunting, but the torchlight picks out only a pair of eyes. Is it the black-and-white king of camouflage, a tapir? Or, against all odds, one of the park's remaining 40-plus Sumatran Rhino? The experience afforded by the five animal hides in **Taman Negara** ㉕ is among the attractions that have made it arguably the best-known of Malaysia's protected areas. This granddaddy, which simply translates to "National Park", sprawls over 430,000 hectares (100,000 acres) across three states, with the bulk being in Pahang. Looming over all this is the central massif of Gunung Tahan, the peninsula's highest peak.

BELOW: Taman Negara at dawn.

These banana-like fruits which grow from this tree trunk in Taman Negara look inviting but are unsafe to eat.

Taman Negara offers everything from a leisurely 2 days' fishing to a 2-week jungle safari, a muddy crawl through bat-infested caves to a splashy ride through Sungai Tembeling's rapids. The park's hundreds of kilometres of trails are kept cleared and well-marked, and meander through fascinating lowland diptero-carp and riverine forests, climbing to stunted montane vegetation.

Bird-watching is a delight. Kingfishers, bee-eaters, fishing eagles and osprey abound, and even if you don't see them, you'd certainly hear them, in particular the hornbills' unmistakable squawk. Besides monitor lizards, the larger denizens such as elephants, black panther, *seladang* wild ox and tigers are virtually impossible to spot, so learn to identify their tracks. Nonetheless, sit quietly in the jungle, and you might be rewarded with the sight of a troupe of long-tailed macaques in the treetops.

The aboriginal Batek communities are no longer a common sight around the headquarters, preferring a nomadic lifestyle deep in the forest. You might occasionally bump into them on a trail or see their temporary huts. The Batek have a natural dignity; don't be too quick to turn them into a tourist spectacle with the click of a camera. But don't be surprised if they demand a fee if you do insist on clicking. The Senoi and Semak Abri tribes outside the park area, however, live more contemporary lifestyles and are more open to visitors.

Riding the Tembeling

BELOW: jungle canopy walk at Taman Negara.

Permits are required to enter the park and there is a fee for cameras – arrange at the Parks and Wildlife Department or your travel agent. Entrance to the park is usually by river from the Kuala Tembeling jetty, although a rough road also goes to the Kuala Tahan *kampung*. However, the covered 14-seater longboat ride is a great way to cover the 35-km (20-mile) journey on Sungai Tembeling. The 2-hour trip can take twice as long if the river level is low; sometimes, passengers have to disembark and wade while the boatmen negotiate the shallow waters.

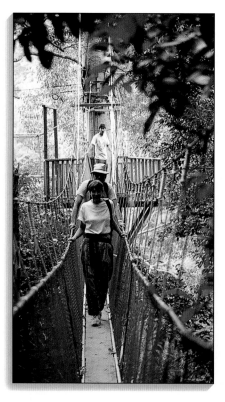

Kuala Tembeling is accessed from Jerantut, where express buses and the Gemas-Tumpat trains stop. From Jerantut, take a 30-minute taxi to the jetty. Tours to the park that operate from major cities and Jerantut include transfers to and from the park.

Accommodation in the park ranges from campsites to luxurious chalets under the Taman Negara Resort. Budget accommodation is available outside the park in the *kampung* and at Nusa Camp. There is a 50-sen river shuttle between the park and the *kampung*, and a riverbus run by Nusa Camp services the main jetties on Sungai Tembeling. Boats within the park must be arranged through the Wildlife Department.

At Kuala Tahan, visitors can book accommodation, arrange trips and get information and maps at either the Wildlife Department or the Taman Negara Resort. The resort and Nusa Camp have good maps and guides to the park, and provide information to non-guests as well. They also rent out camping and fishing gear if you make prior arrangements.

The park's excellent interpretation centre, squashed into the resort grounds, provides a great introduction to the park, including information on trails and rainforests in general. Videos are screened at 2pm and 8.45pm. Short trails can be done yourself, or you can hire nature interpretation guides. Guides are compulsory on the major trails, and guided tours are included in packages.

Map on page 240

Walks in the wild

The most popular walk is the half-hour trek to the **canopy walkway** (open 11am–3pm; entrance fee), a rope-and-ladder bridge among the tops of trees, up to 27 metres (80 ft) up. The 400-metre (1,300-ft) long walkway gives visitors a rare chance to experience the shoots, fruits and pollinating insects of the canopy at close quarters. This trail is part of the longer loop which goes to **Tabing Hide** and **Teresek Hill** with its views of Gunung Tahan.

Another popular trek is to **Gua Telinga**, a wet, ear-shaped cave (hence its name *telinga*) where you crawl through guano beneath bats clustered on the low ceilings. The lucky could spot a cave racer, a long white snake that feeds on the bats. Fist-sized toads and insects like spiders and cockroaches are plentiful too. Although they may be unnerving to many people, all the fauna in the cave are harmless to humans.

A leisurely alternative is to glide under arches of trees up the small pretty **Sungai Tahan**, and soak in **Lata Berkoh**, a natural jungle jacuzzi formed by a bank of cascades. Lata Berkoh is popular with anglers, as is **Sungai Keniam**, which can be reached on foot or by boat. The trail to the latter, Rentis Keniam, takes in the large caves of Gua Luas, Gua Daun Menari, Gua Kepayang Kecil and Gua Kepayang Besar, which also boast prolific cave fauna. It's a good 2-day trek, camping out at the caves or the popular **Kumbang Hide**.

For long-haulers, two options are the **Air Terjun Empat Tingkat** (Four-Step

TIP

Taman Negara Resort and Nusa Camp run buses (RM25 one way) daily between Kuala Lumpur (departing 8am) to Kuala Tembeling (departing 1.30pm), which are open to non-guests, but book beforehand.

BELOW: sun-baked boulders at Sungai Tahan.

Map on page 240

TIP

The best time to fish in Taman Negara is during the drier months from February to March, and June to August; equipment can be hired. For bait, local fishermen use riverside fruits.

BELOW: Malayan Tapir.
RIGHT: face to face with pandanus plants, Lake Cini.

Waterfall) and the ultimate, **Gunung Tahan**. Each involves a 7-day trip where you need to carry your own camping gear and food. Both follow the same route along Sungai Tahan until the Teku tributary fork. There are numerous river crossings and a stretch where you have to climb 27 hills – all in 1 day.

The waterfall is a major tributary of Sungai Tahan that plunges down the eastern flanks of Gunung Tahan and Gunung Gedong. The undulating trek up to the Tahan peak, at 2,187 metres (7,175 ft), involves an exhilarating climb through montane oak and cloud forests. There is an alternative route to the peak, which takes 3 days, but it starts at Merapoh town north of Jerantut.

Other trails snake around the 36 hectares (90 acres) of forest bordering the park that belong to Nusa Camp. There are a couple of waterfalls, and the steep Bukit Warisan trek has great sunrise and sunset views of the rainforest canopy with its amazing diversity of trees.

The jungle by night

A night in an animal hide is your best chance to observe wildlife, much of which is nocturnal. These huts-on-stilts are near salt-licks, where animals come to drink. Arrive at the hides early, say around 5pm. Cooking is not allowed, so bring a packed supper, a powerful flashlight, and insect repellent, and settle down to wait. Binoculars are handy. Take turns to "watch", shining the torch every 10 minutes or so. Nosy jungle rats will help keep you awake.

As night falls, the forest comes alive with sounds and ghostly "spirits" flitting between the trees – fireflies and beetles with fluorescent wings and tails. Deer and tapir are the most common sightings, and you'll see lots of spiders and snakes moving about in the undergrowth. An alternative would be to go on a night walk, where you can pick out luminous mushrooms or a slow loris, flying squirrel or civet cat.

Southwest of Taman Negara is the lesser known but no less interesting **Kenong Rimba Park** ㉖, whose specialities are birds and insects. From dawn, the 128-sq. km (49-sq. mile) park is alive with the sounds of birds, including the unique call of the white-rump shamma and the thwack of the Malayan whistle thrush smashing its breakfast of snails on a rock. You might even spot the *belalang dewa* in action, grasshoppers which display locust-like behaviour in travelling in groups, decimating vegetation in one go.

A 2- to 3-hour trail loops around the park, taking in Kenong Rimba's many limestone caves and types of vegetation. There's **Gua Batu Tangga**, a huge cave believed to provide shelter for elephants. **Gua Hijau** is named after its mossy green walls, while **Batu Kajang** has folkloric connections: according to legend, it is a boat carrying a king's messenger that had been turned to stone. A more challenging route is the undulating 5-day trek to **Gua Batu Putih**, which has a delightful crystal-clear stream.

Kenong can be accessed from **Kuala Lipis**, the old Pahang capital. Kuala Lipis is also on the Segamat-Tumpat train route (get off at Batu Sembilan). A 20-minute longboat ride down Sungai Jelai goes to the park at Tanjung Kiara where there are chalets and a campsite. Tours can be arranged at Kuala Lipis. ❏

THANK YOU FOR
NOT SMOKING

SARAWAK

Once, the much-feared tribes of Sarawak were after enemy heads. Nowadays, they're chasing tourist dollars

Even today, the name Borneo evokes a sense of the exotic – of adventure and a journey into the unknown. Visions of impenetrable jungle, of headhunters and jungle-dwelling tribes, of white *rajahs* (kings) and great riches refuse to fade. And yet today's Sarawak, in the heart of Borneo, is a fast-changing reality.

As loggers move ever further into the wild, deep and dark jungles become accessible, their secrets lost forever. Express boats bring once remote settlements and longhouses within reach, and trips that used to take weeks of battling fast-flowing rivers have been reduced to as many hours as powerful engines churn upriver.

While the white rajahs and headhunters are long gone, Sarawak's tradition of open hospitality continues, making Kuching Southeast Asia's friendliest city. You'll always be made welcome, whether by Chinese women offering free samples in the market, or in an Iban longhouse, where you might sit chatting with the chief over a glass of heady *tuak*, Sarawak's ubiquitous home-brewed rice wine.

While Sabah and Sarawak share a common heritage, each with a history that involved the British, their developments took different paths. Sarawak's white rajahs had great respect for their Dayak subjects and their rule took their predilections into account. Sabah grew as a trading post, with a more pragmatic and certainly less romantic attitude towards its native inhabitants. As a result, modern Sarawak retains its cultural integrity and pride in traditions.

This sprawling state makes a great introduction to Borneo. Even those with little time to spare can gain a rudimentary understanding of the country and the cultures of its people by visiting the award-winning Sarawak Cultural Centre just outside Kuching. But those with more time can look forward to some rich experiences: the enigmatic caves of Niah, with their relics of cave dwellers from 40,000 years ago; the World Heritage Site of Mulu with caves so large that their statistics astound the senses; further afield, the cool Bario Highlands, which bring contact with the warm hospitality of the Kelabits and the chance to trek through pristine jungle.

After a longboat trip upriver, visiting a longhouse, and perhaps even witnessing a longhouse celebration or *gawai,* the taste of Borneo is firmly instilled. If you are lucky enough to hear the haunting music of the *sape* and witness the dance of the hornbills, memories of Sarawak will live in the heart forever. ❑

PRECEDING PAGES: "The Pinnacles" – razor-sharp granitic formations at Sarawak's Mulu National Park.
LEFT: Iban warriors in battle gear strike a pose. Thankfully, headhunting is not practised any more.

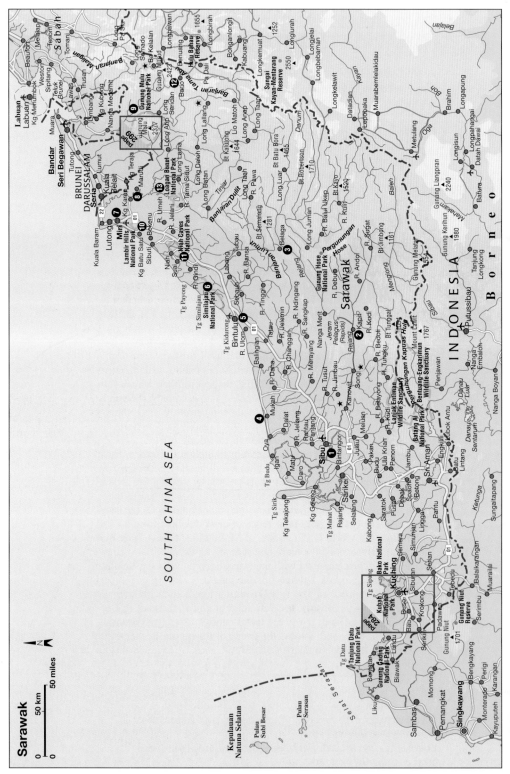

KUCHING AND THE SOUTHWEST

Maps:
Area 284
City 278

Kuching has held on to much of its original character while new development spreads further away from the old town centre. The result is one of the most charming towns in Southeast Asia

When British adventurer James Brooke made his way up the winding Sarawak River in his ship, the *Royalist*, he had little idea what was in store for him, or that in a few short years he would be ruling a whole country. It was 1839 and an uncle of the Sultan of Brunei asked Brooke to help settle disputes amongst the country's fighting factions. To the amazement of all, he managed to talk both sides into a harmonious truce. Even more incredible to the Brunei overlords was his insistence that the lives of the rebels be spared and that they be allowed to return to their villages. Thus, Brooke gained the friendship of the Dayaks, the Malays and the Chinese. In return, the Sultan agreed to Brooke's demand that he be given the title of Governor and Rajah of the Sarawak region, thus initiating the "rule of the White Rajahs" – a rule that lasted three generations and over 100 years. Brooke's admiration for the character of the Dayaks led to a long and fruitful relationship, and the novelty of the Brookes' rule became its essence: justice without favouritism.

Exploring Kuching

Winding through lowland *nipah* swamps, the Sarawak River has always been the focal point for Sarawak's capital city, **Kuching ❶**. This delightful old trading town is suffused with old memories, enhanced by the many colonial buildings that have withstood the march of 20th-century progress. People are friendly and hospitable with time to stop for a chat. Amid the noisy traffic, the shophouses squeezed between the bustling markets of the main bazaar and the stately old buildings give the capital an elegant and dignified air. History has always seemed close to the present in Kuching and until the early 1990s, the town centre had changed little from a century ago, when pressures to modernise led to new roads and improvements to the riverfront.

Scattered around Kuching's colonial heart stand the buildings that played such an important part during the Brookes' rule. A Heritage Walk has been devised that covers many of these buildings. The best time to make an on-foot exploration is early morning, or break it up and continue after 4pm, when the heat of the day has begun to pall. Alternatively, hop on to the free City Tram that stops at key tourist spots and hotels (10am–9pm).

Take one of the gaily painted *tambang* – the small ferry boats leave as soon as they have sufficient passengers – from the various jetties or *pangkalan* along the Kuching Waterfront. First stop is the **Astana ❶**. Built in 1870 for the newly married second Rajah, Charles Brooke, it is now the official residence of Sarawak's head of state. Several renovations later, it

BELOW:
Orang Ulu woman.

Cat sculpture outside the Hilton hotel in Kuching. According to one theory, Kuching was named after the fruit 'buah mata kuching' (cat's eyes), which grows locally.

consists of three bungalows, supported by square brick pillars, with the low, spreading roof giving shade to the interior. You cannot enter the building, but you may walk in the grounds.

Fortified town

A little further downriver is **Fort Margherita B** (open Tues–Sun 10am–6pm; closed public holidays) which holds a commanding position overlooking the town. The first of a series of forts that lined Sarawak's main rivers, Fort Margherita was built in 1879, at a calm and peaceful time. The fort was never used for its intended purpose during the Brooke era; the only time it came under attack was during a Japanese air raid in World War II. No severe damage was caused, however, and since the war, the quaint fort has been used mainly as a barracks by the police force. It also houses the surprisingly interesting **Police Museum** (open Tues–Sun 10am–6pm). The best time to visit is in the morning; for security reasons, you may be asked to produce a passport or ID to enter.

Back across the river is Kuching's **Square Tower C**, (no formal opening times, tel: 082-426 093 for an appointment) an imaginative building built in the same year as Fort Margherita. Its architecture harks back to the Victorian era's fascination with medieval culture. Although equipped with a real dungeon for prisoners, the tower later came to be used as a popular dancing hall.

Next door, also at the beginning of the Kuching Waterfront park, is the renovated **Sarawak Steamship Building**, which houses a number of souvenir stalls and next to that is the Sarawak Tourist Information Centre, which offers brochures, advice and information in a cool air-conditioned haven.

Map on page 278

Once a collection of godowns and trading stores, the old waterfront was greatly transformed in 1993 to become the **Kuching Waterfront**, a kilometre-long stretch of recreational areas, gardens, walkways, stalls and restaurants, dominated by the impressive white edifice of the **Hilton Hotel** right at the end of the walk – the beginning of the main upmarket hotel area. The park is extremely popular with locals, who can be seen enjoying themselves here at all hours of the day and night. At the down-river end of the Waterfront Park, the one-time Chinese Chamber of Commerce building has been transformed into an interesting **Chinese History Museum** (open Sat–Thurs 9am–6pm).

Crossing the road from the Waterfront one reaches Sarawak's oldest, and possibly prettiest, Chinese temple. Devoted to **Tua Pek Kong** , its construction in the late 18th century marks the strong Chinese presence in Sarawak. The Chinese community trades not only in the main towns and cities, but also up-river, with trade boats stocked like floating supermarkets, or others attached to remote longhouses, supplying down-river goods and building up a network of trade and news wherever they go.

The street facing the Waterfront is known as **Main Bazaar**, its shops now forming the main tourist area – a shopping mecca not just for touristy souvenirs but with pieces to interest serious collectors. Many of the old shophouses are taken over by travel companies, handicraft and antique stores specialising in primitive arts.

Continue along Main Bazaar until you reach the former **Court House** **E** – a quietly impressive colonial building, standing stolidly beneath shading trees. Arguably the most beautiful colonial building in Kuching, the building has been converted into the **Sarawak Tourism Centre**, and now houses a Visitor

BELOW:
Fort Margherita was named after Charles Brooke's wife.

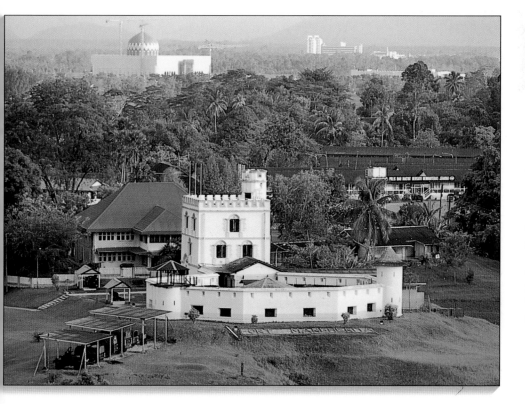

Naturalist Eric Mjoberg who was the first to climb Sarawak's highest mountain, Gunung Murud in 1922, was one of the more famous curators of the Sarawak Museum.

Information Centre on the ground floor, and a Lebanese restaurant on the first floor. Built in 1874, the clock tower was added in 1883. The **Charles Brooke Memorial** stands facing the courthouse, erected in 1924. On closer scrutiny, this unimposing obelisk reveals four superbly crafted copper plaques depicting in turn, an Iban warrior, a Chinese courtier, a British soldier and a Malay warrior.

Next to the Court House in Jalan Tuan Abang Haji Openg is the odd-looking **Round Tower ⑤**, built in 1886 to house the town dispensary. Brooke seems to have had a predilection for fortifications; the Round Tower was meant to double up as a fort in times of attack. The Round Tower is now occupied by the **Sarawak Handicraft Centre**, where craftsmen and craftswomen can be seen making mats, weaving textiles, and embroidering. A good range of quality handicrafts is also on sale. Adjacent is the **Pavilion**, with its elaborate frontage – very different from Kuching's other colonial buildings.

Victorian treasure trove

Across the road is the impressively-columned **General Post Office** (open 9am–5pm), built in 1931 by Vyner Brooke, the last rajah. The road continues up, past the grassy square of the Central Padang to the **Sarawak Museum ⑥** between Jalan McDougall and Jalan Tun Haji Openg (open daily 9am–6pm).

This is perhaps the most important place of interest for the visitor. Naturalist and co-founder of the theory of evolution along with Charles Darwin, Alfred Russell Wallace spent many months in Borneo, exploring and collecting specimens. He became a particular friend of Rajah Charles Brooke, who with Wallace's encouragement, built the museum to house a permanent exhibition of native arts and crafts, and specimens from Wallace's own extensive collection.

BELOW: the Sarawak Museum is dedicated to the soul of Borneo.

The Brookes were steadfast in their sense of justice. They suppressed crime and established peace in the state, but wisely refrained from imposing any "civilised" versus "primitive" comparisons upon the native cultures. The Rajahs insisted upon capable curators, whose Western expertise was to serve only to illuminate the ethnological richness of Borneo and the vivid expressions of the societies it nourished. The facade of the old wing of the museum, however, betrays another influence. Its architecture was influenced by Charles Brooke's French valet, after a house in Normandy.

Map on page 278

Spirit of Borneo

While its sense of mystery disappeared along with the marvellous old teak floors during its modernisation, the museum still invites hours of exploration. It is divided into two buildings, separated by busy Jalan Tun Haji Openg. But the museum's exhibits take you far beyond the paved streets of Kuching and into the heart and soul of Borneo.

One display case in the museum is devoted to the Kenyah people, who have names for 60 varieties of ancient glass beads, each one with a special value. Another houses figurines carved 2,000 years ago by the now-extinct Sru Dayaks. An entire corner of the museum has been transformed into a walk-in replica of an Iban longhouse, with simulated fires, human skulls hanging from the rafters, as well as a warrior's elaborate headdress and weaponry resting at his bedside; you almost expect him to walk in and sound the battle cry.

The Sarawak tribespeople's great love of adornment is reflected in the high walls of the interior, painted with flowing designs. A museum employee found one end of a Kenyah longhouse at Long Nawang completely covered with a majestic mural celebrating "The Tree of Life" and he returned to Kuching and commissioned painters to reproduce it.

In the days of head-hunting, human skulls were hung from the rafters of Iban longhouses; the skulls were said to contain a powerful magic.

BELOW: art on display at the museum.

The old wing of the museum has an eclectic character that recalls a succession of spirited curators, as well as the great diversity of Sarawak. The enthusiastic influence of scholar Tom Harrisson, who first came to explore Sarawak in the 1920s as an Oxford undergraduate (and later returned to make his home here) can be seen in many of the collections. There is a human dental plate on display that was found in the stomach of a 6-metre (20-ft) crocodile. A rhinoceros horn cup that can detect poison is another item. If the drink was contaminated, the liquid bubbled to the top: since princes were always trying to poison one another, rhino horn was in high demand during the days of the dynasties.

The old museum is joined by a footbridge over the road to the new **Museum Annex** completed in 1983. Here galleries display more of this cultural treasure trove; the lifestyles and customs of the nation's various tribes are well documented, and there is a reconstruction of the Niah caves where people lived 40,000 years ago. Videos and slide-shows cover such Sarawakian topics as the Great Golden Hornbill (Sarawak is often referred to as the "Land of Hornbills"), life in the jungle, and popular tribal dances.

TIP

Late afternoon on the Kuching River is best enjoyed from a *tambang*, the colourful local waterboats. Negotiate with the boatman for an hour's charter – pay no more than a few dollars – and sit back as he takes you on a leisurely ride past Kuching's bustling riverside.

BELOW: Kuching Mosque overlooking Sarawak River.

Continue down Jalan Barracks, past the Padang and the Central Police Station and turn left into **Jalan India Mall**, a colourful jumble of shops and small businesses, little changed from 50 years ago.

Veer left into Lebuh Market, the old market street that leads to the golden domes of decorative **Masjid Bandaraya** (Kuching Mosque), which overlooks the river. Built in 1968, it replaced the much older wooden structure built in 1852 that burned down. Retrace your steps along Lebuh Market to Jalan Gambier, where opposite the market, a spicy aroma emanates from the open sacks of spices on display. This collection of colourful shops marks what was once the main trading area. Indian Muslim traders, following the Chinese example in the 18th century, headed for Sarawak to set up textile shops and money-lending stalls; the area still exudes a faint aura of the exotic east. Across the street are a few examples of the old buildings that once lined this end of the Main Bazaar.

The **Masjid India** (Indian Mosque), in between Lebuh India and Jalan Gambier, was built by Indian Muslim traders in 1876. The streets around the mosque are a labyrinth of small Indian shops and spicy curry-scented restaurants. Continue the walk through this colourful area back to the Courthouse.

Chinese influence

Like many Malaysian towns, Kuching has its share of ornate Chinese temples. Apart from the Tua Pek Kong temple mentioned earlier, there is the **Kuek Seng Ong Temple** on Lebuh Wayang. Built in 1895, the temple is the traditional place of worship for Henghua fishermen, praying for good catches and a safe return from the sea. The temple is dedicated to the god Kuek Seng Ong, whose

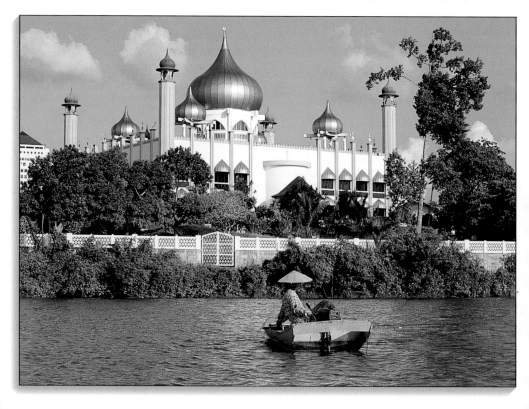

Maps:
Area 284
City 278

figure is placed on a sedan chair on the 22nd day of the second moon, and carried through the town's main thoroughfare.

Worthy of note is one of the oldest buildings in Kuching, the sprawling **Bishop's House ❶**, located behind the temples and shophouses of Chinatown, It was built in 1849 by James Brooke for the Rev. Thomas Francis McDougall and his wife. With his typical astuteness, Brooke selected McDougall as the first Anglican Bishop of Kuching because he had previously been a surgeon. Nearby is **St Thomas's Cathedral**.

The popular **Sunday Market ❶**, which attracts Dayak tradesmen from the surrounding countryside, is situated on the outskirts of town at Jalan Satok. The stallholders arrive and set up market on Saturday afternoon and continue until midday Sunday. All manner of strange foodstuffs – jungle produce, wild boar, bats, lizards, monkeys and turtles – are on sale here, alongside fruit, vegetables and fish.

A more recent addition to the Kuching cityscape is the blue- and gold-domed **Masjid Negara** (National Mosque), an example of modern Islamic architecture which stands across the river at a newer part of town (Petra Jaya).

Temple detail from Kuching's Kuek Seng Ong temple, dedicated to protecting fishermen.

Sarawak's western beaches

Sun worshippers, beach lovers and golfers head for **Damai Beach ❷** near Santubong, just 30 minutes by road from downtown Kuching. The pioneer resort here, Holiday Inn Damai Beach, has been joined by the Holiday Inn Damai Lagoon and the Santubong Resort. As well as the various watersports offered by the resorts, an 18-hole golf course and jungle walks on Mount Santubong increase the recreational options.

BELOW: fruit stall, Kuching.

TIP

There are traditional
dance performances
at the Sarawak
Cultural Village
at 11.30am and
4.30pm each day.
Call 846-411 for
more information.

For a fine introduction to Sarawak's varied cultures, visit the state's award-winning **Sarawak Cultural Village** ❸ (open daily 9am–5.30pm; entrance fee), adjacent to Damai Beach. Spread across 6 hectares (15 acres) of jungle at the foot of Santubong Mountain, the park has authentic dwellings of the six main cultural groups, staffed by friendly helpers wearing the appropriate dress. The village offers demonstrations of traditional arts and crafts, as well as daily cultural shows which incorporate Iban, Kayan, Kenyah, Melanau and Malay, Chinese and Bidayuh dances.

The fishing village of **Santubong** ❹ is also worth a visit. The village dates back to the Tang and Sung dynasties, between the 9th and 13th century, when it was an important trading centre. Ancient rock carvings of Hindu and Buddhist influence have been discovered around the river delta. Other beach resorts further along the coast include the Santin Holiday Beach Resort, hidden among mangroves 30 km (20 miles) west of Kuching. Tour buses leave the capital and take you to the jetty, where a boat zips you to the resort, which is inaccessible by land. There are boats to take you snorkelling and a fine beach lined with casuarina trees. With prior permission, you may be allowed to visit the green turtle sanctuary of **Pulau Satang Besar** ❺, north of Kampung Telaga Air, where precious turtle eggs are closely guarded. During the northeast monsoon season, especially December and January, the rough seas make it difficult to get there.

Sarawak's national parks

An abundance of nature can be enjoyed at the many national parks accessible from Kuching. Some parks can be enjoyed as day trips, although all deserve a longer visit. Gazetted in 1957, **Bako National Park** ❻ (Taman Negara Bako)

BELOW:
Sarawak Cultural
Village hostess.

Kuching Environs

SOUTH CHINA SEA

was Sarawak's first, and it offers some of the best chances to see native animals in the wild. Situated on a peninsula at the mouth of the Sarawak River, Bako's relatively small area of 30 sq km (10 sq miles) is uniquely rich in both flora and fauna, offering examples of almost every vegetation group to be found in the state. Primary rainforest covers one side of the peninsula, while the other side offers a picturesque coastline of steep cliffs and sandy bays with beaches for swimming. Mud flats and sand bars support a great diversity of sea birds, as well as peculiar red crabs and mud skippers.

Map on page 284

While it is possible to visit Bako on a day trip, the rewards are greater if you stay for one night at least – a visit of two or three nights is recommended. Some people stay for a month, relaxing in the natural environment and exploring all the park has to offer. Catch the sun setting over the coloured limestone karsts of the main beach, and enjoy the unearthly experience of walking in the luminous forest at night.

The dry plateau is home to the bizarre insect-eating flowers known as *nepenthes* or pitcher plants; eight species exist within the park's confines. The coastal swamp forest is a favoured retreat of Borneo's endemic proboscis, or long-nosed, monkey, the long-tailed macaque, bearded pig and sambar deer, some of which find their way down to the beaches. Within the park is a good system of well-marked paths; ask for a guide map at the Park Ranger's Office. Settle down and get ready to explore the wonders of Bako.

A magnificent plankwalk leads through a tidal mangrove forest that changes character throughout the day with the rise and fall of the sun, and the ebb and flow of the tide. Here in the early morning, when the water is low, lucky visitors may encounter the shy proboscis monkey or the silver leaf monkey, feast-

BELOW: Orang-utan at Semonggoh.

TIP

Feeding times at the Semonggoh Orang Utan Sanctuary are from 8.30–9am and 2.30–3.30pm so time your visit carefully.

ing on the young leaves. Tread quietly and keep your eyes wide open. The popular **Lintang Trail** leads through nearly all the vegetation types and up to the arid plateau where pitcher plants can be found among the scrub.

Within the park, accommodation is available at the resthouse, dormitories and chalets at the headquarters at **Teluk Assam**. A small shop supplies basic provisions which you can cook yourself, or the canteen offers a perfectly acceptable menu. Beware the cheeky long-tailed macaques who will try their best to find their way into your chalet kitchen or even steal food right off the table in the main dining area. They are a basketful of trouble, providing high entertainment for onlookers. Book accommodation with the helpful staff in Kuching at the Visitors' Information Centre, close to Sarawak Museum.

Some 22 km (14 miles) southwest of Kuching is the **Semonggoh Orang Utan Sanctuary** ❼ (open daily 8am–4.30pm) where you'll find Sarawak's first dedicated reserve for these jungle creatures. This is another must-visit excursion and a great chance for an encounter with these delightful animals. Rehabilitation for orphaned babies and adult animals who have been kept as domestic pets is an ongoing process as they are taught to climb trees, find food, make nests and otherwise survive in the wild. Semonggoh is also the home for hornbills, monkeys and honey-bears.

Parks and islands

In Sarawak's southeast corner you'll find **Kubah National Park** ❽, a small park of 2,230 hectares (5,500 acres), which is only 21 km (13 miles) from Kuching along good roads, making it easily accessible. Within its confines are streams, waterfalls and bathing pools. A 5–6 hour return trail leads to the park's highest peak, **Gunung Serapi,** while the most popular, the waterfall trail, leads through dipterocarps with plankwalk sections in front of the waterfall. Kubah makes a good day trip from the capital; chalets are available for longer stays.

The **Matang Wildlife Centre** ❾ some 14 km (9 miles) further along, is home to a number of orangutan and other local fauna which are contained in large enclosures found within the rainforest.

The little-explored western part of the state has more surprises for those who want to visit. The now reasonable road west leads to **Lundu** and **Sematan** where remote beaches – try Pandan Beach near Lundu – are only one of the attractions. Out from Sematan, a relaxed little fishing village, are several deserted islands, one of which, **Talang Talang** is a turtle sanctuary. Permission to visit the far west of the state can be obtained from the local district officer; accommodation in self-contained chalets is available.

More national parks can be visited in the northwest. The town of Lundu is the access point to **Gunung Gading National Park** ❿. Gazetted in 1983, the mountainous park covers an area of over 41,000 hectares (101,100 acres), on both sides of the Lundu River. Within the park are waterfalls and a trail to the summit of Gunung Perigi, a trek that takes about 8 hours. Giant Rafflesia blooms, growing up to a metre (3 ft) can be found in the park, and chalets are avail-

BELOW: sunset in Bako National Park.

Map
on page
284

able. According to legend, Gunung Gading (Ivory Mountain) is named after a Javanese princess who used to bathe at one of its numerous waterfalls; the trails are steep but it's worth hiking them to see both Rafflesia blooms and the falls, especially Waterfall 3 and 7.

Gazetted in 1994, **Tanjung Datu National Park** ⓫ is one of Sarawak's newest and smallest parks, covering an area of just 1,379 hectares (3,400 acres). Right at the westernmost tip of the state, the park has clear rivers and fine coraline beaches with unspoiled reefs. It is accessible by boat from Sematan and the whole journey takes around 3½ hours – but there is no accommodation available.

Batang Ai National Park and **Lanjak Entiman Wildlife Sanctuary** are favoured haunts of orang-utan, gibbons, barking deer, leaf monkeys and wild boar as well as several hundred species of birds. Both areas are located in the Sri Aman Division, north of the **Batang Ai Dam**. The Batang Ai River, a tributary of the Batang Lupar, was dammed to create Sarawak's first hydro-electric power plant, which became operational in 1985. A subject of great controversy at the time, the dam flooded over 10 longhouses belonging to the Iban and Orang Ulu, and also affected the flora and fauna in the area. During the drier times of the year, the dam is not a pretty sight as thousands of dead trees protrude from the water. The dam is fed by several tributaries where many longhouses are found.

Once past the Batang Ai dam – a 4-hour trip from Kuching – the journey to the park takes about 2 hours upriver by longboat. There are no facilities in these two reserves as yet, but Borneo Adventure (*see page 360*) has accommodation at **Nanga Sumpa** and **Wong Tibul**, on the boundary of Batang Ai National Park; excursions into the park can be arranged from there. ❏

BELOW:
an Iban dancer

LONGHOUSE TOURS FROM KUCHING

A visit to a longhouse in Sarawak – mostly found in the Skrang or Batang Ai regions – is a must (*see page 294–5*). You get to see an integrated community living under one roof, and the Iban people are generally great fun and very hospitable. The Iban and most of the Orang Ulu build their dwellings near rivers, which once offered their only means of access. Today, many are accessible by road.

Visitors were previously encouraged to head out on their own, but now, unless you are invited by a longhouse host, it is advisable to use a tour operator. Many longhouses have tourist accommodations nearby, ensuring privacy for both the longhouse dwellers and visitors.

One of the best longhouse experiences is offered by Borneo Adventure (*see page 360*) at the **Rumah Along** longhouse at Nanga Sumpa, near the Batang Ai Dam some 275 km (170 miles) north of Kuching. The longhouse inhabitants have benefited from their visitors and earn a little cash without compromising their lifestyle. Sarawak's other longhouse experience is the **Hilton's Batang Ai Longhouse Resort** (*see page 381*). Opened in 1994, the upmarket resort with air-conditioning and hot water features "longhouse living with all the modern conveniences", but it lacks a community atmosphere.

SIBU AND CENTRAL SARAWAK

Map on page 276

Sibu is the bustling gateway to the Rejang, Malaysia's mightiest river. A trip upriver will reward you with a glimpse of the lives of the Orang Ulu and Iban peoples of the region

Beyond Kuching, cosmopolitan city life fades away and the innumerable rivers that mark Sarawak's green interior become the highways to remote inland settlements. **Sibu ❶**, capital of Sarawak's third and largest district, is an easy-going and predominantly Chinese town, where the fish markets overflow with gigantic freshwater species such as carp and the much-prized *kolong,* which finds its way to the elegant dining tables of Hong Kong. Timber money has made Sibu rich and the sprawling town, abounding with glitzy hotels and karaoke bars, is home to some of Sarawak's wealthiest families. Visitors tend not to linger in Sibu – often just staying overnight after arriving from Kuching by boat, before leaving to travel upriver the next morning.

The express boat port and surrounding market area is the town's busiest spot, presided over by the imposing seven-tier pagoda that is part of the **Tua Pek Kong Temple**. From the top of the pagoda is a magnificent view of dozens of express boats lined up along the wharf, with boards in front denoting their destinations and a clock showing their departure times. The busy atmosphere lends a hint of adventure and of journeys into the unknown.

Although it is possible to take a bus from Kuching to Sibu, your bones will be considerably rattled by the time you arrive. It is far more pleasant to take the express boat, which heads down the Sarawak River, out to the South China Sea, and then up the **Rejang River** via **Sarikei**. Alternatively, there is a 40-minute flight, giving a wonderful view of the never-ending jungle with its milk-coffee rivers snaking their way through the low-lying *nipah* palm swamps. Flights to further up the Rejang River, to Kapit and Belaga, are also available.

LEFT: tributary of Sarawak's mighty Rejang River.
BELOW: nomadic Penans help to transport goods.

Heading upriver

From Sibu, express boats, long and narrow, rather like wingless 747s, depart regularly. They head downstream to Sarikei and Kuching, and upriver *(ulu)* to Kapit, and also past the treacherous Pelagus Rapids to Belaga. Tourists mingle with an assortment of other passengers: Chinese merchants taking their wares to distant longhouses; river and inland officials (usually Iban) going about their business; the odd longhouse dweller returning home after a visit to the big city, or schoolchildren who attend school in Sibu but return to their family longhouses for the holidays.

Because of extensive logging, express boats now run to several of the major tributaries of the Rejang – a marvellous network that enables visitors to get around at little expense and with great ease – a situation much changed from the heady and hilarious days of Redmond O'Hanlon's explorations in *Into The Heart Of Borneo*. Other, much earlier travellers had to do it all the hard way, by hiring boats themselves. Although expressboat prices are fixed, hire of longboats is expensive (even for locals) and heavily dependent on the water level, weather, time of day, river currents and how willing the boatman is to hurry his journey to fit your schedule. For foreigners, prices will naturally be much higher and a spot of astute but friendly bargaining is in order. Unless you take a direct express to Kapit, the express boat stops along the way at the smaller settlements of **Kanowit** and **Song**, from where local express boats can be taken to visit longhouses up these rivers.

On the river, boats and longboats, and timber tugs work their way up or glide down-river on the Rejang. Sarawak's longest river is also the natural highway for the timber industry, and you may see huge rafts stacked with logs floating downstream. Should one of these hazards become waterlogged, they present considerable danger to outboard motors; with that very danger in mind, the express boats have their undercarriage lined with steel and there is always a spare propellor shaft lashed to the roof.

Kapit – the upriver capital

The day starts early in **Kapit ❷** as the siren call of the first express boats sound through the misty dawn. As the boats fire up their throbbing and powerful engines, passengers down their last cups of morning coffee, ready to start their journeys on the river.

To those who live far up the Rejang River, the bustling market town is the big city. Kapit has electricity 24 hours a day, shops (selling goods at considerably higher prices than back in Sibu), hotels equipped with luxuries like TV and air conditioning and fast food outlets selling fried chicken, pizza, ice cream and

BELOW:
the Rejang River in
the glow of dusk.

Map on page 276

other doubtful big city delights. As a marked contrast, the daily morning market is filled with tribal women coming to town to sell their produce, before heading off to the local provision shops to buy longhouse necessities.

Only 2½ hours upriver from Sibu, and in spite of all these modern improvements, the sprawling centre still retains the atmosphere of a frontier town, bearing marks of its origins when the Brookes established it as a trading post and fort town. **Fort Sylvia**, built in 1875 by Charles Brooke, was placed strategically to prevent the movement of the Orang Ulu downstream and the Ibans moving further *ulu* or upstream, to avert more full-scale wars. Constructed solidly of *belian* or ironwood, the fort has withstood generations of floods, which in some years reached halfway up the walls. Today the fort houses the **Kapit Museum** (open Mon–Fri 9am–4pm, Sat–Sun 9am–12pm) with excellent ethnographic displays on the main peoples of the area.

Kapit lies in the heart of Iban country, Sarawak's largest indigenous population. Ibans were once the headhunters who gave Borneo its romantic and primitive reputation. Some understanding of their culture will help the visitor to see that they were not merely bloodthirsty in an anarchic way. To bring good fortune to the longhouse, and fame and a bride for themselves, young Iban warriors would (and some still do) set out from home to travel "the world". Status would be acquired in the form of tattoos telling of their bravery, and the heads of a few enemies brought home to imbue the longhouse with protective spirits. Only warriors of equal strength were killed, and never children, women or the old and sick. Sadly, these traditions were much misunderstood by the 19th-century writers who revelled in writing lurid stories about the headhunters of the Iban tribes.

Beyond Kapit is **Belaga** ❸ – the last urban centre on the Rejang, after which

An Iban woman weaving the pua kumbu, a traditional fabric used for ceremonial purposes.

BELOW:
Iban tattoos are heavily symbolic.

TIP

The Sarawak Tourism Board has organised a homestay programme which allows visitors to stay with selected families to sample a slice of traditional Malaysian life. Contact the board at tel: 082-240 620

it is longhouse communities all the way. Reaching Belaga means coursing through the **Pelagus Rapids**, marking the natural boundary between the Iban territory below and the Orang Ulu beyond. These rapids are the most treacherous navigable waterway in the state, and possibly in the whole of Borneo. The 2½ km (1½ miles) stretch is a series of whirlpools and waves as the river rapidly loses altitude. Many lives and boats have been lost in this maelstrom; riding the rapids atop an express boat (ready to jump off in case of trouble) provides high excitement. When the water is low – from May to August – only small longboats can struggle through, although some do try to negotiate the perils in a speedboat.

Just below the rapids is the upmarket **Pelagus Resort**, a designer longhouse-style resort, designed by Kuching luminary and architect, Edric Ong. The resort makes a comfortable base for excursions: to longhouses to see Iban women making high-quality *pua kumbu* or ceremonial blankets; to explore waterfalls and jungle trails; or to just laze by the pool, amid beautiful natural surroundings.

Upstream to Belaga

The real last outpost, Belaga has grown larger, due to incessant logging, but visit the town, with its few small but comfortable hotels to see just what a bazaar of the interior looks like. Some of the old wooden buildings remain, although increasingly they are replaced with ubiquitous concrete shophouses. But sit in a coffee shop, sipping on a mug of thick coffee sweetened with spoonfuls of condensed milk, and watch the passing parade of people: Kayan women wearing heavy metal decorations in their ears which have stretched to their breasts; young warriors who devote their ferocity to football rather than collecting heads; children sent down to school to learn the ways of the other world; a collection

BELOW:
long boats are probably the best means of travel.

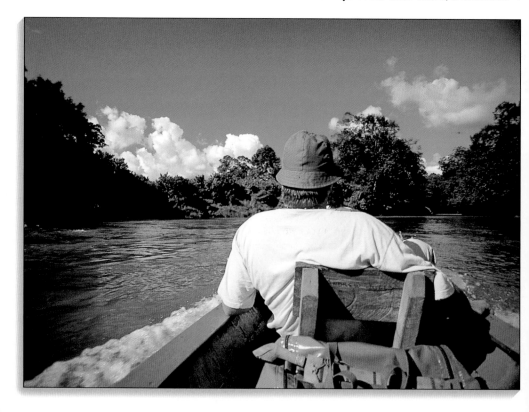

of traders, hustlers, would-be tour guides on the make, and labourers fresh from the logging camps, money burning in their pockets. It's raw and primitive, with an energy you will never find in the city.

From Belaga, express boats head upstream when the water is high, but it really is necessary to find a guide or an invitation before venturing afar to visit an upriver longhouse. In spite of their long traditions of hospitality to travellers on the river, most longhouse folk are just not interested in entertaining people they can't talk to and who have little to offer to their lives. Officially, foreigners wanting to head further upriver from Belaga must obtain a permit from the local police station, and it is neither possible nor desirable to travel near the controversial Bakun hydro-electric dam site.

Map on page 276

Sojourn with nature

Travelling northeast from Sibu along the main highway to Miri, one passes a few worthwhile stops. A good network of buses, taxis and mini buses makes it quite an easy matter to move east by public transport.

The sleepy Melanau fishing village of **Mukah** ❹ is a pleasant layover and offers a relaxed respite from jungle life. The traditional wooden houses are stilted and visitors can watch the fascinating process of extracting sago from the thick trunks of the sago palm. An excursion out to sea with the fishermen is another possibility. The town is home to the enigmatic annual Kaul Festival where ancient Melanau rites appease the spirits of the sea and mark the new fishing season as well as give thanks to the fertility spirits. Several towns hold their own Kaul Festival as well as the official one held in the second week of April.

The burgeoning oil town of **Bintulu** ❺ has developed out of all recognition in the past couple of decades. The old wooden bazaar has given way to new shops and hotels, as well as a deep-water port, chemical factories and a massive liquid petroleum gas (LPG) plant to exploit offshore reserves of natural gas.

BELOW: performing a religious ritual.

About 20 km (12 miles) away from Bintulu is the **Similajau National Park** ❻. Gazetted in 1976, the 7,067-hectare (17,500-acre) national park is less visited than those closer to Kuching or Miri, but its more difficult access makes it no less attractive. Opened to visitors only in 1991, the long narrow park covers a 32 km by 1.5 km area (20 miles by 1 mile) and is bordered by one of Sarawak's most beautiful stretches of unspoiled beach, with jungle trails running into the forest. Small rivers and rapids on the **Sebulong River** also make for interesting exploration. Similajau is home to saltwater crocodiles, so watch your step when walking close to river inlets. Other, less spectacular inhabitants include gibbons, banded langurs, civet cats, porcupines, wild boar and long-tailed macaques, as well as 185 species of birds, including hornbills. Green turtles come to lay their eggs on the quiet beaches between July and September.

Numerous longhouses can be visited up the Kemana River that runs into Bintulu; some of these are accessible by road as well as by river. Further upriver are the Orang Ulu longhouses of the Kenyah and Penan peoples. ❏

THE LONGHOUSES OF SARAWAK

A visit to an Iban longhouse offers a unique glimpse of an ancient way of life that – although changing fast – is still fascinating for outsiders

Longhouse life is a microcosm of a well-run society, where a close-knit community lives together under one roof with one chief, or *Tuai Rumah*, in charge. Within the structure, a kind of horizontal highrise, each family has its own quarters or *bilek*, where they sleep and eat. The main room is often lined with Chinese ceramic jars much prized by the Ibans. At the rear is the kitchen, where a wood fire provides the heat for cooking, adding a distinctive smokey taste to the food and a dark patina to the surroundings.

CHANGING TIMES

Times are changing in the longhouse. Walls which once held faded photographs of the Brookes and Queen Elizabeth II are now adorned with colour magazine pictures of beauty queens, racing cars and the latest pop icons. Many Dayaks have converted from spirit-sensitive animism to Christianity, and evenings once spent performing tribal chants and sacrificial ceremonies are taken up with prayer meetings. Children who once enjoyed carefree days frolicking in the longhouse and the rice fields are ensconced in schools studying Bahasa Malaysia and physics. Yet still the community spirit lives on.

▷ **LIVING OFF THE LAND**
Longhouse life is hard. Men and women spend long hours working in the fields, planting and tending their crops.

△ **ON THE VERANDAH**
Much longhouse activity takes place on the *tanju* and *ruai* – from drying cocoa beans to socialising.

▷ **COCKFIGHTING**
Cockfighting is a popular male pastime. Animistic beliefs and legendary spirits surround many of the festival cockfights.

◁ MULTI-PURPOSE GALLERY
Winnowing grains in the *ruai*, or gallery – the space used for everything from basket weaving to holding community celebrations.

△ LONGHOUSE STAPLE
Drying rice on the longhouse verandah, or *tanju*. Afterwards, the rice is stored carefully in the different family units.

◁ TRADITIONAL SKILLS
An Iban woman displays her handiwork in a *pua kumbu* – a ceremonial cloth used to decorate longhouse walls.

△ IKAT WEAVING
Preparing to dye the threads for a *pua kumbu*. Intricate pieces can use up to five or six colours, and take months to complete.

FIGHTING COCK OR SACRIFICIAL PET?

Cocks play an important part in Iban culture, and they are kept and cossetted as pets while being prepared for their first big fight. The men of the longhouse play with them regularly, engaging them in mock battles with their neighbours, but without the razor sharp spurs attached to their rear claws. Those are reserved for fighting days and can bring a lesser fighter to its death in minutes. Before the fight, the cocks are sometimes given small shots of *tuak*, rice wine, to keep them energised and slightly aggressive.

The cocks and chickens also play an important part in ceremonial issues. Chicken sacrifices are common and the occult powers of a white cockerel are highly respected, in common with many other cultures around the world.

In many ceremonies – for example, in the case of a sick or possessed person – a cock will be sacrificed, and the blood, valued for its purifying quality, sprinkled over a subject. In milder cases, the live chicken is simply waved over the subject or over the ceremony offering plates.

MIRI AND THE NORTHEAST

Just over the border from Brunei, the oil boomtown of Miri is the ideal spot from which to head for the magnificent Mulu caves, or make a visit to a Sarawakian longhouse

Map on page 276

O n the northwest coast of Sarawak lies **Miri ❼**, the first town to come to prominence – and win notoriety – with the growth of the oil industry. But gone are its bad old days as a wild cowboy town – a town of oil money and men chasing it. Miri, which became a city in early 2005, is modern and thriving, with luxurious hotels, including the Miri Marriott Resort and Spa and a Holiday Inn, and restaurants and bars catering to the town's new-found wealth. Miri is also the source of bright lights and salubrious entertainments for the inhabitants of nearby **Brunei**, a short drive across the border. Despite all this, the ambience remains decidedly relaxed in this predominantly Chinese oil town.

While Miri offers few attractions apart from food and relaxation, and more recently some interesting diving, it makes an excellent overnight stop before embarking on a trip to the great caves of Mulu, or to nearby Lambir Hills, Niah Caves or Loagan Bunut.

A feast of seafood

Food in Miri is a pleasure. The town has long been known for its seafood, and has several Chinese restaurants specialising in serving up great piles of fresh and delicious delicacies for the most discerning palate. Don't overlook the Miri Café – opened by an Australian couple, this easygoing café cum bar in an open-fronted shophouse offers basic Aussie dishes and a wide selection of drinks.

On top of **Canada Hill** overlooking Miri is Sarawak's first oil well. Constructed by Shell in 1910, the well was the forerunner of a further 623 oil wells drilled in the area known as the Miri Land Field. It also survived longer than most of the other 623. After more than six decades, and an estimated yield of 600,000 barrels, production ceased in the early 1970s.

Untouched reefs provide excellent scuba diving, about 90 km (60 miles) off the coast. As the reefs are so remote, they have escaped the destructive dynamiting that has ruined many of the more accessible reefs where visibility is often poor. Miri is also the starting point for some of Sarawak's most exciting and adventurous upriver trips. Longhouses are scattered from the coast all the way up the Baram River.

The paved road to **Kuala Baram**, the mouth of the Baram River, and continues towards the Sultanate of **Brunei**. From there, a ferry will take you to the duty-free island of **Labuan**. A road also heads up the northern side of the Baram River to the trading town of **Marudi ❽**.

While most visitors stop just long enough to catch the next expressboat on their rush upriver to Mulu, for a taste of outback Sarawak, Marudi is worth a day or two of exploration by itself. One of the older of

LEFT: bats take flight in Mulu.
BELOW: fish-seller in Miri market.

An elaborate Kenyah headdress.

the Brookes' fort posts and the main supply centre or "bazaar" for the Baram region, Marudi is a fast-spreading town which retains the atmosphere of a trading post. Upriver Iban, Kenyah, Kayan and Penan tribal folk come to sell their wares to the Chinese traders of the town. A lively daily market makes a pleasant diversion and the provision shops stock everything an uplander could need – from chainsaws to chicken feed, plastic buckets to pullovers and even handicrafts. A day or two can be very pleasantly spent wandering about the town, or sitting in a local coffee shop near the express boat jetty to watch the passing parade of people and produce as boats come and go.

A visit to the Rajah Brooke's **Fort House** is almost mandatory. Erected in 1901 and overlooking the Baram River, the fort was built to control migrations (and wars) up and down river. The fort burned down in the early 1990s, but has been faithfully reconstructed and turned into an interesting little museum.

From Marudi, there are flights to Gunung Mulu National Park and to Bario, in the cool Kelabit Highlands, but book well in advance as seats are scarce.

Marvellous Mulu

A trip to **Gunung Mulu National Park** ❾, together with a visit to a longhouse, are two of Sarawak's most memorable experiences. If the trip to or from Mulu follows the old **Headhunters Trail**, using forest paths and longboats, it becomes unforgettable. With the advent of several daily flights to Mulu, getting to the park became much faster and more efficient, but not necessarily more pleasurable, and those with time and a love for travel still prefer to go by boat from Kuala Baram. Flying over part of the park, however, does give you a good idea of its vastness and of the variety of the terrain.

BELOW: guides resting at "The Pinnacles", Mulu.

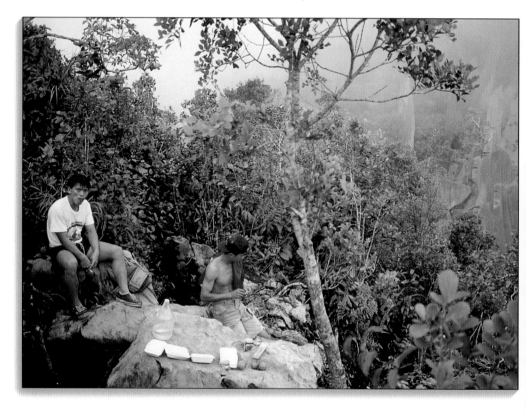

Covering 53,000 hectares (130,600 acres), Mulu is Sarawak's largest park. Gazetted in 1974, it is home to a great variety of flora ranging from flowers and orchids, fungi, mosses and ferns, as well as 10 species of pitcher plants. Ten species of hornbills flourish within the vast park.

A number of tour operators in Miri and Kuching offer package tours, which include transport as well as meals and accommodation in simple lodges just outside the park boundaries. There is also accommodation within the park – the chalets at the headquarters are ideally located – while nearby, the luxurious Royal Mulu Resort comes complete with a small swimming pool. Action sports fans will find roped climbing walls, as well as canoeing and rapids shooting.

Visitors who are not on a package tour (which includes a guide) are obliged to hire a park guide. These independent travellers also pay a high price for transport by boat within the park, unless they join forces with others. Even though a trip to this World Heritage Site is not necessarily cheap, it is worth every cent.

World-class caves

For many visitors, the centre of attraction is the magnificent caves. While over 150 km (100 miles) of caves have already been surveyed, specialists estimate that only 20 to 30 percent of this massive system has been documented. The caves are accessible by short longboat rides between the park headquarters and the various sites, and jungle plankwalks make walking easy, freeing your eyes from watching your step and giving you a chance to enjoy the surroundings.

The sheer scale of these caves will please even the most discerning statistician; within their dank confines lies the world's largest natural cave chamber, allegedly big enough to hold 16 football fields or 40 jumbo jets and to earn a

Maps:
Area 276
Park 299

Gunung Mulu's primary jungle contains astonishing biodiversity; every scientific expedition that has visited its forests has encountered plant and animal species previously unknown to man.

BELOW: hornbill at Mulu National Park.

Gunung Mulu National Park

*Subterranean
animals that inhabit
the Mulu caves
include poisonous
cave scorpions,
huntsman spiders,
albino crabs and
snakes which dine on
swiftlets and bats.*

place in the Guiness Book of World Records. Clearwater Cave at 75 km (47 miles), is the longest cave in Southeast Asia.

Exploring the caves

Only four of the 25 caves so far explored are open to public viewing, but this is plenty to gain an idea of the immensity and complexity of this cave system. Most often visited is the **Deer Cave Ⓐ**, named after long-vanished deer. The site is accessible by a 3-km (2-mile) plankwalk from the **Park HQ Ⓑ**, passing through a peat swamp forest where orchids thrive and an ancient Penan burial site. This massive hall is 2,160 metres (7,090 ft) long and 220 metres (720 ft) deep. The plankwalk cuts a path over the mounds of guano – a tonne of which is made each day – and leads through to the **Garden of Eden**, an enclosed valley where the vegetation has existed undisturbed for millennia.

It is from near the entrance to Deer Cave that one of the most spectacular sights of Mulu can be enjoyed – the nightly bats' exodus. Around 5.30pm, as the lowering sun turns the limestone walls to gold, the first flutterings can be seen, followed by an ever increasing number of bats circling their way out of the cave, up and over the trees on their nightly forage for food. The dramatic spectacle (which unfortunately does not take place during rainy weather) lasts for a good 20 minutes, and is a sight to awe the most jaded of visitors.

Close by Deer Cave is **Lang Cave Ⓒ**, whose well-lit stalactites and stalagmites make it one of the most beautiful of all the caves.

Clearwater Cave Ⓓ on the way to Camp 5 is located off the main river, a 30-minute boat ride from Park HQ. The 355-metre (1,165-ft) deep cavern is very dark inside, but with a strong torch you'll be able to see the marvellous lime-

BELOW: stunning Lang Cave in Mulu National Park.

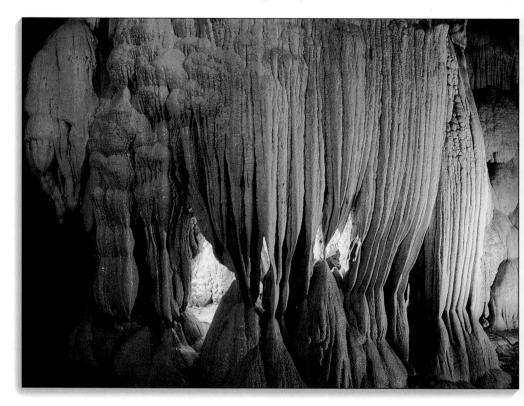

stone formations, and creatures including scorpions, frogs and centipedes. An exquisitely clear river flows out of the cave from under a sheer rockface, providing a popular spot for bathing. Keep an eye out for beautiful butterflies, including the iridescent green and black Rajah Brooke's Birdwing.

Map on page 299

Just a few minutes away, and accessible via a cliff-hugging walkway, is the dramatic **Wind Cave E**, far smaller but filled with limestone stalactites and stalagmites with plankwalks passing the most spectacular examples.

Sarawak Chamber F, reputedly the largest cave in the world, is only accessible to scientists, museum experts and special adventure groups, much of it being extremely dangerous. Gaining access to the cavern involves a 4-hour trek through the jungle from the nearest river point, to the small entrance from where you slide into the dank inky blackness. An exciting excursion, but definitely not for the faint of heart.

Other excursions

Apart from pleasant walks along jungle trails, there are two peaks to be conquered. **Gunung Mulu G** at 2,377 metres (7,800 ft) and **Gunung Api H**, which at 1,750 metres (5,600 ft) is Malaysia's highest limestone mountain. The stiff ascent of both these mountains is only recommended for very experienced (and very fit) climbers.

Caving in Mulu National Park is an unrivalled experience.

The strange limestone spikes, known as **The Pinnacles**, on an alternative path on Gunung Api, can be tackled by anyone of reasonable fitness in about 2 to 3 days. The razor sharp peaks, some standing 45 metres (150 ft) high make a magnificent sight, almost worth the effort of ascending the mountain. The journey there begins with a satisfying longboat trip upriver from the National

BELOW: plankwalk to Deer Cave.

TIP

It is recommended that you wear gloves, long-sleeved shirts and long trousers when climbing The Pinnacles; the sharp rocks can cut easily.

Park HQ, and a short stop-off to visit the Clearwater Cave. A 4-km (2½-mile) walk through lowland forest brings you to the **Melinau River Gorge ❾** and **Camp 5** – a simple hut shelter and campsite overlooking the Melinau River, and the overnight base camp for the climb to the Pinnacles,

The steep climb, which takes 3 to 6 hours depending on fitness level, starts early morning. This allows enough time to reach the viewpoint by lunch, and to make the descent before dark. The ascent is only to be attempted with experienced guides as the limestone pinnacles are razor sharp. The rough trail passes through the mossy forest where dwarfed trees are festooned with hanging mosses, and numerous pitcher plants, while the often misty environment adds an ethereal air.

The trip to Mulu can be combined with the **Headhunter's Trail**, either starting, or finishing at **Limbang**. The trail, used by Kayan headhunters in the 19th century is a 5- or 6-day journey through the backwoods, either entering or exiting by Camp 5, although leaving from Mulu is the easier option. You'll need a tour company or, at the very least, a guide to arrange the boat transport and longhouse accommodation along the way from Limbang (*see Travel Tips*).

Stone-age secrets

Back in Miri, there are a couple of side-trips which are the main attractions that draw most travellers to Sarawak. **Lambir Hills National Park ❿**, which is just south of Miri, is the world's most ecologically diverse park. It makes a pleasant day trip although chalets are available for longer stays. The park's highlights are waterfalls with natural swimming pools as well as a climb up **Bukit Lambir**.

BELOW: the morning market at Batu Niah.

Much more famous, and with more to offer, is **Niah Caves National Park ⓫**, which while less dramatic than Mulu, offers the freedom for visitors to explore on their own; guides are available if needed.

The limestone caves and their past inhabitants are the attraction here. In the 1870s, animal collector and adventurer, A. Hart Everett, came across the caves – already well-known and protected by the local people – only to dismiss them as "rather dull". It was not until the 1950s that the Sarawak Museum heard of the caves being an archaeologist's gold mine. Sure enough, when the curator dug down 5 metres (16 ft) he found the skull of a young *Homo sapiens* who had lived here possibly up to 40,000 years ago. The Deep Skull, as it was known, was what remained of the earliest known community of modern people in the East. It contradicted the haughty theories which insisted that humanity's true ancestor originated on the west side of the Middle East and only later "wandered" over to this part of the world.

As the archaeologists looked elsewhere, they found haematite paintings, featuring stick figures with strange little boat-like objects. Other discoveries revealed that people living here worked with instruments made from bone and shell, made pottery, cut stone adzes and carved wooden coffins or burial boats. Many agreed that these discoveries were as significant as the unearthing of Java Man. More recent objects, canoe-shaped coffins and paintings found in the cave known as the **Painted Cave**, date from only 1,000 years ago.

When the Iron Age reached Borneo in AD 700, the Niahans were trading hornbill ivory and edible birds' nests for Chinese porcelain and beads. They decorated enormous earthenware urns and placed them beside the graves of special men. Then in 1400, they appear to have entered a tropical Dark Age, which forced them to desert the caves. They then vanished from history.

Local delicacy

The Niahans may have been the forefathers of the nomadic Penan, whose elders still maintain beliefs and rituals that allude to those in the pre-historic graveyards of the Great Caves. The Penan rediscovered the caves in the 19th century, and found them to be unbelievably rich in edible birds' nests of the millions of swiftlets that inhabit the bowels of the Niah Caves. The glutinous saliva with which they build the nests is believed to be medicinal, and makes the nests the most expensive Chinese delicacy in Borneo. In the markets of Hong Kong and Singapore, the nests can fetch up to US$1,000 per kg (2¼ lbs).

The astronomical cost is almost understandable when you learn the way in which the nests are collected. A typical day's work might entail scurrying up 60 metres (200 ft) on a slender bamboo pole, scraping the nests off rock ceilings and from within deep crevices – and keeping one's balance where any fall could be fatal. You could say that the high cost of nests takes a man's life insurance into consideration.

Naturally, nest collectors guard their trade jealously, and pass their inherited territory on only to their sons. The hundreds of chambers, chimneys and

Maps:
Area 276
Park 299

BELOW: the Niah Caves are thought to have had human inhabitants 40,000 years ago.

Birds' nests, made from the hardened saliva of swiftlets, are treasured by the Chinese for their medicinal and fortifying qualities.

sub-caves where the tiny swiftlets nest are divided into sectors, each privately owned. Some yield but a few hundred nests, others several thousand. The cave owners live in villages and longhouses situated in the park area, and during harvesting – normally two or three times a year, sometimes more – they bring the entire family along to help gather up the riches.

To get to the Niah Caves, you must drive or take a bus or a taxi from either Miri or Bintulu, the former being much closer. From **Batu Niah** village, a short trip along the river brings you to the **Niah Caves Visitor Centre**.

There are several small hotels at Batu Niah, but you'll have to backtrack down the river after you visit the caves – a pleasant boat trip or a 45-minute walk. It is much more convenient to stay at the government-run hostels right in the park if you plan to spend time there. The hostels are friendly and relaxed, providing cooking facilities on request, bedding, toilets and showers with hot water, and electricity. The canteen serves perfectly acceptable, freshly-cooked local food.

Walking the planks

BELOW: entrance to the Great Cave at Niah.

The plankwalk to the caves begins from **Pangkalan Lubang**, just across the river from the park accommodation. A museum is located right at the beginning of the walk – entry is free and the information available is useful. The 3-km (2-miles) long path is built of the mighty *belian* or ironwood, a timber so dense that it will not float. You should get to the caves in about 45 minutes if the planks are dry. Sensible shoes are preferable to sandals both for the plankwalk and the caves. Other necessities include a strong torch (with spare batteries), some waterproof clothing and a water bottle.

Map on page 276

It is well worth stopping during the walk to absorb the atmosphere of the forest and to listen to the jungle chorus. Down one of the forks in the plankwalk, you can visit a collectors' longhouse, although they may charge you to have a look around their home.

Birds and bats

At the end of the plankwalk you will arrive at a series of steps and the **Trader's Cave**, and a heap of forlorn bamboo scaffoldings where once the traders set up camp during the collecting season. The **Great Cave** is the main area for birds' nest collection – and also for another interesting substance. Besides the three species of swiftlets of which there are said to be around 4 million, there are 12 species of bats, also countable in the millions. The strong-smelling guano lines the cave floor and is collected almost as avidly as the birds' nests – for it is a rich fertiliser. In fact, you may encounter guano collectors on the plankwalk up to the caves, lugging heavy sacks on their backs on their way to Pangkalan Lubang, where it is weighed and then sent down-river to Batu Niah and to the markets beyond.

With a strong torch you will be able to pick out the creatures that inhabit the caves. Only two of the caves are open to visitors without a guide, and the second, the **Painted Cave**, can only be entered with a permit issued by the National Park Office in Kuching.

The most spectacular sight of all at Niah makes it worth taking camping equipment along. At 6pm, the swiftlets return into the caves to sleep in their nests, while the bats, being nocturnal animals, sweep past them out of the entrance of the cave into the night. While far less spectacular than the great

Eight species of bat live in the Niah Caves. Most common are the horseshoe and fruit bats, but other rare residents include the bearded tomb bat and Cantor's roundleaf horseshoe bat.

LEFT: Iban tribesman.
BELOW: guano harvesters in Niah.

Map
on page
276

Mulu exodus, it is quite an experience sitting at the cave mouth, surrounded by dense, green jungle, watching the show. The reverse "shift" takes place at daybreak. It is a sight that humans must have watched and wondered at even 40,000 years ago.

Several other interesting day- or overnight trips can be arranged from Miri. **Bario** ⑫ is the sleepy "capital" of Kelabit country, in the midst of the Bario Highlands, a place right out of time with the industrialised world. A small airstrip, one of a series across the highlands, provides access – when the weather is right – and apart from the daily flights, Bario is remote and untouched. Tom Harrisson described his wartime experiences in the region in his book *The World Within*, and little has changed since. Surrounded by pristine forest, the cool highlands are the perfect place for trekking, stopping at longhouses along the way. One of the best treks is from Bario to **Ba Kelalan**, a 3- to 4-day walk.

Warm welcome

While the culture of the Kelabits has long since given way to the mores of a fundamentalist Christianity, the Kelabits are the kindest and most hospitable people you are ever likely to encounter. The Kelabit community is split across the border between Sarawak and Kalimantan, who are little troubled with the formalities of immigration check points. Visitors are taken to an immigration checkpoint, and the simple formalities are generally ironed out with ease (or a few dollars). From Bario, and with the help of Kelabit guides, it is possible to climb **Gunung Murud**. At 2,423 metres (7,949 ft), this is the highest peak in Sarawak, and you need 5 clear days to ascend and descend the mountain, starting from Bario – a memorable experience. Kelabit guides and porters will also take you on a 6-day walk back to **Long Lallang**, from where you can fly back to the other, hectic and more hurried world. For the fit and adventurous, one of these expeditions is definitely worth experiencing.

Lawas and **Limbang** are the two forgotten parts of Sarawak, two fingers that are interspersed with the Sultanate of Brunei. **Limbang** is the starting point (or finishing point) for those following the Headhunters Trail to Mulu.

Two hours' drive from Miri, on a turnoff before reaching Niah, is **Loagan Bunut National Park** ⑬. Also known as Bunurung, this national park was gazetted only in 1991. The park centres around a mysterious lake that rises and falls with the seasons. In the dry season, it disappears completely, leaving a cracked lake bed and an abundant fish population that hides in the mud. The fish are very easy to catch, a fact that has not escaped the local population of 32 families who are permitted to fish here, or the vast numbers of birds that visit to capitalise on all that fish.

There is little to disturb the peace in this remote place. One old Berawan man tends a guest house that can hold 16 guests, and there is also a park hostel that can accommodate 56 visitors. After arriving by car, the journey can be made into a round trip by taking a longboat and returning via the Baram River and an expressboat to Marudi, then beyond to Kuala Baram and Miri. ❑

BELOW: a soon-to-bloom fern bud.
RIGHT: copper relief of an Iban warrior.

SABAH

Stunningly beautiful, with an air of mystery, Sabah has now become home to a new breed of people seeking adventure

Today's Sabah is a far cry from the romantic days of old. As part of the mysterious Borneo, it inspired visions and wild dreams. It was a land of myth and adventure, of headhunters and strange pagan rites, and the source of buckles of "golden jade" to adorn the imperial belts of Chinese Emperors.

Sabah's ancestors spring from dozens of tribal groups, some deriving from millennia-old migrations from the north of China. Chinese traders sailed to Borneo before the days of Kublai Khan, in quest of kingfisher feathers, hornbill ivory and bezoar stones; others arrived much later, with the British, as coolies and farmers.

Many of today's visitors do not care about Sabah's romantic past. They are here to experience excitement and adventure, whether it is diving in unspoilt coastal waters, driving a four-wheel-drive vehicle cross-country, or scaling one of Asia's highest mountains.

Sabah has become a serious adventure destination, whose main attractions glitter bright as stars. It takes a minimum of a 10-day visit to do it any justice at all, and for most visitors, longer is better. The state offers such stellar attractions as Gunung Kinabalu (Mt Kinabalu), one of the highest mountain peaks between the Himalayas and the Andes, primal jungle retreats, wild whitewater rafting, and river cruising to spot wild elephants or the endemic proboscis monkey. Add some of the best diving in Asia – the prime spot, Pulau Sipadan, is rated as one of the world's top five wall dives – and it's no wonder that Sabah is becoming a favoured destination.

And these are only the highlights of this varied state. For those who like to tread more softly, there are secrets to be revealed in the misty jungles and lonely plains.

Remote coral islands are the destination of green turtles, where almost every day of the year, visitors can witness these remarkable creatures laying their eggs in the clean white sands – after making their mysterious odyssey from half-way across the world, following some ancient call of nature.

Sabah may lack the longhouses and diverse tribal communities of Sarawak, but it has remarkable natural assets, with reserves of pristine rainforest and tracts of virgin forest to explore. Places like the untouched Danum Valley exist nowhere else, and the goverment has gone to lengths to preserve this natural heritage, instilling pride in this unique environment into the hearts of the people who live here. ❑

PRECEDING PAGES: Gunung Kinabalu's dramatic rockface framed by swirling clouds.
LEFT: Bajau horsemen of Sabah, "cowboys of the east".

KOTA KINABALU AND THE WEST

Map on page 312

Sabah's capital is dominated by stunning vistas of the towering Gunung Kinabalu. Nearby are burgeoning new beach resorts to try before heading into the interior

The state capital on the northwest coast, **Kota Kinabalu ❶** is a modern city with little old world charm. Facing the west coast, it affords splendid sunsets over the offshore islands, sunsets which reflect Kota Kinabalu's history – a litany of heated passions, fights and fires – before the town reached its present, easy-going ways.

The British North Borneo Chartered Company established the first settlement in 1882, on nearby **Pulau Gaya** (Gaya Island) in the bay of the present city, in line with a British colonial penchant for offshore island bases. But it was attacked and burned to the ground by the rebel Bajau, Mat Salleh in 1897. Moving to the mainland, the Chartered Company then set up Jesselton, named after the company's vice-chairman, Sir Charles Jessel. The name remained until 1967, when shortly after independence, a new Malaysian consciousness gave the settlement yet another new name.

What's in a name?

The old name for the location of Kota Kinabalu is *Api Api* (literally, "fire, fire"). This does not, however, commemorate bygone arson, but rather the name of a local mangrove tree in which the fireflies twinkle at night. For a short time, the town was called *Singgah Mata* ("Where the Eye Lingers") before becoming Kota Kinabalu, in honour of the great mountain whose craggy peaks lend a magnificent backdrop to the city.

As a trading post, the town grew to be important enough to be bombed to ruins in 1945, in order to prevent the Japanese from setting up a base in this strategic position. Over the following decade, Kota Kinabalu grew into an undistinguished town, occupied with covering up the scars of World War II.

Ever since it was chosen as the site for British North Borneo's west coast base, the town has continued to encroach on the sea. Reclamation was the answer to the shortage of flat land, a process that continues as the need for this precious commodity grows. Even the "coastal highway" was pushed inland by the reclamation of huge areas of shallow sea, and one of the few remaining water villages, which was known by the generic name of **Kampung Air**, was demolished in 2003.

More recently, Kota Kinabalu has mushroomed. New high rise buildings and a rash of plush hotels are changing its face from the bland, uninspiring sprawl of 1950s concrete shophouses and stilt villages perched over the sea.

BELOW: Sabahan girls in ceremonial dress.

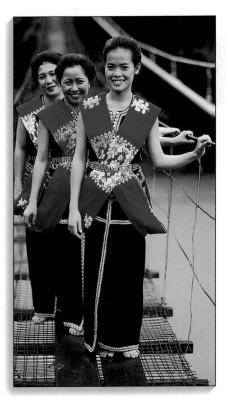

One of the most impressive of these new buildings is the gleaming tower of the **Menara Tun Mustapha** (Tun Mustapha Tower), formerly known as Sabah Foundation (Yayasan Sabah), an institution created with the timber royalties of the state. Situated to the north of the city at Likas Bay, it is one of the few "hanging" structures in the world and this 72-sided polygon rises up some 30 storeys.

Look out for burial poles called sininggazanak at the Sabah Museum. When a Kadazan man dies without an heir, a sininggazanak – said to resemble the deceased – is built in his honour and placed on his land

Architectural digest

To the south, the monumental **Masjid Sabah** (Sabah Mosque) on Jalan Tunku Abdul Rahman is an example of fine contemporary Islamic architecture. The mosque's gilded dome is visible from the city, although it is located some distance from the city centre. You can visit at any time other than prayer times, but remove your shoes before entering quietly. Nearby, the **Sabah Museum** (open Mon–Thurs 10am–6pm; Sat–Sun 9am–6pm), is built in a stylised version of traditional Rungus and Murut tribal architecture. The museum has a good collection of Chinese ceramics and the ethnological and textile sections are growing. The section on Sabah's fascinating flora and fauna helps to make sense of the bewildering variety of wildlife in the state. Within the complex is also a science centre with an exhibition on the oil and petroleum industry, and an art gallery. One of the museum's most striking exhibits is a collection of 10 life-sized traditional houses set in the museum gardens, each depicting the architecture of a different ethnic group. A restaurant, coffee house, an ethno-botanical garden with an artificial lake and a souvenir shop complete the complex.

The town itself is a blend of ultramodern structures and old Chinese shophouses. Walk along **Jalan Gaya** to spot the town's few remaining traditional provision shops, where a delightful jumble of groceries, canned foods and

Map on page 314

sacks of rice displayed as artfully as a film set, invite closer inspection. Few older buildings remain in town but take note of the **Atkinson Clock Tower** ❶ at the end of the Padang, and **Sabah Tourism Board** (open Mon–Fri 8am–5pm; Sat 8am–noon) on Jalan Gaya. Once the main post office, its solid white stone walls and colonial architecture make a pleasing contrast to the concrete shop-houses. Adjacent, also in Gaya Street, is the renovated **Jesselton Hotel** ❷, the town's first hotel which now exudes more old world charm than it ever did before. A charming stop for lunch or dinner, if not overnight.

The bustling **Central Market** ❸ sits midway along the waterfront, best seen early in the morning as fishermen unload their catch directly onto market tables. Kadazandusun women display their exotic range of fresh fruit and vegetables, some, like young fern leaves, never seen before. One section specialises in tobacco and betel nut products, while yeast tablets for making the local rice wine, *tapai*, hang in strings like big, white beads. Adjacent is the **Handicraft Market** (open daily 9am–6pm) – a casual affair where handicrafts and souvenirs, mostly from the Philippines, are sold in rows of small stalls. Watch your purse as you practise your bargaining skills.

At the other end of the day, Kota Kinabalu's restaurants come alive, and some of the best food in the state is served in small coffee shops dotted around the town. As with towns in Peninsular Malaysia, night markets are ever present, selling clothes and curios, as well as local delicacies. On Sunday mornings, there is the very popular **Gaya Street Fair** (open daily 8am–noon) – a city version of the traditional weekly *tamu* – markets that are held in venues across the state. Cheap clothes, plants, foodstuffs and, occasionally, bargain local handicrafts or antiques can be found.

Fern tips, lightly stir-fried are a Sabahan delicacy.

BELOW: a Filipino Market vendor.

TIP

The best reefs in Tunku Abdul Rahman Park are on the southwest of Pulau Sulug. You can hire a glass-bottomed boat from the Marina at Shangri-La's Tanjung Aru Resort to get a closer look at the coral and marine life around Sapi – without getting your feet wet!

For a good idea of what Kota Kinabalu looked like in the post-war years, the view from **Signal Hill ⓖ** affords a vast expanse of concrete, the only two pre-war buildings still standing being the Tourism Board and the Clock Tower. Situated at the eastern end of the city, you can reach the hill by foot, or by car, taxi or tour bus. For a more contemporary view, go up to the top floor of the **Sutera Harbour Resort** – part of the RM2.2 billion Sutera Harbour Complex comprising two luxury hotels, golf and yacht clubs and an array of recreational facilities – at the western end of town. From this vantage point are vistas of both the sea and offshore islands and also of the golf course, across to Tanjung Aru stilt villages and the city beyond, and a distant Gunung (Mount) Kinabalu.

South of town, past the airport road, is the famous **Tanjung Aru Beach**. The sea here is generally calm, the sand is clean and the coastal food stalls and restaurants offer delicious local seafood. The huge orange-roofed complex at the tip of the cape is the popular **Shangri-la's Tanjung Aru Resort**.

Marine park paradise

Offshore from Kota Kinabalu, surrounded by azure waters, are the five islands of **Tunku Abdul Rahman Park ❷**, a popular destination whether for day trips or longer. The marine park headquarters is on Pulau Gaya, the largest of the islands and home to the **Gayana Resort**, (located outside the park boundaries), with its stilted village-style accommodation. The other islands that make up the park are **Manukan**, **Mamutik**, **Sapi** and **Sulug**. Snorkelling can be enjoyed on all of these, and is best on remote Sulug. Pulau Manukan, the most developed of the islands, has chalets, a restaurant and swimming pool.

All the islands except Sulug have nature trails. Wildlife can be spotted on

BELOW:
Sutera Harbour Resort with Tunku Abdul Rahman Park in the distance.

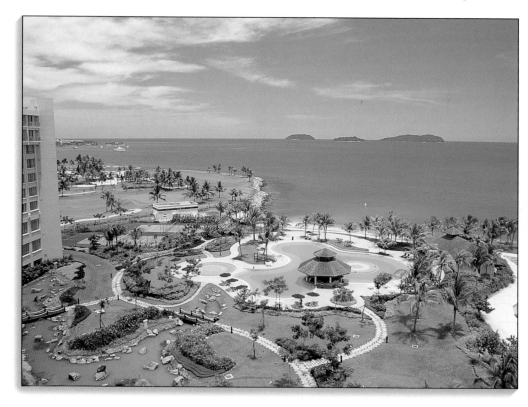

occasion, sometimes closer than you'd like; watch out for the thieving macaque monkeys that proliferate on Pulau Sapi. Pied hornbills, sea eagles and megapode birds can sometimes be seen on Pulau Gaya.

You can camp on any of the islands but you must obtain a permit from the Sabah Parks office. Boats to the islands leave from the **Ferry Terminal**, and this is located at the end of Jalan Haji Salim.

Maps:
Area 312
City 314

Heading north

Sabah's long west coast stretches all the way from the Sarawak border to the northern tip at **Kudat** and **Pulau Banggi** in the Sulu Sea, almost meeting the southern Philippines boundary. This area is ideally explored by car, with the freedom to stop at will. Although some areas outside the city may require a four-wheel-drive vehicle, the trunk road linking Kota Kinabalu with **Sandakan** in Sarawak and the east coast is bitumen and a cursory exploration of the state by road presents no difficulty at all.

The road north of Kota Kinabalu leads towards **Tuaran ❸**, passing en route several ceramics factories near Telipok where visitors are welcome to stop for a look and maybe make a purchase or two. At a large roundabout, you can either head north to Tuaran and a couple of beach resorts, or turn right towards **Ranau** and **Kinabalu Park**.

Bajau men, well-known for their horse riding skills, are mainly found in the Kota Belud area.

Tuaran is a small town known for its colourful Sunday *tamu*. Get there early morning to enjoy the market at its best. It is also noted for a local culinary speciality known as *Tuaran mee* – a delicious mixture of fried noodles, vegetables, pork and pork crackling, and egg. Enjoy it in one of the shops of the main street before heading to the *tamu*. **Kampung Surusup** is about 15 minutes from Tuaran. There, negotiate a price with the boatmen at the jetty, who will take you by motorised canoe to visit **Kampung Penambawan** – a traditional Bajau fishing village.

BELOW: mosque, Kota Belud.

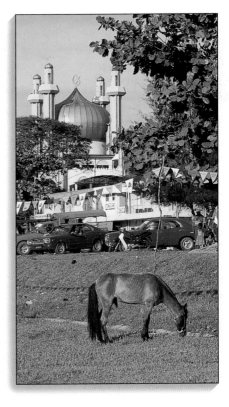

About 40 minutes north of town are a couple of beach areas with luxurious resorts and golf courses. **Pantai Dalit** – a long strip of white sand backed by forested hills is the location for the popular Shangri-la's Rasa Ria Resort while on nearby **Karambunai Beach** is the plush Nexus Resort. In the vicinity, by a road just before Tuaran, is the **Mengkabong Water Village**, a rambling Bajau sea gypsy complex of raised stilted pathways and dozens of attap-thatched stilted huts built over an estuary. Transport around the village is by canoe, although many houses are also connected to one another by precarious-looking plank walks.

On the road leading towards Ranau is the old world village of **Tamparuli ❹**, where the original shopping area consists of traditional wooden buildings, a sight fast fading across the country. Tamparuli is also the site of a Wednesday *tamu* – a colourful traditional market. Beyond Tamparuli is the **Kiulu River**, a scenic area where the waters run clean. Kiulu is very popular as a scenic rafting destination, and it offers a more docile ride than the raging waters of the Padas River to the south.

Kota Belud ❺ is only slightly more than one

The Rungus people align their longhouses west to east, and facing Gunung Kinabalu, believing that position to be the most auspicious for good health.

hour's drive north from Kota Kinabalu and has two claims to fame. Firstly, it is renowned for the Bajau "cowboys", famed for their rearing and handling of horses and buffalo. Secondly, it is the scene of one of Sabah's most colourful weekly *tamus*. Bajau and Kadazandusun market women, their faces crinkled by the harsh sun, squat beside their wares – tobacco wrappers, piles of fresh vegetables or sugary doughnuts for hours on end, constantly chewing the omnipresent betel nut, which stains their gums and teeth a vivid red. There is always more on sale at the *tamu* than mundane necessities – an entire market row is devoted to the accoutrements of betel nut chewing. These women use the *tamus*, not just to sell their wares, but also for a chance to catch up on the latest news and gossip.

Tourist backwater

From Kota Belud, the road heads north towards Kudat, and **Rungus** country – home to perhaps the most traditional and talented craftspeople in the state. **Kudat ❻** was the state's first capital (albeit for a mere two years), and once an important port in the trade between China and Europe. A British adventurer took advantage of this position and set up a trading post on Balembangan Island in 1773. However, this was plagued by lack of water and continual pirate raids and the area was abandoned for less troubled waters.

Today, Kudat has become the peaceful centre for the northwestern administrative district, and is also an active fishing port. Although the Kudat region has escaped the attention of tourists in the past, the traditional cultures of the Rungus and the long stretches of white sandy beaches, unspoiled and unpopulated, are making it an increasingly popular destination.

BELOW: Rungus woman from Kudat.

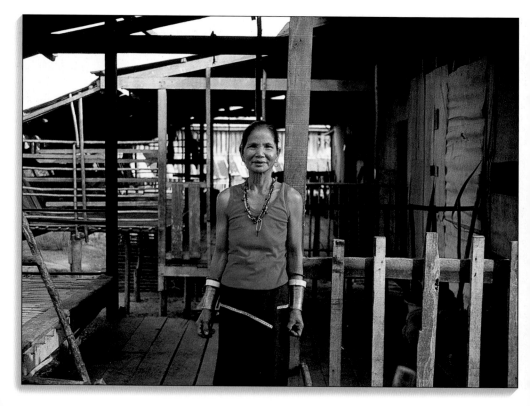

The Rungus people are traditional agriculturalists, and a subgroup of the Kadazandusun tribe. Known for their excellent weaving and beadwork, the Rungus tend to live in small communities and in simple longhouses. The architectural style of their buildings (with their outward-leaning walls) is mirrored in the state museum in Kota Kinabalu.

Map
on page
312

The Rungus have retained their traditional spiritualistic and animist beliefs, much longer than have the other tribes of Sabah. They are also famous for the long brass coils once used by women to decorate their necks, arms and legs. Nowadays, this practice has been discontinued – although you might still see forearm coils on older women. While the women continue to weave shoulder sashes, other woven textiles are rare; these days, people tend to wear decorated black cloth instead. Their excellent beadwork is quite visible in many of the *tamus* in the area.

Older Rungus women are fond of wearing long brass coils around their necks, arms and legs. The practice, however, is dying out with the younger women.

Rungus life

It is possible to visit a Rungus longhouse and some have been constructed especially for visitors. Built in a green valley, **Kampung Bavanggazo 7**, not far from the road leading to Kudat, has two purpose-built tourist longhouses where visitors will get to see Rungus women at work, weaving and making handicrafts. In the evening, enjoy a performance of Rungus dance and a chance to sample the local food and rice wine. At nearby **Kampung Sumangkap**, traditional gong-making is the major activity and at **Kampung Gombizau**, villagers have taken up beekeeping and produce wax, honey and royal jelly. Contact Sabah Tourism in Kota Kinabalu for details.

There is also a large Hakka Chinese community living in Kudat, the first area to be inhabited by the Chinese in the 1880s; many of them are Christians

BELOW:
a Rungus-style
longhouse in Kudat.

and farmers by tradition. On the fishing island of **Banggi**, right at Sabah's northern tip, lives a small tribe long thought to be of Dusun extraction, but their dialect contradicts this ancestry. They remain apart, living much as they have done for the last several hundred years. It is possible to visit the island, although there is no tourism infrastructure.

The ideal way to explore the region is in a four-wheel-drive vehicle, as some of the roads leading to the beaches are little more than dirt tracks. If you don't fancy staying overnight in a longhouse, then a good range of new hotels is available in Kudat.

If you are looking for the beach while visiting Kudat, you're likely to be directed to the local favourite, **Bak Bak**, which is equipped with toilets and picnic tables. However, much lovelier beaches, some with tiny lagoons, can be found all along the west coast, particularly near the village of **Sikuati**, at Pantai Kelambu and Pantai Terongkongan.

Highest mountain

Everyone in Malaysia knows about the mysterious **Gunung Kinabalu**, at 4,093 metres (13,428 ft), one of the highest peaks between the Himalayas and New Guinea. The closer one journeys towards its famous jagged profile – which is often wreathed in feathery clouds – the better one understands the meaning the mount has for the local Kadazandusun people. They call it *Aki Nabalu,* or Revered Place of the Dead. It is believed that the spirits of the tribe's dead ancestors dwell among the forbidding peaks, and in the past no one had dared climb to the top for fear of disturbing and angering them.

In spite of the taboos and myths surrounding the mountain, Hugh Low, a young British officer, was still keen to reach the top. Climbing Gunung Kinabalu in 1851, Low was accompanied by a local chief and his guides. Struggling through the intense tangle of vegetation, which covers the lower slopes of the mountain, Low eventually reached the summit plateau, but owing to a faulty barometer, was unable to locate the true summit. He made a second unsuccessful attempt on the summit in 1858. The honour of reaching the small peak of the summit actually ended up going to naturalist John Whitehead, who named it Low's Peak in honour of the earlier climber.

The mountain is said to still be growing, at a rate of half a centimetre a year. Relatively young, its jagged crown was sculpted by the last ice age, about 9,000 years ago. Although Kinabalu's peak is below the snow line, it grows cold enough here in December for ice to form in the rock pool at the base of the summit, and snowflakes sometimes fall. Dropping away 1,800 metres (5,900 ft) straight downwards is the terrifying **Low's Gully**, its name being a typical piece of British understatement.

To get to the top, there is no need to spend days cutting through tropical rain forest just to reach the granite slopes, like Hugh Low's torturous first ascent. Well-laid trails with steps and rails made of wood help today's climber ascend and descend the mountain in just two days.

Allied bombers used Gunung Kinabalu's peak as a navigational aid to assist their raids on Japanese targets during World War II.

BELOW: sure-footed Kadazandusun women porters

Accommodation is available both at the Park Headquarters, and in basic huts on the mountain slopes. Cooking facilities and sleeping bag-hire is available at the latter. However, Laban Rata has a restaurant and centrally-heated rooms. At the headquarters, accommodation ranges from hostels to chalets. There are two restaurants, and a shop selling basic food supplies for climbers. In the main administration building, there is an exhibit on mountain flora and fauna; in the basement is a film about the park. There is also a range of accommodation on the eastern side of Kinabalu Park, at **Mesilau Nature Resort**.

The easiest way to reach **Kinabalu Park** ➑ now designated a World Heritage Site, from Kota Kinabalu is by mini-bus. From 7am onwards, the bus leaves for Ranau from the long-distance bus station near the Padang. The trip takes a little under 2 hours and the driver will turn off the main road to drop travellers at the park entrance.

Map on page 312

Tips for the top

Before leaving the city, you should book accommodation at Kinabalu Nature Resorts at Wisma Sabah. At certain times of the year, namely July and August and on public holidays, accommodation is tight and bookings need to be made in advance. Alternatively, you can book a package tour through any of Kota Kinabalu's tour operators. Stock up on food if you want to do your own cooking, as the shop at headquarters is limited mainly to noodles and chocolate. Other useful equipment includes a hat and gloves, as it can be extremely cold on the summit, and some kind of waterproof garment to protect you from the frequent rainfall. If possible, leave your luggage at a hotel and take a light pack only, or use the luggage storage area at the Park Headquarters. The air is thin-

BELOW: looking down at the world from Low's Peak.

Hardy womenfolk lugging firewood for cooking.

ner up on the mountain, and even the lightest pack can feel heavy after a while. A torch is also useful for the final ascent, which starts long before dawn.

On the way to Kinabalu Park, you will pass by Tamparuli, 50 km (30 miles) north of Kinabalu (*see page 317*). Less than a kilometre past this town, say goodbye to the level ground as the road begins to ascend the foothills. Although the landscape is often swathed in clouds, the mountain can't be far away because ears begin to pop. Further along, surrounded by the Kinabalu foothills, is the hamlet of **Nabalu**, where a *tamu* is held every Thursday. Kadazandusun women arrive early morning, their goods carried on enormous baskets on their backs. Nabalu is also a popular stop for tour buses, as it is a good place to see genuine native handicrafts and baskets for sale.

On your arrival at the reception, the staff at **Sutera Sanctuary Lodges** (formerly known as Kinabalu Nature Resorts; www.suterasanctuarylodges.com) will confirm bookings, including those for the huts on the mountain. Maps, books, souvenirs and camera films are available at the souvenir store. You might choose not to climb the same day you arrive, so make yourself comfortable in your accommodation, acclimatise to the cool air, check out the exhibition centre with displays on the park and the mountain, and explore the fascinating **Mountain Garden** near the administration building.

Peak of fitness

BELOW: granite slabs are a sight to behold near the summit.

Although Kinabalu is one of the easiest mountains to climb in terms of equipment needs, a certain degree of fitness is required. It would be foolish to head straight from the office, hop onto a plane, and then expect to be able to run up the trail. Some regular exercise is recommended before the actual climb so that

Map on page 312

you don't come off the mountain a wreck of cramps, headaches and fatigue.

Just before the trail begins, there is a rather forbidding notice placed by the park authorities, listing ailments not recommended for those intending to climb the mountain: hypertension, diabetes, obesity, chronic asthma, heart disease, arthritis, anaemia, ulcers, hepatitis, muscular cramps and epilepsy.

Climbing 1,500 metres (4,950 ft) in one day – from the power station above the headquarters to Panar Laban hut – does take inordinate reserves of strength and zest for those who lead sedentary lives. Although experienced and intrepid climbers have climbed to the summit and back in less than 3 hours in the Kinabalu Climathon, most people have an interest not just in getting to the top, but in fully savouring the views, and the area's flora and fauna.

Attached to the headquarters, but not directly employed by them, are a team of local guides, who for a fee will accompany visitors up the mountain. If interested in the mountain flora, you should be sure that your guide is knowledgeable and also speaks passable English (which is not often the case). Porters can be hired at park headquarters and will carry luggage as far as Panar Laban hut. Here they stop and await for your exhilarated but exhausted faces to appear the following morning before beginning the descent. Fees depend on how heavy your luggage is; anything over 10 kg (22 lbs) will cost more.

From Panar Laban, climbing usually begins at 2am, although you can request your guide to start at 5am to avoid the crowd at the summit. Make sure you have a bar or two of chocolate in your pocket; it's not a luxury but a necessity here, as a provider of instant energy for the climb and the cold. You should also bring some headache tablets; as you will be climbing to a great height very quickly, you may suffer from headaches because of the altitude.

Passing the welcoming gate at the power station (with the slogan *Selamat Mendaki* – "Happy Climbing!" written over the arch), the first steps lead down into a small, lush valley with a waterfall. After the waterfall, the climb begins, at first gently, later steeply through tropical rainforest.

A panoply of habitats

All around you are some of the park's 1,500 species of orchids, clinging to mossy tree trunks and surrounded by swinging vines. Steep and arduous stairs leading ever upwards are happily spaced out between gentler paths. Small rest huts and viewpoints are positioned all the way up the trail to give the out-of-breath climber an excuse to stop and admire the view. Don't bother to bring water, as there is pure mountain water available at all rest stops. At 1,300 metres (4,200 ft), the vegetation on either side of the trail begins to change from lowland rainforest into oak and chestnut forests of more temperate flora, like ferns and flowering plants.

Proceeding up to the next level of vegetation, one has the feeling of growing larger the higher one climbs. The trail began with huge trees towering above; now the trees have shrunk and you are almost the tallest thing in the landscape. At 2,600 metres (8,500 ft), you'll see small gnarled trees, twisted and wrinkled by the mountain air; despite their size, some

BELOW: Laban Rata Resthouse, Panar Laban.

TIP

Before you embark on
your trek of Gunung
Kinabalu, get hold of
the intoductory leaflet,
*Mount Kinabalu: A
Guide to the Summit
Trail,* published by
Sabah Parks.

BELOW:
the mountain
forest takes on
a dream-like
quality at dawn.

are more than 100 years old. The soil is poor here, and lichens cling desperately to the little trees.

The soil disappears altogether at 3,300 metres (10,800 ft) and the granite body of the mountain reveals itself. Only sedges, grasses and tiny alpine-looking flowers cling to the rocky crevices where a bit of soil might remain.

Just when you thought you'd left all civilisation far below on the trail – now a hazy ribbon in the afternoon mist – you arrive at a series of huts and the rest-house where you will spend the night.

A leisurely climb should get you here by around 2pm. At Panar Laban, you can retreat into the cosy **Laban Rata Resthouse** with its magnificent balcony looking up to the peak. There is a simple restaurant, as well as warm rooms and hot water. A little further up the slope is **Gunting Lagadan Hostel**, which has dormitory rooms, sleeping bags for hire, and a basic kitchen equipped with cooking utensils and electricity. Once you've stopped climbing, you may begin to feel the cold, so even if you don't feel like it, have some hot soup and filling food. You will now be able to rest and think about your achievement so far – but alas! – the path you so strenuously climbed has been lost in the mountain mists.

Some climbers may find it hard to sleep on the mountain because of the thin air and the headaches caused by the altitude. Yet, you will need to go to sleep extra early to be able to struggle out of bed at 2am (your guide will wake you). Take a hot drink before starting the climb around 3am. If you have a thermos flask, heat some water and fill the flask with sweet tea for a reviving drink at the summit. Don't forget to stuff some chocolate into your pocket and bring your raincoat. Other than cameras, everything else can be left at the hut for retrieval on the way down.

Map on page 312

Rocky mountain high

Soon you will be climbing rock faces of granite in the pitch black as you hold onto the rope systems that guide the way. The steepness of the incline is difficult to gauge in the dark, though, and the granite slopes can be slippery after a night's rain. With an early start, you will be labouring up the slabs of granite with the peak in sight just as the skies begin to lighten. Here the granite rock, bared to the winds, is crumbling and broken, but at last Low's Peak arises.

Venturing a look down into the depths of Low's Gully, the view is awe-inspiring. This does indeed seem a place for spirits, for few mortals could long endure the harsh weather that sweeps away the offerings of sacrificial chickens, eggs, tobacco, betel nut, *sireh* leaves, limes and rice left here by the Kadazandusun. Depending on one's guide and the strength of his beliefs, he may decide to make offerings while you are gushing over the landscape's beauty. The guide may also be carrying personal charms: special pieces of wood, human teeth and other items with protecting properties.

The descent can be more leisurely, especially by climbers still glowing with success of having reached the summit, but appearances can be deceptive. While it is easier on the lungs, the descent is hell to pay on the knees and in the end, can be even more painful than the climb up and the relentless steps leading ever downwards can soon turn even firm legs into jelly!

After collecting your belongings from Panar Laban, you'll continue down through unique vegetation, such as the pitcher plants – some of the nine varieties of *nepenthes* – that were probably missed on the ascent. On your arrival at Park Headquarters, you can rightfully claim your badge commemorating your ascent, only for sale to those who have made it to the top; this is (your guide can act as witness).

Many climbers leave the park the same day or the day after they have made the climb. But if time permits, stay in the area a couple of days more, both to rest and to explore the jungle around the headquarters, which is neatly laid out in trails for nature lovers.

There is a second 5.5-km (2.8-mile) trail up the mountain that starts from the Mesilau Nature Resort, further up the road from the park. This is a tougher, steeper climb which the hard-core mountaineer will relish. The Mesilau trail joins the main summit trail near the rest stop at Layang Layang. Make your bookings for Mesilau at Kinabalu Nature Resorts.

Amazing species

A guide can introduce you to Kinabalu's magnificent flora and fauna, some of it unique to the region. Among the rare plants found here is the famous Rafflesia, the largest flower in the world, which can measure up to a metre (3 ft) across, and nine species of pitcher plants. In 1858, the explorer Spencer St John chanced upon a huge specimen of the latter that contained approximately 1 gallon (4 litres) of rain water – as well as a dead rat.

The park's 750 sq km (300 sq miles) are unique in the world of flora, containing plants from almost every area on earth: the Himalayas, China, Australia, New Zealand, alpine Europe and even America. There are 1,500 species of orchid, 26 kinds of rhododen-

BELOW: wild orchids.

Stick insects in the jungles of Sabah are notoriously difficult to spot as they blend so easily against the bark of trees.

dron and 60 types of oak and chestnut, as well as 80 species of fig tree. Animals found here include orang-utan, gibbons, leaf monkeys, tarsiers, pangolin (scaly anteaters), wild pig and deer. There is also a whole host of "flying" animals, some rarely found in other parts of Malaysia, including flying squirrels, lemurs, snakes and lizards. Also found here – but seldom seen – is the incredibly rare clouded leopard.

The 518 species of birds include several kinds of hornbills, the scarlet sunbird, the mountain bush warbler, the pale-faced bulbul, the mountain blackeye, and the mountain's own Kinabalu Friendly Warbler. Around the area's waterfalls, look for the lovely butterflies, some as large as birds, and the less easy-to-see stick insects, well camouflaged to the human eye. You might also catch sight of squirrels, lizards, tree-shrews and bats.

A steaming, hot bath

Although the park holds all these fascinating sights and more besides, many climbers will be too tired to appreciate the beauty of a pleasant stroll through the forest. Head for **Poring** ❾, 45 km (30 miles) to the east beyond Ranau. Here, natural hot sulphur springs will soothe those tired muscles, plus a canopy walkway and butterfly park may pique your interest.

Pleasant chalets with cooking facilities, and a couple of hostels are available, but few visitors rest long before making straight for the baths. There is nothing like a good long soak in the mineral-rich waters to ease aching limbs and restore one's sense of well being. The baths themselves are set in park-like grounds with hibiscus bushes and frangipani trees, with the untamed jungle above and beyond. They were originally built during World War II by the Japanese, with their love

BELOW: a wreathed hornbill.

of communal bathing giving them the impetus to tame the jungle, and channel in both hot and cold water – the latter to temper the heat of mineral water.

Despite aching muscles (if you've climbed the mountain), it is well worth checking out Poring's 140 metre-(460 ft) long canopy walkway strung high above the ground between giant dipterocarp trees, which literally offers a bird's-eye view of the forest. From time to time, a Rafflesia appears in the jungle areas around Poring. Near the baths you'll find the butterfly park, filled with beautiful local species and some remarkable insects.

The area around **Ranau** ❿ is Kadazandusun country and also the market garden of Sabah, situated on Kinabalu's cool foothills. At the weekly *tamu* in Ranau, you'll see rural people dressed in a mix of traditional dress (black *sarong*) and western attire.

Heading south from Kota Kinabalu, follow the signs from Putatan to the **Monsopiad Cultural Village** (open Mon–Sat 9am–5pm; cultural shows by arrangement; entrance fee), a reconstructed Kadazan village in traditional style built on the same site where the great headhunter Monsopiad lived about 300 years ago. His collection of skulls still hangs in the rafters and the centre is run by his direct descendants. The centre is open all week, while cultural shows featuring Kadazandusun dances to an authentic band are held on Saturday. The participants live on site and the emphasis is on a "living museum" where Kadazandusun culture can survive and be promoted.

About 20 km (12 miles) south of Kota Kinabalu is **Papar** ⓫, situated on the mouth of the Papar River. Paddy fields surround the town and on the coast is a pleasant stretch of sand called **Pantai Manis**, or Sweet Beach. The Sunday *tamu* is a lively scene, as Kadazandusun traders bring their wares from the surrounding hills. The best way to get to Papar is by local train; Borneo's only railway goes from Tanjung Aru near Kota Kotabalu to Beaufort and onwards to Tenom in the interior. The journey is even more memorable – albeit more expensive – on the new restored diesel train known as the North Borneo Railway. Relive the colonial days as you steam through the paddy fields on a 3½ hour ride, enjoying a curry tiffin lunch on the way. The main highway continues on to the town of **Beaufort** ⓬ and beyond to Sipitang, then to Sindumin on the Sarawak border.

Beaufort is a busy highway junction, and an important stop on the railway line. It is also the staging point for whitewater rafting trips on the **Padas River** (*see page 328*) which is directly accessed by rail. Even if you don't participate you can watch rafts hurtling down the rapids from the comfort of your rail carriage.

Offshore millions

Beaufort is on the edge of a swampy peninsula with isolated fishing villages. Just offshore is **Pulau Labuan** ⓭, an international banking centre and an island that hopes to give Bermuda, Cayman and the Channel Islands a run for their money. A British naval station was established on the island in the 1870s and the Japanese forces in Borneo surrendered here in 1945, but other than those two events, little of significance transpired on the island.

Map on page 312

TIP

Train buffs will be keen on the twice-weekly steam train journey on the North Borneo Railway from Tanjung Aru to Tenom. Built in 1896 it is powered by the last of the 60-year-old, wood-burning, British Vulcan steam engines.

BELOW: having a soak at Poring Hot Springs.

TIP

If you haven't yet experienced the highly distinctive *durian* fruit, try it while in Tenom; it is reckoned to be the best in Sabah, smell notwithstanding.

After independence, Labuan was part of Sabah state until 1984, when it was ceded to the federal government for development. Tax-free status came into effect in 1991 and the Malaysian government is keen to attract banks, insurance companies and fund management brokers to Labuan, in addition to offshore holding companies and corporate headquarters. A number of steps have been taken to attract business, including preferential tax laws. The island is also being developed for tourism and a number of wrecks off the coast are said to be worthwhile.

Located right at the end of Borneo's only railway, **Tenom** ⓮ is the centre of Murut country and a rich agricultural centre. The Muruts or "Men of the Hills", have always lived in this region. Young warriors still take their hunting dogs out for a "stroll" in the jungle to catch supper, hunting with a *parang* (large sharp knife) and a shotgun, rather than a blowpipe. Although many young people of the tribe have adopted the trappings of the fast-encroaching western civilisation creeping in from the capital, some still prefer life in remote areas. Others have turned to cultivating the countryside and growing crops.

A popular festive pastime in the few remaining longhouses is jumping on the *lansaran*, a huge trampoline-like structure supported by a wooden platform. The largest can hold 40 people – perhaps the entire population of the longhouse – the basis for a wild party. The best longhouses can be found around Kamabong, south of Tenom.

Riding the raging river

Tenom is also close to the starting point for the Padas River ride, run by several tour operators out of Kota Kinabalu. After arriving at **Kampung Pangi** on the train from Beaufort, having passed through the dramatic Padas Gorge, rafters

BELOW: wild white-water kayaking.

disembark. Rafts are carried to the river, there is time for a brief lesson and donning of safety gear before taking the plunge. The 1½-hour ride is filled with thrills passing through some hefty waves, deep in the gorge, especially when the river is high. The ride finishes at **Kampung Rayoh** where lunch is served before you catch the train back to Kota Kinabalu.

Map on page 312

Tenom is also known for its **Agricultural Research Station**, 18 km (11 miles) northeast of town. The station has grown from its humble beginnings as a centre for cocoa research, to include a full scale agri-park known as **Taman Pertanian Sabah** or **Sabah Agricultural Park**. The **Tenom Orchid Centre** is also part of the park, where numerous species of orchids can be seen. British botanist Tony Lamb is largely responsible for the success of this growing project. Tenom's one classy hotel, the Perkasa, sits on the hill overlooking the town, although accommodation is also available within the park.

Orchid blooms at Tenom Orchid Centre.

Some 40 km (25 miles) south of Tenom, at **Batu Bunatikan Lumuyu** close to Kampung Tomani, are Sabah's only rock paintings. Strange distorted faces and enigmatic figures are painted on massive boulders. These impressive paintings are thought to be around 1,000 years old.

From Tenom, travel north through Keningau and Tambunan, and from there follow a rough road to Ranau and Gunung Kinabalu or follow the road over the Sinsuron Pass to Kota Kinabalu, thus completing a round trip.

Keningau is the centre of the interior timber industry of west Sabah, with its many sawmills and log-holding depots. The town has prospered from its timber industry, and has several hotels and a sports complex for the management staff visiting their logging sites.

BELOW: intricate Rungus bead work.

Keningau and beyond

Driving southeast of Keningau, you come first to **Nabawan**, the last outpost of the government administration, and then to the settlement at **Sapulut ⓕ**. From here, you can take a rough track to **Agis**, from where a pleasant 4-hour boat ride leads to the border and a fairly easy crossing into Kalimantan at the **Pagalunggan** checkpoint (obtain a visa first) and the traditional longhouse of **Kampung Selungai**, only half-an-hour away. This remote area is well worth exploring, but logging, El Niño and forest fires have taken a toll on the area in the last few years. Traditional longhouses sit along these riverbanks, where boats are built and the women engage in weaving, making intricate rattan mats and elaborate beadwork. Travellers are most welcome to stay the night, and the Muruts are renowned for their hospitality. Remember that it is polite to accept a drink when offered, as it is a host's duty to please guests with a cup of *tapai*. If you don't drink alcohol, simply touch the cup with your lips or the tips of your fingers and ask your guide to explain that you don't wish to partake of the fiery liquid. Gifts of food for the adults and toys for the children are customary, and items from your own country will be even more welcome than a product available in Kota Kinabalu.

Sarawak is not the only state with limestone caves. In Sapulut it is possible to hire a local canoe along

Map
on page
312

the **Sapulut River**, for a 2–3 hour boat journey to **Batu Punggul** ⑯, a large limestone outcrop soaring 200 metres (600 ft) upwards from the encircling jungle. Local guides will show you the way to the top of Batu Punggul, a rough climb but well worth it for the spectacular view from the top. Another half-an-hour's walk through the forest leads to the less impressive **Batu Tinahas**, which is almost entirely obscured by the forest. This limestone massif was only recently discovered by a team from the Sabah Museum. Although not as high as Punggul, its cave and tunnel system is enormous and rivals the Gomantong Caves in east Sabah (*see page 336*).

A rough road leads from Keningau to **Tambunan**, passing by an old stone on a grassy plain marking the site of Mat Salleh's last stand. Here, Sabah's most renowned hero built an underground fortress in the middle of the jungle. He might have survived longer than 1900, had not a villager betrayed his location to the British forces, who promptly severed his water supply, and surrounded the fort. Mat Salleh and his followers were massacred when they emerged, ending the rebellion of a native lord who refused to pay tax to foreigners.

The route back to Kota Kinabalu from Tambunan passes through the Crocker Range National Park, with the **Rafflesia Forest Reserve** ⑰ located not far from the summit at **Sinsuron Pass** which crosses the range at 1,649 metres (5,410 feet). The attractive **Rafflesia Information Centre** (open Mon–Fri 8.45am–12.45pm and 2–5pm; Sat–Sun 8am–5pm) has displays on this extraordinary parasitic flower and rangers can advise visitors if any are blooming in the 20 or so identified plots within the reserve.

BELOW: underwater hideout, Sipadan.
RIGHT: Poring's canopy walkway.

Delirious Diving

Sitting at the southern tip of the Spratley Islands, 250 km (155 miles) northwest of Kota Kinabalu, **Layang Layang** is part of the disputed territory that is being contested by a number of countries in the region – including China, Vietnam, Indonesia and Malaysia. In the meantime, Malaysia is putting the island to good use as a tourist destination – the only country to do so – as well as laying a claim that may become important in future negotiations.

This 7 km by 5 km (4 miles by 3 miles) oceanic reef is as much a draw for migratory seabirds, as it is for the big game fishermen, who are attracted by the richly-populated waters. Layang Layang is also the site of some of the best diving in Malaysia. Because of the distance from the the main island, the waters are particularly clear and untainted by any amount of pollution, and the divers who come can enjoy spectacular coral walls, which drop down 2,000 metres (6,560 ft) to the coral below. Sharks and pelagic fish are common sights in these unspoiled waters, and schools of hammerhead sharks can often be seen in the months of March and April.

The island has a tiny airport, and just next door is the comfortable Layang Layang Island Resort, which is dedicated to divers and has a fully-serviced dive centre, a desalination plant, air-conditioned rooms, a restaurant, and even a swimming pool. A 45-minute flight from Kota Kinabalu covers the journey. ❏

SANDAKAN AND THE NORTHEAST

Map on page 312

The lively Chinese trading town of Sandakan is the tourism focus of Sabah's east coast, and the jump off point for Sepilok Orang-utan Rehabilitation Centre

I n its heyday, people called the logs bobbing in the Sulu Sea "floating money". Logs were floated down the Segama and Kinabatangan rivers from timber concession areas near and far into the hands of Chinese entrepreneurs, who shipped them to Japan. So prosperous was **Sandakan** ⓲, that at one time many investors thought the town would become another Hong Kong, but the speed of deforestation of the Sandakan region has quenched that dream. Now the logging industry is but a shadow of its former self, and the derived wealth has been moved to places far beyond. Sandakan remains the same – a medium sized, predominantly Chinese town and the base for tourist exploration of the east.

The capital of North Borneo from 1883, Sandakan was completely razed during the bombings of World War II; the modern town was built on these ruins. The nucleus of the original town began as a gunrunning settlement.

The gunrunners were mostly Germans, although later a Scotsman called William Clarke Cowrie ran guns for the Sultan of Sulu, setting up a camp on Pulau Timbang which he named "Sandakan", the old Sulu name for the area. Later he became the first managing director of the North Borneo Chartered Company, whose main settlement was established here on the fine harbour of Sandakan Bay.

At one time, Sandakan was a major trading centre. Jungle products from the interior – bird's nests, beeswax, rhinoceros horn, hornbill ivory along with marine products like sea cucumber (*trepang*) and pearls were valuable trade items which attracted a cosmopolitan collection of traders from all over the world: Europeans, Arabs, Japanese, Dusun, Javanese, Bugis, Chinese – even Africans came to engage in the wealth-generating business of trade.

Many visitors to the east stay at the Sabah Hotel just outside town. Built on the site of the town's most historic hotel, it caters to the burgeoning tourist trade. Alternatively, stay at the new Sepilok Nature Resort, or one of the other lodges at Sepilok rather than in the town itself.

Around town

The first Sandakan flight from Kota Kinabalu arrives early morning, allowing ample time for an exploration of the town before heading out. An Asian breakfast can be enjoyed in one of the Chinese *kedai* or coffee shops before a visit to the colourful **Sandakan Central Market**. At its busy best in the early morning, the bustling market is an important source of local vegetables and fresh seafood which is exported across the state and over to Singapore and Hong Kong. Other

LEFT: orang-utan at Sepilok.
BELOW: Sandakan was a major logging centre.

TIP

Pulau Selingan, the largest of the Turtle Islands, has everything you could ask for: coconut palms, sandy beaches, with chalets nearby. However, accommodation is limited and must be booked in advance. See Travel Tips.

BELOW: Sepilok is the largest of three orang-utan sanctuaries in the world.

town sights include the **Agnes Keith Museum**, once the home of a famous American writer, who wrote lovingly on Sabah in the 1930s and 1940s, and the adjacent **English Tea House**, a restaurant with a stunning view and even a croquet lawn.

Several Chinese temples are dotted around – the most spectacular being the huge modern **Puu Jih Shih Buddhist Temple** on a hilltop south of town. Outside Sandakan, the **Sandakan Memorial Park** (formerly the Australian Memorial) is built on the site of a Japanese prisoner-of-war camp, and commemorates the Allied soldiers and locals who lost their lives during World War II.

Sandakan's main source of tourist fame is the **Sepilok Orang-utan Rehabilitation Centre** ⑲ (daily 8am–4.30pm, feeding time 10am and 3pm; entrance fee), a 20-minute drive westwards from town. In 1964, 4,000 hectares (9,880 acres) were designated a reserve for these lovable creatures. It takes but a little interaction to fall in love with these most "human" of primates. The orang-utan reportedly shares 96 percent of its genes with a human being, while its intelligence level can reach that of a six-year-old child. The centre assists orphaned orang-utans, or those who have been forced to live in captivity, to adjust gradually to jungle life and return to the wild. Instruction to the animals includes encouraging them to climb, building nests in trees (something wild orang-utans do each night) and foraging for food in the jungle. Gradually they are weaned from the milk and bananas provided, and taught to fend for themselves.

Those who stay longer than the obligatory hour-long feeding stop will find nature trails set around the park, where the stunning vegetation is the main feature, although you may spot birds, squirrels and macaques. Visit the nature centre and watch a video show on orang-utans in the wild. Adjacent to the centre are several lodges of various standards. Right next to the Sepilok Forest Reserve is the tasteful Sepilok Nature Resort, where trekking tours, birding and visits to the rehabilitation centre can be arranged. The Sepilok Jungle Resort provides a pleasant, cheaper alternative.

Map on page 312

Life of the turtle

Pulau Selingan, Pulau Bakkungan and Pulau Gulisan are the Sabah islands which make up the **Turtle Islands Marine Park** ⓴, a 1,740-hectare (4,300-acre) tropical paradise in the Sulu Sea, about 40 km (25 miles) north of Sandakan. Green (*Chelonia mydas*) and Hawksbill turtles (*Eretmochelys imbricata*) or *sisik,* as the locals call them, come here to lay eggs nearly every night of the year, but the best time to watch is between July and September. Rangers will take you out to the beaches where you can observe female turtles after they have commenced laying their eggs. Later, the eggs are scooped into plastic buckets and reburied at a nearby turtle hatchery, where they are safe from predators. Earlier in the evening, if you are lucky and a previous batch of eggs has hatched, you can witness their release and watch them begin their struggle for life as they make their way down the beach to the sanctity of the sea. Only some 3 percent of these turtles will reach maturity.

The best time to visit Turtle Islands Marine Park is between July and September when green turtles converge on the island to hatch their eggs.

Another 40 km (25 miles) due north is the exclusive and reclusive tropical retreat known as **Pulau Lankayan** ㉑, a previously uninhabited coral island. The Lankayan Island Resort is a tranquil place of white sand beaches that provides a wonderful escape – and utter peace. It is particularly good for divers, with accessible wrecks to explore, and vivid marine life of hard and soft corals. Only one dive resort is established on the island.

BELOW: an endangered turtle in motion.

Map
on page
312

Bats galore can be seen in **Gomantong ㉒**, where some of Sabah's largest caves are found. These caves are also home to one million swiftlets, whose nests are collected to furnish the tables of Cantonese restaurants both in town and abroad. Collectors scale the hanging *rotan* (cane) and bamboo ladders which hang from the cave roof up to heights of 90 metres (300 ft) above the bat guano-covered ground, to collect these treasures in the vast caves. The bats are only in evidence at dusk, as they make their nightly flight out to forage for food, just as the swiftlets return home. The huge, odorous guano pile is gradually raising the cave floor level. At one time the guano was harvested for use as fertiliser, but the cave's swift population declined so quickly that the guano now stays in an ever-mounting carpet, alive with cockroaches and other tiny cave dwellers. A wooden boardwalk makes is possible to tour the main **Simud Hitam** cave with ease. If visiting these caves, bring a flashlight and mosquito repellent. The fastidious might wish to bring a pair of gloves.

River journey

An enjoyable excursion is a trip up the **Kinabatangan River**. Now one of Sabah's most popular tours, the river is dominated by tour operators who shuttle guests, by bus, to **Sukau ㉓** or **Bilit**, stopping off at the **Sepilok Orang-utan Rehabilitation Centre** as well as the **Gomantong Caves** along the way. It is also possible however, to charter a boat and explore the river, beginning from **Sandakan Bay**.

BELOW: Gomantang Caves near Sukau.
RIGHT: Kadazandusan girls all dolled up for a concert.

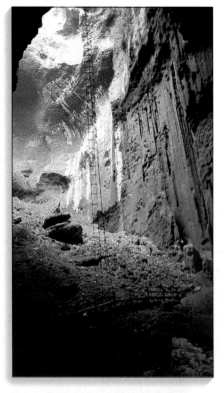

After crossing Sandakan Bay, the first stage of the journey is dominated by mangrove swamps and twisting waterways of the lowland floodplain. The occasional Orang Sungei (river people) settlement of stilted houses can be seen along the banks. Much of the original forest along the river has been replaced by oil palm, yet pockets still remain. Its role as an important wetlands area – the biggest in Malaysia – has been recognised by the WWF. The region has recently been gazetted as the **Kinabatangan Wildlife Sanctuary**.

The Kinabatangan and its tributaries are famed for the wildlife, not least of which is the long-nosed, pot-bellied proboscis monkey. The best place for close up sightings of these unique animals is the swampy forest along the small Menanggol River, a tributary of the Kinabatangan, just upstream from Sukau. Boats leave in the cool of the afternoon (around 3.30pm to 4pm) in time to catch the monkeys as they crash through the trees, making their way to the riverside, for their nightly sojourn.

Even more exciting to many visitors are the wild elephants that roam thorough the Kinabatangan area. Sightings of elephants along the river are not uncommon and recently, some pleasing encounters with a group of 40 or so elephants were reported by some very happy tourists.

The ox bow lakes, formed as the river has changed its slow course over the years, are exceptionally rich sources of birdlife, and you're likely to find a visit particularly rewarding. More than 100 species of bird live in these habitats, including waterfowl, snake birds and hornbills. ❏

TAWAU AND THE SOUTHEAST

Right in the southeast tip of Sabah, near the border with Indonesia, the regional centre of Tawau provides an access point to world-class diving and some beautiful jungle habitats

Map on page 312

F lights from Kota Kinabalu and Sandakan arrive at **Tawau** ㉔, Sabah's main town of the southeast. As well as being the hub of an important timber and cocoa growing area, this busy little town has a very mixed population, where Muslim Filipinos from Mindanao and Indonesian estate workers have helped create a different atmosphere to the towns of the west coast. As well as the present timber capital of the state, Tawau is also the home of a reforestation programme situated at **Kalabakan**, where 30,000 hectares (70,000 acres) have been planted with fast-growing trees such as *Albizia facalaria*; the fastest is said to have soared 30 metres (100 ft) in just five years.

However, Tawau's real pride is the cocoa plant, which thrives in the region's volcanically-rich soils, making Sabah the largest cocoa-producing state in Malaysia; oil palm is grown, too, in huge estates that stretch mile after mile across the country. Tawau also boasts several good hotels, and **Tawau Hills State Park**, a nature reserve where hot springs and waterfalls can be found.

Stilts and seafood

Tawau's main interest to the thousands of scuba divers who pass through each year is its proximity to **Semporna** ㉕, the gateway to Pulau Sipadan – Malaysia's only oceanic island and famous with the international diving fraternity as one of the world's five best dive sites. A 1½-hour drive east of Tawau brings visitors to the small settlement, where Bajau fishermen, Suluk tribespeople, and Chinese traders lend a village atmosphere and a far-flung feel. Fringing the town are numerous settlements built on stilts over the water, an architectural style utilised by many of the newer resorts being built in the vicinity. The rich marine life around Semporna yields delicious seafood, which can be bought (often live) at the restaurant at **Dragon Inn**. Prepared by Chinese chefs in any style you wish and served with fresh, locally-grown vegetables, it is among the best seafood found in Malaysia.

Semporna's main jetty, where Dragon Inn's restaurant and chalets perch over the shallow waters, is always a hive of activity, with locals from the nearby islands coming and going in narrow wooden boats, and sleek speedboats leaving for dive resorts. Various dive companies maintain their offices on the jetty, while a couple of hotels, a souvenir shop and an air-conditioned restaurant cater to those en route for the nearby islands.

While Pulau Sipadan is the most exceptional dive site off Sabah's east coast, the jade and sapphire seas around Semporna are dotted with countless idyllic islands, surrounded by coral reefs. Unfortunately, dynamiting by fisherman has caused considerable

LEFT: wild banana bloom.
BELOW: keeping sentry at Kapalai.

Moray eels can turn out to be vicious creatures if you stick your arm too far up their resting holes.

destruction, but since the deportation of large numbers of illegal immigrants, the reefs are slowly regenerating.

The large islands of **Bodgaya** and **Bohey Dulang** to the northeast of Semporna, and several surrounding isles, have been gazetted as the **Tun Sakaran Marine Park**. As yet, facilities have not yet been developed, but the region promises to be a magnet for divers in the near future. Not far from Bodgaya, **Mataking**, the last island before the international border with the Philippines, is shared by an exclusive diving resort and the Malaysian army, which – along with navy patrols – ensures security along the entire east coast.

South of Semporna, **Pulau Sipadan** ㉖ is Malaysia's only oceanic island. A pinnacle of limestone and coral rising up 600 metres (2,000 ft) from the floor of the Celebes Sea, it spreads out like a mushroom cap to form a 12-hectare island. The first divers to Sipadan in the 1980s slept in tents, disturbed at night only by nesting sea turtles burrowing in the sand before laying their eggs.

The stunning visibility and the incredible range of marine life – including large pelagic fish, brilliantly colourful hard and soft corals and underwater caverns – greatly impressed the late marine ecologist and diver, Jacques Cousteau. It also impressed the first foreign divers who stayed with the pioneer operator, **Borneo Divers**. Tales of schooling barracuda, mating sea turtles, huge jacks, moray eels, white-tip reef sharks and shimmering schools of exquisite reef fish soon spread. Perhaps inevitably, tiny Sipadan eventually became over-run with dive resorts and divers. In an effort to avoid environmental degradation of Sipadan and its surrounding reefs, the Malaysian government closed all resorts on the island in December 2004, permitting divers to dive in the surrounding reefs but not land on the island. Limited day visits may be permitted in future.

BELOW: snorkelling in Sipadan.

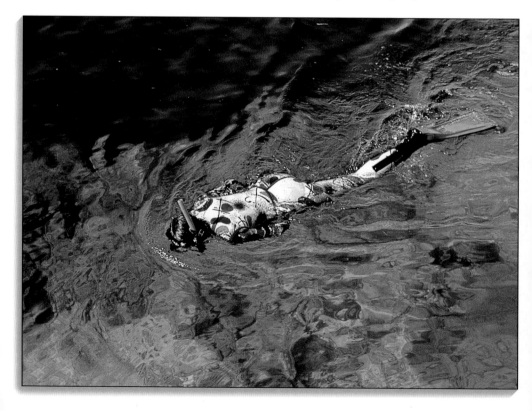

Most dive operators have transferred their resorts to the nearby low-lying island of **Mabul** , while **Kapalai** is occupied by a single beautiful resort perched on stilts. Both Mabul and Kapalai are renowned "muck diving" sites, great for macro life and all kinds of unusual critters that won't be seen on Sipadan.

Map on page 312

Subterranean settlements

An hour's drive north from Tawau and Semporna towards **Lahad Datu**, leads to the **Madai Caves** ❷, where you'll find a limestone outcrop with large caves just 2 km (1½ miles) off the main road. Outside the caves is a village that may be deserted except for a small nucleus of caretakers, but will be packed twice a year when harvesters come to gather the valuable edible nests built by swiftlets in the caves.

A flashlight is necessary for exploring the caves; although sunlight filters down through crevices in the limestone roof of some caves, many of the deeper caves are pitch black. Remains found at Madai prove that people lived in the area as long as 15,000 years ago.

Further evidence of ancient settlement in the region – in this case going back some 20,000 years – can be found 18 km (11 miles) west of Madai. **Baturong** is another limestone outcrop, situated near what was once a lake known as Tingkayu, which drained away 16,000 years ago. With a guide from Lahad Datu or Kunak, you can visit this fascinating massif. The journey involves an hour's drive through cocoa and oil palm plantations to a mud volcano.

Lahad Datu is another of Sabah's "cowboy towns", known for its lawlessness. Situated close to the Sulu Islands of the Philippines it is, like the Semporna area, subject to occasional pirate attacks on shipping.

BELOW:
aerial walkway
at Danum Valley.

Map on page 312

Southwest of the town is the important **Danum Valley Conservation Area ㉙**, a 440-sq km (170-sq mile) reserve established by the Sabah Foundation for conservation and research. The inner area is totally unlogged, and has numerous walking trails through a pristine rainforest filled with waterfalls, streams and abundant wildlife. Morning starts early with the dawn chorus, as cicadas begin the chant, followed by the calls of some of the park's 270 bird species, echoed by the cries of gibbons. Hidden within this jungle paradise are rare Sumatran rhino, gibbons, mousedeer, barking deer, sambar deer, bearded pigs, giant flying squirrels and wild elephants. The conservation area houses the highly-regarded **Danum Valley Field Research Centre**, which is open to day visitors. Tourists are required to stay in the "eco-resort" – the Borneo Rainforest Lodge. The charming lodge has a huge open lobby with restaurant and bar looking across the Danum River to the rainforest and comfortable stilted chalets nestling beneath the trees.

Local guides, with an intimate knowledge of their subject, can take guests on nature walks; if you are lucky, they can show you how to call the different animals, and pick out a bird hidden in the jungle at a hundred paces. Many guides grew up in the region and have turned their well-honed hunting skills to better use, tracking down animals to photograph. But you'll need plenty of time and patience, standing silently, hoping to catch a glimpse. On the more remote trails, a total disregard for leeches is also an advantage during the wet months.

One of the most popular short excursions is an early morning walk to the canopy walkway, strung high between giant dipterocarps. It can be a rewarding experience to sit for an hour or so and watch for hornbills and honeyeaters, and possibly even the Asian paradise flycatcher – one of Danum's most exotic inhabitants. Night drives in an open jeep will often reveal deer, bearded pigs and other creatures, caught in the beam of the strong spotlight.

BELOW: wild elephants at Tabin.
RIGHT: waterfall in the Danum Valley.

More wildlife

To the east of Lahad Datu is the **Tabin Wildlife Reserve ㉚**. Although logging encroached on the area in the 1970s and 1980s, the re-growth has provided a home for larger mammals such as the elephant, rhino and banteng (wild ox). Comfortable chalets with fans and a restaurant are available, with nature trails for exploring the environment.

From the Tawau district, the north coast can be reached by road via Keningau (over the Crocker Range), and via Sapulut in the interior, travelling close to the Indonesian border along logging tracks passing by the **Maliau Basin**. Four-wheel-drive vehicles, which have obtained permission to carry passengers through the logging concessions, make the trip daily. The drive from Tawau to Keningau takes between 8 and 10 hours, depending on the condition of the tracks. The road north to Sandakan is easy and open, passing through mile after mile of oil palm plantations on what was once rainforest. Buses – which travel north almost to Sandakan before heading west across the Crocker Range – take 12 hours to Kota Kinabalu, and cost half the price of the airfare, although the flight takes just 40 minutes. ❑

Travel Tips

☀ INSIGHT GUIDES Phonecard

One global card to keep travellers in touch. Easy. Convenient. Saves you time and money.

It's a global phonecard

Save up to 70%* on international calls from over 55 countries

Free 24 hour global customer service

Recharge your card at any time via customer service or online

It's a message service

Family and friends can send you voice messages for free.

Listen to these messages using the phone* or online

Free email service - you can even listen to your email over the phone*

It's a travel assistance service

24 hour emergency travel assistance – if and when you need it.

Store important travel documents online in your own secure vault

For more information, call rates, and all Access Numbers in over 55 countries, (check your destination is covered) go to www.insightguides.ekit.com or call Customer Service.

JOIN now and receive US$ 5 bonus when you join for US$ 20 or more.

Join today at

www.insightguides.ekit.com

When requested use ref code: **INSAD0103**

OR SIMPLY FREE CALL 24 HOUR CUSTOMER SERVICE

UK	0800 376 1705
USA	1800 706 1333
Canada	1800 808 5773
Australia	1800 11 44 78
South Africa	0800 997 285

THEN PRESS ⓪

For all other countries please go to "Access Numbers" at www.insightguides.ekit.com

* Retrieval rates apply for listening to messages. Savings based on using a hotel or payphone and calling to a landline. Correct at time of printing 01.03

(INS001)

powered by ⊛ *ekit*

"The easiest way to make calls and receive messages around the world"

CONTENTS

Getting Acquainted

The Place

Area 342,000 sq. km. (132,000 sq. miles) comprising Peninsular Malaysia, and Sabah and Sarawak on Borneo island.

Situation North of the equator, with the peninsula bordered by Singapore in the south and Thailand in the north. Sabah and Sarawak border Indonesia (Kalimantan).

Time Zone Malaysia's standard time is 8 hours ahead of Greenwich Mean Time.

Population 25 million.

Language The official language is Bahasa Malaysia (Malay), but English is the language of business and technology. The Chinese also use Mandarin and various Chinese dialects, while the Indians use Tamil and other Indian languages. The indigenous people retain their own languages.

Currency Ringgit and sen. RM1=100 sen. Coins come in denominations of 5, 10, 20, and 50 sen, and RM1, and notes in RM1, RM2, RM5, RM10, RM50, RM100, and RM500.

Weights and Measures Malaysia follows the metric system, but people in rural areas might still use miles (*batu*) rather than kilometres for distance.

Electricity 220 volts, 50 cycles. American products do not work here, but most supermarkets stock adapters. Major hotels can supply an adapter for 110–120 volt, 60 Hz appliances.

International Dialling Code To call Malaysia from abroad, dial 00 60 followed by the local code, omitting the initial zero, then the number you want. (*For local dialling codes see Practical Tips, page 353*).

Climate

Malaysia's weather is generally hot and sunny all year round, with temperatures wavering between 32°C during the day and 24°C at night. Humidity is high at 80 percent. The temperature in the highlands is slightly lower.

The onset of the monsoon season from May to September brings with it rain to the west coast of Peninsular Malaysia. The east coast of the peninsula and Sabah and Sarawak experience their monsoon season between November and February.

The inter-monsoon periods experience the heaviest rainfalls. Otherwise, light showers come and go, helping to relieve the heat from the sun.

Public Holidays and Festivals

Many of Malaysia's public holidays relate to cultural festivals, the dates of which are not fixed but follow the lunar or Muslim calendar. These include Hari Raya Puasa, the main Muslim festival, a 2-day holiday celebrating the end of the Muslim fasting month of Ramadhan; Hari Raya Haji, celebrating the annual Muslim pilgrimage season; Awal Muharam, the Muslim New Year; and the Birthday of Prophet Muhammad, during which prayers and Quran recitals are held at mosques.

Some festivals are observed only in certain states; for example, the birthday of the respective state sultans. If a public holiday falls on a Saturday or Sunday, the following Monday is a holiday; likewise if a holiday falls on a Thursday or Friday in the states that follow the Muslim week, the following Saturday is a holiday. Check with Tourism Malaysia for specific dates.

School holidays occur during the months of March, May/June, August, November/December. When planning your holiday, avoid these periods.

People

A blend of the great Asian cultures of the world, Malaysians comprise Malays and the indigenous tribes, which make up some 60 percent of the population, Chinese fewer than 30 percent, Indians fewer than 10 percent, and a potpourri of other ethnic groups.

The main and official religion is Islam, adopted by the Malays, but religious tolerance sees the open practice of Buddhism and Taoism among the Chinese, Hinduism among the Indians and Christianity among non-Malays. Some indigenous people retain their animist beliefs.

This diversity has seen the flowering of Malaysia's places of worship, colourful festivals, variety

- **January** New Year's Day (1st); Thaipusam, the Hindu festival of penance, celebrated colourfully in Kuala Lumpur and Penang.
- **January/February** Chinese New Year, a 2-day holiday for the main Chinese festival celebrated over a 15-day period. Make sure to visit Kuala Lumpur's Chinatown during this period.
- **April** Pesta Kaul, a Melanau festival celebrated in the fishing communities around Mukah on Sarawak's north coast.
- **May** Labour Day (1st); Vesak Day, temple celebrations to mark Buddha's birth, death and enlightenment; Harvest Festival, a 2-day holiday, the main festival for the different tribal groups of the state of Sabah.
- **June** Gawai, a 2-day holiday that is the main official festival for the different tribal groups of Sarawak; Birthday of the Yang Dipertuan Agung (king) (5th).
- **August** National Day (31st), celebrated with parades.
- **October/November** Deepavali, Hindu festival of lights.
- **December** Christmas (25th), midnight mass, celebrated in churches all over.

of food, and their particular brand of English. A Malaysian custom during major festivals is the "open house", whereby practitioners of the various religions open their doors to visitors all day. This is when people of different races visit each other to wish each other *Gong Xi Fa Cai* during Chinese New Year, *Selamat Hari Raya* during the Muslim New Year, and *Happy Deepavali* during the Hindu Festival of Lights.

Economy

Electrical and electronic goods, manufactured goods, textiles, clothing and footwear, palm oil, natural gas, petroleum, timber and rubber are the main exports. Malaysia's main trading partners are the United States, Singapore and Japan. Tourism also ranks among the top three contributors to the economy.

Despite the economic crisis that began in 1997, the unemployment rate is relatively low. The stabilisation of the ringgit and stimulation of domestic demand are expected to help resuscitate the economy.

The government's ambitious information technology-based Multimedia Super Corridor (MSC) project, is also viewed as an important springboard in helping the country to achieve developed nation status by 2020.

Government

Malaysia is a constitutional monarchy comprising 13 states and a federal territory. Independent from British colonial rule since 1957, the Malaysian government is regulated by the Parliament comprising the Yang di-Pertuan Agung (king), who is elected for a five-year term from among the sultans of the states, and two houses: the House of Representatives, to which members are elected once every five years, and the Senate, to which members are nominated.

The executive functions of the government are carried out by the cabinet, led by the prime minister. The current prime minister in Malaysia is Dato' Seri Abdullah Ahmad Badawi, who came into office in October 2003. The political entity which has been in power since Independence is the Barisan Nasional (National Front) coalition representing numerous race-based parties.

Business Hours

In an Islamic nation with a British colonial past, the definition of the "working week" varies. In the former British Federated States, it runs from Monday–Friday and Saturday morning. However, the formerly semi-autonomous states of Kedah, Perlis, Terengganu and Kelantan retain the traditional half-day on Thursday and are closed on Friday, not Sunday. Every first and third Saturday is when government offices and banks are closed.

The working day begins at 8am and ends at 4.30pm with time off on Friday from noon–2.30pm for communal prayers at the mosque. Most private businesses stick to the nine-to-five routine. Shops start to close at 6pm, but large supermarkets, department stores and shopping malls are open 10am–10pm.

Planning the Trip

Malaysia's tourism industry is well-established and caters to both the individual traveller as well as groups. While the major peninsula destinations could be covered in a fortnight, distances in Sabah and Sarawak are far greater, and attractions more remote, therefore requiring a little more planning.

Finding accommodation and transport is generally not a problem, except during school holidays and public holidays when it is best to book ahead. In places that are popular with Singaporeans, you should take into account Singaporean holidays, too, when these places can be crowded. Local favourites such as waterfalls near towns can also be crowded with picnickers at the weekend.

Packages are popular with locals, and are usually a better deal than making separate arrangements for accommodation and transport, although they are less flexible. Packages usually include a guided tour, and can be booked through tour agents in the major towns.

The peninsula's west coast is good to visit all year round, although temperatures can be uncomfortably high at the end of January and beginning of February.

The peninsula's east coast usually experiences heavy rain between November and February, and, apart from Chinese-run eateries, food is almost impossible to obtain during the day in the Muslim fasting month of Ramadhan.

Sabah and Sarawak are fine to travel in all year round, although eastern Sabah and Sarawak can be wet during December–January.

A good time to visit the country

is during the major festivals when towns and people get prettied up, unusual goodies are on sale, and tradition flaunts itself.

Passports & Visas

Valid passports or internationally-recognised travel documents valid for at least 6 months are required for entering Malaysia. Remember that Sabah and Sarawak are treated like separate countries, and you will have to go through customs again there, both from Peninsular Malaysia and between the two states.

A social single-entry visa valid for 3 months can be applied for at Malaysian diplomatic missions overseas. Check www.tourism.gov.my for details about formalities and visa requirements. Citizens of most Commonwealth countries, Ireland, Switzerland, Netherlands, San Marino and Liechtenstein do not need a visa to visit. The following countries do not need a visa for a visit not exceeding 3 months: Austria, Italy, Japan, South Korea, Tunisia, United States, Germany, France, Norway, Sweden, Denmark, Belgium, Finland, Luxembourg and Iceland. You are not allowed to be employed with this visa.

Extensions may be applied for at any *Pejabat Imigresen* (Immigration Office):

Kuala Lumpur
Headquarters Office,
Pusat Bandar Damansara
Tel: 03-2095 5077
Alor Setar
Kedah, Wisma Persekutuan,
Jalan Kampung Baru
Tel: 04-733 3302
Ipoh
Perak, Bangunan Sri Kinta,
Jalan Sultan Idris Shah
Tel: 05-254 9316
Johor Bahru
Johor, Wisma Persekutuan,
Jalan Air Molek
Tel: 07-224 4255
Kangar
Perlis, Menara Kemajuan PKNP,
Jalan Bukit Lagi

Tel: 04-976 2636
Kota Bharu
Kelantan, Wisma Persekutuan,
Jalan Bayam
Tel: 09-748 2120
Kota Kinabalu
Sabah, Bangunan Penerangan
Tel: 088-280 700
Kuala Terengganu
Terengganu, Wisma Persekutuan,
Jalan Paya Bunya
Tel: 09-622 1424
Kuantan
Pahang, Wisma Persekutuan,
Jalan Gambut
Tel: 09-514 2155
Kuching
Sarawak, Bangunan Sultan Iskandar,
Jalan Simpang Tiga
Tel: 082-245 661
Labuan
Sabah, Jalan Tanjung Kobang
Tel: 087-412 298
Melaka
Wisma Persekutuan,
Jalan Hang Tuah
Tel: 06-282 4955
Pulau Pinang (Penang)
Jalan Lebuh Pantai
Tel: 04-261 5122
Seremban
Negeri Sembilan,
Wisma Persekutuan,
Jalan Dato' Abdul Kadir
Tel: 06-762 0000
Shah Alam
Selangor, Kompleks PKNS
Tel: 03-5519 0653

Customs

Import duties seldom affect the average traveller, who may bring in 250 g (½ lb) of tobacco, 50 cigars, or 200 cigarettes, and a 1-litre bottle of liquor duty-free as well as personal cameras, watches, cassette players, cosmetics, etc.

On rare occasions, visitors may be asked to pay a deposit for temporary importation of dutiable goods (up to 50 percent of the value) which is refundable upon departure. Be sure to get an official receipt for any tax or deposit paid.

Pornography, weapons and walkie-talkies are strictly prohibited. Exporting antiques requires a

licence from the Museum Department. The duty-free guidelines do not apply on domestic flights, or from Singapore.

Note Possession of narcotics and other illegal drugs carries the death sentence.

What to Bring

There is very little need to worry about leaving something important behind when you visit Malaysia. Toiletries, medicines, clothes, film, suntan lotion and straw hats are all readily available in most towns, and definitely in the large cities. So, travel lightly.

If you are planning to visit the hill stations, a light sweater would be a good idea for the cooler evenings. In more remote areas, you will not have the luxury of a shaving point, but disposable razors are widely available, or you can buy a battery-operated razor. Sanitary products for women are also available, but tampons are not easily obtainable in small towns.

In Malaysia's tropical climate, think cotton. Malaysians are fairly informal but they do dress up for dinner or a night out, especially in the cities. In fact, the fancier establishments have a dress code. Moreover, since this is a predominantly Muslim and conservative country, observance of local customs is important. T-shirts and longish shorts are fine, except in rural areas and especially if you go off the beaten tourist track, in which case, keep your legs and upper arms covered. Check the required attire before entering any house of religious worship.

Cheap clothes are everywhere – colourful batik shirts and "I was here" T-shirts make good souvenirs, too. Large shoe sizes could be a problem though.

Toilet paper is still not widely available, even in cities, so unless you are familiar with the local pail or hose-and-water method, pack a roll, or carry tissue paper with you.

Health and Insurance

Travellers have little to worry about in a country where the health standards are ranked among the highest in Asia. Water in cities is generally safe for drinking, but it is safest to drink it boiled. Bottled drinks are also widely available. Avoid drinking iced water from roadside stalls. It is important to drink sufficiently to avoid dehydration; drink more than you would normally if you're from a temperate country. Cooked stall food is generally safe to eat.

The sun is deceptively strong in Malaysia: one hour of sunbathing a day for the first few days will get you a lasting tan without giving you sunstroke.

If you are visiting remote rainforest areas, it is advisable to take protection against malaria. See your doctor before leaving home. Malaria tablets are only available on prescription in Malaysia. To keep mosquitoes at bay, use insect repellents, mosquito coils and mosquito nets at night.

Treat open cuts and scratches immediately as infection in humid climates can delay healing, and at worst, cause tropical ulcers. It is advisable to read up about which rainforest and marine creatures to be wary of.

Medical supplies and treatment are readily available in Malaysia, in pharmacies and hospitals as well as at 24-hour private clinics.

It is advisable to buy travel and health insurance before arriving in the country.

Emergencies

Emergency services numbers are:
999 – police and ambulance
994 – fire and rescue
991 – civil defence.

Money Matters

Carry a combination of cash and travellers' cheques and/or a credit card. Cash is imperative in rural areas, but you can change travellers' cheques and use credit cards in urban areas and established tourist areas.

Most currencies can be exchanged for ringgit, but the popular ones are US dollars (to which the ringgit is pegged), British sterling and Singapore dollars. Licensed money changers (open from early morning until late at night) offer better rates than banks, while hotels and shopping centres levy a service charge (usually 2–4 percent).

Local and international banks handle the gamut of transactions, and automated teller machines, from which you can use your credit card to withdraw cash, are widespread in towns.

In the more flashy quarters of the larger towns, in department stores, shops, first-class restaurants and hotels, travellers' cheques can be exchanged easily. Have your passport ready when changing cheques.

Banking Hours

Banking hours are Monday–Friday 9.30am–4pm, Saturday 9.30am–noon (closed on first and third Saturdays of the month).

Credit Cards

The most widely used credit cards are Visa and MasterCard. Diners Club and American Express are less welcome, but accepted, too. Make sure you have enough cash before you leave a city.

Taxes

There is no general sales tax on purchases, but there is a government tax of 10 percent. While service tax has been abolished, some establishments still charge 5 percent. Hotels are obliged to list net prices, but restaurants generally do not.

Overseas Tourist Offices

Tourism Malaysia (www.tourism.gov. my) has a network of overseas offices. For information in each country, contact:

Dressing for the Jungle

Going into the rainforest requires extra preparation. It is much more humid in the rainforest, so packing light is even more imperative, as you could find yourself getting tired easily. Be prepared to get wet, so a light raincoat is a must. A rainpack could be useful, but line your backpack with a plastic bag anyway, and check that everything is waterproof, because river-crossings are almost inevitable. Long-sleeved cotton shirts and cotton trousers are comfortable and protect you from thorny rattan and insects.

Leave your heavy-duty leather boots behind – after a river-crossing, your feet will feel like lead. Sports sandals or light sneakers with a good grip are a better bet.

Temperatures can drop to 0°C on the mountain peaks, such as Mount Kinabalu and Mount Mulu, so warmer clothing and even gloves are a good idea.

Also, pack a water bottle, purifying tablets (or boil all your water), insect repellent, sunscreen, a cap, small towel or sarong, and your own energy supplements such as chocolate and sweets – these can double as goodwill gifts to any children you might meet. Leech socks come in handy, too.

If you travel with a tour company, everything else will be provided. Otherwise, tents, sleeping bags and cooking utensils can be hired in places such as Taman Negara, but book beforehand.

Note that while bikinis might be fine in the beach resorts, they are considered offensive in the more remote areas, particularly in the presence of Orang Asli or native guides, who consider some of their places sacred. So, you can also forget about going starkers.

Australia (Sydney)
Tourism Malaysia
Level 2, 171 Clarence Street,
Sydney, NSW 2000
Tel: 02-9299 4441/2/3
Fax: 02-9262 2026
e-mail: mtpb.sydney@tourism.gov.my
Canada (Vancouver)
Tourism Malaysia
830 Burrard Street, Vancouver, BC,
Canada V6Z 1X9
Tel: 604-689 8899
Fax: 604-689 8804
e-mail:
mtpb.vancouver@tourism.gov.my
www.tourism-malaysia.ca
Germany (Frankfurt)
Tourism Malaysia
Rossmarkt 11,
60311 Frankfurt Am Main
Tel: 069-283 782/3
Fax: 069-1337 9121
e-mail:
mtpb.frankfurt@tourism.gov.my
Singapore
Tourism Malaysia
#01-01B/C/D, 80 Robinson Road,
Singapore 068898
Tel: 02-6532 6321/51
Fax: 02-6535 6650
e-mail:
mtpb.singapore@tourism.gov.my
Thailand (Bangkok)
Tourism Malaysia
Unit 1001, Liberty Square, 287
Silom Road, Bangkok 10500
Tel: 0662-631 1994/5/6
Fax: 0662-631 1998
United Kingdom
Tourism Malaysia
57, Trafalgar Square,
London WC2N 5DU
Tel: 020-7930 7932
Fax: 020-7930 9015
e-mail:
mtpb.london@tourism.gov.my
United States (New York)
Tourism Malaysia
120, East 56th Street, Suite 810,
New York, NY 10022
Tel: 212-754 1114/5
Fax: 212-754 1116
e-mail: mtpb.ny@tourism.gov.my
www.visitmalaysia.com
United States (Los Angeles)
Tourism Malaysia
Suite 970, 9th Floor, 818 West
Seventh Street, Los Angeles,
CA 90017 U.S.A.

Tel: 213-689 9702
Fax: 213-689 1530
e-mail: mtpb.la@tourism.gov.my

Photography

Beware of the heat if using a
conventional film loaded camera.
Exposure of film or camera
equipment to hot sun causes
changes in the chemical emulsions
of the film, which detract from
natural colour. Whenever possible,
store your camera and film in a cool
place; if not in an air-conditioned
room, at least in the shade. Also,
buy film in the cities, or where you
can see that film is properly stored.

Get your films processed as
soon as possible. You can do this
everywhere in Malaysia where it is
cheaper than in Western countries,
with fairly good to excellent results.
All outlets will process colour print
film, sometimes in as little as half
an hour. Bigger shops handle slides
and APS-processing, too, while
black-and-white takes approximately
48 hours.

Only photography shops in the
bigger cities stock accessories, but
those that do offer a good gamut,
from tripods to the latest types of
film and cameras.

Note that rainforest trips are
camera-killers because of the
humidity. Bring a plastic bag for
your camera; likewise wrap film
tightly in a plastic bag. Pack a dry,
non-lint cloth. When you reach your
campsite, wipe your camera dry,
and leave it out to air. If you can,
bring silica gel to absorb moisture.

For rich colours, snap your shots
before 10.30am or after 3pm. At
noon, the light is too strong. Early
morning or late afternoon sidelights
give softer contrasts and deeper
colour density. And you perspire
less as well.

Most Malaysians are more than
amiable about having their pictures
taken. It usually takes a gang of
schoolchildren about 15 seconds
before they merrily begin jabbing
peace signs in front of your 20 mm
lens. Mosques and temples are
rightly more reserved about
photographers posing their subjects

in front of altars. Whatever the
situation, you should always ask for
permission. This is imperative
during religious ceremonies, where
you should keep a respectful
distance. Likewise with tribal
people, ask your tour guide. You
should also ask if you should pay –
this is controversial, but don't be
surprised if payment is demanded.

Carry sweets for the children. If
you can bear to carry one, a zoom
lens is a solution, ensuring your
slideshows back home comprise
your best memories.

Getting There

Malaysia is served by a large
number of airlines. It can be
reached by road from Singapore
and Thailand, and ferries and boats
connect the coastal towns.

BY AIR

Malaysia is well connected by about
41 airlines to all continents.
Besides **Kuala Lumpur International
Airport (KLIA)** at Sepang, the hub
for most international flights, the
other international airports are at
Penang, Langkawi, Johor Bahru,
Kuching, Kota Kinabalu and Labuan.

Direct flights from Singapore
connect with Kuala Lumpur,
Penang, Kuantan and Tioman in the
peninsula, and Kuching and Kota
Kinabalu in East Malaysia.
Likewise, direct flights from
Bangkok (Thailand) and Bandar Seri
Begawan (Brunei) connect with
Kuala Lumpur and other cities.

Malaysia Airlines (MAS), the
national airline (www.malaysia
airlines.com), handles international
(about 120 destinations worldwide)
and a wide range of domestic
routes. MAS and Singapore Airlines
run shuttle services between Kuala
Lumpur and Singapore about every
half an hour – just go to the airport
and take a number and you will be
put on the first available flight.
Although this is cheaper than
confirmed seats, early-morning and
late-night flights are popular and
sell out quickly.

Domestic Flights

All **Malaysia Airlines** domestic flights also depart from KLIA while smaller domestic airlines such as **Berjaya Air** operate from the old airport at Subang.

There is also a budget airline called **Air Asia** (www.airasia.com) which connects to popular tourist destinations in various Southeast Asian countries, including Malaysia.

Enquire about special multi-sector air passes in your own country – these apply only if you purchase your ticket there. The peak season is over Christmas when overseas students flock home for the holidays. Summertime in Europe and the United States are also busy periods. Make sure you confirm your return ticket. You will have to pay airport tax and surcharges.

International Airlines

Malaysia Airlines
Tel: 1300 88 3000 (24 hours)
Air Asia
Tel: 03-8660 4333
Air New Zealand
Tel: 03-2142 1199
British Airways
Tel: 1800 88 1260
Cathay Pacific
Tel: 03-2078 3379
China Airlines
Tel: 03-2142 7344

Continental
Tel: 03-2142 4375
Emirates Air
Tel: 03-2058 5838
Eva Air
Tel: 03-2162 2981
Garuda
Tel: 03-2162 2811
Japan Air
Tel: 03-2161 1722
KLM
Tel: 03-2711 2300
Lufthansa
Tel: 03-2052 3428
Philippine Airlines
Tel: 03-2141 0767
Qantas
Toll free: 1 800 88 1260
Royal Brunei Air
Tel: 03-2070 7166
SAS
Tel: 03-2142 6044
Singapore Airlines
Tel: 03-2692 3122
Thai Airways
Tel: 03-2031 2900
Northwest Airlines
Tel: 03-2161 5901
United Airlines
Tel: 03-2161 1433

BY RAIL

The railway runs north from Singapore through Malaysia to Bangkok. **Malaysian KTM** trains operate night and day services from Singapore to Kuala Lumpur and to Tumpat near Kota Bharu on the east coast. The journey to Kuala Lumpur takes 7–10 hours; 12–15 hours to Tumpat.

From Bangkok, the Thai-owned **International Express** leaves daily for Butterworth (Penang) where you change trains for Kuala Lumpur. From Haadyai in southern Thailand you can travel all the way south. This journey takes about 2 days. Trains from Haadyai connect to Malaysia's east coast line. You can travel in a first-class air-conditioned sleeper, a second-class non-air-conditioned sleeper, or in upright seats, third class. For reservations, contact the station in Bangkok (Hualamphong), or Kuala Lumpur's new Sentral station (03-2274 7435).

Sabah has only one railway that runs from Kota Kinabalu to Beaufort in the interior.

BY ROAD

There are two road links to the peninsula from Singapore and a plethora from Thailand, just as numerous points link Sabah and Sarawak with Kalimantan in Indonesia. From Singapore, there are links across the **Causeway** from Woodlands to Johor Bahru, and **Linkedua (Second Link)** from Tuas to Tanjung Kupang. In Singapore, buses to Peninsular Malaysia depart from Beach Road (outside

To and From KLIA

Kuala Lumpur International Airport (KLIA) is located some 80 km (50 miles) from Kuala Lumpur city centre. The most convenient door-to-door option is by **airport taxi**. Tickets to the city centre cost RM67 for budget taxis and RM92 for the more comfortable premier taxis. All tickets must be purchased inside the Arrival Hall. Journey time is about one-hour but subject to the peak-hour traffic crawl in the city.

Airport express coaches depart from the KLIA basement every hour from 5am–10.30pm for the Jalan Duta stop. Tickets cost RM20 per person. Passengers can also ask to be dropped off at major city hotels. Coaches also go to the Chan Sow Lin stop, leaving hourly from 6.30am–9.30pm.

Another option is to take the **KLIA Ekspres** (tel: 03-2267 8000), the Express Rail Link (ERL) that runs every 30 minutes. Fares are RM35 one- way and RM65 return. It takes 28 minutes to reach **KL Sentral**, the city's main transportation hub. To get to your hotel, hop into a taxi or take a connecting LRT or KTM intra-city train.

When departing KL, you can request to be picked up by the airport express coach from any major hotel in KL, although bookings must be made at least one day before your flight (tel: 03-6203 3064/3067). Alternatively, call the airport taxi service (tel: 03-9223 8080) or hail any cab off the street. Expect to pay the fare on the meter plus surcharges and toll fees.

Malaysia Airlines and Cathay Pacific passengers can also check in at the **KL City Air Terminal** at KL Sentral two hours before their flight departs. The first train departs at 5am while the last train at 1am.

Golden Mile Centre), Lavendar Street and Queen Street. If you opt for long-distance taxis, take the bus no. 170 to Johor Bahru and get a taxi from there.

The main routes from Bangkok or Haadyai in Thailand are across the border at Padang Besar (Perlis), Bukit Kayu Hitam (Kedah) and Rantau Panjang (Kelantan). Buses and taxis serve these routes.

From Pontianak in Kalimantan regular buses go to Kuching, Sarawak (10 hours). Miri is the jump-off point to Brunei's Bandar Seri Begawan. In Sarawak there is a road from Kuching to Kalimantan (Pontianak) and a long coast road joins Miri with the Brunei capital of Bandar Seri Begawan.

Direct to Singapore

Plusliner coaches (tel: 03-2272 1586; www.plusliner.com) operates an efficient coach service 15 times a day from the KL Railway station to Singapore's Copthorne Orchid Hotel, and vice versa. The journey takes over 4 hours and travel is on board the Nice Executive Coach. With only 26 seats on board a regular-sized coach, this means ample leg roon for passengers. In addition, refreshments and a simple meal is served during the trip. Tickets cost RM60 one way while a premium service on board the double decker Nice 2 coach costs RM70 one way. The premium service only operates five times a day. Plusliner also operates coach services from KL to various cities in the peninsula.

BY SEA

Malaysia has a number of authorised entry points by sea. Singapore has ferry links to Tanjung Belungkor and Kukup in Johor, and a high-speed catamaran to Tioman. Satun in south Thailand has a regular ferry or longboat service to Langkawi. Penang connects to Medan in Sumatra, Indonesia and Melaka connects to Dumai further

south on the same island. Ferries also connect Port Klang and Tanjung Balai in Indonesia.

In Sabah, Tawau connects to Tarakan in Kalimantan, Indonesia; Brunei is linked to Labuan, and Limbang and Lawas in Sarawak. Sabah has ferry services from Kota Kinabalu to Labuan from where a boat can be taken across to the Sarawak side.

Overseas Tour Operators

United Kingdom

Footprint Adventures
5 Malham Drive, Lakelands
Lincoln LN6 0XD
Tel: 01-522 804 929
Fax: 01-522 804 928
e-mail:
info@footprint-adventures.co.uk
Specialist in jungle trekking, birdwatching trips, and butterfly and wildlife safari holidays.

Kuoni Travel Ltd
Kuoni House, Dorking,
Surrey RH5 4AZ
Tel: 01-306 740 888
Fax: 01-306 740 328
e-mail: fareastsales@kuoni.co.uk
Winner of the Tourism Malaysia Travel Awards 1998 for the "Best Overall Tour Programme to Malaysia". Tailor-made service also available.

Travelbag Plc
12 High Street, Alton,
Hampshire GU34 1BN
Tel: 01-420 546 312
Fax: 01-420 821 33
e-mail: freequotes@travelbag.co.uk
Specialist in providing tailor-made service, with single or multicentre-holidays to Malaysia.

United States

ABSORBtours Inc
545 Eighth Avenue, 18th Floor
New York, New York 10018
Tel: 212-584 1194
Fax: 212-714 1768
e-mail: info@absorbtours.com
www.absorbtours.com
Dedicated to creating customised, private tours for the independent traveller with special interests.

Practical Tips

Media

Newspapers and Magazines

The main daily newspapers are in Bahasa Malaysia and English. There are also Chinese and Tamil language newspapers. The *New Straits Times* is the voice of the government, but it is difficult to be otherwise when all media have to apply annually to renew their operating licence under the Printing and Presses Act. The other big English language national daily is *The Star* and the main business weekly is *The Edge*. The *Malay Mail* is an afternoon tabloid with a more chatty, local slant. Sabah and Sarawak have their own papers, including *The Sabah Times*, *Sabah Daily News*, *Daily Express*, *Sarawak Tribune* and *Borneo Post*.

Most of these papers have online editions; *The Star Online* is one of the most popular websites for Malaysian news. There is also a large number of local magazines, from leisure to entertainment and business. Foreign newspapers and magazines can be purchased in large cities.

Radio and Television

The radio can be heard everywhere, blaring out a wild assortment of different sounds; a flick of the dial will tune you to Malay rock or heavy metal, Tamil numbers or Western classical music, Canto-pop or the latest hits from Britain or the United States. The main national English language radio stations are: Hitz FM, Mix FM, Light & Easy (format radio stations which play a mix of local and international numbers), THR – which specialises in traffic updates – and the government-run Radio 4.

Television is the most popular medium in Malaysia, watched in international hotel rooms and longhouses with the same enthusiasm. Programmes are cosmopolitan and American sit-coms and documentaries are shown alongside Indonesia's hottest films and Koran reading competitions. Sports are given generous amounts of air-time.

The government television stations are RTM1 and 2, the private operators are TV3, 8TV and NTV7, while the subscription-only satellite TV broadcaster, Astro, offers 44 channels, including MTV and CNN. The news in English is broadcast at 6.30pm on RTM1 (also known as TV1) and 12am on TV3 and NTV7. Most hotels offer an in-house cable station as well as selected Astro satellite channels. Check the local newspaper for programme details.

Postal Services

Malaysian postal services are reliable, and there are post offices everywhere. Post offices are open Monday–Saturday, 8am–5pm (closed first and third Saturday each month), while a handful in large housing estates are open until 10pm. The full range of services is available, including PosLaju courier and overnight Pos Ekspres services.

Most large hotels provide postal services; and stamps and aerogrammes are often sold at the small Indian sweet and tobacco stalls on street corners.

Telecommunications

Three telephone companies operate coin-operated public phone services. These also accept credit cards and/or telephone cards, which are sold at many small shops. **Telekom Malaysia** is the main national operator with Time dot Com as a relatively new competitor.

Home country direct calls can also be made from public phones. Off-peak periods for inter-state calls are 7pm–7am.

The access codes for US phone companies are as follows: MCI: 1800-800 012; Sprint: 1800-800 016; AT&T: 1800-800 011.

Since 2000, phone numbers in most parts of Kuala Lumpur have changed from seven to eight digits. As this was an on-going exercise at time of press, check with Telecom Malaysia (www.telecom.com.my) if you cannot get through the phone numbers listed in this guide. In Malaysia, call 103 for operator assistance.

Faxes can be sent through Kedai Telekom Bureaufax centres and Pos 2020 outlets in the major towns.

Medium to luxury hotels provide in-room telephones with local and international connection as well as public telephones in the foyer.

Telephone Codes

Malaysia country code 60
Johor 07
Kedah 04
Kelanan 09
Kota Kinabalu 088
Kuala Lumpur 03
Kuching 082
Labuan 087
Melaka 06
Miri 085
Negeri Sembilan 06
Pahang 09
Penang 04
Perak 05
Perlis 04
Selangor 03
Terengganu 09
Singapore from Malaysia 02

Internet

Cybercafés can be found in all the capitals and some towns and tourist areas, including several in Kuching and Kota Kinabalu. Many are in the large shopping centres. Backpacker hotels seem to be more advanced in providing this service than some of the medium-class ones. Major hotels offer an Internet service at a high cost in their business centres, and business-class international hotels offer it in the room.

Tourist Information

Tourism Malaysia (www.tourism. gov.my) has offices in every state. TM offices vary in the amount of literature available, but there are usually comprehensive brochures on each state and sometimes local places of interest, and the officers are informed and helpful. The regional offices can also be contacted for information on reliable tour and travel operators, who have to be registered with them.

In addition, both Sarawak and Sabah have their own state-run tourism offices:

Tourist Offices
TM – Head Office
24–27th & 30th Floor, Menara Dato' Onn, Putra World Trade Centre, 45 Jalan Tun Ismail, KL
Tel: 03-2615 8188
e-mail: enquiries@tourism.gov.my
Malaysia Tourism Centre (MTC)
109 Jalan Ampang, KL
Tel: 03-2164 3929
e-mail:
mtpb.enquiries@tourism.gov.my
TM – East Coast Region
5th Floor, Menara Yayasan Islam Terengganu, Jalan Sultan Omar, Kuala Terengganu
Tel: 09-622 1893
e-mail: mtpbkt@tourism.gov.my
TM – Northern Region
Level 56, KOMTAR, Penang
Tel: 04-261 0058
e-mail: mtpbpen@tourism.gov.my
TM – Southern Region
L3–26, Level 3, Bagunan JOTIC
2 Jalan Ayer Molek
Johor Bahru
Tel: 07-222 3591
e-mail: mtpbjhb@tourism.gov.my
TM – Sabah
Ground Floor, EON CMG Life Building
1 Jalan Sagunting, Kota Kinabalu
Tel: 088-248 698
e-mail: mtpbbki@tourism.gov.my
Sabah Tourism Board
51, Jalan Gaya, Kota Kinabalu
Tel: 088-212 121
e-mail: info@sabahtourism.com
www.sabahtourism.com
TM – Sarawak
2nd Floor, Rugayah Building, Jalan Song Thian Cheok, Kuching

Tel: 082-246 575
e-mail: mtpbkch@tourism.gov.my
Sarawak Tourism Board
6th Floor Bangunan Yayasan
Sarawak, Jalan Masjid, Kuching
Tel: 082-423 600
e-mail: stb@sarawaktourism.com
www.sarawaktourism.com

Embassies and Consulates

Australia
6 Jalan Yap Kwan Seng
Tel: 03-2146 5555
Canada
17th Floor, Menara Tan & Tan
207 Jalan Tun Razak
Tel: 03-2162 2363
China
229 Jalan Ampang
Tel: 03-2142 8495
Denmark
22nd Floor Wisma Denmark
86 Jalan Ampang
Tel: 03-2032 2001
France
192–196 Jalan Ampang
Tel: 03-2053 5500
Germany
3 Jalan U Thant
Tel: 03-2170 9666
India
Jalan Taman Duta, off Jalan Duta
Tel: 03-2093 3510
Indonesia
233 Jalan Tun Razak
Tel: 03-2145 2011
Italy
99 Jalan U Thant
Tel: 03-4256 5122
Japan
11 Pessiaran Stonor
Tel: 03-2142 7044
Myanmar
1 Lorong Ru Kedua, off Jalan Ru,
Ampang
Tel: 03-4257 0680
Netherlands
7th Floor, The Amp Walk,
South Block, 218 Jalan Ampang
Tel: 03-2168 6200
New Zealand
Level 21 Menara IMC,
Jalan Sultan Ismail
Tel: 03-2078 2533
Norway
53th Floor Empire Tower
Jalan Tun Razak

Tel: 03-2175 0300
Philippines
1 Changkat Kia Peng
Tel: 03-2148 9989
Singapore
209 Jalan Tun Razak
Tel: 03-2161 6277
South Korea
9 Jalan Nipah, off Jalan Ampang
Tel: 03-4251 2336
Sri Lanka
12 Jalan Keranji 2, Ampang Hilir
Tel: 03-4256 8987
Sweden
6th Floor Wisma Angkasa Raya
123 Jalan Ampang
Tel: 03-2148 5433
Switzerland
16 Persiaran Madge
Tel: 03-2148 0622
Thailand
206 Jalan Ampang
Tel: 03-2148 8222
United Kingdom
186 Jalan Ampang
Tel: 03-2148 2122
United States
376 Jalan Tun Razak
Tel: 03-2168 5000
Vietnam
4 Persiaran Stonor
Tel: 03-2148 4036

Women Travellers

Travelling alone is fairly safe for women, but no thanks to Hollywood. Western women do have the image of being "easy", so a wedding ring helps, or a "Yes, I'm married" to the inevitable query. Ignore wolf whistles and catcalls. If you are approached, be polite but firm. Mostly people are just being friendly, even if some might be hoping for something more; if you start feeling uneasy, walk away. Be careful about being over-friendly with your tour guide.

Malaysians stare – both men and women – but wearing revealing clothes in areas that are newer to tourism will invite harassment. In Malaysia's rural societies, young women rarely approach or speak to male strangers, and travel is virtually unheard of, let alone travelling alone. Topless and nude sunbathing is prohibited.

Travelling with Kids

There are enough attractions to keep children occupied when travelling in Malaysia. However, children might be more susceptible to heat and food-and-water related ailments. Food could be a problem off the beaten track. Malaysian infrastructure is not at all baby-friendly, even in the cities. There are no mother's rooms or nappy-changing tables in toilets, and it can be difficult to buy infant products in rural areas. Public transport and public areas are unsympathetic to pushchairs. Yet Malaysians love children, so a helping hand is never far away.

Tipping

In most hotels and large restaurants, a 10 percent government tax and 5 percent service tax is added to the bill, so tipping is not obligatory. However, it is appreciated and is common, but only in the cities and major tourist spots. In large hotels, bellboys and porters usually receive tips from RM2 to RM5 depending on the service rendered. In smart restaurants you can just leave behind the loose change. Tourist guides expect a tip. Otherwise, a simple thank you (*terima kasih*) and a smile will do.

Religious Services

Minarets, spires, domes and steeples adorning the skylines reflect a rich diversity of faiths in Malaysia. However, churches might be difficult to locate outside urban centres and in the predominantly Muslim east coast of Peninsular Malaysia. Check with your hotel.

Security and Crime

Like anywhere else, pickpockets will be your biggest worry. Unless you are in a luxury hotel, do not leave valuables in your room, except in a safe. Carry your passport and money with you at all times – even for a bout of sunbathing – or keep them in the main hotel safe. Sling your camera around your body, and make sure your backpack is firmly strapped on. If you are going diving or snorkelling or taking part in any other adventure sport, put valuables in a small backpack which you can leave with the operators. Travelling on public transport is safe – just keep an eye on the luggage that is taken out whenever your interstate coach stops. Walking around at night is safe; women should be a little more careful, especially in tourist areas, but groups are fine.

Hitch-hiking is uncommon and hence can be frustrating and dangerous. Public transport, if slow and erratic in some places, is cheap and plentiful.

Etiquette

Malaysians smile a lot, and are more often than not polite and helpful. Cities and entrenched tourist areas have a more liberal atmosphere, but if visiting rural areas, and especially someone's private home, it helps to know something of local norms.

Seniority is much respected. The oldest male member of a family is greeted first, often sits in the best and highest seat, and is consulted first on any matter.

If you are a man, greet the men first, then the women. Women usually greet other women first. It is not uncommon for women not to shake hands with male strangers. Although handshakes are common, particularly in the cities, do not be offended by what is a limp handshake by Western standards. The Malay style of greeting is to touch the other's palm and then his heart, "I am pleased to meet you from the bottom of my heart."

Hugging and kissing are foreign among non-family members, so except for children, refrain from doing so, no matter how fond you become of someone. Necking or fondling each other in public is a no-no, too, particularly in rural areas. In traditional homes, it is rude to cross your legs when you sit down in front of the host, particularly for women.

Drinks and snacks are always served to guests. Never refuse. At the very least, take a nominal sip or one biscuit. Use the right hand to pass or accept anything. The left is traditionally "dirty" because of its washroom connections.

Pointing with the finger is considered very rude and a whole hand is used to indicate a direction, but never a person. To point to a person, close the right hand into a fist with the thumb on top and then aim it at the subject.

Malaysians remove their shoes at the door to keep the house free from dirt. You can always tell if there is some kind of get-together at someone's house by the number of shoes and sandals scattered around the front door.

Old Customs – New Lifestyles

Leisure and tourism are relatively new concepts to Malaysians. As an industry, tourism was established only in the 1960s, which was also when Malaysians started travelling on holiday. Today, tourism is one of the top three revenue-earners for the country, and the industry comes under a federal ministry which spends millions on infrastructure and promotions. This investment is most evident in ease of access and range of accommodation.

The industry's Achilles' heel is service. Therefore, sometimes, a complaint might receive a less than satisfactory response, or staff at a three-star resort might be slow or ignorant. The key is to be patient and firm – often, making a joke out of a situation gets a quicker response than anger.

Punctuality, or the lack thereof, is the other point to note. Malaysians follow "Malaysian time", which translates to anything from a few minutes to hours late. Rarely does a bus or boat leave ahead of schedule, and almost never without a passenger. Have a cuppa and wait. Detailed information about an area is also scarce, although it is improving; but locals are always happy to regale you with a local legend, or point out "must-sees".

Because of the incipience of tourism, particularly in the rural areas, great is the danger of cultural pollution. Satellite television notwithstanding, age-old traditions, lifestyles, and morals are crumbling before the holy grail of the so-called better life. Tourism can rent the fragile social fabric of a family and community through something as simple as what a foreigner wears (or often, does not), to more direct interaction and infusion of ideas.

Visitors to the country are also, more and more, encountering another breed of locals: the Malaysian on holiday. To many

Malaysians, spending money on leisure is still anathema to their frugal, Asian work-based ethos. Malaysian Chinese, in particular, holiday only once a year during Chinese New Year, and often go overseas; otherwise, those running their own businesses in particular, work 7 days a week. On the other hand, leisure is important to the city-bred, middle-income baby-boomers of the 1990s, and especially those exposed to Western norms.

Malaysians generally like to travel in big groups and thus tend to be noisy – it is a cultural trait. They like crowds, and will try to replicate home by bringing along their stereos, card games and mahjong sets. They also enjoy karaoke, even in a rainforest or cave. On the other hand, Malaysians do not generally sunbathe in the nude or wander about drunk, yelling obscenities – generally, nor do tourists.

Getting Around

On Arrival

Buses, public and private, taxis and limousines operate from major airports in Malaysia. Many airports have a taxi desk, where you purchase a coupon; the price is fixed. Kuala Lumpur's railway station also uses a coupon system. Tolls are paid by the passenger. Elsewhere, inquire about fares at the information desk. Taxi fares from airports are higher than around the town.

Sarawak and Sabah

Please note that although Sarawak and Sabah are part of Malaysia, it is necessary for both Malaysian and foreign visitors, whether coming from other parts of Malaysia or from another country, to go through immigration procedures on arrival.

By Air

Travelling by air is the best way to cover the great distances in Sabah and Sarawak, and in some cases, the only way – other than days of walking – to access the high hills and deep rainforests. Locals hop on and off planes like they do buses.

Touting for Business

The airport is where you are likely to meet your first tout. Unlicensed taxi operators, called *teksi sapu* or *kereta sapu*, hang around airport, train, bus and boat terminals, and will charge a flat rate, usually higher than official rates. They sometimes go round gathering a few passengers before they depart. Opt for a licensed cab if you can.

The most extensive network of flights is operated by **Malaysia Airlines (MAS)**. In the more remote areas, its Fokker 50s and Twin Otters are the fastest link to capitals. Airport tax (RM$) for domestic flights is collected at all airports. Check in no later than 45 minutes before departure. You may check baggage through to your final destination. All flights are non-smoking.

MAS has a night tourist fare which is 30 percent cheaper on Kuala Lumpur sectors to Alor Setar, Penang, Kota Bharu, Johor Bahru, Kuching and Kota Kinabalu. Other discounts on selected routes (mainly from Johor Bahru, Kuala Lumpur, Kuching and Kota Kinabalu) include a special one-way fare (less 20 percent) if you pay up 7 days' in advance; a special round-trip fare (less 30 percent) if you stay between 3 and 30 days; and a group fare (less 50 percent) for travel between the peninsula and Sabah or Sarawak if you are in a group of three, pay up 7 days' in advance, and remain in the destination between 3 and 30 days; other restrictions apply. There is also a special rate for families. Enquire at the nearest MAS office.

Malaysia Airlines Offices

Call 1300-88 3000 (within Malaysia) or 603-7846 3000 (outside Malaysia) for inquiries or check www.malaysiaairlines.com. Note: In Kuala Lumpur, all MAS domestic flights operate out of Kuala Lumpur International Airport (KLIA).
Alor Setar Lot 180, Kompleks Alor Setar, Lebuhraya Darulaman, Kedah
Tel: 04-731 1107; 04-731 1186
Ipoh Lot G-01 Bangunan Seri Kinta, Jalan Sultan Idris Shah, Perak
Tel: 05-253 0278
Johor Bahru Suite 1.1, Level 1, Menara Pelangi, Jalan Kuning, Taman Pelangi, Johor
Tel: 07-331 0035
Kota Bharu Ground Floor, Komplek Yakin, Jalan Gajah Mati, Kelantan
Tel: 09-748 3477
Kota Kinabalu Ground Floor, Kompleks Karamunsing
Tel: 088-239 310/297

Kuala Lumpur Bangunan MAS, Jalan Sultan Ismail
Tel: 03-7846 3000 (24 hours)
Kuala Terengganu 13 Jalan Sultan Omar, Terengganu
Tel: 09-622 9279
Kuantan 7 Ground Floor, Wisma Persatuan Bolasepak Pahang, Jalan Gambut, Pahang
Tel: 09-515 6030
Kuching Lot 215, Jalan Song Thian Cheok, Sarawak
Tel: 082-244 144
Labuan Level 2, Airport Terminal Building, PO Box 23, Sabah
Tel: 087-431 737
Langkawi GF5/GF44, Langkawi Fair Shopping Mall, Jalan Persiaran Putra, Kedah
Tel: 04-966 8611/0332
Melaka Lot 1 & 2, Block A, Ground Floor, Century Mahkota Hotel, Jalan Mardeka, Melaka
Tel: 06-282 9597
Miri Lot 239, Beautiful Jade Centre, Sarawak
Tel: 085-417 315
Penang 2nd Floor, Menara KWSP, 38 Jalan Sultan Ahmad Shah, Penang
Tel: 04-217 6330

Other Airlines

Two smaller airlines service limited destinations and offer cheaper rates.
Air Asia (tel: 03-8660 4333; www.airasia.com) offers low-fare, no-frills flights a la Virgin Airways to most main tourist destinations such as Penang, Langkawi, Kuching, Kota Kinabalu and Kota Bharu. The airline also offers a small selection of holiday packages to selected destinations. The airline operates out of Kuala Lumpur International Airport (KLIA).
Berjaya Air (tel: 03-2145 2828; www.berjaya-air.com) is the only airline to offer flights to islands such as Tioman and Pangkor. Using 48-seater Dash 7 aircrafts, Berjaya Air mainly operates from the Sultan Abdul Aziz (Subang) Airport to the two islands. The airlines also offers flights from Singapore to the islands.

Sandakan Mezzanine Floor, Sabah Building, Jalan Pelabuhan, Sabah Tel: 089-273 970
Sibu 61 Jalan Tuanku Osman, Sarawak
Tel: 084-321 055
Tawau First and Second Floor, TB 319 Block 38, Jalan Haji Sahabudin Fajar Complex, Sabah
Tel: 089-950 888

Border Shuttle Service

MAS operates a coach shuttle service between Johor's Senai Airport, Johor Bahru, and Copthorne Orchid Hotel in Singapore, tel: 02-6250 3333 (Singapore), 07-599 3976 (Senai), 07-599 4737 (airport).

Tours

MAS's subsidiary, **MAS Golden Holidays**, offers a range of holiday packages including flights, transfers, accommodation, meals, and guided tours. There are options of fly-drive and coach holiday packages, as well as golf, scuba diving, and adventure packages. Tel: 03-2165 5124, 03-7846 3000 (24-hours); fax: 03-2165 5060.

By Rail

Malaysian Railways (KTM Berhad) runs right from Singapore through the peninsula and into Thailand in the north. Express services call only at major towns; the others stop everywhere. Malaysian trains are comfortable and equipped with restaurant cars. There are extremely cold air-conditioned first- and second-class coaches and bunks on the night trains. Third-class coaches are fan-cooled. Book in advance during peak periods.

The west coast line goes through Kuala Lumpur to Butterworth (Penang) and joins Thailand at Padang Besar, Kedah. The Ekspres Rakyat (ER) departs every morning from Singapore to Butterworth and vice-versa. Ekspres Sinaran (XSP) is the other morning service and links Kuala Lumpur and Butterworth.

The night trains are the Ekspres Senandung Malam sleepers (ESM) servicing Kuala Lumpur–Singapore and Kuala Lumpur–Butterworth, and Ekspres Langkawi (EL) Kuala Lumpur–Haadyai.

The east coast line branches off at Gemas in Johor, plunges through the central forests and emerges at Tumpat in Kelantan, near the border to Thailand. Only night trains do this route, the Ekspres Timuran (XST) Singapore–Tumpat and Ekspres Wau (XW) Kuala Lumpur–Tumpat (via Gemas).

For foreign tourists, KTM offers a railpass which entitles the holder to unlimited travel in any class and to any destination for a period of 10 or 30 days. Sleeping berths are extra.

For more information, call KTM: Tel: 03-2267 1200/2263 1267; Fax: 03-2710 5716; e-mail: passenger@ktmb.com.my; www.ktmb.com.my

Touring by Train

KTM offers good value rail packages to various destinations in Malaysia, which include train tickets, transfers, accommodation, some meals and tours. Try the Langkawi, Penang, Perlis or the popular Haadyai (Thailand) package, tel: 03-2267 1200; fax: 03-2710 5716.

The **Eastern & Oriental Express** is the ultimate in luxury rail travel, complete with mahogany marquetry and Burmese rosewood inspired by the 1932 Marlene Dietrich film *Shanghai Express*. The 132-passenger train travels 2,000 km (1,260 miles) over 2 nights from Singapore through Kuala Lumpur to Bangkok (or vice versa) with side trips to Penang and Kanchanaburi. For reservations, tel: 02-6392 3500 (Singapore); e-mail: oereservations.singapore@ orient_express.com.

By Boat

On the peninsula, boats are the chief means of travel to the islands and in the interiors. Regular ferries service the islands of Pangkor (6.30am–7pm), Penang (6am–midnight) and Langkawi (8am–6pm). Boats out to islands on the east coast generally do not follow schedules, and in the monsoon season (November–February), services may stop altogether. Note that the sea can be choppy just before and after the monsoon period.

In the north, services run from 8.30–9am and stop between 2–2.30pm. Other than during public and school holidays, it is generally fine to arrive on the Perhentian Islands (from Kuala Besut) and Kapas (from Marang) without having booked accommodation, but safer to pre-book accommodation and therefore boats at Redang and Tenggol (from Merang).

In the south, Mersing services the bulk of the Johor islands and Tioman, while Tanjung Leman is the staging point for the Sibu isles. Scheduled ferries depart Mersing only to Tioman (arrive at Mersing as early as possible) and Rawa (one service at midday). Other services can be a little confusing (*see chapter on Mersing and Isles, page 241*). Tioman can also be accessed from Tanjong Gemok and Singapore. The Tanjung Leman boats depart daily at 11am, 1.15pm and 4.30pm.

In the interior, Taman Negara is the only destination with scheduled boats (9am and 2pm). It is generally all right to arrive at Kenyir, Kenong and Cini without booking, but Temenggor (for Belum) and Bera must be pre-booked.

SARAWAK

There are no scheduled shipping lines to Sarawak, but within the country express boats and local river craft are still the main form of transport to the interior.

In recent years logging companies have opened up previously inaccessible areas. There is a lot of traffic on the rivers inland throughout most of the year as roads are still few and far between and are generally in poor condition.

On the Rejang River, regular boats run between Sibu and Kapit, and if the waters are high enough, they go on to Belaga to longhouse territory. Express boats travel to many of the smaller rivers stopping at remote longhouses along the way. Chartered boats can be fearfully expensive.

Bigger boat services operate between Kuching and Sibu – daily departures with a three- to four-hour ride. Regular ferry services also connect Kota Kinabalu in Sabah with the tax-haven island of Labuan and then on to Brunei and the Sarawak divisions of Lawas and Limbang.

Cruises

Short-term cruises on the peninsula have been a hit with a niche market, mainly because of on-board gambling in international waters. Besides casinos, ships are usually equipped with a swimming pool, cinema, disco and karaoke. There is usually a live band or cabaret-style shows, ballroom dancing classes and other activities, and packages are full-board. The 2,000-passenger ship *Virgo* departs from Singapore and offers 4-day/3-night packages to Phuket/Langkawi, a 3-day/2-night Kuala Lumpur cruise to Melaka and Port Klang, and a 6-day/5-night Straits of Melaka package. Book with **Travel Malaysia** (tel: 03-2070 8667) or **Mansfield Travels** in Kuala Lumpur, which also handles international liners, tel: 03-2142 8980; fax: 03-2142 8992; Penang, tel: 04-262 1233; fax: 04-262 1835.

By Road

Malaysia's inter-state (outstation) buses and taxis are a fairly comfortable and convenient way of covering the country. Both the roads and public transport are better in the peninsula than Sabah and Sarawak, but good networks link capital cities and major towns. Sarawak's road system is pleasant enough to explore the areas surrounding Kuching and up to the Kalimantan border. The longer northern road to Miri is driveable, but not yet in perfect condition.

Inter-state Buses

Three types of inter-state buses operate in Malaysia: the non-air-conditioned buses plying between the states, the air-conditioned express buses connecting major towns, and the non-air-conditioned buses that provide services within each state. With the exception of the express buses, the others seldom adhere to the schedule, but are frequent between 9am–6pm.

Express buses usually connect two or three major towns, and will break the journey for a toilet stop at a restaurant (serving fairly inedible local food with the occasional burger stall) for half an hour – even in the early morning. Driving on the highway is not so bad, but the single-lane trunk roads bring out the devil in people and you would need to steel yourself for dicey overtaking, taking corners too quickly, and other such tricks.

There are several classes of buses: the VIP or business-class coaches have the most legroom and do not cost that much more (recommended for longer journeys).

At bus stations, you will inevitably be accosted by touts selling tickets for unlicensed operators. Tickets might be cheaper but these buses do not depart until enough passengers are rounded up; they also make numerous stops.

Different operators handle different towns – information and fares are displayed at the counter window. Outside public holidays, you don't need to purchase your ticket beforehand (bookings are rarely taken). The popular routes are serviced hourly.

There are three bus terminals in Kuala Lumpur. North and southbound services are at the old and bustling **Puduraya** bus station and the old **Kuala Lumpur railway station**; coaches to the east coast and Tasik Kenyir depart from the **Putra** bus station (opposite the Putra World Trade Centre); and the interior destinations such as Kuala Lipis are serviced from **Hentian Pekeliling**, at the ring road off Jalan Tun Razak.

Coaching It

Plusliner coaches (7.30am–9pm; tel: 03-2272 1586; www.plusliner.com) operates an extensive network of coach services to different destinations in Peninsular Malaysia. Plusliner's fleet of comfortable and air-conditioned coaches depart daily from KL's Puduraya station. Its more expensive Nice Executive Coaches services only Penang and Singapore, with several departures daily from the old KL Railway Station. These coaches feature only 26 seats on board a regular-sized coach, with refreshments and a simple meal served on board.

SARAWAK

Sarawak has no main bus station, but there are small bus terminals in Kuching, close to the river, and each bus company has its own operating area. For southwest Sarawak, the Sarawak Transport Company can take you to Semonggoh and other points west. The distinctive green and yellow buses leave from Leboh Jawa. Petra Jaya Transport buses go to Damai, Santubong and Kampung Bako and leave from the bus area near the open-air market.

SABAH

A network of buses and mini buses operates in Sabah. In Kota Kinabalu the buses to Kinabalu Park leave from the Long-distance Bus Station near the Padang. In rural areas, mini-buses operate effectively and faster than the larger yellow town buses.

Inter-state Taxis

These "share" taxis go to any destination and are quicker than buses. They are old Mercedes Benz vehicles and some are air-conditioned. However, you have to wait until there are four passengers, unless you want to pay for the whole cab – remember, you do not have to charter the whole taxi. So turn up early and be prepared to wait; you wait longer in the afternoon. If you book a cab to yourself, the driver will pick you up from your hotel for free if you are close to town.

Note that there is a quota for how many taxis can ply a route. During public holidays, this quota could be full, in which case you would be asked to pay extra for non-quota taxis because the driver would not be allowed to pick up passengers on the return leg. Sometimes, if the traffic is heavy, particularly on the busy Karak Highway, you might have to pay more, so make sure you sort all this out with your driver. Night

journeys have a surcharge. Long distance taxi stands are usually near the inter-state bus stations. In Kuala Lumpur, the stand is at the Puduraya bus station.

City Transport

Buses and Taxis

All towns have public buses and taxis. Buses usually charge according to distance except in Kuala Lumpur, where the fare is standard. Timetables are a mystery, and listings of stops and routes elusive, except for the signs on the front of each vehicle. However, buses are a great way to rub shoulders with the locals.

Taxis can be hailed at taxi stands or by the roadside. In larger cities, taxis are usually metered but in

smaller towns, bargain on an agreed price before you get in.

Trishaws

Trishaws are found in Kota Bharu, Kuala Terengganu, Georgetown, Penang and Melaka. These three-wheeled contraptions are a memorable way to cover a city as their slow pace allows you to see points of interest along the way, providing more photographic opportunities. The bicycle is usually at the side of the carriage, except in Penang, where the two passengers sit in a sun-hooded carriage in front of the cyclist. Trishaw drivers will warn you to hold on to your bags firmly for fear of snatch-thieves on motorcycles. Incidences of this kind, however, are rare. Fix the price before you get

Kuala Lumpur City Transport

Taxis

Kuala Lumpur is well served by a system of highways which bring commuters, taxis, buses and cars into the centre of the city. While traffic jams have not yet reached Bangkok's disastrous gridlocks, they are well on the way.

Look out for the Teksi lamp on the roof for cabs that are available. They offer a convenient and economical means of moving around the city, and drivers usually speak at least a smattering of English.

Air-conditioning and fare meters are compulsory in all taxis. Make sure the meter is switched on after you get in. Rates are RM2 for the first 1km (½ mile) and 10 sen for each additional 150m (490 feet). There is a surcharge of RM1 for booking a taxi by phone. There is also a 50 percent surcharge on the meter fare between midnight and 6am. If there are more than two passengers per taxi, 20 sen per additional passenger is levied.

City taxis cannot legally pick passengers up at the airport where a coupon system is in use but you can take a city taxi to the airport.

It is fairly easy to get a taxi

either by queueing at taxi stands, flagging one down by the street, or booking one by telephone. Note: it will also be difficult to get a taxi in heavily jammed areas during rush hours.

Half- and full-day taxi charters to places in the Klang Valley range from RM30–35 per hour, excluding toll charges. You can also book with reliable taxi companies such as **Comfort** (tel: 03-8024 2727) and **New Supercab** (tel: 03-7875 7333); call at least four hours beforehand.

Buses

There are several local buses to choose from in KL, including **Rapid KL** and **Metrobus**. Fares are from 90 sen upwards; prepare exact change. Enquire about multi-ride fares.

The inner city bus stops are Puduraya, the Klang Bus Station near Chinatown, Bangkok Bank behind Central Market, Lebuh Ampang, and the Jalan Tuanku Abdul Rahman/Jalan Ipoh intersection in Chow Kit. Buses can be packed like sardine cans during peak periods, so watch your wallets.

Train and Light Rail

KTM Berhad also administers the Rawang to Klang **KTM Komuter** electrified commuter rail service, which transports commuters and travellers within greater Kuala Lumpur and the Klang Valley.

Within the city, the **Light Rail Transport** (LRT) is an integrated monorail system operated by two concessionaires, Putra and Star. Air-conditioned and very convenient, the LRT services areas such as Jalan Ampang, Chow Kit, Petaling Jaya and Bangsar. Feeder buses go to suburbs and shopping centres. Ask for maps at any station. The **Monorail** covers the Bukit Bintang, Kampung Bahru, Chow Kit and Titiwangsa areas.

The fare range for LRT is 70 sen to RM2.50; Monorail RM1.20 to RM2.50; and KTM Kommuter trains RM1 to RM4.30 (to Port Klang). Enquire about multiple-ride and off-peak rates. Services run from 6am to midnight.

The central transport hub for all these services is the modern **KL Sentral** (tel: 03-2279 8888; www.stesensentral.com), where you can also catch the KLIA Express train to the airport.

on. You could try renting the trishaw for a period, say, half-a-day.

Tour Companies

The whole gamut of tours is available in Malaysia, from city and night tours to week-long packages that cover several destinations, and any combination of fly, drive and coach choices with accommodation and sometimes transfers and food. Ask at your hotel, the tourism information centre, or check newspapers for the latest listings.

KUALA LUMPUR

Kuala Lumpur-based operators include the following

Anjung Holidays
Tel: 09-697 4095
Fax: 09-697 8679
e-mail:
reservation@pulauperhentian.com.my
www.pulauperhentian.com.my
Provides various packages to Kelantan and Terengganu. Go island-hopping, caving, diving or fishing. You can also experience the Malay village lifestyle through the homestay package.

Asian Overland Services
Tel: 03-4252 9100
Fax: 03-4252 9800
www.asianoverland.com.my
A nationwide pioneer, which started with nature/adventure tours 30 years ago. It has broadened its scope to incorporate leisure,

Nature Society

The **Malaysian Nature Society (MNS)** has chapters in every state, and a very active Selangor branch, which organises trips for members in caving, hiking, etc. MNS also runs nature education courses in Kuala Lumpur, Cameron Highlands, Kuala Selangor and Endau-Rompin in Johor.
Tel: 03-2287 9422
Fax: 03-2287 8773
e-mail: natsoc@po.jaring.my
www.mns.org.my/mns

sightseeing, and other tour packages. Solid philosophy, trained guides, innovative ideas, tailor-made itineraries covering the whole country, good for long-haul journeys.
Mayflower Acme Tours
Tel: 03-6252 1888
Fax: 03-6257 5717
www.mayflower.com.my
Mudtrekker Adventure Travel
Tel: 03-7882 0701/02/03,
Fax: 03-7804 4662
www.mudtrekker.com.my
Offers eco-tours and adventure tours. Also offers tailor-made programmes, covering various areas such as Endau-Rompin, Ulu Slim, Lata Kijang, Penyabong Islands, Taman Negara and Kuang.
Ping Anchorage
Tel: 09-626 2020
Fax: 09-622 8093
e-mail: patrvl@tm.net.my
www.pinganchorage.com.my
This is your best bet for the east coast, especially Terengganu, offering innovation and variety.
SA Tours
Tel: 03-2142 9155
Fax: 03-2142 9420
www.satours.com
Utan Bara Adventure Travel
Tel: 03-4022 5124
Fax: 03-4022 6125
www.ubat.com.my
Specialises in jungle adventure and eco-tourism in lesser-known areas such as the upper Tenor river system in Taman Negara, Ulu Yam and Ulu Kemansah forests in Selangor, Ulu Cheh and Ulu Terong forests in Perak. Also brings visitors to the Elephant Sanctuary in Kuala Gandah, Pahang.

SARAWAK

In Sarawak, tour companies are very helpful when it comes to longhouse visits and trekking tours. Unless one speaks at least a little Malay, it is not recommended to visit longhouses without a guide, who will make a trip far more enjoyable and meaningful.
Borneo Adventure
55 Main Bazaar, Kuching
Tel: 082-245 175

Fax: 082-422 626
e-mail: info@borneoadventure.com
www.borneoadventure.com
Known for its eco-tourism specialities, although it handles almost every type of tour. They also have an office in Kota Kinabalu, Sabah.
Borneo Transverse
15 Ground Floor, Jalan Greenhill Kuching
Tel: 082-257 784
Fax: 082-421 419
e-mail: bntv@po.jaring.my
www.borneotransverse.com
Ibanika
Lot 435, Ground Floor, Section 62 Lorong 9, Jalan Ang Cheng Ho Kuching
Tel: 082-424 022
Fax: 082-424 021
www.ibanika.com
e-mail: ibanika@ace.cdc.abu.com
Offers longhouse and general tours and can tailor a tour to suit your requirements.
Seridan Mulu
Lot 273 Brighton Centre
Jalan Temenggong Datuk Oyang Miri
Tel: 085-415 582
Fax: 085-412 469
e-mail: info@seridanmulu.com
www.seridanmulu.com
Miri-based adventure tour outfit offering white water rafting, rock climbing, tribal trekking and caving; Mulu Cave specialist.

SABAH

Many excursions in Sabah are difficult without the help of a tour company, or at least a guide, and destinations are often geared to tour groups.
Discovery Tours
Wisma Sabah, Jalan Tun Fuad Stephens, Kota Kinabalu
Tel: 088-221 244
Fax: 088-221 600
e-mail: distour@po.jaring.my
www.infosabah.com.my/discovery
An energetic company with many interesting tours. It also has offices at the Shangri-La's Tanjung Aru Resort and the Rasa Ria Resort.

Borneo Eco Tours
2nd Floor, Shop Lot 12a, Lorong
Bernam 3, Taman Soon Kiong,
88300 Kota Kinabalu
Tel: 088-438 300
Fax: 088-438 307
e-mail: info@borneoecotours.com;
www.borneoecotours.com
Block J, 1st Floor, Lot 74
Bandar Pasar Raya
Jalan Utara Mile 4, Sandakan
Tel: 089-220 210
Fax: 089-213 614
Run by one of the leading tour
operators in Sabah, this award-
winning company specialises in
environmentally oriented tourism,
with trips focusing on the flora and
fauna of Sabah. The company also
runs a eco-friendly lodge at Sukau
on the Kinabatangan River.

Traverse Tours
2nd Floor, Gaya Centre
Jalan Tun Fuad Stephens
Kota Kinabalu
Tel: 088-260 501
e-mail: sales@traversetours.com
www.traversetours.com
Adventure tourism specialist,
including Riverbug's white water
rafting.

Wildlife Expeditions
Shangri-La's Tanjung Aru Resort,
Kota Kinabalu
Tel: 088-268 309
Fax: 088-231 758
e-mail: enquiry@wildlife-
expeditions.com
www.wildlife-expeditions.com
Room 903, 9th Floor, Wisma Khoo
Siak Chiew, Sandakan
Tel: 089-219 616
Fax: 089-214 570
Tours to most Sabah destinations
including Mt Kinabalu, Sepilok,
Tenom Rafflesia Centre, Padas
River rafting, Rungus longhouses,
Turtle Islands, Danum Valley and
Kinabatangan.

Driving

Driving is the best way to see
Peninsular Malaysia, which has an
excellent network of trunk roads
and a dual-carriageway highway on
the west coast. Driving is also
enjoyable in Sabah and Sarawak,
but you need a stauncher vehicle or
even a four-wheel drive and lots
more time.

Having your own transport gives
you the freedom to go off the
beaten track at your leisure. Visitors
need an international driving licence
and it is advisable to buy travel
insurance. Local car hire firms are
found in major cities in both the
peninsula, Sabah and Sarawak.

Driving is on the left-hand side of
the road. The speed limit is 50 kph
(30 mph) in towns, 80 kph (50 mph)
outside towns, and 110 kph (68
mph) on highways. Slow down when
you go through a *kampung* – keep
your eye out for children, livestock
and bicycles, especially at night.
Keep left unless overtaking. The
wearing of seat belts in the front is
compulsory. Breaking traffic rules
incurs a flat-rate fine.

International traffic signs apply
along with local ones (*see box,
above right*). Local drivers have
developed a few signals; there are
individual variations so watch what
other motorists do. If the driver in
front flashes his right indicator, he
is signalling to you not to overtake.
This is usually because of an
oncoming vehicle or a bend in the
road, or he himself might be about
to overtake the vehicle in front of
him. If he flashes the left indicator,
this means to overtake with
caution. A driver flashing his
headlamps at you is claiming the
right of way. At roundabouts or
traffic circles, the driver on the right
has the right of way.

Road Signs

Awas **Caution**
Bahaya **Danger**
Berhenti **Stop**
Bulatan **Roundabout**
Di hadapan **In front**
Jalan **Road**
Jalan Sehala **One-way street**
Kanan **Right**
Kiri **Left**
Kawasan/Zon Kemalangan
  Accident Zone
Lencongan **Diversion**
Lorong **Lane**
Pusing **Turn**
Tutup **Closed**
Utara **North**
Selatan **South**
Barat **West**
Timur **East**

Malaysian drivers can be speed
maniacs and bullies – the bigger
the vehicle, the more so. Give way.
In towns, motorcyclists can shoot
out from nowhere or hog the road.
Don't lose your cool: count to 10
instead. Heavy rain can be
hazardous, so switch on your lights,
drive slowly and be prepared for
delays on smaller roads as entire
roads are sometimes washed away.
At worst, pull over until the
downpour lightens up.

Petrol Stations
Petrol can be found in or around the
fringes of towns and along the
highway, where there are also
eateries and toilets. Many operate
24 hours (*24 jam*) and accept credit
cards. Stations in major cities are
self-service.

Maps
Road maps are becoming more
accurate, but road signs can be
frustratingly misleading, and asking
for directions even more so – be
patient. The names of tourist
attractions are highlighted in green
writing on signs, while the highway
is illustrated with a graphic.

Breakdown Services
The Automobile Association of
Malaysia (AAM) is the national

motoring organisation and has offices in most states – it has a prompt breakdown service for members, tel: 03-2161 0808.

Main Routes

Peninsular Malaysia's North-South Highway starts at the causeway connecting to Singapore and runs north along the west coast to the Thai border. The old trunk road runs roughly parallel to that through small towns, and branches off to interesting nooks and corners, but you could be stuck behind a long queue waiting to overtake a series of rattling lorries.

Several main routes link the east and west coasts through the spectacular Main Range. From Kuala Lumpur, the busy Karak Highway goes to Kuantan (3 hours), the dual carriageway ending midway at Karak town. A fork at Bentong heads north through Kuala Lipis to Kota Bharu on the Gua Musang road (9 hours). Kota Bharu is also linked to Penang via the East-West Highway (5 hours), and Kuala Kangsar in Perak at the Grik fork.

From Johor Bahru, the Segamat Highway goes to Kuantan (4 hours), but the more scenic and much longer route hugs the east coast north from Desaru all the way to the Thai border. A parallel inland road with less traffic runs from Kuantan to Kota Bharu.

SABAH AND SARAWAK

In Sabah and Sarawak, motorways run along the coast connecting major towns. Roads leading to more remote areas inland are often unpaved or rough, and a four-wheel drive is advisable for these interior routes; unless you want to explore jungle tracks and logging routes, a little Suzuki Jimny or the equivalent can handle most conditions with ease. For day trips to Santubong, Damai, or west towards Lundu and beyond along the coast, a normal saloon car can be used. In Sabah, too, most of the main destinations along the coast are trouble free, as

is the road to Kinabalu Park and northwest to Kudat.

Car Rental

Car rental firms have branches in the main towns throughout Malaysia and at big airports. Rentals are usually based on time rather than mileage and most allow you to pick up a car from one place and drop it off at another. Credit cards are preferred; a large deposit is required if you pay cash.

Kuala Lumpur
Avis Rent A Car
Tel: 03-9222 2558
(Freephone: 1-800 882 054)
Fax: 03-9222 2109
KLIA
Tel: 03-8787 4087
Pacific Rent A Car
Tel: 03-2287 4118/9
Fax: 03-2287 1126
KLIA
Tel: 03-8787 4393
Hertz Rent A Car
Tel: 03-2148 6433
Fax: 03-2148 8481
KLIA
Tel: 03-8787 4572
National Car Rental
Tel: 03-2148 0522
Fax: 03-2148 2823
KLIA
Tel: 03-8787 3890 (Depot)
Tel: 03-8776 4541 (Arrivals Hall)

SARAWAK

Kuching
Mayflower Car Rental
Lot 4, 24A
4th Floor Bangunan Satok
Jalan Satok
Kuching International Airport
Tel: 082-410 110/410 117
Pronto Car Rental
1st Floor
98 Jalan Padungan
Tel: 082-236 889/237 889
Fax: 082-236 889
A wide range of vehicles, including Landcruisers, Mercedes and Hondas.

SABAH

Kota Kinabalu
Padas Jaya Rent A Car
G20 Ground Floor, Wisma Sabah
Tel: 088-239 936
Fax: 088-239 937
e-mail: padas_jaya@yahoo.com
Kinabalu Rent A Car
3rd Floor, Kompleks Karamunsing
Tel: 088-232 602/3, 088-248 233
Fax: 088-242 512
e-mail: krc@sabah.com.my
www.kinabalurac.com.my

There are rent-a-car booths at the airport, or for better rates ask your hotel concierge.

Where to Stay

Choosing a Hotel

The economic meltdown and glut of hotels means that high-quality accommodation has become remarkably affordable. This has unfortunately pushed some medium-priced accommodation out of the market, but there is always plenty of budget accommodation.

Choose your location then the price category. Always enquire about packages, which include a buffet or local breakfast with the room, and if you stay more than one night, you can try bargaining for better rates. Most hotels are fine with triple-share. Hotels are supposed to display net rates (including the 10 percent service and 5 percent government tax).

Cities and main tourist destinations offer the range. At the lowest end are dormitories at RM15–40 depending on location and whether the room has air-conditioning, or a ceiling fan.

Then come the simple Chinese-run Rumah Tumpangan motels which you can find in almost every town, and beachside Malay *kampung*-type chalets; these go for RM40 to more than RM100 and are sometimes equipped with TV, air-conditioning and hot showers.

Medium-class hotels come in traditional hotel blocks or chalets, and are popular with locals (RM100–300). The higher end ones in this category generally have full room facilities and services, including air-conditioning, ensuite baths with hot showers, colour TV, IDD telephones, laundry, mini bar, coffee-making facilities, room service, and a restaurant and/or coffee house. The world's top hotel chains and resorts are also here,

complete with the usual full room facilities and services, saunas and gourmet restaurants (RM200–400, luxury hotels can be upwards of RM800). Incidentally there is local and international accreditation (five-star, four-star, etc.). Options in the medium to upper range are the condotels or apartment hotels, although rarely is cooking allowed.

Check-in times are between 1–3pm, check-out 11am–noon, late checkout requests until 2pm; some hotels do not accept guests between midnight and 7am. Sometimes, a 50 percent deposit is needed to secure bookings, rooms are held up to 6pm. Book well in advance if your stay coincides with public holidays and school holidays in Malaysia *(see page 346)*.

Price Guide

Prices are for a standard double room during peak periods.
$$$$: more than RM400
$$$: RM200–400
$$: RM100–200
$: less than RM100

Hotel Listing

KUALA LUMPUR AND ENVIRONS

Kuala Lumpur

Kuala Lumpur's budget hotels are mainly located in the Chinatown area and Jalan Tunku Abdul Rahman, while the medium-class to luxury accommodation is in the business and shopping areas along Jalan Sultan Ismail and Jalan Bukit Bintang.

Carcosa Seri Negara
Taman Tasik Perdana
Tel: 03-2282 1888
Fax: 03-2282 7888
www.carcosa.com.my
For a taste of colonial splendour, the 13 extravagant suites in this former British governor's residence have butlers, a gorgeous restaurant overlooking huge landscaped gardens, and a bar. The "in thing" is to have high tea and curry tiffin on the terrace. **$$$$**

J W Marriott
183 Jalan Bukit Bintang
Tel: 03-2715 9000
Fax: 03-2715 7013
www.marriott.com
Centrally located luxury hotel (rooms underwent a major make-over in 2004) with fabulous spa, and well-known Shook restaurant with four kitchens – Japanese, Italian, Chinese and grills. Also has Marriott Café on the adjacent Bukit Bintang Walk and a well-known tapas bar. **$$$$**

Mandarin Oriental
Kuala Lumpur City Centre
Tel: 03-2380 8888
Fax: 03-2380 8833
www.mandarinoriental.com
Set within the office/shopping complex featuring the world's tallest twin buildings, this hotel has 643 luxurious rooms and executive apartments, six restaurants including a grill and bar, a fusion Japanese restaurant and a Cantonese restaurant specialising in seafood. **$$$$**

Regent of Kuala Lumpur
160 Jalan Bukit Bintang
Tel: 03-2141 8000
Fax: 03-2142 1441
www.regenthotels.com
KL's most elegant hotel sits on the fringes of bustling Bukit Bintang, and is well-known for its service and opulence. Classical music welcomes you in the lovely lounge; the gym has Roman baths; and the 469 rooms are tastefully furnished. **$$$$**

Shangri-La Hotel
Jalan Sultan Ismail
Tel: 03-2032 2388
Fax: 03-2070 1514
www.shangri-la.com
Newly-renovated hotel with 701 rooms, French restaurant and grill, well-stocked deli that is packed at lunchtime, English-style bar, cafe, tennis, squash, health centre, and a lobby lounge with a resident pianist. **$$$$**

The Ritz-Carlton
Jalan Imbi, Bukit Bintang
Tel: 03-2142 8000
Fax: 03-2143 8080
www.ritzcarlton.com
Award-winning boutique style hotel

with exceptional service (24-hour butler service) and large rooms, close to the shopping hub. **$$$$**

Concorde Hotel
Jalan Sultan Ismail
Tel: 03-2144 2200
Fax: 03-2144 1628
www.concorde.net
Central, busy hotel close to nightlife and trendy eateries. It has 673 rooms, and a popular coffee shop and lounge attracting spill-over weekend crowds from the nearby Hard Rock Café. For better rooms, book the Premier wing. **$$$**

Crowne Plaza Mutiara Kuala Lumpur
Tel: 03-2148 2322
Fax: 03-2144 2157
www.crowneplaza.com
Extensively renovated 563-room hotel within walking distance of Bukit Bintang. Spacious rooms, luxurious rain shower; fine dining at Indochine restaurant, which is popular for business lunches, and good family buffets at the Planter's Inn. **$$$**

Federal Hotel
35 Jalan Bukit Bintang
Tel: 03-2148 9166
Fax: 03-2148 2877
www.federal.com.my
Hotel shares the same age as Malaysia with a colourful history, situated right on Bukit Bintang. It has 450 rooms, a revolving lounge, decent Chinese restaurant, full-window café that is great for people-watching, supper club showcasing golden oldies stars, and an 18-lane bowling alley. **$$$**

Grand Plaza Parkroyal
Jalan Sultan Ismail
Tel: 03-2142 5588
Fax: 03-2141 5524
www.parkroyalhotels.com
Recent renovations have given this 348-room hotel – in the heart of the Bukit Bintang shopping district – a fresh and contemporary look. Good range of restaurants and bars. **$$$**

Hotel Istana
73 Jalan Raja Chulan
Tel: 03-2141 9988
Fax: 03-2141 0111

www.hotelistana.com.my
Right in the heart of the Golden Triangle, this extravagantly "palatial" hotel has 516 rooms, a Italian restaurant, lounge overlooking a garden and a health centre. **$$$**

Hotel Nikko
165 Jalan Ampang
Tel: 03-2161 1111
Fax: 03-2161 1112
www.hotelnikko.com.my
A five-star hotel with 470 rooms, a gymnasium, spa, health centre and a large swimming pool with a spacious sundeck. Famous for its Benkay Japanese Restaurant which is set in a classic Japanese ambience, and which serves the best and freshest seasonal Japanese delicacies. **$$$**

Pan Pacific Kuala Lumpur
Jalan Putra
Tel: 03-4042 5555
Fax: 03-4041 7236
www.panpac.com
Oldish hotel opposite the Mall and next to the Putra World Trade Centre

Alternative Accommodation

Government resthouses were established during the colonial era for travelling administrators. They were found in most towns on the west coast, and provided cut-price accommodation with colonial style charm, but most of them, except for a handful, have now closed and been replaced by the Seri Malaysia chain to fill the void in quality medium-class hotels. These are in prime locations, close to transport or attractions. They have air-conditioning, attached baths, hot showers and a restaurant. Look for the red roofs.

The Seri Malaysia chain of hotels is listed below:

Central reservation number:
03-2161 8223 (Kuala Lumpur)
e-mail:
central@serimalaysia.com.my
www.serimalaysia.com.my

Alor Setar
Jalan Stadium
Tel: 04-730 8737
Fax: 04-730 7594

Genting Highlands
Tel: 03-6100 2525
Fax: 03-6100 1125

Ipoh
Jalan Sturrock, off Jalan Ipoh
Tel: 05-241 2936
Fax: 05-241 2946

Johor Bahru
Jalan Langkasuka
Tel: 07-221 1002
Fax: 07-221 1006

Kuala Terengganu
Jalan Hiliran (Balik Bukit)
Tel: 09-623 6454
Fax: 09-623 8344

Kuantan
Jalan Telok Sisek
Tel: 09-513 6666
Fax: 09-514 7788

Marang
Kampung Paya
Tel: 09-618 2889
Fax: 09-618 1976

Mersing
Jalan Ismail
Tel: 07-799 1876
Fax: 07-799 1886

Port Dickson
Jalan Pantai Batu 4
Tel: 06-647 6070
Fax: 06-647 6028

Penang
7 Jalan Mayang Pasir, Bayan Baru
Tel: 04-642 9452
Fax: 04-642 9461

Rompin
Tanjung Gemok
Tel: 09-413 2723
Fax: 09-413 2732

Seremban
Jalan Sungai Ujong
Tel: 06-764 4181
Fax: 06-764 4179

Sungai Petani
Seksyen 21, Jalan Pasar
Tel: 04-423 4060
Fax: 04-423 4106

Taiping
4 Jalan Sultan Mansor
Tel: 05-806 9502
Fax: 05-806 9495

Temerloh, Jalan Hamzah
Tel: 09-296 5776
Fax: 09-296 5711

with all-glass elevators on the exterior providing good views of this part of the city. It has 554 rooms, and is busy during conventions. **$$$**

Renaissance Hotel
Corner Jalan Sultan Ismail
Jalan Ampang
Tel: 03-2162 2233/2163
Fax: 03-2163 1122
www.renaissance-kul.com
The Renaissance tries to capture European splendour with plush decor of black marble and crystal chandeliers, but targets the business sector. It has a Mediterranean restaurant and shares the car park and pool with the slightly more modest New World Hotel wing. **$$$**

Swiss Garden Hotel
117 Jalan Pudu
Tel: 03-2141 3333
Fax: 03-2141 5555
www.swissgarden.com
Situated on the busy Jalan Pudu, within walking distance to Puduraya and Bukit Bintang without being in the thick of it. This is a small but pleasant hotel, with 306 rooms and a Chinese restaurant that serves good *dim sum*. **$$$**

Corus Hotel
Lot 2, Jalan Ampang
Tel: 03-2161 8888
Fax: 03-2161 2393
www.corushotelkl.com
Opposite the KLCC, of which some of its 378 rooms and its swimming pool have a grand view, this business hotel offers in-room broadband Internet access and a wide range of secretarial services. **$$**

Hotel Capitol
Jalan Bukit Bintang
Tel: 03-2143 7000
Fax: 03-2143 0000
www.capitol.com.my
Part of the Federal group, this 225-room hotel is smack in the middle of Bukit Bintang. The hotel underwent a recent stylish makeover. Rooms are small but tastefully furnished; good restaurant and a café with gourmet sandwiches and coffee. **$$**

Heritage Station Hotel
Bangunan Stesen Keretapi
Jalan Sultan Hishamuddin

Tel: 03-2273 5588/1688
Fax: 03-2273 2842
Sitting among the graceful cupolas of the Kuala Lumpur Railway Station, this hotel has been extensively renovated. Although the rooms are smaller now, some of the old-style charm is retained in the furnishings and furniture, including its restaurants. **$$**

The Royale Bintang
Jalan Bukit Bintang
Tel: 03-2143 9898
Fax: 03-2145 9558
www.royale-bintang-hotel.com.my
Located in the heart of the Bukit Bintang shopping area with 214 rooms, plus a restaurant with international and local fare. **$$**

Backpackers' Travellers' Inn
2nd Floor, 60, Jalan Sultan
(opposite Furama Hotel)
Tel: 03-2032 1855
Fax: 03-2032 1988
Right in Chinatown, close to food and transport, some air-conditioned rooms with own bathrooms, laundry, kitchen, left luggage facilities. **$**

Chamtan
62 Jalan Masjid India
Tel: 03-2693 0144
Fax: 03-2693 2422
In bustling Little India with its *sari* and curry shops, this has 44 rooms with air-conditioning and hot showers, and a restaurant with tasty, but spicy, local fare. **$**

Coliseum Hotel
100 Jalan Tunku Abdul Rahman
Tel: 03-2692 6270
Tiny and very old 10-room hotel with shared baths, it is mentioned in every guidebook because of its historical importance. The café is popular for its good steaks and infamously bad service; bar patrons are determined to keep up its colourful character. **$**

YWCA
12, Jalan Hang Jebat
Tel: 03-2070 1623
Fax: 03-2031 7753
e-mail: ywcakl@po.jaring.my
Small, clean, 12-roomed facility for women, couples and families only. It has a small restaurant, and is within walking distance of the heart of Chinatown. **$**

Price Guide

Prices are for a standard double room during peak periods.
$$$$: more than RM400
$$$: RM200–400
$$: RM100–200
$: less than RM100

Selangor

The Mines Beach Resort
Jalan Dulang, Sri Kembangan
Tel: 03-8943 6688
Fax: 03-8943 5555
www.mbr.com.my
Part of The Mines rehabilitated mining pond theme park and development, this classy 481-roomed hotel has an artificial beach, ferries to the Wonderland theme park, a spa, and a shopping and conference centre. It has four restaurants, but a rather stuffy lounge. **$$$$**

Palace of the Golden Horses
Jalan Kuda Emas, Mines Resort City
Sri Kembangan, Selangor
Tel: 03-8943 2333
Fax: 03-8943 2666
www.PalaceoftheGoldenHorses.
com.my
This opulent Indian-influenced hotel at which heads of governments reside and meet, has 480 rooms and seven restaurants, and lovely gardens; it's a pity the same attention is not extended to the car park. **$$$$**

Sunway Lagoon Resort Hotel
Persiaran Lagoon, Bandar Sunway
Petaling Jaya
Tel: 03-7492 8000
Fax: 03-7492 8001
www.sunway.com.my/hotel
This plush hotel is next to the Sunway Lagoon theme park, the country's most successful rehabilitated mining pond, as well as the Egyptian-themed Sunway Pyramid shopping centre, complete with sphynx. The hotel has 439 rooms, a large and popular disco, and excellent Chinese, Japanese and American-Italian restaurants. **$$$**

Jungle Lodge
Alang Sedayu (Gombak)
Tel: 03-4252 9100 (Asian Overland Services)
Fax: 03-4252 9800

About half an hour from Kuala Lumpur, this large timber lodge sits in 2 hectares (5 acres) of green grounds with streams and ponds. There are two river-fed swimming pools, treks, canoes, old war tunnels nearby and supervised outdoor activities. There is also a hostel for 60. **$$**

Kuala Selangor Nature Park
Kuala Selangor
Tel: 03-3289 2294
Wake up to the sound of birds: these new budget chalets and dormitories at the park entrance have hours of trails on the doorstep; booked out at weekends. Food is available at Kuala Selangor town a short walk away. **$**

NORTHWESTERN PENINSULA

HILL STATIONS
Maxwell Hill (Bukit Larut)
(accessible from Perak state)
All accommodation and transport come under the Bukit Larut Hill Resort, tel: 05-807 7241/3. Book in advance. The bungalows have to be booked in their entirety: Beringin (two rooms or eight people), Cendana (three rooms or eight people) and Tempinis (four rooms or 10 people, highest point). **$$**

Double rooms are available at the Maxwell Hill Resthouse and Gunung Hijau (four rooms each). **$**

Meals have to be pre-arranged. Dogs, pork, or unmarried Muslim couples sharing a room are prohibited.

Cameron Highlands
(accessible from Perak state)
If you get stuck for the night in Tapah, you could try the Rest House Tapah (tel: 05-401 1190) or N.H. Hotel (tel: 05-401 7288), both close to the train station. **$**

Heritage Hotel
Jalan Gereja, Tanah Rata
Tel: 05-491 3888
Fax: 05-491 5666
www.heritage.com.my
This boxy, 165-room hilltop hotel is the first when you reach Tanah Rata. Ask for a room with a view of the charming little garden. Cantonese

restaurant, coffee house, bar, and a health centre. **$$$**

The Lakehouse
30th Mile, Ringlet
Tel: 05-495 6152
Fax: 05-495 6123
www.lakehouse-cameron.com
The first hotel on the Cameron's road, 1 hour from the toll gate, opposite the Sultan Abu Bakar lake. It features Tudor architecture, cosy, English antique furnishings, 18 rooms/suites with four-poster beds, a restaurant overlooking the lake, fishing and jungle walks. Isolated from towns. **$$$**

The Smokehouse Hotel
Tanah Rata
Tel: 05-491 1215
Tel: 03-2163 3136 (KL)
Fax: 05-491 1214
Fax: 03-2161 2044 (KL)
www.thesmokehouse.com.my
Built in 1939, this is a beautiful replica of an English Tudor inn complete with lush English country garden, log fires, antique furnishings, 13 family suites (most overlooking the golf course), dining and tea rooms, two bars and a restaurant; packed sandwiches and pies are available for your jungle walk. **$$$**

Strawberry Park Resort
Tanah Rata
Tel: 05-491 1166
Fax: 05-491 1949
www.malaysiahillresorts.com
Mock-Tudor blocks at the top of a steep, windy road, with great views from the hotel's 127 rooms and apartments (no cooking). It has an indoor heated pool, Chinese restaurant, coffee house, grill, bar, disco, racquet sports, travel service, and is popular with locals and Singaporeans. **$$$**

Bala's Holiday Chalet
Lot 55, Tanah Rata
Tel: 05-491 1660
Fax: 05-491 4500
e-mail: balasch@hotmail.com
Former backpackers' hotel in an English cottage which has gone upmarket. The hotel is set in a lovely green location 10 minutes from Tanah Rata (free shuttles), close to walks. Recently renovated, re-carpeted and newly-furnished, the

hotel has 33 different types of rooms – some with balconies – a lounge, restaurant, laundry and it offers tours. Book one week in advance. **$$**

Merlin Inn Resort
Tanah Rata
Tel: 05-491 1211
Fax: 05-491 1178
Once *the* place to stay in Camerons, it may be old but it is still decent. Golfers favour this resort for easy access to the golf course opposite. It has 64 rooms, full room facilities, restaurant and bar, karaoke, disco, pool tables and tennis. Enquire about golf packages. **$$**

Price Guide

Prices are for a standard double room during peak periods.
$$$$: more than RM400
$$$: RM200–400
$$: RM100–200
$: less than RM100

Rosa Passadena
Brinchang town
Tel: 05-491 2288
Fax: 05-491 2688/902
Right in town next to the bank and bakery. This is an average, no-frills hotel with 120 rooms, a restaurant with big city prices, karaoke, lounge, laundry, tours, babysitting by arrangement, basement parking, sports facilities. **$$**

Father's Guesthouse
Jalan Gereja, Tanah Rata
Tel: 05-491 2484
e-mail: fathersonline@hotmail.com
Basic but very popular 25-year-old backpackers outfit with variety of twin-sharing rooms and dorms, and lovely garden; tucked a little away from town; local and western breakfast and dinner available. **$**

Twin Pines Chalet
2 Jalan Mentigi, Tanah Rata
Tel: 05-491 2169
Fax: 05-491 5007
e-mail: firhill@tm.net.my
This friendly and clean backpackers' hotel is located behind new town development, offering hot showers, laundry,

tours, travel arrangements, telephones and Internet. There are free kitchen facilities, a spacious lounge area with TV and videos, a restaurant, travellers' notebooks, free book exchange, indoor games, a safe for valuables; free pickup. **$**

Fraser's Hill
Accessible from Selangor and Pahang.
Silver Park Holiday Resort
Tel: 09-362 2888
Fax: 09-362 2185
Blocks of 115 apartments that fail to blend with the surroundings. **$$$**
Fraser's Hill Bungalows & Chalets
Tel: 09-362 2248, 03-262 8561
Fax: 09-362 2273
Run by the Fraser's Hill Development Corporation, there are about 60 rooms in old stone bungalows, with 3–4 rooms each, all with ensuite bathrooms. Make arrangements with the caretaker for food; day-use available. **$$**
The Smokehouse Hotel
Tel: 09-362 2226
Fax: 09-362 2035
www.thesmokehouse.com.my
Colonial style Tudor hotel with beautiful gardens, antique-filled interiors, famous Devonshire teas, all very pricey, but very atmospheric and a great retreat. **$$$**

Genting Highlands
Accessible from Kuala Lumpur.
Awana Golf and Country Resort
Tel: 03-2718 1118
Freephone: 1-800 881 328
Fax: 03-2718 1888
www.genting.com.my
Much quieter surroundings, 10 km (6 miles) down the hill, with an 18-hole golf course, nice views, full room facilities including jacuzzis, and outdoor activities. Packages include rides and use of facilities. **$$$**
Genting Highlands Resort
Tel: 03-2718 1118
Freephone: 1-800 888 228
Fax: 03-2718 1888
www.genting.com.my
A casino and theme park with large hotels on the hilltop, including Genting Hotel, Highlands Hotel and apartments. Full room facilities, but

rooms are cheap, especially off-peak. Restaurants of every variety, including buffet, dinner theatre and excellent Western fare at the Sails Grill. Health centre with jacuzzi and sauna, bowling alley, disco. Packages include rides and use of facilities. **$–$$$**
Gunung Jerai Resort
Gunung Jerai
Tel: 04-423 4345/0599
Fax: 04-423 2957
This 1920s building has 30 rooms, including two-bedroom chalet-suites with cooking facilities. Good views, landscaped gardens; quiet. **$**

PERAK
Ipoh
Casuarina Hotel
18 Jalan Gopeng
Tel: 05-255 5555
Fax: 05-255 8177
e-mail: gmcaspr@tm.net.my
A little out of town, this is Ipoh's swankiest hotel with 200 luxurious rooms, full room facilities and an Italian restaurant. **$$$**
The Syuen
88, Jalan Sultan Abdul Jalil
Tel: 05-253 8889
Fax: 05-253 3335
e-mail: syuenht@tm.net.my
Central hotel, reminiscent of an enormous white wedding cake, with 290 rooms, Cantonese restaurant, spa facilities and Shiatsu massage, popular disco, and poolside bar. **$$$**
Heritage Hotel
Jalan Raja Dihilir
Tel: 05-242 8888
Fax: 05-242 4959
www.heritage.com.my
Pleasant new hotel, overlooking the Turf Club, with 265 rooms, Continental grill, a branch of a famous Chinese restaurant chain, and a health club. **$$**
Hotel Excelsior
43, Jalan Sultan Abdul Jalil
Tel: 05-253 6666
Fax: 05-253 6912
www.hotelexcelsior.com.my
Ipoh's first international hotel, a bit run-down but popular with business travellers because of its central location. Good Cantonese restaurant, and affordable buffets. **$$**

Majestic Hotel
Ipoh Railway Station
Tel: 05-255 4242
Fax: 05-255 4217
www.majesticstationhotel.com
Famous colonial hotel in the best tradition of railway station hotels, with huge verandahs, original lights, and an old-style restaurant. **$$**
Rega Lodge
131 Jalan Raja Ekram
Tel: 05-242 5555
Fax: 05-241 1555
On the fringes of the town centre, but secluded. It has 93 rooms, a restaurant-cum-pub with Italian and local cuisine, and air-conditioned rooms with ensuite baths. **$**
YMCA
311 Jalan Raja Musa Aziz
Tel: 05-254 0809
Fax: 05-241 2093
Fringes of town next to park. Clean budget-class rooms with air-conditioning and ensuite baths and hot showers; basic canteen. **$**

Pulau Pangkor
Accommodation is on the west coast, with clusters at Pasir Bogak and Teluk Nipah. Tour companies and taxi drivers receive a commission for recommending accommodation, so unless it is peak period, the best bet would be to pick a beach, get dropped off on the main road and walk around until something catches your fancy. However, some tour agents can offer better prices – select from their photograph albums. At Teluk Nipah, the chalets are virtually identical and so are the prices; many do not offer food during the low season. During the busy periods, go for a room further back from the beach – it's quieter.
Pangkor Island Beach Resort
(previously Pan Pacific Resort)
Teluk Belanga (Golden Sands)
Tel: 05-685 1091
Tel: 03-2287 6868 (KL)
Fax: 05-685 1852
Fax: 03-2287 6869 (KL)
Isolated hotel with great private beach and lush forest, and its own ferry from Lumut. There are 240 rooms (top floor has nice views), bungalows and chalets,

watersports, restaurants, bars, barbecue on beach, children's activities, traditional massage, tours. Day-trippers are allowed to use the beach and facilities. **$$$**

Teluk Dalam Resort
Pulau Pangkor
Tel: 05-685 5000
Fax: 05-685 4000
www.tdr.com.my
Lovely setting, with 163 chalets, bungalows and luxury villas sprawled over 16 hectares (40 acres) of beachside and forested land. There are cute seashell showers at the swimming pool. Restaurants, pubs, special jungle trails, and tours. The beach is only suitable for swimming at high tide. **$$$**

Pangkor Holiday Resort
Lot 41, Pasir Bogak
Tel: 05-685 3321/685 3626
Fax: 05-685 3627
Unassuming but clean, with a beautiful jungle and orchard backdrop, 54 air-conditioned chalets and 108 rooms and 15 quads; no beach. Cafétéria offers local fare and DIY BBQ. Popular for group retreats, especially churches. **$$**

Pulau Pangkor Laut

Pangkor Laut Resort
Tel: 05-699 1100
Tel: 03-2145 9000 (KL)
Fax: 05-699 1200
Fax: 03-2418 7397 (KL)
www.pangkorlautresort.com
One of the country's poshest luxury hotels sits on its own island and has its own ferry from Lumut. It has the gorgeous Emerald Bay beach to itself. There are 178 luxurious rooms in hillside or beachfront Malay-style villas as well as suites on stilts over the sea, swimming pools, six restaurants, a library of books and CDs, and a watersports centre. On the other side of the island is Pangkor Laut Estates, 8 secluded, walled estates with their own pool, outdoor jacuzzi, bedrooms and living and dining rooms. Built of stone and wood in the virgin forest or facing a private beach, each has its own chef and butler – all at a price of course. **$$$$**

Lumut

Orient Star Resort
Lot 203 & 366, Jalan Iskandar Shah
Tel: 05-683 4199
Fax: 05-683 4223
e-mail: tosrlso@po.jaring.my
Lumbering facility at the edge of town with traditional Malay house entrance; 150 recently upgraded rooms (odd numbers are sea-facing), restaurants, lounge, swimming pool with bar; mainly Navy patronage. Also manages the Lumut International Yacht Club with its five small but fully-equipped cabins (**$**). **$$$**

Price Guide

Prices are for a standard double room during peak periods.
$$$$: more than RM400
$$$: RM200–400
$$: RM100–200
$: less than RM100

Swiss-Garden Resort
Jalan Damai Laut
off Jalan Telok Senangin
Tel: 05-618 3333
Fax: 05-618 3388
www.swissgarden.com
Isolated in enormous grounds with ocean, mangrove, river, rainforest and oil palm surrounds, the resort is 20 minutes by ferry from Lumut, or over 1 hour by road. It features a beautiful pool overlooking the sea, 300 rooms, 18-hole golf course, disco, karaoke, and every sort of resort facility, including children's activities. Ask about a golf package with unlimited rounds; day-trippers are allowed use of facilities. **$$**

Blue Bay Resort
Lot 4, Jalan Titi Panjang
Tel: 05-683 6939
Fax: 05-683 6239
Block-ish accommodation with 66 decent rooms, swimming pool, garden and esplanade at the back, seafood restaurant. **$**

Lumut Country Resort
331, Jalan Titi Panjang
Tel: 05-683 5109
Fax: 05-683 5396
Built in the 1980s with colonial-inspired architecture and now fraying at the edges, but still

decent. The 44 motel-style rooms surround the swimming pool. A bistro serves so-called "country fare", such as Beef Stroganoff and Chicken Maryland. **$**

Kuala Kangsar

Seri Temenggong Resthouse
Jalan Bukit Kerajaan
Tel/Fax: 05-776 3872
One of Malaysia's prettiest resthouses, with views of the Perak River and 17 rooms of various sizes with ensuite baths and hot water. An open-air restaurant, serving local and Western meals, overlooks the lake. The resthouse is within walking distance of attractions, so is very popular; make sure you book ahead. **$**

Temenggor/Belum

Banding Island Resort
36 km (22 miles)
Grik East-West Highway
Tel: 05-792 1791
Fax: 05-792 1793
Lakeside motel that is very quiet unless there's a fishing competition, with 28 spacious rooms, a restaurant overlooking the lake, karaoke, fishing, boating, and jungle trekking; camping permitted. **$$**

Rumah Rehat Gerik
682, Jalan Haji Meor Yahya
Tel: 05-791 1454/791 2305
Fax: 05-791 2288
Basic and old hotel, but with clean and spacious rooms, some air-conditioned, for 50 guests. Restaurant serves traditional Malay, Thai and Western fare. **$**

Taiping

Legend Inn
2 Jalan Long Jaafar
Tel: 05-806 0000
Fax: 05-806 6666
Close to the bus station, this is the best hotel in town, set against Bukit Larut, with 88 rooms with bathrooms, hot showers and TV, and a café with a view. **$**

Hotel Panorama
61–79 Jalan Kota
Tel: 05-808 4111
Centrally located, next to a large supermarket, with 70 rooms, baths and hot showers; car rental. **$**

PENANG

The city's powerful preservation lobby has seen some of Penang's older buildings preserved as "nostalgia" and boutique hotels. Georgetown's bigger hotels cater to the business sector, while budget and backpackers' accommodation is along Lebuh Leith and Lebuh Chulia. These are mainly Chinese hotels that need facelifts, but many have great atmosphere, and sit amid eateries, travel and tour agencies, and motorbike and bicycle rental firms.

E & O (Eastern & Oriental) Hotel
10 Lebuh Farquhar
Tel: 04-222 2000
Fax: 04-261 6333
www.e-o-hotel.com
Situated at the best site in Georgetown overlooking the sea, this extensively-renovated hotel still retains the ambience of its former self. The "premier hotel east of the Suez" was patronized by Noel Coward, Douglas Fairbanks, Rudyard Kipling, Somerset Maugham and Herman Hesse during its early years. Sea-view suites are the best. Enjoy devonshire teas in The Conservatory, steaks at the 1885 Grill. Also boasts a new pool overlooking the sea and a gym. **$$$$**

Equatorial Penang
1 Jalan Bukit Jambul, Bayan Lepas
Tel: 04-643 8111
Fax: 04-644 8000
www.equatorial.com
Catering to the Free Trade Zone industrialists, this beautiful hotel with its impressively high-ceilinged lobby and lovely landscaping has 655 guestrooms and suites, and 22 apartments, restaurants, and sports facilities, including an 18-hole golf course. **$$$$**

The Northam
55 Jalan Sultan Ahmad Shah
Tel: 04-370 1111
Fax: 04-370 2222
www.northam-hotel.com.my
The town's fanciest business hotel with a resort feel, towering 38 floors high, with all business and non-business mod-cons, such as jacuzzis with a view of the ocean in its 233 suites, including a whopping 96 presidential suites, in-suite massage, and fine dining in Italian, Indian and Chinese restaurants.

Penang's Beach Hotels

The beach hotels in Penang are among the country's oldest seaside resorts. Many have been refurbished and renovated. Sea-view rooms are pricey during peak season; otherwise stiff competition makes them absolutely affordable.

Mutiara Beach Resort
1 Jalan Teluk Bahang
Tel: 04-886 8888
Fax: 04-885 2829
www.mutiarahotels.com
Luxurious, large, and the last resort on the stretch, with tasteful use of local motifs; 440 rooms, full resort facilities. **$$$$**

Grand Plaza Parkroyal Penang
Jalan Batu Ferringhi
Tel: 04-881 1133
Fax: 04-881 2233
www.parkroyalhotels.com
Recently refurbished hotel with 330 large contemporary rooms and 30 suites, beautiful freeform swimming pool and right on the beach. Two restaurants, pool-side cafe and a bar. **$$$**

Lone Pine Hotel
97. Jalan Batu Ferringhi
Tel: 04-881 1511/1512
Fax: 04-881 1282
www.lonepinehotel.com
Feringghi's first hotel is now a boutique hotel, refurbished for a 1970s feel. There are verandahs for all 50 rooms, some of which have Balinese-style courtyards. **$$$**

Casuarina Beach Hotel
Jalan Batu Ferringhi
Tel: 04-881 1711
Fax: 04-881 2155
www.casuarina.com.my
Pleasant hotel, sea-view rooms. Excellent Italian restaurant. **$$**

Copthorne Orchid
Jalan Tanjung Bungah
Tel: 04-890 3333
Fax:04-890 3303
www.millenniumhotels.com

Aptly situated on "Millionaires' Row", it assumes the colonial road name. Small swimming pool, gymnasium, spa. **$$$$**

One of the first hotels on the stretch, beautifully breezy, 318 sea-view rooms with balconies, Cantonese and Szechuan restaurant; no beach. **$$**

Ferringhi Beach Hotel
Jalan Batu Ferringhi
Tel: 04-890 5999
Fax: 04-890 5100
www.ferringhi.com.my/
Bridge links the hotel to a nice beach, windy lounge, 350 rooms with sea view, grill. **$$**

Golden Sands Resort
Batu Ferringhi Beach
Tel: 04-881 1911
Fax: 04-881 1880
www.shangri-la.com
Adjoining Rasa Sayang, an old hotel with pool, 395 rooms, sea views, Italian restaurant. **$$**

Holiday Inn Penang
Batu Ferringhi Beach
Tel: 04-881 1601
Fax: 04-881 1389
www.penang.holiday-inn.com
Beach hotel with 352 rooms, good steakhouse. **$$**

Paradise Sandy Bay
527 Jalan Tanjung Bungah
Tel: 04-899 9999
Fax: 04-899 0000
www.paradisehotel.com
Pleasant all-suite hotel with 200 sea-facing rooms; popular nightspot, good Italian fare. **$$**

Ali's Guest House & Restaurant
53 Batu Ferringhi
Tel: 04-881 1316
Friendly accommodation on the beachfront near Parkroyal. Nice restaurant/pub in the garden. Fan and shared facilities, some rooms air-conditioned with own bath. **$**

Shalini's Guesthouse
56 Batu Ferringhi
Tel: 04-881 1859
Budget accommodation with homestay feel. Shared bathrooms. Fans, good local meals, kitchen, self-service laundry. **$**

Shangri-La Hotel
Jalan Magazine
Tel: 04-262 2622
Fax: 04-262 6526
www.shangri-la.com
Next to KOMTAR, therefore its top floors offer some of the same great views of Georgetown rooftops, this mainly business sector hotel has 442 rooms, a decent Chinese restaurant, disco, car rental. **$$$$**

Sheraton Penang
3 Jalan Larut
Tel: 04-226 7888
Fax: 04-226 6615
www.sheraton.com/penang
Smack in the centre of the shopping district, with 295 rooms, grill, coffee house, bars, swimming pool, health centre, disco. **$$$**

Bellevue Hotel
Penang Hill
Tel: 04-892 9600
This is Penang Hill's only hotel with fine views of Georgetown; built in the colonial style with a garden terrace. Quiet and cool because of the altitude, with an aviary at entrance. **$$**

City Bayview Hotel
25A Lebuh Farquhar
Tel: 04-263 3161
Fax: 04-263 4124/160
www.bayviewintl.com
Fringing the main shopping area, within walking distance of Leith Street pubs, the hotel has a new wing, good Malay restaurant, a charming café serving hawker fare, and a revolving restaurant. **$$**

Hotel 1926
Jalan Imigresen
Tel: 04-228 1926
Fax: 04-227 7926
Saved from demolition (and the

Penang on a Budget

Lebuh Chulia in Penang is chock-a-block with backpackers' accommodation, from dilapidated to decent. Most are basic and fan-cooled, with coffee house downstairs serving breakfast and snacks, and offering some help with travel arrangements. Best bet is to walk around and check them out.

erection of yet another modern shopping complex), this former government quarters has been conserved as a medium-budget boutique hotel with Penang's longest corridor, which also doubles as a sort of art gallery. The 94 rooms come in different sizes, but are all air-conditioned and have ensuite baths. Café, Malay restaurant, and lounge. **$$**

YMCA of Penang
211 Jalan Macalister
Tel: 04-228 8211
Fax: 04-229 5869
e-mail: ymcapg@streamyx.com
Clean hostel within walking distance of food stalls, hospitals and gardens. **$**

Butterworth

An uninteresting place, stay the night only if you're stuck here. Try Butterworth Travel Lodge, 1 Lorong Bagan Luar, tel: 04-333 3399 (**$$**) or Sunway Hotel Seberang Jaya, 11 Lebuh Tenggiri 2, tel: 04-370 7788, fax: 04-370 0555, www.sh.com.my (**$**)

KEDAH

Alor Setar

Grand Continental Hotel
134–141 Jalan Sultan Badlishah
Tel: 04-733 5917
Fax: 04-733 5161
www.grandcontinental.com.my
The town's fanciest hotel, central, with 130 rooms. Restaurant serves good local fare. **$$**

Hotel Grand Crystal
40 Jalan Kampung Perak
Tel: 04-731 3333
Fax: 04-731 6368
www.grandcontinental.com.my
Good value in central location, 145 rooms, swimming pool, sauna and coffee house. **$**

Sungai Petani

Swiss-Inn Sungai Petani
1 Jalan Pahlawan
Tel: 04-422 3333
Tel: 03-2141 5333 (KL)
Fax: 04-422 3423
www.swissgarden.com
Lovely hotel with 101 rooms. Restaurant overlooks nice landscaped pool. **$**

Price Guide

Prices are for a standard double room during peak periods.
$$$$: more than RM400
$$$: RM200–400
$$: RM100–200
$: less than RM100

Tasik Pedu

Desa Utara Pedu Lake
KB2 Kuala Nerang, 6300 Kedah
Tel: 04-732 8888
Fax: 04-732 4999
www.desautara.com
Kampung-style two- and three-room chalets with balconies, some with views of the lake, well spread out in forested area. **$$$**

Mutiara Pedu Lake Resort
KB1 Kuala Nerang
Tel: 04-730 4888
Tel: 03-2142 1601 (KL)
Fax: 04-730 4488
Located on two islands and accessible only by boat, there are 180 Kedah-Thai style chalets and a pleasant restaurant. **$$$**

Pulau Langkawi

Everything is here, from some of the most impressive hotels in the country, to budget accommodation. Kuah is very built-up, so the beach hotels are certainly more pleasant, but the town has more eateries and shops. Book ahead during the peak season and especially in December when the *Lima Maritime* exhibition takes place.

Four Seasons Resort
Jalan Tanjung Rhu
Tel: 04-959 2888
Fax: 04-959 2889
Lovely hideaway amid Moorish inspired grounds on wide beachfront, its 91 pavilions and villas provides the ultimate in luxury pampering, hospitality and personal services. **$$$$**

Langkawi Lagoon
Lot 78, Jalan Kuala Muda,
Padang Matsirat
Tel: 04-955 8181,
Tel: 03-2283 1122 (KL)
Fax: 04-955 8881,
Fax: 03-2283 6622 (KL)
www.langkawilagoonresort.com

An upscale resort, with charming wooden villas built over the sea and spacious hotel suites. **$$$$**

The Andaman Datai Bay
Jalan Teluk Datai
Tel: 04-959 1088
Fax: 04-959 1168
www.ghmhotels.com
Exclusive luxury resort in rainforest surroundings, shares beautiful beach and views of Thailand's islands with the Datai (see below). Both resorts, managed by the GHM group have excellent spas and restaurants in both beach and forest settings. 188 rooms with five restaurants, including Mediterranean and Japanese cuisine. Close to 18-hole golf course; children's activities. **$$$$**

The Datai
Jalan Teluk Datai
Tel: 04-959 2500
Fax: 04-959 2600
www.ghmhotels.com
Award-winning Balinese-inspired luxury resort in isolated lush surroundings, with a beautiful private beach. It has 106 villas and rooms, three restaurants, and an adjacent 18-hole golf course. **$$$$**

Pelangi Beach Resort
Pantai Cenang
Tel: 04-952 8888
Fax: 04-952 8899
www.pelangibeachresort.com
At a splendid curve of the beach, with a gracious lobby, these traditional-style bungalows and chalets with 331 rooms are best known for having housed the Commonwealth heads of government, including Britain's Queen Elizabeth. **$$$$**

Sheraton Langkawi Beach Resort
Teluk Nibong
Tel: 04-955 1901
Fax: 04-955 1968
www.sheraton.com/langkawi
Luxury wooden resort set in rainforest surrounds with 231 rooms, including chalets with ocean views. A cascade of stairs lead down to the swimming pool. The sea-facing Captain's Grill serves seafood; popular disco. **$$$$**

Sheraton Perdana Resort
Jalan Pantai Dato' Syed Omar
Tel: 04-966 2020
Fax: 04-966 6414
www.sheraton.com/perdana
Isolated from other hotels, the resort is situated just past the yacht club within walking distance of the jetty. There are 200 rooms. Although there is not much of a beach, the sports facilities are excellent, including salt and freshwater swimming pools, watersports, jogging track, bicycles, top-class gym, and squash. **$$$$**

Tanjung Rhu Resort
Tanjung Rhu
Tel: 04-959 1033
Fax: 04-959 1899
www.tanjungrhu.com.my
This luxury resort is peacefully situated on a secluded northern beach amid a lush mangrove forest. Beautiful landscaping and intelligent use of its sprawling grounds. Tasteful rooms featuring lots of wood and simple lines are huge. There is a 2.5-km (1½-mile) private beach. Three restaurants, two swimming pools and spa. **$$$$**

Awana Porto Malai Langkawi
Tanjung Malai
Tel: 04-955 5111
Fax: 04-955 5222
www.awana.com.my
Built on reclaimed land with a marina, the hotel has 175 sea-facing rooms, a nice boardwalk café and casual fine dining. Next door is a gruesome 16-lane bowling alley. Cruise liners unleash thousands of passengers here regularly. **$$$**

Mutiara Burau Bay Resort
Pantai Kok
Tel: 04-959 1061
Fax: 04-959 1172
www.mutiarahotels.com
On one of the island's loveliest beaches and close to lush forest, the resort has 150 rooms in tent-style cabins, karaoke, and traditional massage. The restaurant, however, is uninspiring. **$$$**

Beach Garden Resort
Pantai Cenang
Tel: 04-955 1363
Fax: 04-955 1221
Small, pretty 13-room outfit with thatched roofs, run by a German couple and popular with foreigners. Beachfront eateries, including good Italian fare and margaritas. **$$**

Bon Ton Resort
200 Pantai Cenang
Tel: 04-955 3463/6787
Fax: 04-955 4791
www.bontonresort.com.my
Charming, authentic thatched Malay-style kampung houses reconstructed from old wood, with verandahs, basic bathrooms and fans-only. There is a very good restaurant and a good Asian curio shop. **$$$**

The City Bayview Hotel
Jalan Pandak Mayah 1
Pusat Bandar Kuah
Tel: 04-966 1818
Fax: 04-966 3888
www.bayviewintl.com
Like a white monolith, this 250-room city hotel rises from among the roofs of the market. Great value rooms, ask for promotional rates. The top floors have sea view, swimming pool, sauna, and a gym. **$$**

The Gates Langkawi Resort
Jalan Persiaran Putra, Kuah
Tel: 04-966 8466
Fax: 04-966 9466

Kuah on a Budget

Budget and backpackers' accommodation can be found at Kuah and Pantai Cenang/Pantai Tengah. In Kuah, try the family-owned basic **Gaya**, tel: 04-966 7704, or the friendly **Iska Travellers Guesthouse**, Taman Seri Pelang, tel: 04-966 8879. One of the original budget places at Cenang is **Langkawi Sandy Beach Motel**, tel: 04-955 1308, fax: 04-955 1762, which now offers air-conditioned chalets alongside the original A-frames; other popular ones include **Semarak Langkawi Beach Resort**, tel: 04-955 1377, fax: 04-955 1595, and **Grand Beach Motel**, tel: 04-955 1457. Right at the end of Pantai Tengah are **Charlie's**, small but clean, with a popular bar, tel: 04-955 1200, **Sunset Beach Resort**, popular bar and restaurant, tel: 04-955 1751 and **Tanjung Mail Beach Resort**, tel: 04-955 1891.

Close to Kuah, opposite the jetty. It doesn't have a beach but there are great views from its hilly location. *Kampung* chalets, 170 rooms, decent restaurants with good local, Thai western and Italian fare, and a shuttle to town. **$$**

Tanjung Sanctuary
Jalan Pantai Kok
Tel: 04-955 2977
Fax: 04-955 3978
www.tanjungsanctuary.com.my
Quiet, 32-room, all-suite wooden chalets with balconies, well spread out among the trees; some are beach-fronting. Restaurant has 270-degree view of the sea. **$$**

Perlis

Putra Palace Hotel
135 Persiaran Jubli Emas Kangar
Tel: 04-976 7755
Fax: 04-976 1049
e-mail: putrapalace@netscape.net
The state's fanciest hotel with 146 rooms and standard facilities; Asian and Continental restaurant featuring buffets. **$$$**

SOUTHERN PENINSULA

MELAKA
Melaka City

Room prices are lower by 30 percent on weekdays. Hotels are located in a so-called "hotel zone" in the Jalan Bendahara area, just outside the historic hub, and in the Old Town across the bridge.

Backpackers' accommodation is on Jalan Parameswara and the Taman Melaka Raya, but be careful about these, especially if there are girls hanging around downstairs. You'll also find some lovely renovated accommodation that successfully maintains a degree of old-world charm.

Century Mahkota Hotel
Jalan Merdeka
Tel: 06-281 2828
Tel: 03-2162 2999 (KL)
Fax: 06-281 2323
Fax: 03-2162 8644 (KL)
www.centuryhotel.com
Sitting on reclaimed coastal land near the historic centre and the Mahkota Parade shopping mall, this massive 590-room hotel has landscaped swimming pools and a host of activities. Rooms in contrast are uninspiring and dull. Appeals to mainly tour groups. **$$$$**

Renaissance Melaka Hotel
Jalan Bendahara
Tel: 06-284 8888
Fax: 06-283 5351
www.renaissance-melaka.com
Towering over the city, this 295-room luxury hotel is beautifully-furnished, centrally located and has great views of the town, Melaka River and the sea. Swimming pool on the 9th floor, Chinese restaurant, coffee house, lounge-cum-library, disco. **$$$$**

Price Guide

Prices are for a standard double room during peak periods.
$$$$: more than RM400
$$$: RM200–400
$$: RM100–200
$: less than RM100

City Bayview Hotel
Jalan Bendahara
Tel: 06-283 9888
Fax: 06-283 6699
www.bayviewintl.com
Situated near St Peter's Church, this hotel has good views, 182 rooms, swimming pool, a Chinese restaurant and a coffee house. **$$$**

Equatorial Hotel
Jalan Bandar Hilir
Tel: 06-282 8333
Fax: 06-282 9333
www.equatorial.com
High-rise luxury hotel, totally out of place with Melaka's heritage surroundings but in a good location with swimming pool and six restaurants. **$$$**

Emperor Hotel
123 Jalan Munshi Abdullah
Tel: 06-284 0777
Fax: 06-284 0787
e-mail: empehtl@tm.net.my
Decent and central, the hotel has 235 rooms, some with views of the sea, a Chinese restaurant with good *dim sum*, a coffee house, a swimming pool and sauna. **$$**

Heeren House
1 Jalan Tun Tan Cheng Lock
Tel: 06-281 4241
Fax: 06-281 4239
e-mail: herenhse@tm.net.my
Lovely, cosy six-room restored shophouse in the Old Town overlooking the Melaka River and facing the historic centre. It has air-conditioned rooms with ensuite baths, and a café offering Peranakan and Portuguese fare. **$$**

Straits Heritage Lodge
591-A Taman Melaka Raya
Tel: 06-282 3950
Fax: 06-282 3957
Beautifully-renovated Peranakan interior that belies its boring facade; 20 minutes' walk from the historic hub. There is a lovely open-air fountain courtyard which serves as a reading area. Rooms are air-conditioned with ensuite baths. The Portuguese pub downstairs serves food and wine. **$$**

Hotel Portugis
12–20 Jalan Melaka Raya 20
Tel: 06-292 4100
Fax: 06-292 9300
Loud and heavy on the kitsch, but decent standard rooms and wonderfully-decorated VIP rooms which are nonetheless still affordable. Portuguese restaurant, 24-hour food court, karaoke. **$–$$**

Baba House
125–7 Jalan Tun Tan Cheng Lock
Tel: 06-281 1216
Fax: 06-281 1217
Pretty Peranakan house in the Old Town serving as backpackers' accommodation, with clean simple rooms, some with air-conditioning and ensuite baths, few with views, no restaurant. **$**

Hotel Puri
118 Jalan Tun Tan Cheng Lock
Tel: 06-282 5588
Fax: 06-281 5588
www.hotelpuri.com
Carefully restored 1819 Peranakan house in the quaint "Millionaires' Row", which belonged to an eminent philanthropist. Marble and wood abound. There are 50 rooms, a decorated original airwell, beer garden and L-shaped new wing; near the Kochee Café. **$**

Melaka Coast
Riviera Bay Resort
10km Jalan Tanjung Kling
Tel: 06-315 1111
Fax: 06-315 3333
www.meritus-hotels.com
Showy Roman gateway, 450 sea-facing suites, three restaurants, pub, swimming pool that is a better bet than the sea, and lots of facilities. **$$$$**
Shah's Beach Resort
9km Jalan Tanjung Kling
Tel: 06-315 3121/315 2120
Fax: 06-315 2088
e-mail: vera@po.jaring.my
Famous old motel overlooking the Melaka Straits. Wood chalets, pool and good restaurant. Very popular with Singaporeans and expats on the weekends and holidays when booking ahead is essential. **$$**
Tanjung Bidara Resort
Tanjung Bidara, Masjid Tanah
Tel: 06-384 2990
Fax: 06-384 2995
Beachside resort of ocean-facing chalets (85 rooms), restaurant, lounge, swimming pool, but no public transport. **$$**

Ayer Keroh
A'Famosa Resort
Alor Gajah
Tel: 06-552 0888
Fax: (+6) 06-552 0811
www.afamosa.com
Sprawling theme park hotel with Cowboy Town, Animal World Safari and Water World, they also have comfortable bungalows and condos. Golf course nearby. **$$**
Air Keroh Country Resort
Tel: 06-232 5211
Fax: 06-232 0422
A green and secluded chalet resort next door to Mini Malaysia, with swimming pool and restaurant; jungle-trekking and car hire can be arranged. **$$**
Air Keroh d'Village Melaka
Tel: 06-232 8000
Fax: 06-232 7541
e-mail: village@tm.net.my
Oldish resort with 274 motel rooms/chalets, seafood restaurant, coffee house, pool, terrace, sports facilities, bicycle hire. **$$**

NEGERI SEMBILAN
Seremban
Allson Klana Resort
Jalan Penghulu Cantik, Taman Tasek
Tel: 06-762 7888
Fax: 06-767 7788
www.allsonklana.com.my
Facing the pretty lake, this upmarket hotel has 223 rooms, full room facilities and service, Japanese and Chinese restaurants, coffee house, bars, business centre, fitness centre, swimming pool. **$$$**
Royal Adelphi
Jalan Dato AS Dawood
Tel: 06-766 6666
Fax: 06-766 6000
www.royaladelphi.com
Luxury hotel which offers the usual comforts with a good Chinese restaurant, swimming pool and outdoor jacuzzi. **$$$**
Carlton Star Hotel
47 Jalan Dato' Sheikh Ahmad
Tel: 06-763 6663
Fax: 06-762 0040
Central location near the bus and taxi station as well as food stalls, with 34 rooms, air-conditioning, Chinese restaurant, coffee house. **$$**

JOHOR
Johor Bahru
Hyatt Regency
Jalan Sungai Chat
Tel: 07-222 1234
Fax: 07-222 9234
www.johorbahru.regency.hyatt.com
Luxurious hotel with 406 rooms, some with views of the Straits of Johor and Singapore, two-tier swimming pool, Roman spa. Within walking distance of town. **$$$$**
Mutiara Johor Bahru
Jalan Dato' Sulaiman
Tel: 07-332 3800
Fax: 07-331 8884
www.mutiarahotels.com
Within walking distance to large malls, this luxury hotel targets families with its junior club suite featuring double-decker beds, Playstation and games and soft toys. **$$$**
Puteri Pan Pacific
Jalan Abdullah Ibrahim
Tel: 07-223 3333

Johor Islands
Accommodation on the islands is divided into what are termed resorts – the bigger air-conditioned and hot-shower operations – and chalets, which can be dormitory-style. All have restaurants and snorkelling facilities. Some are diver-friendly. Operations have a habit of changing management and ownership. Some have their own offices or agents in town, but tour agencies can book you into any of the islands – they receive a commission, so be firm. Ask to see their photo album of resorts and boats. Enquire about 3-day/2-night packages, which include boat transfers, accommodation, all meals and a snorkelling trip.

Fax: 07-223 6622
www.panpacific.com
Massive, central hotel, close to shopping malls, with 476 rooms, some with views of the straits and Singapore, Italian restaurant. **$$$**
Straits View Hotel
1-D Jalan Skudai
Tel: 07-224 1400
Fax: 07-224 2698
Out of town hotel with upstairs rooms overlooking the straits; 30 air-conditioned rooms, open-air seafood restaurant. **$**
Wadi Hassan Traveller's Home
52E Jalan Wadi Hassan
Clean backpackers' hotel with dormitories and family rooms, fan-cooled, laundry, tours and information. **$**

Kota Tinggi
Kota Tinggi Resort
16 Jalan Lombong
Tel: 07-883 6222
Fax: 07-883 1146
Resort comprising 63 chalets and rooms by the waterfalls with air-conditioning and ensuite baths; mostly Singaporean clientele. Weekday rate 20 percent cheaper, also much quieter. **$$**

Desaru

Accommodation here is classy, and expensive because of the mostly-Singaporean clientele. Weekend rates are about 20 percent higher. All eateries are in the hotels or the coastal villages a drive away. Seaview rooms are at a premium. All resorts have swimming pools, sea-sport facilities and bicycles.

Desaru Impian Resort
Tanjung Penawar
Tel: 07-2240 827
Fax: 07-2228 306
www.marinathemepark.com
Like Disney's Sleeping Beauty's castle whose towers are topped by flags that don't flutter, this gigantic theme-park hotel at the entrance to Desaru has staff dressed as pirates, a water park surrounded by 16 blocks of 356 well-furnished all-suite family apartments (cooking allowed), two swimming pools – one in a Taj Mahal clubhouse on the beach – mini zoo and sports facilities. Day use allowed. **$$$**

Desaru Perdana
Tanjung Penawar
Tel: 07-822 2222
Fax: 07-822 2223
www.desaruperdana.com.sg
Blocks harbouring 200 rooms around beautiful pool with waterfall; nice landscaping. **$$$**

Sebana Golf and Marina Resort
Tanjung Penawar
Tel: 07-826 6688
Fax: 07-826 6677
www.sebanacove.com
The approach road winds through an 18-hole golf course, past the yacht clubhouse and the beautiful marina which is overlooked by the resort's tavern. There are 64 rather small rooms, some with marina views. Pub lunches at the bar, nominal fee for recreational facilities, river cruises. Ask about packages. **$$$**

Desaru Golden Beach Resort
Tanjung Penawar
Tel: 07-822 1101
Fax: 07-822 1480
www.desaruresort.com
Oldie resort with 1970s feel, but decent; 100 rooms in chalets, including newer sea-fronting villas. The famous golf course is just down the road. **$$**

Desaru Leisure Camp
Tanjung Penawar
Tel: 07-822 1211
Fax: 07-822 1937
www.desaruresort.com
Most basic offering but not good value, with rooms and tiny chalets with mattress. Camping permitted with equipment for rent; friendly staff, food on request only, popular with groups. Mountain biking pit nearby; day use allowed. **$**

Tanjung Balau Fishing Village
Tanjung Balau
Tel: 07-822 1601
Fax: 07-822 1600
Next to a modern fishing village, this new government venture has 115 family and double rooms and 20 triple-share dormitories, and a local restaurant. Traditional fishing is seasonal only, but there's a good fishing museum and nice uncrowded beach. **$**

PENINSULA'S EAST COAST

MERSING AND ISLANDS

Mersing

Hotel Timotel
837 Jalan Endau
Tel: 07-799 5888
Fax: 07-799 5333
e-mail: timotel@tm.net.my
Situated past the bridge north but within walking distance of the jetty, the hotel is clean with 44 rooms, local and Western food. **$$**

Mersing Inn
38 Jalan Ismail
Tel/fax: 07-799 1919
Next to a supermarket in a central location with clean, air-conditioned rooms, ensuite baths and hot water. **$**

Omar's Backpackers' Hostel
Jalan Abu Bakar
Tel: 07-799 5096, 019-774 4268
Opposite the post office is Mersing's arguably best-established backpackers' hostel. Situated on the first floor with dormitories for 10 only; kitchen, tours, walking distance of jetty. **$**

Pulau Besar

Aseania Resort
Tel: 07-799 4152
Fax: 07-799 1413
Smartest hotel with 50 beach-fronting (premium) and hill-view coconut-framed chalets arranged in clusters for *kampung* feel, with hot showers, lush grounds, 24-hour electricity, bar, sea-sports, a 45-minute cross-isle jungle trek from back of huts; no TV, no karaoke, or dive shop. **$$**

Endau-Rompin National Park (Johor)

Staging Point and campsites
Tel: 07-223 7471 (Johor Park Corporation in Johor Bahru)
Fax: 07-223 7472
The Staging Point at Endau-Rompin National Park has chalets (20 people) and dormitories (100 people – men and women separate), otherwise there are campsites: Kuala Jasin, Kuala Marong, Upih Guling, and Batu Hampar (maximum 200 visitors) with some shelters and basic toilets. Booking ahead is imperative. Bring everything in, including food and cooking gas. Limited equipment may be hired. The area is accessible by boat from Felda Nitar (jump-off point Mersing or Kahang). Permits are required (and for cameras). A guide can be arranged.

Nature Education and Research Centre (NERC)
Tel: 03-2287 9422 (Malaysian Nature Society in Kuala Lumpur)
Fax: 03-2287 8773
e-mail: mas@streamyx.com
The centre offers 4-day/3-night nature courses (minimum groups of 10, maximum 40), including full board and excellent meals (student concessions available).

D'Coconut Island Resort
Tel: 03-4296 5753
Fax: 03-4291 1808
www.dcoconut.com
New, *kampung* environment with 20 air-conditioned chalets with ensuite baths, satellite TV and mini fridge, mountain bikes, watersports, dive shop. **$$**

Nirwana Beach Resort
Tel: 07-799 1606
Fax: 07-799 5294
Basic chalets, some air-conditioned, all with ensuite baths, dormitories for 6–10 people, bar. **$$**

White Sand Beach Resort
Tel: 07-799 4955/2582
Fax: 07-799 2572
Established outfit with beach-fronting chalets, dive packages. **$$**

Pulau Rawa

Rawa Safaris Island Resort
Tel: 07-799 1204
Fax: 07-799 3848
www.rawasfr.com
One-island-one-resort tagline, with 53 wood-and-attap A-frames, chalets and bungalows on beach and hill, some with air-conditioning and ensuite bathroom. A quiet spot with a lovely beach, electricity until midnight (lanterns provided), bar, sea-sports, scuba gear for hire but no dive master. **$$**

Pulau Tinggi

Tinggi Island Resort
Tel: 019-7433 252, 07-224 0063
Fax: 07-861 2005
www.tinggiislandresort.com.my
25 no-frills twin-sharing rooms on hillside and beach next to the Marine Parks museum; aircon, attached bath, snorkelling and fishing trips. Both room-only and packages with meals are available. **$$**

Pulau Pemanggil

Basic accommodation and only packages are available, usually for groups of 10 or more. Enquire at the travel agencies. The biggest operation is **Pemanggil Holiday Heaven**, tel: 07-799 4360 with 13 chalets and a 10-room longhouse; **Ranting Resort** is fairly big; other smaller operators with chalets and

dormitories are **Pemanggil Baru Chalet**, tel: 07-799 2363 and **Pulau Pemanggil Mini Resort**, tel: 07-799 2660. **$$$**

Pulau Aur/Dayang

Another packages-only destination, the prettiest beaches are on Pulau Dayang: chalets and longhouses available at **Blue Water Holiday Resort**, tel: 07-799 4027; **Dayang Blues**, tel: 07-799 4558; and on Aur, **Mahmood's Chalet**, tel: 07-799 4217. Enquire about the smaller operations at tour agencies; packages. **$$$**

Pulau Tioman

Tekek beach is lined with small virtually indistinguishable resorts – you can check out each one until you find something you like. At the end of the stretch is **Berjaya Tioman Beach Resort**, tel: 09-419 1000; fax: 09-419 1718; www.berjayaresorts.com, the largest – and only luxury – resort, with 400 rooms and suites, golf and all the facilities expected of a resort. **$$$**

Peladang is well-kept, *kampung*-style accommodation with roomy chalets in pretty gardens, but sits across the road near the mini market and has no beach. **$**

Air Batang (ABC) and Juara are backpacker and A-frame beaches, Salang also has budget accommodation as does Mukut, while Paya and Genting cater to locals and Singaporeans and have more up-market accommodation.

There are dive shops at Tekek (Tioman Reef Divers and Scuba Point), ABC (B&J Dive Centre), Salang (Dive Asia and Fishermen Dive Centre), Penuba (Bali Hai Divers).

Japa Mala Resort, tel: 09-419 6001, fax: 09-419 6002, a boutique hotel boasts deluxe villas and chalets.

Pulau Sibu Besar

(accessible from Tanjung Leman)
Sea Gypsy Village Resort
Tel: 07-222 8642
Fax: 07-221 0048
www.siburesort.com

Lovely resort set in a 5-acre coconut-fringed site with 23 sea-facing Malay chalets with ensuite baths and verandahs. Bar, barbeque on Saturdays, dive shop, full-board. **$$**

Sibu Island Cabanas
Tel: 07-331 7216/1920
www.sibuislandcabanas.com
Comfortable, 18 fan-cooled chalets with ensuite baths, dive shop, full-board. **$$**

There is plenty of basic accommodation, mainly A-frames and huts. **Sibu Coconut Village Resort** (tel: 010-761 2761) and **Junansa Villa** (www.sibuisland.com.my) offers *kampung*-style hospitality; **Twin Beach Resort** (www.sibuisland.com.my) commandeers the middle of the island, and therefore two beaches.

Price Guide

Prices are for a standard double room during peak periods.
$$$$: more than RM400
$$$: RM200–400
$$: RM100–200
$: less than RM100

Pulau Sibu Tengah

Sibu Island Resort
Tel: 07-223 1188
Fax: 07-223 1199
www.sibuisland.com.my
Fancy resort and the island's only one with 171 air-conditioned chalets and a host of facilities and activities including batik-making classes, tennis courts, sunken pool bar; *teh tarik* stall in the shape of a boat, selling Indian breads and tea at night. **$$$**

PAHANG, TERENGGANU AND KELANTAN

Resorts are usually open all year round, but during the monsoon season, some offer a free stay if it rains during your visit. Sea-view rooms are premium; weekends and public holidays are 20–30 percent more pricey. Transfers from airports can be arranged by the bigger hotels.

PAHANG
Kuantan

All the town hotels are medium range, clustered around the centre and cater to the business sector, offering the same facilities; air-conditioning, TV, IDD phones, hot-water baths and breakfast. Among them are **M.S. Garden Hotel**, Lorong Gambut, tel: 09-517 7899 (202 rooms), **Vistana**, Jalan Telok Sisek (en route to Teluk Cempedak), tel: 09-517 8000, **Classic Hotel**, Jalan Besar, tel: 09-516 4599 (33 rooms), **Hotel Pacific**, Jalan Bukit Ubi, tel: 09-514 1980 (60 rooms), **Mega View**, Jalan Besar, tel: 09-517 1888 (105 rooms), **Citiview**, Jalan Haji Abdul Aziz, tel: 09-555 3888.

Teluk Chempedak Beach
Hotel Kuantan
Tel/fax: 09-517 7899
Distinct 1960s feel with high ceilings, colonial fan-cooled restaurant and bar, tiled floors, some rooms with air-conditioning and hot showers, tiny bathrooms, upstairs rooms with balcony and bathroom. Friendly, family-owned. **$**
Hyatt Regency Kuantan
Tel: 09-566 1234
Fax: 09-567 4677
www.kuantan.regency.hyatt.com
Grand old lady of the beach, with 336 rooms, restaurant with commanding ocean view, pizzas by the pool or on the beach, fun pub, tours. **$$$$**

Beserah
Le Village Beach Resort
Lot 1260 Sungai Karang
Tel: 09-544 7900
Tel: 03-983 2268 (KL)
Fax: 09-544 7899
e-mail: fal@tm.net.my
Mature is the word for this resort 14 km (9 miles) north of Kuantan, with wooden chalets and blocks of rooms amid lush foliage. Water sports, tours and car rental available. **$$**
Swiss-Garden Resort
2656–7 Sungai Karang, Balok
Tel: 09-544 7333
Fax: 09-544 9555
www.swissgarden.com

This 304-room hotel 13 km (8 miles) from the Kuantan airport has a beautifully breezy lounge area and lovely garden terrace. **$$**
De Rhu Beach Resort
152 Sungai Karang
Tel: 09-557 9000
Fax: 09-557 9002
www.derhu.com
Oldish hotel that has changed hands several times, with a beautiful beach beneath the casuarinas, large grounds, huge pool with sundeck, disco. **$**

Cherating
Club Med
Batu 29, Jalan Kuantan/Kemaman
Tel: 09-581 9133
Tel: 03-2161 4599 (KL)
Fax: 09-581 9172
Fax: 03-2161 7229 (Reservation)
www.clubmed.com
Just north of Kampung Cherating is Asia's first Club Med, spread out in carefully preserved forested surroundings, with a lovely private beach, the usual organised activities, including racquet sports, circus acts, rock-climbing, archery and watersports in non-monsoon period. Wide range of international food from Japanese to French, Rio-type carnival with live band every weekend. Day visitors from 10am–12pm, 2–6pm. **$$$$**
Impiana Resort Cherating
32km Jalan Kuantan-Kemaman
Tel: 09-581 9000
Fax: 09-581 9090
www.impiana.com
Situated just beyond Cukai, this is a graceful and tasteful adaptation of traditional Malay architecture, with an interesting pond design merging into a lounge and 120 rooms. Outdoor jacuzzi, lessons in arts and craft, full sports facilities. **$$$**
Legend Resort
Lot 1290, Sungai Karang
Tel: 09-581 9818
Fax: 09-581 9400
www.legendsgroup.com
Average hotel whose brochures are much more impressive than the reality, with 152 rooms. **$$$**
Cherating Holiday Villa
Lot 1303 Sungai Karang
Tel: 09-581 9500

Fax: 09-581 9178
e-mail: chv@tm.net.my
www.holidayvilla.com.my
The first resort north from Beserah to Cherating. Established, lovely ambience with 130 rooms, including a unique *kampung* section with a chalet cluster based on architecture from each state, two open-air jacuzzis, steak house, full watersports facilities. **$$**

For budget travellers, there are many cheap and cheerful chalets for rent along the entire stretch of Cherating beach. The price varies with the duration of the stay – bargaining is expected and advised.

Turtle-watching

At Rantau Abang, prices are higher by about 30 percent during the turtle season of May–September. However, sightings can be rare these days. The beach and the beautiful lagoon behind it are still worth a stay though.
Awang's Beach Bungalows & Restaurant
Tel: 09-844 3500
Long-time "turtle tourism" resort near Turtle Information Centre, it has 37 bungalows with terraces, and dormitories, and a self-service laundry. **$**
Dahimah's Guest House & Restaurant
Tel: 09-983 5057/09-845 2843
Clean, different-sized *kampung*-style chalets with verandahs, a little away from the beach. The river-fronting huts are nice. Restaurant open only during turtle season. **$**
Ismail Beach Resort
Tel: 09-844 1054
Right in front of the Turtle Museum, similar to Awang's, with choice of fan or air-conditioning. **$**
Rantau Abang Visitor's Centre
Batu 13 Jalan Dungun
Tel: 09-844 1533
Fax: 09-844 2653
Minimum quad-share traditional huts and chalets overlooking the lagoon, some air-conditioned. **$**

Price Guide

Prices are for a standard double room during peak periods.
$$$$: more than RM400
$$$: RM200–400
$$: RM100–200
$: less than RM100

Kampung Cherating

There is a host of accommodation here, now also called Cherating Lama ("old Cherating"). Many are still backpackers' hostels and budget-class hotels, but upmarket developers are gradually moving in.
Cherating Cottage
Tel: 09-581 9273
Fax: 09-581 9279
Classy chalets and double-storey block around a lotus pond, some rooms with air-conditioning and TV, open-air bar. **$**
The Shadow of the Moon
Tel: 09-581 9186
At the northern entrance, this is an established backpackers' hostel with attitude. Rustic fan-cooled and, imperatively, mosquito-netted, chalets are set amid much greenery on a hillside, all with baths. There is a wonderful restaurant/bar/reading area that is completely open – bring insect repellent. **$**

TERENGGANU
Kuala Terengganu
Permai Park Inn
Jalan Sultan Mahmud
Tel: 09-622 2122
Fax: 09-622 2121
www.parkinnkt.com.my
Within walking distance of Batu Buruk beach, comfortable, pleasant hotel with 130 rooms, and a nice pool. **$$$**
Primula Beach Resort
Jalan Persinggahan
Tel: 09-622 2100/623 3722
Fax: 09-623 3360
www.primulabeachresort.com
Town's fanciest hotel, renovated, with a sandy beach; 248 rooms, some with sea view; grill, cosy Italian restaurant, tours. **$$$**
Pura Tanjung Sabtu
Kampung Tanjung Sabtu
Tel/Fax: 09-615 3655

(mobile) 019 983 3365
www.puratanjungsabtu.com
A beautiful complex of traditional old wooden palaces have been re-created in an orchard upriver from Kuala Terengganu. Run by the famous songket-weaving prince, Tengku Ismail Tengku Su, it offers package deals with transfers, accommodation, home-cooked meals and sightseeing trips. **$$$**
Grand Continental
Jalan Sultan Zainal Abidin
Tel: 09-615 1888
Fax: 09-625 1999
www.grandcontinental.com.my
Beachside but close to the town centre, 200 pleasant rooms, swimming pool, pastries and cakes, live bands. **$$**

Diving Camps

Redang Aquatic Adventures, tel: 09-623 8188; fax: 09-623 0225, also ties up with Redang Beach Resort and arranges outings to Lang Tengah and Perhentian.

Hotel YT Midtown
Jalan Tok Lam
Tel: 09-623 5288
Fax: 09-623 4399
Right in the heart of town, a decent new hotel with 141 air-conditioned rooms with ensuite baths, good value set lunch and dinner; supper special of local bread, *roti jala*, with curry. **$$**
KT Mutiara
67 Jalan Sultan Ismail
Tel: 09-622 2655
Fax: 03-623 6895
Centrally located with 51 clean, decent-sized rooms arranged around a central airwell with koi pond that looks better at night; hot water. **$**
Ping Anchorage
77A Jalan Dato' Isaacs
Tel: 09-623 2141
Fax: 09-622 0851
www.pinganchorage.com.my
Central, small, clean backpackers' hostel with rooms and dormitories atop the town's best travel agency; sunny rooftop café and bar. **$**

Dungun
Tanjong Jara Resort
8th Mile off Jalan Dungun
Tel: 09-845 1100
Fax: 09-845 1200
www.tanjongjararesort.com
Award-winning traditional Malay all-timber resort located 13 km (8 miles) north of Dungun on a 17-hectare (42-acre) site. There are 100 beach cottages and sea-facing hotel rooms (great views from second floor rooms) with 1.5 km (1 mile) of private beach. Restaurants, two swimming pools, hot spa, library, "well-being" centre with stress-release programmes, massages. **$$$$**
Awana Kijal Golf & Beach Resort
Km 28, Jalan Kemaman-Dungun
Tel: 09-864 1188
Fax: 09-864 1688
www.awana.com.my
Only one word for this place; huge. There are 343 rooms, nine food and beverage outlets, a massive swimming pool and nine holes of golf fairways on either side. Cruise ships unload passengers here. **$$$**

Marang
Anguilla Beach House Resort
Kampung Tanjung Rhu
Tel/fax: 09-618 1322
Opposite beach with 34 clean chalets in 2 hectares (5 acres) of well-kept grounds facing Pulau Kapas. Garden shelters, set meals, laundry, boat service. **$$**
Kamal's
Kampung Tanjung Rhu
Tel: 09-618 2181
Facing the lagoon is the original backpackers' hostel and therefore entrenched as the place to stay; dormitories and chalets in a pleasant garden. **$**

Pulau Gemia
Gem Isles Resort
As there are no scheduled boats and the resort takes people booked on packages only, book through a travel agent such as Ping Anchorage, tel: 09-626 2020. The 52 air-conditioned chalets have views of the alcove and Pulau Kapas. Snorkelling, diving, non-motorised watersports, deep-sea

fishing and squid fishing (*candat sotong*) all available. Small turtle hatchery. **$$$**

Merang
Aryani Resort
Jalan Rhu Tapai-Merang
Tel: 09-653 2111
Fax: 09-653 1007
www.thearyani.com
Wonderful, and very exclusive heritage Terengganu house-suites by the same architect as the Floating Mosque; each house has a courtyard and an outside bath. **$$$$**

Sutra Beach Resort
Kampung Rhu Tapai, Setiu
Tel: 09-653 1111
Fax: 09-669 6410
www.sutrabeachresort.com
Traditional-style chalets gathered together in *kampung* clusters overlooking the islands; nice gardens. **$$**

Price Guide

Prices are for a standard double room during peak periods.
$$$$: more than RM400
$$$: RM200–400
$$: RM100–200
$: less than RM100

Pulau Redang
There are no scheduled boats to Redang, so resorts offer packages which include boat transfers from Marang jetty, accommodation, meals and snorkelling trips and gear. Dive packages are available. Pickups from airports can be arranged. Book with the resort or tour agency. Resorts listed are in Pasir Panjang unless stated otherwise.
Berjaya Redang Beach Resort
Tel: 09-697 3988
Fax: 09-697 3899
Toll-free: 1 800 88 8818
www.berjayaresorts.com.my
Luxury hotel in Teluk Dalam on stunning pure white beach with crystal clear turquoise waters. **$$$**
Coral Redang Island Resort
Tel: 09-623 6200, 09-692 0110
Fax: 09-623 6300/690 2112

www.coralredang.com.my
The nicest hotel on Pasir Panjang, with 40 chalets and standard rooms with air-conditioning and hot water, around swimming pool with bar. Local and continental dishes, dive shop. **$$$**
Redang Beach Resort
Tel: 09-623 8188
Tel: 03-2031 5079 (KL)
Fax: 09-623 0225,
Fax: 03-2026 2013 (KL)
www.redang.com.my
Rooms in two-storey wooden block, nice breakfasts, deck chairs, DIY batik, jungle-trekking, fishing and *candat sotong* (squid fishing), dive shop. **$$$**
Redang Kalong Resort
Tel: 09-622 1591
Fax: 09-622 8186
www.redangkalong.com
Beach-facing rooms in a longhouse with air-conditioning and hot showers also ensuite baths, but this beach is rather corally. Dive shop. **$$$**
Redang Reef Resort
Tel: 09-626 2020
Fax: 09-622 8093
Perched on rocks, this hotel has 24 air-conditioned rooms in a two-storey block with ensuite baths. Large wooden deck for dining overlooks the bay, also used for karaoke. Dive shop. **$$$**
Redang Pelangi Resort
Tel: 09-624 2158, 626 1189
Fax: 09-623 5202
www.redangpelangi.com
One of the better resorts, located at the centre of Pasir Panjang beach between Coral Redang and Ayu Mayang, Redang Pelangi offers air-conditioned twin (4 units) or quad sharing (37 units) rooms with attached bathrooms; dive shop. Activities include snorkeling, scuba diving, fishing, jungle-trekking, squid fishing and beach volleyball. **$$–$$$**

Pulau Lang Tengah
Square Point Resort
Tel: 09-623 5333
Fax: 09-623 9533
www.langisland.com.my
Peaceful and basic, this resort has 56 rooms in longhouses, all air-

conditioned and with ensuite baths; snorkelling, house reef good at high tide. Dive shop. **$$$**
Blue Coral Island Resort
Tel: 09-622 0851
Tel: 03-4257 8587 (KL)
Fax: 04-4257 4103 (KL)
www.aseaniaresortsgroup.com.my
Facing a lovely quiet beach are 55 rooms with air-conditioning and hot water. Also swimming pool, library, movies, karaoke and grocery shop. Fishing and diving tours and instruction available; house reef good for snorkelling. **$$**

Pulau Perhentian
Facilities notwithstanding, these islands have never outgrown their original backpacker mentality. The smaller outfits have no proper reception area or management as such, so do not be surprised to be faced by grumpy and/or ignorant staff. Water is also a problem during the dry months.
For online information and bookings, try these sites: **Ping Anchorage:** www.pinganchorage.com.my **Paradise Tropical Discovery:** paradise.com.my or **Anjung Holidays:** www.pulauperhentian.com.my

Perhentian Besar
Coral View Island Resort
Tel: 09-697 4943
Fax: 09-690 2600
The next upmarket resort to PIR, it has 71 pretty chalets on two beaches, though only the rockier one is good for swimming. Some chalets are air-conditioned. Breezy restaurant, dive operation pioneer. **$$$**
Perhentian Island Resort
Tel: 09-697 7562
Tel: 03-2144 8530 (KL)
Fax: 09-697 7199
www.perhentian-island-resort.com
The island's only three-star resort with 104 beautifully-furnished chalets and bungalows with ensuite bath and air-conditioning, some on the private beach. No problem with water. Excellent fresh grilled fish and dinner buffet, but food here is on the pricey side; dive shop, non-

Perhentian Besar on a Budget

Budget accommodation at Perhentian Besar is found south of Coral View. Among the established hostels is **Mama's Chalet & Restaurant** with basic chalets and a dive shop. The nearby **Watercolours Resort** (tel: 010-981 0930) also has a dive centre. There is more accommodation on Teluk Dalam, the southern beach over the headland – get off at the jetty at Ibi Chalet and walk around. Among

operations here are the pretty **Flora Bay**, tel: 09-697 7266, with chalets, some air-conditioned, money changing, 20 hours of electricity a day, dive shop. Other operators include **Coco Hut's A-frames**, tel: 011-972 085; **Rosli Chalets, Dormitories and Rooms**, tel: 09-691 0155; and **Samudra Beach Chalet** (tel: 010-984 2920). **Seahorse Divers** are beside the basic ABC Chalet.

motorised sea-sports, tennis and swimming pool, circular jungle trek behind the resort, tours. Cheaper rates from tour agencies. **$$$**

Perhentian Kecil
Bubu Long Beach
Tel: 03-2142 6688 (KL)
Fax: 03-2141 0080 (KL)
www.buburesort.com.my
Fancy resort that signals the upmarket direction in which this backpacker stretch is heading; 39 sea-fronting rooms with balconies, aircon and hot showers; restaurant with local and western cuisine; karaoke and dive centre; packages available. **$$$**

The rest of the island is backpacker haven, both at Teluk Aur and Pasir Panjang. Around the jetty at Teluk Aur where the best picture-postcard sunset scenes are, sit six chalet operators, including **Rajawali's** (tel: 010-980 5244) on the headland in the north, with A-frames and great views of the bay.

There are eight operators fronting the famous Pasir Panjang (Long Beach), where it all began. There is no jetty so you have to wade in, or small boats will charge to bring you in if you have not decided on a resort. The original **Pasir Panjang Chalet** (tel: 010-985 3589) has been upgraded to chalets with ensuite baths (11 chalets), some with air-conditioning; local food and nightly BBQ.
Mohsin Chalet
Tel/fax: 010-333 8897
Tel: 09-623 5915

e-mail: marhms@pc.jaring.my
Newer accommodation, set back from the beach with 30 hillside chalets with ensuite baths, great views from the restaurant which serves local and Western fare, use of telephones and Internet, friendly staff. **$**

The Perhentian Dive Centre and Turtle Bay Divers are at this beach. The snorkelling site of D'Lagoon in the northeast has some budget accommodation comprising of chalets, A-frames and dorm rooms.

KELANTAN
Kota Bharu
Diamond Puteri Hotel
Jalan Post Office Lama
Tel: 09-743 9988
Fax: 09-743 8388
New high-rise with great river views in centre of town. Ask for promotion package deals, includes dinner and breakfast. Great deals during Ramadan. Popular buffets at the riverview café. **$$$**
Renaissance Kota Bharu
Jalan Yahya Petra
Tel: 09-746 2233
Fax: 09-746 1122
The city's only international hotel is within reach of the State Museum, has 298 rooms and suites, business centre, pool, racquet games, Chinese restaurant. **$$$**
Juita Inn
Jalan Pintu Pong
Tel: 09-744 6888
Fax: 09-744 5777
e-mail: hotel@tm.net.my

Popular moderately priced small hotel with 70 rooms and good café in central location. **$$**
Perdana Resort
Pantai Cahaya Bulan
Tel: 09-774 4000
Fax: 09-774 4980
www.perdanaresort.com.my
Situated on the famous PCB Beach about a half-hour drive from Kota Bharu with chalets well spread out along the beach, great sunsets, decent Chinese and Western restaurants. **$$**

Budget accommodation in the form of dormitories and rooms is offered by: **City**, 2nd Floor, Jalan Pintu Pong; **Ideal Traveller's Guest House**, Jalan Padang Garong, tel: 09-744 2246 (52 rooms); **Rebana Hostel**, 1218, Jalan Sultanah Zainab (40 rooms).

Kuala Besut
Primula Besut Beach Resort
Tel: 09-697 1563
Very run-down hotel on the quiet beachfront with large rooms, swimming pool, restaurant and disinterested staff. **$**
Putra Inn
Tel: 09-695 6919, 019-981 2919
A 20-minute walk from the Kuala Besut jetty. New adaptation of lovely wooden handicraft centre that didn't take off; 10 air-conditioned rooms with *kampung* furnishings, ensuite bathrooms and hot water, free transport to jetty, friendly management.

EASTERN INTERIOR
Tasik Kenyir
Each resort is close to a waterfall and trek routes and is pretty much isolated from the others. Most are very basic floating chalets moored to the mainland, which means that if a group comes along and decides to make merry, there isn't much you can do about claiming back peace and quiet on the deck or in your room. Otherwise, the setting is truly tranquil. Meals are Chinese-style and buffet. Generators are usually switched on only at night.
Kenyir Lake Resort
Tel: 09-514 6002
Fax: 09-513 5687

Chalets with ensuite bathrooms and hot water in an upmarket setup, which is developing animal viewing hides. A free-form swimming pool is fed by continuously flowing natural springs; there is a fish farm for anglers and many activities. **$$$**

Kenyir Lakeview Resort
Tel: 09-666 8888
Tel: 03-2052 8441/2/3 (KL)
Fax: 09-666 8343
www.lakekenyir.com
A secluded retreat amid lush greenery for those who love the great outdoors. Stay in one of the 150 rustic timber chalets and enjoy fishing, nature walks, picnics beside waterfalls, and breathtaking views. The resort has a restaurant serving Western/Malaysian fare, and also a poolside restaurant. **$$$**

Lake Land Resort
Tel: 03-6273 2213 (KL)
Tel: 019-278 2939
Recently upgraded, this remote resort comprises 20 green-roofed chalets (4–6 people per chalet) on an island. There is basic accommodation on a floating deck, 24-hour electricity, satellite TV, karaoke, 3-hour trail to Ulu Terang. Camping is sometimes available. Two dining halls, ice and bar. **$$$**

Uncle John's Resort
Tel: 09-622 9564
Fax: 09-622 9596
e-mail: ujohnresort@yahoo.com
Small floating concern close to Lasir Waterfall, with lovely design of varnished split bamboo and open deck, 12 rooms, karaoke, videos, accessible from main dam jetty. **$$**

Tasik Cini

Kijang Mas Gumum Resort
Kampung Orang Asli Gumum
Tel: 09-422 1448
Basic lakeside chalet outfit run by the Aborigines Affairs Department, set within the modern village of Kampung Gumum and accessible by road and boat. There are 10 chalets and dormitories for 32; shared facilities, tours. **$**

Rimba Resort Tasik Cini
Tel: 09-477 8037
Fax: 09-477 8036
Rather run-down government-owned 13-year-old resort on the banks of a lake that is lotus-covered from June to September. Decent-sized chalets with balconies, some with air-conditioning; dormitories and campsite. Jungle-trekking (two guides) and boat trips by arrangement. Decent restaurant, karaoke, TV in lounge. Walkway leads to jetty of private boat operators. **$**

Price Guide

Prices are for a standard double room during peak periods.
$$$$: more than RM400
$$$: RM200–400
$$: RM100–200
$: less than RM100

Tasik Bera

Persona Lake Resort
Kompleks Pelancungan Tasik Bera
Tel/Fax: 09-276 2505
Set in the wilderness of oil palms, this simple lakeside resort has 50 rooms, dormitories for 40, and a campsite for 200, including eight riverine huts. Interesting Orang Asli homestay programme is among the numerous tours led by trained guides. **$$$**

TAMAN NEGARA

Kuala Tahan

Mutiara Taman Negara
Tel: 09-266 3500
Tel: 03-2145 1601 (KL)
Toll-free: 1800-88 3838
Fax: 09-266 1500
Fax: 03-2142 9822 (KL)
www.mutiarahotels.com
Fancy resort, somehow a little too civilised for a wild jungle reserve. Malaysian-styled wooden chalets with balconies, 110 rooms, dormitories, nice camping ground with limited equipment for hire, pricey restaurant and cafeteria, tours, guides, helpful information desk. There are 10 lodges upriver in Keniam and Terengganu respectively, not very well maintained and have a small restaurant. **$$**

Nusa Camp
Tel: 09-266 2369
Fax: 09-266 4369
e-mail: spkg@tm.net.my
Comprising 36 hectares (90 acres) of park buffer zone across the river; located upriver, with its own trails. Basic accommodation at 20 chalets and A-frames, dormitories for 40, and a camping ground (tents supplied). Restaurant with a great view of the river, and guided tours. **$**

Kampung Kuala Tahan

The tiny village opposite the Park Headquarters outside the park has been invaded by a host of budget accommodation, some with dubious sewerage facilities and management; the village is accessible by boat or by dirt road from Jerantut. Accommodations include: **Ekoton Chalet**, tel/fax: 09-266 9897, air-conditioned chalets and dormitories in pretty *kampung* set-up with laundry, safe deposit box; pioneer **Tembeling Lodge** overlooks the river, and has dormitories with bamboo walls that open at the top and useful mosquito nets, table and chair outside, lawn on which to hang out, complete with hammock; **Teresek Hill View**, tel: 09-266 3065, consisting of A-frames and basic chalets in a quiet location away from the river. **$**

Jerantut

Jerantut Rest House
Jalan Benta
Tel: 09-266 6200
Fax: 09-266 6200
This basic motel, which also has dormitories, sits 500 metres (550 yds) from the bus/taxi station, and operates free pick-ups within town. It also handles Taman Negara bookings. Food is available from 7am–11pm. **$**

Hotel Sri Emas Jerantut
Guest House
Bangunan MUIP, Jalan Besar
Tel: 09-266 4499/88/77
Fax: 09-266 4801
e-mail: tamannegara.8m.com
Doubles as pro-active travel agency offering nightly briefings on Taman Negara; agent for some resorts in the village. Dormitories and restaurant. Foreigner-only hotel. **$**

Kenong
Persona Rimba Resort
Kenong Rimba Park
Tel: 09-312 5032
Fax: 09-312 1421
Basic chalets on stilts among trees
accommodating 32 people.
Activities include jungle trekking,
mountain climbing, river activities,
cave exploration; guides available;
packages only. $$

SARAWAK

Kuching
Kuching abounds with
accommodation on all levels. We
have chosen the best – most have
been personally tried or
recommended by others.
Crowne Plaza Riverside Kuching
Jalan Tunku Abdul Rahman
Tel: 082-247 777
Fax: 082-425 858
e-mail: cprk@po.jaring.my
www.ichotelsgroup.com
Established hotel situated between
the Hilton and the Holiday Inn. $$$
Hilton Kuching Hotel
Jalan Tunku Abdul Rahman
Tel: 082-248 200
Fax: 082-428 984
www.hilton.com
The imposing white facade of
Kuching's best hotel looks out
across the Kuching River and
magnificent sunsets over the old
trading town. Facilities and service
are as good as expected. $$$
Hotel Grand Continental
Jalan Ban Hock
Tel: 082-230 399
Fax: 082-255 099
www.grandcontinental.com.my
Situated a little out of the old town
centre, popular with local
businessmen; good facilities. $$$
Holiday Inn Kuching
Jalan Tunku Abdul Rahman
Tel: 082-423 111
Fax: 082-426 169
Popular hotel that looks out over
the Kuching River. Good facilities.
$$$
Borneo Hotel
Jalan Tabuan
Tel: 082-244 122
Fax: 082-254 848

Kuching's oldest established hotel
with a friendly staff but small
rooms. $$
Harbour View Hotel
Lorong Temple
Tel: 082-274 666
Fax: 082-274 777
www.harbourview.com.my
New good value hotel in great
position overlooking the river and
Chinatown. Excellent buffet
breakfast included in room price. $$
Telang Usan Hotel
Jalan Ban Hock
Tel: 082-415 588, 425 316
Fax: 082-254 848
www.telangusan.com
A small, comfortable hotel with
traditional Kenyah décor and
informative staff. $$
Green Mountain Lodging House
Jalan Green Hill
Tel: 082-416 320
Fax: 082-246 342

Longhouse Resorts

Hilton Batang Ai Resort
Batang Ai Dam
Tel: 083-584 388
Fax: 083-584 399
www.hilton.com
A longhouse-styled resort with
standard Hilton facilities, 4½
hours from Kuching. It offers a
gentle introduction to longhouse
living. Close enough to real
longhouses for excursions. $$$
Regency Pelagus Resort
Rejang River
Tel: 084-799 050
Fax: 084-799 060
www.theregencyhotel.com.my/
pelagus
A resort situated just below the
treacherous Pelagus Rapids in
an untouched area of
longhouses. Offers river safaris
and nature excursions. $$$
Bukit Saban Resort
Paku River, Betong
Tel: 083-477 145
Fax: 083-477 103
www.sedctourism.com/hotel_
saban.html
About 4½ hours from Kuching with
excursions to local plantations,
longhouses and nature treks. $$

Popular with backpackers and
travellers, situated in a convenient
location. Rooms are air-conditioned
with hot water. $

Damai Beach
Holiday Inn Resort Damai Beach
Teluk Bandung Santubong
Tel: 082-846 999
Fax: 082-846 777
www.holidayinn-sarawak.com
Long-standing popular resort with
comfortable atmosphere. The
hilltop chalets overlook panoramas
of the sea and mountains; has a
scenic pool. $$$
Holiday Inn Resort Damai Lagoon
Teluk Penyu Santubong
Tel: 082-846 900
Fax: 082-846 901
www.holidayinn-sarawak.com
Big hotel blocks near the sea with
full range of watersports and
facilities. $$$
Santubong Kuching Resort
Tel: 082-846 888
Fax: 082-846 666
A smaller family-style resort with
watersports and activities. $$$
Damai Rainforest Resort
Pantai Damai Santubong
Tel: 082-846 490
An outdoor activity centre with log
cabins, tree houses, camping
facilities and a rainforest location.
$–$$

Lundu
Lundu Gading Hotel
Lundu Bazaar
Tel: 082-735 199
Fax: 082-735 299
Small hotel with air-conditioned
rooms and bathrooms – a fine base
to explore the Lundu area. $$

Sibu
Sibu is usually a stopover on the
way upriver, but most visitors stay
overnight and visit the colourful
morning market near the river.
Kingwood Hotel
12 Lorong Lanang 4
Tel: 084-335 888
Fax: 084-334 559
www.sarawak.com.my/kingwood
Sibu's biggest hotel complete with
plush granite tiles and views of the
Rejang River. $$$

Tanahmas Hotel
Jalan Kampung Nyabor
Tel: 084-333 188
Fax: 084-333 288
www.tanahmas.com.my
One of Sibu's best hotels, well run
and popular with local
businessmen; good restaurant. **$$$**
Hotel Capitol 88
19 Jalan Wong Nai Siong
Tel: 084-336 444
Fax: 084-311 706
Clean rooms and a 10-minute walk
from the expressboat jetty. Good for
early morning departures upriver.
$$

Kapit

The first upriver town, Kapit has an
array of accommodation, mostly
small hotels. This is the last chance
for pizza or ice cream.
Greenland Inn
463 Jalan Teo Chow Beng
Tel: 084-796 388
Fax: 084-796 708
A small hotel with comfortable
clean rooms and ensuite bathrooms
– especially welcome after a journey
upriver. **$$**
Ark Hill Inn
Jalan Penghulu Geridang
Tel: 085-796 168
Fax: 085-797 168
Small friendly hotel with clean,
reasonably-priced rooms. **$**

Belaga

This upriver bazaar town has a few
simple hotels.

Bee Lian Hotel
Belaga Bazaar
Tel: 085-461 416
Small hotel with air-conditioned
rooms of an adequate standard. **$**
Belaga Hotel
Tel: 086-461 244
A friendly hotel with restaurant
downstairs and some air-
conditioned rooms. **$**

Mukah

An idyllic little fishing community
with well-preserved fishing villages
on the way to Bintulu, about 2
hours from Sibu.
King Ing Hotel
Mukah River
Tel: 084-871 400
Located near the town's colourful
old bazaar and a Chinese temple.
For character and local flavour it is
the best place to stay. **$**
Lamin Dana
Kampung Tellian, Mukah
Tel/fax: 082-241 735
e-mail: info@lamindana.com
Has an excellent homestay
programme that enables guests to
experience authentic Melanau
culture. Located near the river, it is
the ideal base from which to take
part in the local festivals, the
biggest being *Pesta Kaul* in April. **$**
Pantai Harmonie Beach Resort
4km Jalan Mukah Oya
Tel: 084-872 566
Fax: 084-871 010
Pleasant resort by the beach with
some facilities. **$**

Homestays

Homestay in a Sarawak
longhouse or Orang Asli village
are popular options in the
rainforest. These are usually
"tourist-friendly", but if you are
lucky, your hospitable Malaysian
guide might just invite you home
for the real thing – however, be
especially mindful that this is
someone's home, and respect
local mores. Longhouse visits
are arranged though a tour
company, so it's worth asking
around first to find a suitably
interesting one.
    Sarawak Fishing Village
Homestays allows guests to stay
with Malay families fluent in
English, giving a taste of genuine
kampung life. For more
information, tel: 082-245 481;
fax: 082-256 871; e-mail:
gazul@tm.net.my

Bintulu

Mainly known for its fame as an oil
town, Bintulu is close to Similajau
National Park, the spectacular
caves of Niah National Park and
some decent beaches.
Bintulu Plaza Hotel
Jalan Abang Galau
Tel: 086-335 111
Fax: 086-332 742
Bintulu's best hotel with swimming
pool, nice restaurant with Western
food and good value rooms. **$$$**
Hoover Hotel
Jalan Keppel
Tel: 086-335 111
Fax: 086-332 742
A popular moderate hotel. **$$**
My House Inn
Jalan Taman Sri Dagong
Tel: 085-336 339
Fax: 085-332 050
Small, friendly hotel with clean
rooms and air-conditioning. **$**

Miri

This former oil town is becoming
increasingly green and pleasant, and
makes a fine base between visits to
Mulu, Niah and Loagan Bunut
national parks. Restaurants and
nightlife make it a good stopover.

Staying in Sarawak's National Parks

For accommodation in the national
parks, bookings can be made at
the Visitors Information Centre in
Kuching, or for Mulu and Niah, in
Miri. Prices for park chalets and
hostels vary between **$–$$**.
    On arrival at the park,
registration is required and the
payment of additional fees of a
nominal sum for entrance and for
cameras.
    Bookings for Bako, Kubah,
Gunung Gading national parks and
the Matang Wildlife Centre can all

be made at the Visitor's
Information Centre, Lot 31, Jalan
Masjid, Kuching, tel: 082-248
088; fax: 082-416 700.
    In Miri, bookings for Mulu, Niah,
Lambir Hills, Similajau and Loagan
Bunut national parks can be made
at the Visitor's Information Centre,
Lot 452, Jalan Melayu (close to
Miri Bus Station), tel: 085-434
184; fax: 085-434 179;
e-mail: stb@po.jaring.my
    For website, information, click
on www.forestry.sarawak.gov.my

Holiday Inn Miri
Jalan Temenggong Datuk Oyong
Lawai
Tel: 085-418 888
Fax: 085-419 999
www.holidayinn-sarawak.com
Well-run Holiday Inn with excellent
food; by the sea. **$$$**

Mega Hotel
Lot 907, Jalan Merball
Tel: 085-432 432
Fax: 085-433 433
e-mail: info@megahotel.net
www.megahotel.net/
New hotel with good facilities. **$$$**

Miri Marriot Resort & Spa
Jalan Temenggong Datuk Oyong
Lawai
Tel: 085-421 121
Fax: 085-421 099
www.rihgamiri.com
Comfortable and popular, with good
facilities and a large swimming pool
next to the sea. **$$$**

Brooke Inn
Jalan Brooke
Tel: 085-412 881
Fax: 085-420 899
This is a good location for budget
travellers, close to the bus station
and visitor information; friendly
staff. **$**

Marudi
This little trading town is worth at
least a night's stopover and a visit
to the morning market. It's also a
good place to arrange upriver trips.

Grand Hotel
Lot 350 Backlane, Marudi
Tel: 085-755 711/755 712
Fax: 085-755 293
A good hotel with some air-
conditioned rooms, close to the
boat jetty. Useful source of
information for upriver journeys.
$–$$

Mulu
Royal Mulu Lodge
Mulu National Park
Tel: 085-790 100
Fax: 085-790 101
www.royalmuluresort.com
Comfortable, with friendly staff and
close to all the rainforest
attractions; by the river. The hotel
can arrange trips and sporting
activities. **$$$**

Ba Kelalan
Apple Lodge
Tel: 085-285 385
This little lodging house near the
airport is clean and simple,
providing adequate and friendly
accommodation. **$**

Bario
This highland valley is close to
many longhouses and has the
perfect climate for trekking.

Tarawe's Lodge
This small lodge, close to the
airport and main bazaar, provides
friendly service and big older-style
rooms. No phone or fax and only
accessible by plane or on foot. **$**

Price Guide

Prices are for a standard double
room during peak periods.
$$$$: more than RM400
$$$: RM200–400
$$: RM100–200
$: less than RM100

SABAH

Kota Kinabalu
Kota Kinabalu (KK) is burgeoning
with big new hotels, catering to the
high end of the tourist market.
Action-adventure and packaged
nature tours are Sabah's big draw,
as well as the already well known
Mount Kinabalu.

Hyatt Regency Kinabalu
Jalan Datuk Saleh Sulong
Tel: 088-221 234
Fax: 088-225 972
www.kinabalu.regency.hyatt.com
This is a long-established, always
pleasing hotel. Rooms enjoy
magnificent sunset views over the
waterfront and out to the nearby
islands. **$$$**

Shangri-La's Tanjung Aru Resort
Tanjung Aru
Tel: 088-225 800
Fax: 088-217 155
www.shangri-la.com
A very popular and well regarded
resort that has grown in popularity
and size over the last 10 years.
$$$

Sutera Harbour Resort
Tel: 088-318 888
Fax: 088-317 777 (Pacific Sutera)
Fax: 088-312 020 (Magellan
Sutera)
www.suteraharbour.com
Comprising two hotels called the
Pacific Sutera and Magellan Sutera
respectively, this sprawling resort
sits on 384 acres (156 ha) of
reclaimed grounds overlooking a
bay of islands, five minutes from
downtown Kota Kinabalu. With
excellent Mandara Spa, pool, tennis
courts, signing facilities at adjacent
golf and yacht club, and access to
over a dozen restaurants. **$$$**

The Jesselton Hotel
Gaya Street
Tel: 088-223 333
Fax: 088-241 401
www.jesseltonhotel.com
A delighfully restored nostalgic hotel
offering gracious service and good
Western food in a formal dining
room, as well as an informal
coffeeshop. **$$$**

**Backpacker Lodge ("Lucy's
Homestay")**
Lorong Dewan, Australia Place
Tel: 088-261 495
Fax: 088-261 495
A basic backpackers' lodge with
dormitories, in a convenient
location in the city, close to
everything you need before heading
into the interior. **$**

Berjaya Palace Hotel
Jalan Tanki Karamunsing
Tel: 088-211 911
Fax: 088-211 600
www.berjayaresorts.com.my
Located in a quiet part of town,
a short taxi ride away from the
centre. **$**

City Inn
Jalan Pantai
Tel: 088-218 933
Fax: 088-218 937
A popular small hotel, which is
often full; good value. **$**

Kinabalu Pine Resort
Kundasang
Tel: 088-889 388
Fax: 088-889 288
e-mail: k_pine2002@yahoo.com.sg
The most attractive accommodation
outside the park, with chalets facing
Mt Kinabalu. **$**

Kinabalu Park

Accommodation in the park has been privatised, making it necessary to book through Kinabalu Nature Resorts, Lot G15, Ground Floor, Wisma Sabah, tel: 088-243 629, fax: 088-259 552, e-mail: info@kinabalunatureresorts.com, www.kinabalunatureresorts.com.

Within Kinabalu Park, the company manages a variety of lodges and chalets with prices ranging from $$–$$$. Large dormitories with shared kitchen facilities also have budget-priced rooms.

Laban Rata Resthouse can also be booked through Kinabalu Nature Resorts, with prices in the $ range. The company also arranges porter hire and climbing permits. Slightly higher up are the **Waras Hut** and **Gunting Lagadan Hostel** with very basic facilities $. **Poring Hot Springs** has accommodation; prices from $–$$$.

Located just outside the park limits, the **Mesilau Nature Resort** has chalets and lodges with prices ranging from $–$$$.

Rina Ria Lodge
Mile 36, Ranau Road
Tel: 088-889 282
Within walking distance of the park entrance, this hotel is very convenient when the park is full. Hostel and more luxurious accommodation available. $–$$$

Kundasang

Some 5km (3 miles) from Kinabalu National Park, Kundasang is the location for a rash of new hotels and chalets for park visitors.

Perkasa Hotel Mt Kinabalu
Kundasang
Tel: 088-889 511
Fax: 088-889 101
e-mail: phmk@tm.net.my
www.perkasahotel.com.my
The rooms enjoy great views of Mt Kinabalu. Good facilities including tennis and shops. The hotel is also a handy 20-minute drive from Mt Kinabalu Golf Course. $–$$$

Town Inn
Jalan Pantai
Tel: 088-225 823
Fax: 088-217 762
Convenient location, clean with good facilities and good value. $

Pantai Dalit

Pantai Dalit is a 40-minute drive from Kota Kinabalu. A pristine beach area backed by rainforested hills.

Shangri-La's Rasa Ria Resort
Pantai Dalit, Tuaran
Tel: 088-792 888
Fax: 088-792 777/792 000
www.shangri-la.com
A luxurious modern holiday resort with golf course, spa and nature reserve. Activities include crabbing and fishing as well as the more traditional watersports and beach activities. $$$–$

Karambunai

Nexus Golf Resort Karambunai
Menggatal
Tel: 088-411 222/411 030
Fax: 088-411 020/412 028
www.borneo-resort.com
This luxurious resort is about 30 minutes from Kota Kinabalu by road. Situated on a pristine beach with adjacent golf course.

Tunku Abdul Rahman Park

These offshore islands facing Kota Kinabalu have attractive chalet accommodation on Pulau Manukan, with one restaurant serving continental and Asian dishes. Prices are in the $–$$ category.

For bookings, contact Sutera Sanctuary Lodges, Lot G15, ground floor, Wisma Sabah, tel: 088-243 629, fax: 088-259 552, e-mail: info@suterasanctuarylodges.com, www.suterasanctuarylodges.com.

Gaya Island has a privately-run resort and some snorkelling and diving.

Gayana Resort
Pulau Gaya
Tel: 088-264 461
Fax: 088-264 460
e-mail: gayana@tm.net.my
A water resort with stilted chalets built over the sea, backed by rainforest. Watersports facilities and jungle walks. $$$

Tenom

A highland town in the centre of Murut country. It is close to the Agricultural Research Station and the new Sabah Agricultural Park with a magnificent orchid park.

Asrama
Agricultural Research Station
Tel: 087-737 952
Fax: 087-737 571
Dormitory accommodation is available with the Sabah Agricultural Park, near an attractive lake. $

Perkasa Hotel Tenom
Tel: 087-735 811/736 166
Fax: 087-736 134
Overlooking Tenom town, on top of a hill, the seven-storey hotel has full facilities and great views. You can call to be picked up from the railway station and staff are eager to help with local knowledge. $

Labuan

This tax haven island has a well-kept war cemetery.

Hotel Sheraton Labuan
Jalan Merdeka
Tel: 087-422 000
Fax: 087-422 222
e-mail: slabuan@tm.net.my
www.sheraton.com/labuan
Situated opposite the financial park, the Sheraton offers the best in service and cuisine. $$$

Hotel Global
Jalan OKK Aawang Besar
Tel: 087-425 201
Fax: 087-425 180
A new hotel with good facilities; good value. $$

Layang Layang Island Resort
Pulau Layang Layang
Tel: 03-2162 2877
Fax: 03-2162 2980
www.layanglayang.com
Luxury resort on coral atoll 300 kms from Kota Kinabalu. Offers comfortable rooms, swimming pool, and fully serviced PADI dive centre.

Sandakan

Sandakan is the base for visitors embarking on tours to east Sabah. Many people choose to stay outside the town itself, at Sepilok, where it is quieter and probably safer.

Sabah Hotel
Jalan Utara Km 1
Tel: 089-213 299
Fax: 089-271 271
e-mail: shsdkfm@tm.net.my
This one-time colonial governor's house has been rebuilt and upgraded so that the old architecture has all but disappeared. Located slightly out of town in a pleasant hilly location. **$$$**

Hotel Sandakan
4th Avenue
Tel: 089-221 122
Fax: 089-221 100
e-mail: tengis@tm.net.my
www.hotelsandakan.com.my
The newest hotel in town. Conveniently located and with a good range of restaurants. **$$**

Pulau Lankayan

Pulau Lankayan is located north of Sandakan, past the Turtle Islands. The remote coral island has one luxurious dive resort making it a unique hideaway.

Lankayan Island Dive Resort
Langkayan Island
Tel: 089-765 200
Fax: 089-763 575/763 563
e-mail: psrt@po.jaring.my

The Turtle Islands

Located north of Sandakan, the Turtle Islands have egg-laying turtles arriving almost every day of the year. Chalets to accommodate 20 guests are available on the island. **$**

The management of chalets, accommodating up to 20, and the restaurant on Pulau Selingan has been privatised and is managed by **Crystal Quest Sdh Bhd**, tel: 089-212 711, 230 777, fax: 089-212 712, e-mail: cquest@tm.net.my. Tour operators offer package tours to Turtle Islands Park; alternatively, book directly through Crystal Quest. A speedboat departs from the Sabah Parks Jetty on Jalan Buli Sim Sim, Sandakan for Selingan at 9.30am daily, and leaves the island for Sandakan at 7am daily.

www.lankayan-island.com
A luxurious resort on its own coral island in the Sulu Seas north of Sandakan. Good wreck dives and corals nearby. Dives conducted by divers from the resort's dive centre.

Sepilok

This orang-utan rehabilitation centre, located in the jungle, has several standards of accommodation nearby.

Sepilok Nature Resort
2.5km (1½ miles) Sepilok Road
Tel: 089-535 001
Fax: 089-535 002
www.sepilok.com
An upmarket resort adjacent to the orang-utan centre, in a garden setting. It has timber air-conditioned chalets with private verandahs overlooking the gardens. **$$$**

Sepilok Jungle Resort
Sepilok Road
Tel: 089-533 031
Fax: 089-533 029
e-mail: sepilokgr@yahoo.com
The lodge is the handiwork of owners John and Judy Lim. It offers a range of accommodation, from campsites to air-conditioned chalets, set amid beautifully landscaped gardens filled with native birds and butterflies. **$–$$**

Sepilok Resthouse
Jalan Sepilok
Tel: 089-533 031
A small, attractive lodge just by the entrance of the Rehabilitation Centre. **$**

Kinabatangan River

The major concentration of wildlife lodges along the Kinabatangan is near the village of Sukau, although a number of tour operators are now establishing lodges at Kampung Bilit, with a forest lodge further upriver at Danau Girang. All tour operators are able to offer package tours including transport, tours, accommodation and food.

Sukau

Sukau Rainforest Lodge
Tel: 088-234 009
Fax: 088-233 688
e-mail: info@borneoecotours.com
www.borneoecotours.com

Price Guide

Prices are for a standard double room during peak periods.
$$$$: more than RM400
$$$: RM200–400
$$: RM100–200
$: less than RM100

A comfortable lodge operated by Borneo Eco Tours; elephants sometimes seen nearby. **$$$**

Sukau River Lodge
Tel: 088-246 000
Fax: 088-231 758
e-mail: leegn@pc.jaring.my
wildlife-expeditions.com
The pioneer in the Sukau region, Wildlife Expeditions now offers 2 riverside lodges here. **$$**

Sukau Tomanggong Riverside Lodge
Tel: 089-534 900, 534 300, 013-856 0969
Fax: 089-534 900
e-mail: cpu@tm.net.my
Just downriver from Sukau in a beautiful location facing a limestone outcrop, with a riverside restaurant and simple twin rooms. **$$**

Bilit

Bilit Adventure Lodge
Tel: 089-533 031, 533 041, 533 051
Fax: 089-533 029
e-mail: sepilokjr@yahoo.com
A converted riverside house with 9 rooms accommodating 18 guests, operated by Sepilok Jungle Resort. **$$**

Danau Girang

Uncle Tan's Jungle Camp
Tel: 089-531 639
e-mail: eugene@uncletan.com
www.uncletan.com
Basic accommodation, good food and a friendly atmosphere make this lake-side lodge set in the forest very popular with serious wildlife enthusiasts and budget travellers. **$**

Lahad Datu

The gateway to Danum Valley, Lahad Datu has an airport with daily flights to Kota Kinabalu. A good road connects it to Sandakan and Tawau and Semporna to the south.

Silam Lodge
10km Lahad Datu/Tawau Road
Tel: 088-243 245
Fax: 088-254 227
Managed by Borneo Nature Tours, the lodge was built by an American timber company and offers a good alternative for those who want to make day visits to the Danum Valley. **$$**

Executive Hotel
Jalan Teratai
Tel: 089-881 333
Fax: 089-881 777
This hotel is nothing special, but it is fine for an overnight stop in Lahad Datu. **$**

Danum Valley

Sabah's Danum Valley, 483 sq. km (186 sq. miles) of pristine rainforest, has a sole upmarket resort to accommodate visitors. There is a field study centre available only to serious bona fide researchers. The rainforest is teeming with wildlife, although it can be difficult to see it; you'll need plenty of time and patience.

Borneo Rainforest Lodge
Danum Valley
Tel: 089-880 206/7
Fax: 089-885 051
e-mail: ijl@po.jaring.my
www.borneorainforestlodge.com
Inspired by Tiger Tops in Nepal, this pleasing nature resort is located beside the Segama River facing a misty and untrammelled jungle. Built on elevated plank-walks, the chalets are comfortable with good facilities. Guides and talks are available for visitors. **$$$**

Tawau

Marco Polo Hotel
Jalan Clinic
Tel: 089-777 988
Fax: 089-763 739
e-mail: bmph@tm.net.my
Popular with tourists as well as businessmen, it is the best hotel in town and has a good bar. **$$**

Pan Sabah Hotel
Jalan Stephen Tan
Tel: 089-762 488
Fax: 089-763 878
Good value, and a convenient location close to the bus station. **$**

Semporna

The gateway to Pulau Sipadan and the other offshore islands, Semporna is a fine overnight stopover.

Dragon Inn
Semporna Tourist Jetty
Tel: 089-781 088
Fax: 089-781 088
This stilted hotel over the sea has a great location and adequate facilities, including a seafood restaurant. **$**

Pulau Sipadan

All accommodation this world-class dive site was closed by the government in December 2004 in order to protect the environment. Most dive operators previously based on Sipadan now have accommodation on the nearby islands of Mabul and Kapalai, and organise day trips to Sipadan.

Price Guide

Prices are for a standard double room during peak periods.
$$$$: more than RM400
$$$: RM200–400
$$: RM100–200
$: less than RM100

Pulau Kapalai

Kapalai Dive Resort
Kapalai Island
Tel: 089-782 322/765 200
Fax: 089-763 575/763 653
www.sipadan-kapalai.com
An upmarket stilt village built over a reef with comfortable rooms and verandahs looking towards a distant horizon of sea and sky, 15–20 minutes from Pulau Sipadan.

Pulau Mabul

This small flat island, about 20 minutes from Sipadan, has a very basic fishing village. It is now packed with resorts, some of which transferred here when all Sipadan accommodation was closed. Rates differ for divers and non-divers, and vary depending upon whether air transport – from Kota Kinabalu to Tawau – is included.

Borneo Divers Mabul Resort
Tel: 088-222 226
Fax: 088-221 550
e-mail:
reservations@borneodivers.info
www.borneodivers.info
The pioneer operator on Sipadan now has 30 chalets on Mabul, not far from the upmarket Sipadan Water Village Resort.

Sipadan Mabul Resort
Mabul Island
Tel: 088-230 006/7
www.sipadan-mabul.com.my
Located on the island itself, the resort consists of beach chalets that look across to Pulau Sipadan.

Sipadan Water Village Resort
Mabul Island
Tel: 088-221 221
Fax: 088-219 233
e-mail: swv@sipadan-village.com.my
www.sipadan-village.com.my
A stylish water village built on stilts which reaches out over shallow reefs from the main island. Comfortable and quiet with few distractions and a good restaurant and dive shop.

Where to Eat

All of Malaysia's medium-class hotels have decent eateries, the higher-class ones have good restaurants, while hotels at the very top of the range will probably have at least one Western outlet – but these are not listed here unless they are outstanding.

Hotels also usually offer high-tea at the weekend, and their coffee houses would have the usual buffet breakfast, lunch and sometimes dinner, to cater to value-for-money demand. Western fast food chains such as McDonald's, KFC and A&W are everywhere for those who cannot possibly stomach another scorcher of a curry, as are coffee-house chains like Coffee Bean, Starbucks and Gloria Jeans. There are also fairly decent burger stalls, run by Malay boys.

Otherwise, try the local fare, which are not only different according to where you are, but subdivide into regional varieties, too. The best often comes as hawker food, sold at street stalls or in coffeeshops; sometimes you can get authentic preparations in restaurants, but you miss out on the atmosphere of the roadside stalls. Restaurants charge a 10 percent government tax and 5 percent service tax.

Breakfast is served from about 6am, lunch 11.30am–2.30pm, and dinner 6.30–11pm, although some places open until 2am; supper joints close at 3.30–4am.

Restaurant Listing

Restaurants are listed in the same order as they appear in the Places section, but focus on the main tourist destinations. The restaurants are in alphabetical order within price categories, with hawker food at the bottom.

KUALA LUMPUR & ENVIRONS

Kuala Lumpur
Malay
Bijan
3 Jalan Ceylon
Tel: 03-2031 3575
Authentic home style cuisine in a cosy setting decorate with Malay antiques, contemporary paintings and heritage textiles. **$$**
Restoran Seri Melayu
1 Jalan Conlay
Tel: 03-2145 1833
A tourist-targeted outfit complete with Minangkabau roof and nightly cultural performances, but the food is decent; buffet available. **$$**
The Gulai House
Carcosa Seri Negara
Tel: 03-2282 1888
Malay specialities, including satay and spicy curries in colonial setting. **$$**

Hawker Food
The best Malay fare is in Kampung Bahru, from satay to rice porridge, curries and soups, and a chance to sample the cooking styles of the different states. Head towards the stalls at Jalan Raja Mahadi. You'll find good *nasi lemak* at the Benteng stalls by the Klang River in Masjid India, particularly Nasi Lemak Benteng Utama; these stalls are, however, open only at night. **$**

Nyonya
Kapitan's Club
Jalan Ampang
(opposite Standard Chartered)
Tel: 03-2101 0242
A charming restored shophouse with antique furnishing and good Nonya house specials such as the curried Kapitan Chicken. **$$**
Old China Café
11 Jalan Balai Polis
Tel: 03-232 5915
Best time-trip café in KL, where the historical ambiance, old photos and memorabilia and marble-topped tables provide the perfect location

for just as memorable *nyonya* cuisine. Specialities include *laksa* (noodles in spicy gravy) and fish head in tamarind sauce. Try the delicious sago dessert called *gula melaka*. **$$**

Price Guide

These are the prices of meals for two people, including drinks, but excluding alcohol such as wine, which is expensive.
$$$$: more than RM200.
$$$: RM100–200.
$$: RM50–100.
$: less than RM50.

Chinese
Hakka Restaurant
6, Jalan Kia Peng
Tel: 03-2143 1906
Serves superb Chinese Hakka food. **$$**
Lee Wong Kee
239 Jalan Tunku Abdul Rahman
Tel: 03-2692 6285
Chinese specialities such as fried sharksfin with salad leaf appetiser and lemon chicken. **$$**
Spring Court
Melia Kuala Lumpur, Jalan Imbi
Tel: 03-2142 9881
Cantonese and Szechuan specialities, with *dim sum* served both for breakfast and lunch. **$$**
Xin Cuisine Concorde Hotel
Jalan Sultan Ismail
Tel: 03-2144 2200
Cantonese specialities such as spare ribs, shark's fin soup,and abalone concoctions. **$$**
Esquire Kitchen
Level 1 Sungei Wang Plaza
Jalan Bukit Bintang
Tel: 03-2148 4506
A variety of Chinese delicacies; well known for its *woh tieh* or fried dumplings. **$**
Soo Kee Mee Stall
14 Medan Imbi, off Jalan Imbi
Tel: 03-2148 1234
Simple Chinese restaurant that has been here for over 50 years. Serves excellent beef *kway teow* (flat rice noodles), *sang har yee mee* (prawn crispy noodles), fried Hong Kong *kailan* (leafy vegetables) and various Cantonese dishes. **$**

Hawker Food

All sorts of Chinese fare can be found from morning until the wee hours in Chinatown, while the night stalls are on Jalan Alor, and behind Jalan Imbi (especially for *bah kut teh* pork rib soup). **$**

Indian
Bombay Palace
388 Jalan Tun Razak
Tel: 03-2145 4241/7220
Fine Indian food in a beautiful setting; with large variety of spicy and non-spicy meat and vegetable dishes, including North Indian breads. **$$$**

Passage Thru India
235 Jalan Tun Razak
Tel: 03-2145 0366
Cosy interior decorated with Indian collectibles. Best for Tandoori prawns, chicken tikka, naan breads and delicious creamy lassi. Live traditional music played in the evening. **$$$**

The Taj
Crown Princess Hotel
Jalan Tun Razak
Tel: 03-2162 5522
Award-winning restaurant with an excellent menu, including vindaloo, tandoori and Goanese dishes in an authentic Indian setting and often with live music. **$$$**

Hawker Food

The *teh tarik* tea stall with *roti canai* bread and *dhall* (lentils) curry is literally round every corner, and a stall somewhere is bound to be open no matter the time. There are bigger shops which also sell rice accompanied by an array of spicy curries on banana leaves behind Istana Hotel, on Jalan Tunku Abdul Rahman, Masjid India and Brickfields. **$**

Local/Fusion
Shook
Basement of Starhill shopping mall
Bukit Bintang

Fruits of the Land

Though seasonal, there is fruit all year round, cheapest and freshest at a *pasar tani* (farmer's market), *pasar malam* (night market), or rural roadside stalls. Malaysian fruit also features in local *kuih* (cakes) and desserts.

Durian, the football-sized "king of the fruits", emanates a distinct smell that evokes either love or disgust. Passionate Malaysians will travel miles for the best and spend a week's salary on one fruit. Although available all year round, the prime season is June to August. A spiked green casing encompasses a sweet, creamy yellow flesh.

Mangosteens are a traditional accompaniment to the durian, as they are believed to "neutralise" the potent, "heaty" properties of the latter. The size of a small orange, the mangosteen's thick, dark purple skin is squeezed open to reveal five to eight snowy-white segments. The flesh is both astringent and sweet, but mind the rind's staining purple juice.

Rambutan is an egg-shaped red fruit covered in dark thin hair and grows in bunches. A relative of the lychee, the rambutan's translucent white flesh, hugging a flat seed, is extremely succulent and sugary sweet. Open the rambutan by inserting a thumbnail into the thin rind. Rambutans are also canned.

Pomelos are a large sweet grapefruit that the Chinese consider auspicious because it resembles an orange (*kum* meaning "gold"). Beneath the green rind and a thick layer of spongey pith, are the large segments which are gently prised apart. Perak has indisputedly the sweetest and juiciest pomelos in Malaysia.

Starfruit is pale yellow fruit with a waxy edible skin covering a translucent watery flesh. Eaten raw, or juiced for an acidic, slightly sweet thirst-quencher.

Jackfruit (*nangka*) is a large fruit that grows all year round. It is often seen on trees covered with sacks or plastic bags to keep away birds and insects. Averaging 50 by 25 cm (18 by 9 in), its thick rind is bumpy and greenish yellow. Inside are 20–30 oval seeds encased by thick sweet and fragrant flesh, with a firm, plasticky texture. A relative is the **chempedak**, which is smaller, with sweeter, creamier-textured and stronger-smelling flesh. Battered and deep-fried, they make a delicious snack.

Ciku (pronounced "chickoo") looks like a hairless kiwi fruit. Its light brown flesh is unmistakably sweet and smooth, with a pear-like, gritty texture. Flat, black seeds are found in the centre of each fruit.

Guava (*jambu*) comes in two varieties: a smaller, softer pink, or larger, harder white with an edible green casing. Generally, the former are sweeter and juicier, while the latter are crisp and milder-tasting. Locals eat the fruit with various condiments such as a sweet-sour plum powder.

Duku is about the size of a golf ball, and is available from August to September. Its leathery light-brown rind is peeled off to reach the small segments of transparent tangy-sweet flesh around a hard small green seed. **Langsat** is a relative, but with a much thinner, lighter-coloured skin. Also available is *duku langsat*, a hybrid.

Buah susu, literally "milk fruit"; this passion fruit comes in many delicious varieties: crisp-skinned orange from Indonesia, purple from Australia and California, and local ones with soft, velvety yellow skins. The translucent seeds are sweet and juicy.

Custard apples are not apples at all. About the size of a fist, the knobby green skin encloses black seeds wrapped by delicate sweet flesh, which is custardy smooth and fragrant.

Mangoes come in different varieties in Malaysia: small, hard and fragrant jungle types, eaten with salt or a spicy soy sauce dip; sweet, bright orange varieties dripping with juice; and pale yellow, milder-tasting ones of Thai origin.

Tel: 03-2716 8535
Part of the JW Marriott Hotel, this chic inclusion into KL's eating scene has 4 kitchens: Chinese, Japanese, Italian and Grills. It's spacious and contemporary and you can choose food from all the kitchens. **$$$**

The Mango Tree
4 Lorong Maarof, Bangsar Utama
Tel: 03-2284 6268
Pioneer of contemporary cuisine in KL. Try the scamorza cheese on pitta bread, or squid-ink pasta with prawns. **$$$**

Be Be's
Hotel Capitol, Jalan Bukit Bintang
Tel: 03-2143 7000
Affordable East-West meals in a lovely contemporary setting; good selection of wines and beer. **$$**

Sakura
Jalan Imbi
Tel: 03-2142 2319
Hawker fare in a restaurant setting, although the air-conditioning is at sub-zero temperatures. Good *nasi lemak* (coconut rice), *laksa* (noodles in spicy gravy) and desserts; also steak and other Western fare. There are hawker stalls round the corner and a famous beef noodle eatery down the road. **$$**

Telawi Street Bistro
1 Jalan Telawi 3 Bangsar
Tel: 03-2284 3168
In the heart of Bangsar's famous nightlife and restaurant hub, this restaurant serves a wide array of international dishes based on a pan-global concept rather than fusion. Among the dishes served are the usual local favourites, Thai, Japanese, Italian and fine French fare. Very modern, minimalist setting with good ambience. **$$**

Top Hat
7 Jalan Kia Peng
Tel: 03-2142 8611
A gorgeous old bungalow behind the nightspots, with excellent Malay, Peranakan and Western fusion fare such as the Nyonya *pie tee* pastry, chicken and mushroom pie, and grilled rack of lamb. Set meals are good; book ahead. **$$**

Other Asian

Benkay Japanese Restaurant
Nikko Hotel, 165 Jalan Ampang

Tel: 03-2161 1111
Very elegant and authentic Japanese restaurant where the food style follows the decor. The Sushi Bar is especially popular for lunch where the chefs can be seen in action. A great dessert is the green tea ice cream. **$$$**

Rama V
5 Jalan U Thant
Tel: 03-2143 2663
Elegant Thai restaurant in the embassy area is a welcome oasis of lotus-filled ponds. Salads are wonderful, particularly the spicy catfish salad and the mango salad with glass noodles. **$$$**

Tamarind Springs
Jalan 1, Taman Tun Abdul Razak Ampang Jaya
Tel: 03-4256 9300
Like its sister restaurant, Tamarind Hill, this outlet specialises in Indochinese Cuisine – Thai, Laotian, Cambodian and Vietnamese. **$$$**

Price Guide

These are the prices of meals for two people, including drinks, but excluding alcohol such as wine, which is expensive.
$$$$: more than RM200.
$$$: RM100–200.
$$: RM50–100.
$: less than RM50.

Western

Mahsuri
Carcosa Seri Negara, Taman Tasik Perdana, Persiaran Mahameru
Tel: 03-2282 1888
Elegant dining in the main restaurant of this exclusive colonial-style hotel, or a wonderful English-style afternoon tea served on the verandah of the adjacent mansion. **$$$**

Ciao
428 Jalan Tun Razak
Tel: 03-9285 4827
Authentic Italian pasta and pizza in a candlelit bungalow; has some good wines. **$$$**

Lafite
Shangri-La Hotel, Jalan Sultan Ismail
Tel: 03-2074 3900
Fine French fare in contemporary setting. **$$$$**

Marche Mediterranean Restaurant
Rennaisance Kuala Lumpur
Jalan Sultan Ismail/Jalan Ampang
Tel: 03-2162 2233
Buffet of antipasti, *mezze* and tapas, breads and salads; interesting bar and open-grill and wood-oven kitchen; wines. **$$$**

Scalini's
19 Jalan Sultan Ismail
Tel: 03-2145 3211
Where celebrities eat when in KL. Long-time excellent Italian restaurant where the food is authentic and served with style. The antipasto is memorable as is the beef carpaccio sprinkled with truffles. One of KL's best wine lists. **$$$**

Cilantro
Micasa Hotel Apartments
368B Jalan Tun Razak
Tel: 03-2179 8000
Classy establishment serving excellent food and wines. The place to go for fine dining when you want to impress someone. **$$$**

Coliseum Café
98 Jalan Tunku Abdul Rahman
Tel: 03-2692 6270
Lamb and beef steaks with fries in a colonial setting so real it is easy to imagine bushy-moustached white planters at the bar complaining about the heat. **$$**

T.G.I. Friday's
Life Centre, Jalan Sultan Ismail
Tel: 03-2163 7761
Good Western dishes in large portions with an array of alcoholic and non-alcoholic drinks; American paraphernalia on the walls; good music and friendly waiters. **$$**

NORTHWESTERN PENINSULA

Cameron Highlands

The Smokehouse Hotel
Tanah Rata
Tel: 05-491 1215
Delectable cream teas, lunch and afternoon teas on the terrace, which on a fine day offers a peaceful view of the hills. Fine dining of English fare including steaks, pies, seafood; light meals all day long in the conservatory.
$$$$

Bala's Holiday Chalet
Lot 55 Tanah Rata
Tel: 05-491 1660
Old English cottage restaurant, well-known for its homestyle cooking, especially its Indian curries; Western fare also available. **$$**

Fern Restaurant
Rosa Passadena Hotel, Brinchang
Tel: 05-491 2288
Decent Western meals, including steaks and chops, but at KL prices. Chinese meals, steamboat at lunch and dinner; high tea. **$$**

Kafe Palm Leaf
Brinchang
In front of Rosa Pasadena, dishes up good Thai, Western and local dishes at reasonable prices. **$**

Tanah Rata's famous Indian fare outlets sit in a row opposite the bus station. Try **Suria's** banana leaf rice and Indian breads. Opposite are Malay hawker stalls. Western set lunches are at **Café Downtown** and the **Highlander's Grill. Brinchang's** hawker fare is found at the bus terminal and Food Court, and there are stalls throughout town selling Indian breads and curry. Good Chinese at **Kowloon Hotel** and Indian fare at **Shal's Curry House. $**

Frasers Hill
The Smokehouse Hotel
Jalan Jeriau
Tel: 03-362 2226
Excellent high-tea of scones or apple pie on the garden patio or in the cosy tea room. English meals by candlelight in a beautiful dining room. **$$$$**

Hawker Food
Cheap and tasty hawker food, including a *nasi lemak* (coconut rice) breakfast to fill you up before trekking, is available at Malay stalls next to the mosque. There are also small outlets in the shopping centre by the clock tower. **$**

Ipoh
FMS Bar
Jalan Sultan Yusof
Tel: 05-254 0591
This rather worn-down colonial gem by the Padang serves Western-style meals; its bar has hardly changed

Price Guide

These are the prices of meals for two people, including drinks, but excluding alcohol such as wine, which is expensive.
$$$$: more than RM200.
$$$: RM100–200.
$$: RM50–100.
$: less than RM50.

since British administrators sipped at its counters. **$$**

Restoran Yum Yum
5 Persiaran Green Hill
Tel: 05-253 7686
The new gourmet lane of Ipoh is on this stretch perpendicular to Excelsior Hotel, whose eateries are more upmarket than Jalan Leech (*see below*). Among them is this excellent outlet with great Chinese-Nyonya ambience; it serves an excellent grouper in basil, and Yum Yum fried chicken. **$$**

Ipoh Tandoori House
135F Jalan Dato Lau Pak Kuan
Tel: 05-548 0806
Opposite Fatimah Hospital in the Ipoh Garden suburb; good North Indian fare in an air-conditioned restaurant; try the breads. **$**

Ming Court
36 Jalan Leong Sin Nam
Tel: 05-255 7134
This popular and good *dim sum* venue near Excelsior Hotel is packed during breakfast. **$**

Sin Yoon Loong
Jalan Bandar Timah
(near Jalan Silang)
This is the original Ipoh coffeeshop, where a fragrant local brew tastes its best. Watch the regulars at breakfast, and try the excellent home-made coconut jam (*kaya*) and toast. **$**

Hawker Food
Chinese hawker fare is found in old Chinese coffeeshops around Jalan Leech (Jalan Bandar Timah). Kedai Kopi Nam Heong has a good range, particularly the Ipoh speciality of chicken *kway teow* (noodle) soup; also available at the crowded and rather airless Kedai Kopi Kong Meng, which offers good *popiah*

(fresh springrolls), satay, and the sour-spicy Turf Club *laksa*. A little out of town is Wooley Food Centre and the adjoining Gourmet Square in Ipoh Garden. The Stadium has good Chinese and Malay food. More Malay fare is available at the late-night Pusat Penjaja Padang Kanak Kanak, Jalan Raja Musa Aziz.

Pulau Pangkor
Pangkor Island Beach Resort
Teluk Belanga
Tel: 05-685 1091
Western dinners at the Pacific Terrace, happy hour cocktails at the bar, seafood BBQ on Wednesday and Saturday, buffet with daily themes at poolside Hornbill Terrace Restaurant. You can also dine and watch the sun set on a beautiful beach (upon request). **$$$$**

Guan Guan
Pangkor town (near jetty)
Chinese seafood eatery that is good but pricey. **$$**

Yee Lin Seafood Garden
Pasir Bogak
Next to Coral Bay Hotel, established seafood restaurant with typical Chinese decor; serves fresh fish, shellfish and crabs. **$**

Hawker Food
Next to Sri Bayu Hotel in Pasir Bogak, open till the wee hours of the morning, serves excellent Indian *roti* bread and *teh tarik* at night. **$**

Taiping
Bismillah Restoran
(opposite the Town Market)
Enjoy hot, fresh *roti canai* with tea for breakfast and for lunch try Indian *briyani istimewa* (rice and curries). **$**

Jalan Kota
Any number of Chinese seafood restaurants line this road, with fresh produce from the Kuala Sepetang fishing area. **$**

Hawker Stalls
Jalan Panggung Wayang
A multi-ethnic food centre beneath the Fajar Supermarket with delicacies such as *popiah*, satay, *rojak sotong* (squid salad with peanut sauce) and fresh ginger tea. **$**

Penang
Hai Chu Hooi
338 Jalan Tanjung Tokong
Sitting on rocks by the seaside, this secluded basic open-air Chinese restaurant serves superb crabs (try the chilli crabs) and giant prawns. **$$**
Hot Wok
3-H Jalan Pantai Molek
Tel: 04-890 7858
Peranakan fare of traditional dishes in a bungalow with cosy atmosphere amid antiques. Opposite Caltex station and near Island Plaza mall. **$$**
Revolving Restaurant
City Bayview Hotel, Lebuh Farquhar
Tel: 04-263 3161
Award-winning restaurant serving a la carte and buffet meals. Live band music at night and great views of Georgetown. **$$**
Rossmerah
Jalan Chow Thye
Tel: 04-228 2221
Malay dishes and rice buffet style for breakfast and lunch. **$$**
Sigi's By the Sea
Shangri-la's Golden Sands Resort
Batu Ferringhi
Tel: 04-886 1191
Excellent East-West fusion food in a seaside restaurant. **$$**
747 Restaurant
YMCA of Penang
211 Jalan Macalister
Tel: 04-228 8211
Caters both western and local dishes popular with foreigners and Malaysians alike. **$**
B.M. Sagars Restaurant
Lebuh Bishop
Specialises in North Indian vegetarian food. **$**
Coca Steamboat
Level 3 Island Plaza, Tanjung Tokong
Tel: 04-890 6808
Steaming hot soup-based meal. Cook your own food at the table and order from a large selection of meat, seafood, vegetables and soya products. Air-conditioned. **$**
Goh Huat Seng
59A Lebah Kimberly
Tel: 04-261 5646
Known for its tasty rice soups, with a large variety of meats, seafood and vegetables. Also serves *dim sum* and sweet Teochew desserts. **$**

Food Notes

Eat	*Makan*
Drink	*Minum*
Bread	*Roti*
Beef	*Daging lembu*
Chicken	*Ayam*
(pronounced "ah-yarm")	
Fish	*Ikan*
(pronounced "ee-karn")	
Vegetables	*Sayur*
Fried noodles	*Mee goreng*
Fried rice	*Nasi goreng*
Salt	*Garam*
Spicy	*Pedas*
Delicious	*Sedap*
A cup of coffee	*Kopi satu*
A cup of tea	*Teh satu*
Water	*Air*
(pronounced "ah-yayr")	
Less sweet	*Kurang manis*
Without sugar	*Tanpa gula*
Without milk	*Tanpa susu*
Without ice	*Tanpa ais*
(pronounced "ice")	
Not enough	*Tak cukup*
Not hot/cold	*Tak cukup*
enough	*panas/sejuk*
Add	*Tambah*
Big	*Besar*
Small	*Kecil*

Hameediyah Restaurant
164A Lebuh Campbell
Six generations of an Indian-Muslim family have run Hameediyah's. Famous for its chicken curry, *murtabah* (pancake filled with meat), and *briyani* (rice), especially the mutton variety. Air-conditioned room available upstairs if downstairs is full. **$**

Hawker Centres
Persiaran Gurney (Gurney Drive) has the most famous of Penang's foodstalls, selling all of the island's favourites from spicy prawn-based *hokkien mee* to *jiu hoo eng chai* (squid with spinach). They are open from sunset to the wee hours of the morning. Hawker food is also good (and cheaper) at the coffeeshops at Jalan Penang and Jalan Macalister, Pengkalan Weld, and Jalan Burma, up to Pulau Tikus. Fatty Loh's Chicken Rice at Tanjung Bungah has the island's most famous chicken

rice, with moist, succulent meat and "oily rice". The Chowrasta stalls off Jalan Penang are a must for *nasi kandar*. The Esplanade foodstalls overlooking the sea in downtown Georgetown are great for night dining. Try the Indian-Muslim-style *rojak pasembur*, a salad with fried seafood covered in peanut sauce. Also look out for *laksa* (noodles in spicy gravy) stalls along the northern beaches. **$**

Pulau Langkawi
Beach Garden Resort
Pantai Cenang
Tel: 04-955 1363
Worth the splurge for an evening meal on the beach. Steaks, buttered potatoes, herbed salad, waffles and cream and coffee, not to mention the excellent margaritas; the menu changes nightly. **$$$**
Bon Ton
Pantai Cenang
Tel: 04-955 3643
Its Nam Restaurant has a limited menu but wonderful traditional Malay cooking in Western packaging, such as the seafood platter with baked fish in banana leaf, and prawn ravioli in spicy *tom yam* broth. **$$$**
Barn Thai Restaurant
Kampung Belangga Pecah
Long lamp-lit plank-walk through mangrove forest leads to a lovely wooden cabin that serves excellent Thai food. The restaurant also offers mangrove tour packages which include lunch. **$$**
Prawn Village
Kuah
Typical Chinese restaurant set-up with very bright lights, well-known for its seafood, and signature prawn dishes – try the buttered prawns, sweet and sour, or simply steamed. **$$**
Sari Seafood Restaurant
Kuah
Tel: 04-966 6192
Great sunsets from the wooden deck which sits on stilts over the sea; local Malay fare, specialising in seafood. **$$**
The Lighthouse
Pantai Tengah
Tel: 04-955 2586

Great location on the beach with food cooked by famous local chef Shukri Shafi, who also runs cooking classes at his traditional Malay house. Good Malay food and western specialities. Fresh fish and seafood are particularly good. **$$**

Restoran Haji Ramli
Pantai Cenang
At the Pantai Tengah end is a simple open-air Malay restaurant with blinking Christmas tree lights, where you choose your seafood from a boat; raw delectable grilled fish, and Thai-style chilli crab; no alcohol sold. **$**

SOUTHERN PENINSULA

Melaka

Coconut House
128 Jalan Tun Tan Cheng Lock
Tel: 06-282 9128
A restaurant, art gallery, bookshop and art-film venue housed in a beautiful Peranakan house. Specialities are wood-fired pizzas and freshly-baked cakes. Closed on Wed. **$$**

Geographer's Café
83 Hang Jebat
Tel: 06-281 6813
Located in an ambience-filled corner shophouse along one of the historic side-streets, this lovely cafe is a nice place to chill out and partake of local specialities. **$$**

Ole Sayang Restaurant
198/199 Taman Melaka Raya
Tel: 06-283 1966
Excellent authentic Peranakan cooking and great traditional decor, just ignore the morose staff. It is popular with large groups, so go early for lunch or dinner. **$$**

Restoran de Lisbon
Portuguese Square
Tel: 06-284 8067
Good Malaysian-Portuguese fare, such as devil curry, complete with Portuguese brew; on Saturday evenings there are cultural performances. **$$**

Restoran Peranakan Town House
107 Jalan Tun Tan Cheng Lock
Tel: 06-284 5001
Another gorgeous Peranakan showpiece. All the well-known

Nyonya dishes are on the menu and there is a nightly cultural show. The same management runs another heritage restaurant, Nam Hoe Villa, in the coastal town of Klebang Besar. **$$**

Nancy's Kitchen
15 Jalan Hang Lekir
Tel: 06-283 6099
Owners Robert and Nancy cook authentic Peranakan dishes. The *ayam buah keras* (chicken in candlenut curry) is a classic. Open lunch only; closed on Wed. **$$**

Heeren House
1 Jalan Tun Tan Cheng Lock
Tel: 06-281 4241
Set lunches in a cosy and old-world environment, with Western, Peranakan and Portuguese dishes, and delicious cakes. **$**

Hoe Kee Chicken Rice
4 Jalan Hang Jebat
Located just near the bridge and open only from around mid-morning to lunch, it has remained low key despite the fame won by its delicious Hainanese chicken and billiard ball-sized rice balls; good home-made barley drink. **$**

Hawker Food
For Melaka-style Malay home-cooking, particularly in the very spicy-sour *asam pedas* style, head for 35 Jalan Merdeka. A hawker centre sits all the way out at Klebang Besar, with goodies such as satay and Malay baked fish (*ikan bakar*) and tables facing the Straits of Melaka. **$**

Johor Bahru

Eden Floating Palace
Johor Bahru Duty Free Zone
Jalan Ibrahim Sultan
Tel: 07-221 9999
This has the final word on big – a converted passenger ferry with three restaurants on four air-conditioned decks, seating 600 diners and serving duty-free wines. Part of the huge Eden seafood chain, Chinese/Western menu. **$$$**

Jaws 5
Straits View Hotel, Jalan Skudai
Tel: 07-223 6062
Very popular, and therefore pricey, but excellent Chinese style seafood

in a glitzy over-lit environment – good for Drunken Prawns and Chilli Crab. **$$**

Briyani House
Jalan Kebun Teh
Dishes up the Johor speciality of *briyani gam*, a rice dish served with spicy mutton or chicken and pickles. **$**

Capati Corner
Jalan Kolam Air
Home-made *capati* – Indian bread, served with *dhall* (lentils) or curries and vegetables of your choice. **$**

Prawn House
Jalan Kebun Teh
This seafood joint sits along the same road as the Briyani House, with fresh fish cooked in various styles; a speciality is the yam cake dessert. **$**

Tepian Tebrau Food Centre
Jalan Abu Bakar
A favourite among locals for its seafood steamboat, *nasi briyani* spiced rice with mutton or chicken, *ikan bakar* grilled fish, and the delectable Wahid family recipe *mee rebus* with fat noodles. **$**

Hawker food
Go for Johor favourites, *laksa Johor*, noodles in thick fishy coconut gravy, *ikan bakar* grilled fish and *lontong*, rice cubes in a creamy coconut sauce, at the big hawker centres at Lido Beach and Stulang Laut.

PENINSULA'S EAST COAST

Pulau Tioman

Babura Sea View Chinese Restaurant
Babura Sea View, Kampung Tekek
Breezy beachside Chinese restaurant with excellent seafood. **$**

Liza Restaurant
Kampung Tekek
Good selection of Malay and Western dishes. **$**

Mekong Restaurant
Kampung Paya
Good Chinese-style seafood. **$**

Sunset Boulevard
Kampung Salang
Built on stilts over the sea. You can jump off your boat onto the

restaurant itself. Great for a beer and good seafood. **$**

Kuantan
Kampong Restaurant
Hyatt Regency Kuantan
Teluk Cempedak
Tel: 09-566 1234
Built on stilts over the sea, this restaurant serves good Malay and Continental food, and excellent pizzas. **$$**
Pak Su Seafood Restaurant
Batu 6 (6th mile)
Kuantan-Beserah Road
About half-an-hour north of Kuantan, just before De Rhu Beach Resort, sits a breezy Chinese restaurant overlooking the sea, that is well-known for its stuffed crab, salad lobster and spicy-sour *asam* steamed fish. Air-conditioned. **$$**

Hawker Food
Head to Teluk Cempedak, Kuantan's best beach, where a beachside promenade brims with food stalls and outdoor seafood restaurants. Definitely the only place to dine on a hot evening. **$–$$**

Kuala Terengganu
Good Luck Restaurant
11Y & Z Jalan Kota Lama
Tel: 09-622 7573
Popularly known as Lucky Restaurant, it is centrally located, next to a *bah kut teh* (pork ribs herbal soup) eatery, and serves seafood specialities and frogs legs *à la* Cantonese, as well as one-dish noodle and rice dishes. Air-conditioned upstairs. **$**
Restoran Meka
66/16 Taman Seri Intan
Tel: 09-623 1831
Traditional Terengganu Malay cooking with mainly fish dishes in various spicy coconut concoctions and *ulam*, traditional salads eaten with a prawn paste-based chilli condiment called *sambal belacan*. The dishes are laid out in trays. **$**
Nils Restaurant
Pantai Batu Buruk
Renowned Malay seafood restaurant, famous for its *ikan bakar* (grilled fish with *sambal* sauce), right on the beach.

Favourite dining spot with locals including royalty. **$–$$**

Hawker Food
The traditional Malay breakfast of *nasi dagang*, glutinous rice and curry fish is best at Cendering, slightly south of town, but the Batu Buruk beach stalls also cook up a decent meal. There are Chinese hawker stalls behind The Store departmental store and opposite the markets.

Price Guide

These are the prices of meals for two people, including drinks, but excluding alcohol such as wine, which is expensive.
$$$$: more than RM200.
$$$: RM100–200.
$$: RM50–100.
$: less than RM50.

Kota Bharu
Azam
Jalan Padang Garong
North Indian fare, including breads and *dhall* (lentil curry). **$**
Central Market
The bustling first floor is packed with foodstalls selling local Malay rice and curries – try the *nasi kunyit* glutinous rice concoction; also there is a large variety of local *kuih* (cakes), which cannot be bought outside Kelantan. **$**
Kedai Kopi White House
Jalan Sultanah Zainab
Located opposite the State Mosque, it is the best place to enjoy *nasi dagang* – unbleached rice with sweet curry sauce. **$**
Kow Lun
Jalan Kebun Sultan
Chinese set-up with meat and vegetable dishes; piping hot noodles, as well as beer. **$**

Hawker Food
Opposite Central Market next to the bus station, stalls are set up at a night bazaar. You can buy satay and other spicy Malay delectables, including Thai-style spicy-sour noodles. While there try the famous Yati's *ayam percik*, chicken grilled and marinated in rich coconut

sauce, together with *nasi kerabu*, a rice dish with herbs **$**

SARAWAK

Kuching
Recommended
Magenta
Jalan Nanas
Tel: 082-237 878
This beautifully converted and brightly painted old wooden bungalow just 5 minutes from downtown Kuching is popular for its good fusion cuisine. **$$**
Waterfront Café
Hilton Hotel, Kuching
Tel: 082-428 200
Gaze out across the Kuching River in air-conditioned comfort as you enjoy excellent espresso, fresh baked bread, salads and delicious food. The café features different food promotions each day. **$$**
Hornbill's Corner Café
Jalan Ban Hock
Tel: 082-252 670
Both a bar and a restaurant, the Hornbill has the best barbecue steamboat in town with an inexpensive all-you-can-eat buffet. The bar has a friendly clientele; the cold draught beer and satellite-TV soccer attract many foreign visitors. **$**

Western
Beccari's Ristorante
Merdeka Palace Hotel
Authentic Italian fare from an authentic Italian chef, plus the best pizzas in town. Sensible prices. **$–$$**
The San Francisco Grill
Jalan Ban Hock
Good service and good steaks make for a pleasant experience. **$–$$**
The Steak House
Hilton Hotel, Kuching
Tel: 082-248 200
Probably the best steaks in town, plus other excellent dishes with an Italian touch in elegant surroundings. Try the set meal for extraordinarily good value. **$–$$**

Indian
Several Muslim shops in Jalan Carpenter serve *roti canai* – the

delicious fried Indian pancake served with a curry sauce; or equally delicious eaten with sugar. *Murtabak* (meat-filled *roti canai*) is also available, as well as curries and fried chicken.

Bollywood Café
66 Jalan Carpenter
Despite the trendy name, this conventionally located spot is decidedly simple, offering a good range of typical Indian food from 7am until about 6.30pm. Specialties are *biryani*; curries with either rice, *chapati*, *puri*s or flaky *roti canai*; and Indian sweetmeats. **$**

Lyn's Tandoori
Lot 62 No 10G, Lorong 4, Nanas Road
Just a short taxi ride from town. Serves genuine North Indian *tandoori* dishes and *naan*. **$**

Japanese
Minoru
Lot 493G, Section 10, Rubber Road
Tel: 082-251 021
Regarded by many as Sarawak's best Japanese restaurant, Minoru offers a selection of fine Japanese cuisine for both lunch and dinner, and is known for its attentive service. **$$–$$$**

Ten Ichi
(Lok Thian Restaurant)
Bangunan Bee San, Jalan Padungan
Tel: 082-331 310
Somewhat curiously located within a large and very popular Chinese restaurant, this rather elegant Japanese restaurant serves a good

range of typical Japanese cuisine. Open for lunch and dinner, and busy at weekends. **$$**

Chinese
The quaint old streets of Chinatown are lined with *kedai kopi* (coffeeshops) serving fresh Chinese noodle dishes and specialities like roast chicken or pork rice. Wander about until you see a restaurant that looks attractive, find a seat and order up.

Golden Phoenix Restaurant
Ban Hock Road
Tel: 082-415 588
Reasonably priced and eclectic menu with Vietnamese and Thai specialities included. **$–$$**

Meisan
Holiday Inn, Kuching
Tel: 082-423 111. **$–$$**

River Palace
Crowne Plaza Riverside, Kuching
Tel: 082-247 777. **$–$$**

Toh Yuen
Hilton Hotel, Kuching
Tel: 082-248 200
All the above serve excellent Chinese cuisine in elegant and air-conditioned surroundings. **$$**

Seafood
Fresh seafood abounds in Kuching. Look out for *ambal* (bamboo clam), a local speciality. Served steamed or cooked in a mild curry, it tastes far more delicious than it looks.

Benson's Seafood
49 Jalan Abell
Popular spot by the river for fresh seafood, this relaxed place is just

past the Holiday Inn. Simply point to the vegetables and fish, crabs, prawns, etc. of your choice and say how you'd like them cooked. **$–$$**

See Good Food Centre
53 Ban Hock Road
Excellent seafood, fresh and affordable. Delicious noodle dishes are served between main meal times. **$**

Top Spot Food Centre
5th Floor, Jalan Bukit Mata Kuching
An open-air seafood plaza where half-a-dozen eating outlets vie for business with tempting displays of fresh seafood on ice. **$**

Hawker Centres
Kuching has some very good hawker centres offering Chinese and Malay food at remarkably reasonable prices. It's easy to wander about, see what you like, and just point to order it. A favourite is the oddly-named **Open Market**, which is actually covered with a roof and located off Jalan Khoo Hun Yeang near Electra House. Food stalls cluster in front of a Chinese theatre, or *wayang* stage, opposite a temple half way along **Jalan Carpenter**. For those who prefer air-conditioned dining, try the wide selection of local favourites at the **Food Court** in Medan Pelita, just off Main Bazaar.

Sibu
The food in Sibu is as good as elsewhere in Malaysia with plenty of seafood and Chinese restaurants. The strong Chinese population means a variety of Chinese cuisines like Foochow, Szechuan, Cantonese and Teochew.

Golden Palace
Tanahmas Hotel
Jalan Kampung Nyabor
Tel: 084-33 188
Cantonese and Szechuan dishes and plenty of seafood. **$–$$**

Jhong Kuo
13 Jalan Wong Nai Siong
Foochow food, good standard. **$–$$**

Hock Cho Lau Restaurant
Jalan Blacksmith
A popular Chinese restaurant; good for Foochow duck and fried noodle dishes. **$**

Eating Out in Kuching

Good food abounds in Kuching, whether it is such typical Malaysian favourites as *roti canai*, chicken rice, or chilli crab, or the usual Western fare often found in the big hotels. Kuching has its own specialities as well – with influences deriving from Malay, Indian, Chinese and Dayak heritages. The slightly sour-ish Sarawak *laksa* is a big favourite, a noodle dish cooked in chicken stock with coconut cream and

spices, as is *umei* – a Melanau dish of raw, marinated fish blended with limes, chilli and shallots. There are the jungle vegetables like *midin* and *paku* – baby fern served boiled or fried with the spicy addition of *belacan* paste and garlic and perhaps a hint of oyster sauce. Fresh seafood, venison, wild boar, *pansoh manok* – an Iban chicken dish cooked in bamboo tubes with rice wine – are not to be missed.

Hawker Centres

These provide a good source of cheap eating. The Rex Food Centre on Jalan Cross has a good selection of outlets as does the hawker centre in Jalan Market. Close to the expressboat jetty, the Gerai Makanan Muslim offers delicious Malay dishes.

Western
Pepper's Café
Tanahmas Hotel
Jalan Kampung Nyabor
Tel: 084-333 188
Good for both Western and local dishes. **$–$$**
Villa By The Grand
2nd Floor Grand Meridien Building
Jalan Kampung Nyabor
Canadian-run restaurant serving Western food. **$–$$**

Miri

With a large Western population and an affluent Chinese community, Miri has an assortment of eateries and excellent, reasonably-priced seafood. In the old part of town, there are good coffeeshops with hawkers selling an array of delicious fried noodle dishes.

Western
Golden Steak Garden
Gloria Hotel, Jalan Brooke
Good steaks. **$–$$**
Holiday Inn
Jalan Temenggong Datuk Oyong Lawai
Tel: 085-418 888
Serves the best Western food in town. **$–$$**
Café Miri
Taman Yakin Shopping Centre
Jalan Bulan Sabit
Tel: 085-425 122
A few kilometres from the town centre, a relaxed café run by an

Miri's Food Stalls

Take a walk through the old part of Miri where the tour guides never take you – down to the fish market and an old Chinese temple. The Jalan Oleander Food Stalls on the left serve excellent and authentic Malay food.

Australian-Chinese man and his wife. Great array of drinks and plenty of Australian specialities. **$**
Chatterbox Coffee House
Mega Hotel, Jalan Maju
Tel: 085-432 432
Good Western and local food. **$**

Seafood
Ocean Seafood Village
Luak Bay
Located by the beach, this big open-concept restaurant is regarded as the best place to enjoy seafood in Miri. **$$–$$$**
Maxims
Jalan Pujut
Lutong (next to Bintang Plaza)
Open-air evening eatery. Choose your fish from the iced fresh seafood on display and specify the style of cooking. Informal and good value. **$–$$**

SABAH

Dining in Sabah tends to be just as casual as the general lifestyle, with open-fronted restaurants, food stalls and simple coffee shops being very popular. Excellent and relatively inexpensive seafood is particularly popular with visitors.

Kota Kinabalu
Western
Peppino's
Shangri-la's Tanjung Aru Resort
Tel: 088-225 800
Casually elegant restaurant in the city's premier resort, this serves Italian favourites, including plenty of seafood. **$$$**
Gunther's Gasthaus
9/11 Taman Sinar, off, Jalan Tuaran (opposite Kian Kok School)
Tel: 088-217 249
Located in a converted house just off Jalan Tuaran less than 4km from the city, this German-Swiss restaurant is popular for its steaks, sausages and braised pork knuckle. **$$**
Little Italy Pasta & Pizza Corner
Ground Floor, Hotel Capital
Jalan Haji Saman
Tel: 088-232 231
Ideally located in the heart of town, this restaurant offers Italian

Price Guide

These are the prices of meals for two people, including drinks, but excluding alcohol such as wine, which is expensive.
$$$$: more than RM200.
$$$: RM100–200.
$$: RM50–100.
$: less than RM50.

favourites (with the emphasis on pasta and pizza) at reasonable prices. Outdoor and air-conditioned indoor dining available. **$–$$**

Chinese
Supertanker
Grand Industrial Estate, Jalan Bundusan (off Jalan Penampang)
Tel: 088-717 889
This large and popular restaurant, located about 10–15 minutes by taxi from the centre of the city, serves some of the best Chinese food in town. **$$**
Canton House
70 Jalan Gaya (opposite The Jesselton)
Tel: 088-269 399
Bright and bustling, this air-conditioned restaurant specialises in all kinds of noodles, roast meat and poultry, and dim sum; there are some good desserts and drinks also. Very busy at lunch time and Sunday morning. **$**

Japanese
Nagisa Japanese Restaurant
Hyatt Regency Kinabalu, Jalan Datuk Salleh Sulung
Tel: 088-221 234
Reputed to be the finest Japanese restaurant in the city, Nagisa offers Japanese favourites in particularly attractive surroundings. **$$–$$$**

Indian
Naan
Shangri-La's Rasa Ria Resort
Pantai Dalit
Tel: 088-792 888
Refined Indian food is prepared and served with a delightful modern touch in this out-of-town restaurant. Well worth the drive for top quality Indian food; evenings only. **$$$**

Jothy's Restaurant
Block 1, Lot 9, Api Api Centre (near McDonald's, facing Coastal Highway)
The southern Indian food here, both vegetarian as well as meat, poultry and fish curries, is deliciously spicy; other advantages of this simple restaurant is that it's air-conditioned and spotlessly clean. **$–$$**

Malay/Nyonya
Penang Nyonya Kitchen
Lot 5, The Waterfront
Jalan Tun Fuad Stephens
Tel: 088-263 286
Nyonya food is featured in this waterfront restaurant. Don't miss the Penang Asam Laksa, Penang Prawn Mee and the delicious deep-fried rolls, *lobah* and *popiah*. **$–$$**

Sri Sempeleng
Block C Asia City (facing Centrepoint shopping complex)
Open 24 hours a day, 7 days a week, this is one of the most popular Malay/Indonesian restaurants in town. Branches in Wisma Merdeka and Sinsuron shopping complex. **$**

Seafood
Garden Seafood Restaurant
Off Jalan Mat Salleh, Tanjung Aru
Tel: 088-442 222
This huge, open-sided restaurant has an extensive range of seafood, and also sells exotica such as ostrich and venison. The very clear menu helps in ordering either Thai- or Chinese-style dishes. **$$$**

Suang Tain Seafood Restaurant
SEDCO Square, Kg Air
Open daily from 5pm–2.30am, this seafood restaurant dominates a popular open-air evening eatery. A large range of fresh seafood is available and the restaurant known for its reasonable prices. **$$–$$$**

Price Guide

These are the prices of meals for two people, including drinks, but excluding alcohol such as wine, which is expensive.
$$$$: more than RM200.
$$$: RM100–200.
$$: RM50–100.
$: less than RM50.

Sabah's Specialities

Sabah has its own specialties, especially vegetable dishes. Best of all is *sayur manis*, a green leafy vegetable with a slightly crunchy stem and sweet green leaves. Try it in oyster sauce, or for the Asiaphile, in a spicy sauce of *sambal belacan* which has a heady, fishy tang that takes time to get used to.

Thai
Tham Nak Thai
Api Api Centre
Tel: 088-257 328
Part of a chain of Thai restaurants, this has all the usual Thai favourites, well-presented in pleasant surroundings by attractively dressed staff. **$$–$$$**

Sandakan
Sandakan has numerous coffee shops and simple restaurants serving excellent noodle and seafood dishes. The seafood is particularly good and generally less expensive than in Kota Kinabalu.

The English Tea House and Restaurant
Jalan Istana
Tel: 089-222 544
This beautifully-restored colonial-era bungalow overlooks Sandakan and the bay. English favourites, including bangers and mash, and selected Asian cuisine. You can even play croquet. **$$$**

Ocean King Seafood Restaurant
Jalan Batu Sapi (4½ km), Pasir Putih
Tel: 089-618 111, 616 048
A large open-side restaurant built on stilts over the bay. There is a vague menu/price list written on a board on the verandah, but basically, if it swims you can order it. Fish, crabs, prawns, lobster, squid and various shellfish are all available, and the bean curd and vegetable dishes are good. **$$**

Penang Curry House
Lebuh Dua (Second Avenue), next to the AM Finance
Featuring Southern Indian cuisine, including curries, *murtabak*, *roti canai* (flaky bread) and *dosay* (rice-flour and lentil pancakes) and plenty of vegetarian options in a busy open-fronted restaurant. **$**

Restoran Habeeb
There are at least 8 restaurants in this chain featuring Indian and local Muslim cuisine. One of the most convenient is located directly in front of Wisma Sandakan, in Leboh Empat (Fourth Avenue). **$**

Drinks

Alcohol is expensive in Malaysia. A glass of wine may cost as much as a tot of brandy, but the full range is available. Wine bars are becoming increasingly popular, and also sell cigars. While alcohol is forbidden to Muslims, it is freely available at pubs, hotels, restaurants and in Chinese eateries, as well as in supermarkets in towns and tourist areas (except in the Muslim PAS-ruled states of Terengganu and Kelantan). Duty-free wine, beer and other hard drinks are easily available on the islands of Langkawi, Labuan and Tioman.

Fruit juices are available everywhere. If you don't want sugar, ask the waiter not to add the sugar syrup (be warned though that without the syrup, juices are tasteless as they are not pure juices, but have had water added to 'stretch' them); in Kelantan, salt is often added to cut fruits and juices, so ask for plain fruit or juice.

Young coconuts produce a refreshing clear juice which can be drunk straight from the coconut with ice added and a straw stuck into a hole in the top.

Try soya bean milk, barley or Chinese herbal teas (*leong char*). Mineral water is widely available.

Local coffee and tea pack a punch, and are served with condensed milk and sugar. You can also ask for Nescafé. Decaffeinated and flavoured teas are available only in higher-class restaurants.

Ipoh white coffee has won a wide following among avid coffee lovers because of its creamy smooth taste and strong flavour.

American coffee-bar chains are opening up in the cities, which serve finger food, too.

Culture

Museums

All museums in Malaysia are documented in the Places section. Most are open 9am–5pm daily. They close noon–2.30pm on Friday and a half-day on Thursday or Saturday. Admission to museums is free or at a nominal fee. Tours are rare, and information is usually in English and Bahasa Malaysia.

Art Galleries

Malaysia's serious art gained credence only in the 1960s after independence. Art is becoming a popular collectable locally, particularly in Kuala Lumpur, with the increase in number of exhibitions and galleries.

Other than subject matter, there is nothing really to define Malaysian art in terms of style; the diversity is staggering from Chinese brush painting to abstract art and sculpture, although batik would come closest – the artist who pioneered this style, Chuah Thean Teng, has a gallery in Penang.

The best place to see the range of established Malaysian art is at the National Art Gallery, Jalan Temerloh, Kuala Lumpur (tel: 03-2274 0157). Newer artists are featured in smaller galleries throughout the country, with many congregating in the trendy Bangsar suburb in Kuala Lumpur. Check dailies for exhibition listings and art spaces.

Galeri Petronas
KLCC, Kuala Lumpur
Tel: 03-2051 7581
This circular gallery located on the 3rd floor of the Suria Shopping Mall at the base of the Petronas Towers is Malaysia's first international museum-quality display space. It also contains an experimental area. Also here is a good gift shop specializing in Malaysian art works.

Performing Arts

Cultural shows
Authentic cultural performances are difficult to catch these days in Kuala Lumpur. National Day and Malaysia Fest parades in Kuala Lumpur provide some glimpses, while a handful of hotels stage performances, as does Kuala Lumpur's Central Market.

For Malaysian culture, Kota Bharu's Gelanggang Seni (Cultural Centre) is probably the only venue where cultural performances are staged regularly. Competitions held in villages are the best places to watch traditional pastimes and *wayang kulit* (shadow puppetry).

A professional dance troupe has scheduled performances in the Dewan Filharmonik Petronas in Kuala Lumpur, while the Suasana Dance Company is the sole purveyor of the Malay dance-drama.

For traditional Borneo Malaysian native performances, the Sarawak Cultural Village in Kuching has regular shows, but the best performances are in longhouses, the further into the interior the better; the local people are always ready for an excuse to break into music, song and dance. Likewise in the more remote areas in Sabah. The harvest festival in June is the best time to catch the action.

Chinese
Traditional Chinese opera is staged on temporary platforms in the suburbs during special Buddhist or Taoist festivals. Based on mainland Chinese myths and old tales, this sees the use of traditional Chinese costumes and heavy make-up.

Chinese dances are performed only during official functions, but there are many dance groups who use this as a base for modern work.

There are a few classical Chinese orchestras, with Dama being the most professional and creative.

Cinemas

Subtle drama never stays on the billboards long, although *Titanic* wove its magic in Malaysia, too, and the movie that scored as longest-playing was a classic Hindi tear-jerker in the 1970s. Nonetheless, local box-office hits are invariably the action movies, preferably with violence and explosions.

American movies do the circuit in the big urban cinema chains, as well as the odd Hong Kong hit. Otherwise, Bahasa Malaysia, Chinese and Indian language films are screened in the smaller cinemas; English language hits rarely make it to the small towns.

In deference to the official religion of the country, Islam, nude, semi-nude and even kissing scenes between unmarried people are diligently, but not always professionally censored, so that sometimes, vital dialogue disappears, too.

However, the same concern does not always apply to very violent scenes, particularly Hong Kong ghost-story and mafia flicks.

The chain that revived cinema-going and made it fashionable in the early 1990s is Tanjung Golden Village, with its plush multiplexes and prime locations in large shopping complexes. The KLCC also has two THX cinemas.

The huge Mid Valley Mega Mall has several theatres including one that specializes in art-house cinema. Local papers highlight viewings of classic movies and arthouse favourites at various embassies and clubs.

Other chains are upgrading slowly, but for a taste of the original movie theatre, head for Rex, Cathay and Ruby in Kuala Lumpur, where there is first- and second-class seating, groundnut shells under your feet as well as the occasional rat.

Music Venue

World-class international music performances are held at the Dewan Filharmonik Petronas in Kuala Lumpur, tel: 03-2051 7008.

Indian

Classical Indian artforms are well and truly alive, with dance, vocal and instrumental performances held regularly, particularly in temples. The most famous troupe is the Kuala Lumpur-based Temple of Fine Arts (tel: 03-2272 5709), known for its epic productions. It also incorporates contemporary and Malaysian elements in its shows.

Contemporary Arts

The contemporary arts scene is centred in Kuala Lumpur, with some productions in Penang and Ipoh. Contemporary dancers have small companies and some are quite good, training and performing internationally. The most popular contemporary theatre is the comedy revue, attracting trendy urbanites, although drama, some locally written, is also staged.

The established companies are the Instant Café Theatre (tel: 03-2148 5192), particularly for its revues, the Five Arts Centre which pursues the alternative and Malaysian themes, and the Actors' Studio. For listings, check dailies and websites: www.artseefartsee.com and www.kakiseni.com for theatre, and www.mydancealliance.org for dance performances, or call The Actors' Studio, tel: 03-2094 0400, at Level 3 of Bangsar Shopping Centre, in Kuala Lumpur.

Nightlife

Pubs, discos and karaoke dens are places where Malaysians party at night. The best nightlife is in the capital. Elsewhere, the action concentrates in hotel lounges and discos. Other than Kuala Lumpur, people tend not to dress up, but shorts and sandals are definite no-nos.

Nightclubs

Kuala Lumpur

Nightlife has tended to congregate in specific areas. Clubs and discos may be the trendsetters, but they have a shorter shelf-life and pubs stick around longer, particularly the neighbourhood ones. Generally, club crowds swell after 11pm or even midnight, and there is a cover charge on Friday and Saturday, which includes one drink from a limited menu. In most places, jeans, shorts, collarless T-shirts and sandals are not allowed, and yuppies dress to kill.

Live bands are popular and usually play three sets from 10pm onwards. Almost all the larger hotels have bars featuring live music. This is usually broad-appeal, middle-of-the-road music, so hotel lounges are not listed here unless they have a reputation for something different.

Pub- or club-hopping has long been happening in the Jalan Sultan Ismail/Jalan Ampang area. The Rennaisance Hotel's basement bar, **Cream** is a post-dinner hangout. Across the road is the **Hard Rock Café** at Concorde Hotel, with great local and international live acts and a small dance floor. Long queues form at the weekend, so go early or book a table for a meal. Concorde also has a popular lounge with good acts. Down Jalan Sultan Ismail and into Jalan P. Ramlee near the Petronas Twin Towers are a host of sidewalk coffeeshops and eateries, including **Red's Café**, **T.G.I. Fridays**, and **Coffee Bean and Tea Leaf**.

The clubs along this stretch are **Espanda**, a magnet for international DJs and KL's hip crowd, the ever-so-yuppie **Modesto's** and **12SI**, a massive multiple club and pub complex featuring mainly house music. **Nouvo** features 'boutique club' house music flavoured with disco, Latin, Afro and Cuban inflections while fun and zany **Beach Club** attracts a mixed bunch of locals, expatriates and tourists. Flavour of the month is the distinctive dome of **Zouk**, scoring a name as one of KL's hottest dance spots.

The Backroom behind Shangri-La plays techno and house at the front section, and rave at the back, and has a young crowd. At Hilton PJ, the older, more laidback crowd gets groovy on the dance floor after dinner at **Uncle Chilli's Fun Pub**

Bangsar – the Place to Party

The most "happening" place in Kuala Lumpur is a suburb south of the city centre called Bangsar, where the young and not-so-young but totally trendy hang out. Here, neck-to-neck are bars, coffee bars, restaurants and art galleries, whose names you don't bother remembering because the sky-high rents ensure they don't last anyway. This is where the expatriates hang out, and like bees to the honey pot, the so-called *sarong* party girls, whom they pick up (or vice-versa). There's always no parking here, and lots of partying. At one end is a huge all-night hawker centre with Malay and Indian fare, to which the bleary-eyed and not-so-sober retire when the party ends anywhere around town.

and **Restaurant**. For something more exclusive, head for the **Kit Kat Club** at Sheraton Imperial Hotel. A similar crowd hangs out at Istana Hotel's **Musictheque**, with its huge dance floor, karaoke rooms and huge video walls – and a high cover charge.

The Bukit Bintang area has numerous open-air relaxed, café-type joints. **Viper Room** at KL Plaza is a trendy favourite, with a widely-stocked wine cellar that pulls in the sophisticated crowd. **The Palm Beach** caters to an enthusiastic crowd. **Planet Hollywood** has regular live acts featuring local artistes playing to full houses on weekends. **The Club de Macau** is an established joint in Renaissance Hotel, Jalan Ampang, which attracts business executives.

For more nightspots and good food, head out to Desa Sri Hartamas. **Souled Out Café** is an established bistro-style joint that is always packed. Live bands regularly play here. Other nightspots worth visiting are **The Orange** and **Background Pub**, both of which cater mostly to a younger crowd. **Bistro 1957** regularly features live, one-man acts playing to a crowd similar to Souled Out Café's.

Penang

Most of the action in this town tends to centre at The Garage, such as the ever-trendy **Downtown** or **Slippery Senoritas**. The popular **Gurney Drive** along the waterfront also has numerous bistro-type pubs that open till the early hours.

In town, **20 Leith Street**, housed in a beautifully renovated colonial mansion and its walls adorned with scenes by Penang artists and antique clocks, has a beer garden in front and a cosy bar that spins out some great music. Elsewhere in Georgetown's backpacker alley, there are little Chinese watering holes. Bear in mind, however, that some of these are of dubious nature.

Pulau Langkawi

Nightlife concentrates in Pantai Cenang and Tengah, at the little restaurants such as **Beach Garden**, **Champor-Champor** and the beachside, coconut-tree strewn **Charlie's Bar** at the end. Head to **CocoJam**, an established disco at Holiday Villa for some action on the dance floor. Sheraton Langkawi Beach Resort's **Black Henry**, with its regular live acts, remains a favourite.

Cherating

The action focuses on Kampung Cherating, and usually starts at **Pop Inn** at the northern end, where a live band plays from Thursday to the weekend, moves on to the dimly-lit **La Pippin** down the road, and usually ends up in the wee hours at **Nan's Beach Bar**, behind Coconut Inn. The **Moon's Deadly Nightshade** is a tiny hillside bar-restaurant in a rough *attap*-roofed open setting with great ambience.

Kuching

Kuching is a relaxed and very friendly place, where it's easy to make new friends at the city's many night spots. **The Junk**, on Wayang Street, is very popular with locals and visitors alike, and offers food as well as drinks. **Soho**, **Grappa** and **Red Lantern** on Jalan Padungan retain their popularity and are often packed to the rafters at the weekend. Another popular place for both food and drink, as well as pool and darts, is **Eagle's Nest** on Jalan Bukit Mata Kuching. More upmarket is **Victoria Arms**, a lively English pub in Merdeka Palace Hotel.

Kota Kinabalu

A range of bars and Irish pubs in the downtown area known as **The Waterfront** offers drinks and entertainment both indoors and on the boardwalk.

Shopping

General

Shopping malls are found in every city and comprise a supermarket, department store (the big chains sell branded goods), and lots of little shops, including boutiques, shoe-stores, and stores selling watches, electrical goods, computers, mobile phones, music shops, bookshops and/or stationery/magazine stores, sometimes with money changers and tour agencies, cinemas and video-arcades. Some malls specialise in certain items. They usually have eateries, too, including hawker fare-type food courts, Western fast food chains, or restaurants.

Kuala Lumpur

From branded goods to rustic handicrafts, foodstuffs to software, Kuala Lumpur's shops have it all. The shopping area is Bukit Bintang around Jalan Bukit Bintang and Jalan Sultan Ismail. Here you'll find Bukit Bintang Plaza (BB Plaza), which is joined to Sungei Wang Plaza, well-known for its electrical items and photographic equipment. The more upmarket Lot 10 is across the road from Sungei Wang Plaza with mid- to high-priced items and branded goods in the top floor; there's a good bookshop, too. Down the road is the even more upmarket Starhill Centre, with its international shops. Next door at KL Plaza is the American Tower Records, Kuala Lumpur's largest music store. Along Jalan Imbi, Imbi Plaza is the place for computer goods, including software and peripherals.

Central Market is probably the best place for souvenirs, with its two levels offering Malaysiana, Asian

Night Markets

Open-air *pasar malam* (night markets) are good to soak in the local atmosphere and find bargain-price items, including clothes (which you try on in the open), shoes, trinkets, CDs and VCDs (often pirated) and household items. You can usually buy fresh produce, including fruit, and delicious local street food and titbits. The traders are itinerant, so check locations in the local press or at your hotel. There is a *pasar malam* in both Bangsar and Taman Tun Dr Ismail on Sundays from 5.30pm till midnight.

hand-crafted goods and souvenirs, and artwork. Kuala Lumpur's glitziest shopping mall to date is the modernistic Suria KLCC at the base of the Petronas Twin Towers, which houses all the big chains as well as interesting boutique shops, international cuisine and cosy cafés as well as cinemas.

Aseana department store is definitely worth a visit. There's wonderful crafts from all the Asean countries, including a range of gift ideas from Malaysia. The sarong section is excellent, as are its range of Straits Chinese embroidered *kebaya* blouses.

Sogo Kuala Lumpur on Jalan Raja Laut is one of the largest department stores in Southeast Asia with eight floors, a waterfall on the top floor where the restaurants are, and good sales.

Down the road, Pertama Complex sells cheaper goods, but is good for shoes. The Mall on Jalan Putra opposite the Putra World Trade Centre is still popular for *haute couture* and specialist shops; there is a stuffy hawker centre on the top floor and souvenir stalls.

Jalan Tuanku Abdul Rahman has small interesting shops selling Asianware such as Chinese embroidery and antiques. The Globe Silk Store along this road has affordable clothes and textiles. Jalan Tuanku Abdul Rahman is closed to traffic every Saturday 5–10pm and transformed into a *pasar malam* (night market) with bargain goods hawked in stalls.

Jewellery, Indian saris and comfy cotton *kurta*-pyjamas are found behind this road in Masjid India. The famous and crowded Petaling Street *pasar malam* comes to life 5–11pm every evening, with a variety of stalls offering textiles, clothes, leather goods, jewellery, and "designer watches".

Out-of-town shopping malls are also worth a visit. Try Asia's biggest at the Mid Valley Mega Mall, and the trendy 1 Utama, in the suburb of the same name. Be warned though all KLs malls are packed on weekends.

Melaka

Jonker Street, once *the* place to shop in Melaka, has been a victim of money-driven urbanisation in recent years. Traditional craftsmen have been evicted and several historic shophouses have been demolished or else subject to sham restoration projects where only the facades are kept while the interiors been modified beyond recognition. Still, antique collectors and bargain-hunters will find what they want if they search hard enough. Authentic artefacts and relics, some over 300 years old, can be found along with a host of other more recent collectables.

Amid shops selling traditional crafts are trendy modern and creative handicraft shops such as the Orang Utan House at No. 59, run by an artist whose humorous T-shirts and artwork make great souvenirs. Wah Aik Shoemaker, formerly at No. 92, has unfortunately been demolished and moved to No. 103 Jalan Kubu, outside the main conservation area. This shop is famous for its tiny shoes made for Chinese women with bound feet, an ancient Chinese tradition of beauty that has long since died out.

Handicraft stalls are at Taman Merdeka, and there is a *pasar malam* on Sunday at Jalan Parameswara.

The city's biggest shopping mall

Antiques and Curios in Kuching

Shopping is a Kuching speciality. Antiques, Iban textiles, handicrafts, and quality collectables as well as pretty and interesting handcrafted souvenirs are readily available in what is perhaps the best antique market in Malaysia.

Walking down the Main Bazaar can take all day for a shopping enthusiast. Old trading houses and shophouses have been converted and restored into galleries and shops selling a range of goods.

Look out for Edric Ong's gallery with fine range of silk woven *pua* blankets, and scarves with authentic Iban motifs using natural dyes. Nelson's Gallery offers an eclectic collection – even if you don't buy, a meeting with this local character is a must. Margaret Tan (tel: 082-421 881 or 019-889 2181) no longer maintains her famous Galeri M at the Hilton but can be contacted for sales by appointment of fine textiles, beadwork and modern jewellery. Lucas Goh's Atelier opposite the Chinese History Museum is also filled with fine textiles and collectables, while Arts of Asia, in the Main Bazaar, has beautifully crafted wooden bowls, statues, and woodcarvings among its treasures. Richard Yong's Sarawak House has fine top-end pieces.

In addition there are several air-conditioned malls with lots of shops selling food, adventure gear and fashion items.

Don't miss Kuching's Sunday Market which starts on Saturday afternoon. Held at Jalan Satok, the market is filled with Bidayuh vegetable sellers, Chinese and Malay stalls selling all manner of handicrafts, jungle products, wild honey, pets, snacks and plants.

is the Mahkota Parade at Jalan Merdeka, which also has an Asian antique and handicraft centre.

Penang

Georgetown's maze of little shops around Jalan Penang are great for antiques and curios, such as antique clocks, old bronze and brassware, chinaware, Dutch ceiling lamps, old phonographs and Chinese embroideries and porcelain and batik. Saw Joo Aun at 139 Jalan Pintai Tali has a large range of antique furniture.

Elsewhere in Penang, Little India on Lebuh King and Lebuh Queen has brightly-coloured saris and *kurta* (mens' shirts), brassware and jewellery. Chulia Street has good second-hand bookshops.

Chowrasta Market specialises in all kinds of cotton, silk and other materials, as well as dried local foods such as nutmeg and preserved fruits.

More bargain-price Chinese souvenirs are at the Kek Lok Si Temple in Ayer Itam. Batu Ferringhi and Teluk Bahang have brightly-coloured, hand-painted batik sarongs and T-shirt souvenirs; the night market at the former sells fake but decent quality designer clothes and watches.

Modern shopping malls are at KOMTAR, Parkson and Gama on Jalan Penang, the Midlands Shopping Mall on Jalan Kelawei, the suburban Sunshine Square in Bayan Baru and Bukit Jambul Complex, which also has an ice-skating rink.

Terengganu

Jalan Bandar is the place to head for, with the Central Market selling batik and local handicraft.

Teratai Arts and Craft, at No. 151, is a lovely gallery/shop owned by renowned artist Chang Fee Ming. It showcases his depictions of local life, as well as curios from all over Asia, including coconut shell craft and textiles.

The Batik Gallery next to the Chinese temple has contemporary hand-printed batik cotton material and souvenirs as well as interesting clothing designs beyond the usual *kaftan* and shapeless shirts.

Out at the Chendering industrial area is the Noor Arfa batik factory, Malaysia's largest, which welcomes visitors to watch and even participate in batik production. There is an excellent showroom as well. Also out of town along the beachfront to Marang, at Rusila, are numerous batik and basketware shops, as well as vendors of the area's famous salted fish.

Kelantan

Like Terengganu, Kota Bharu's Central Market has copious amounts of batik and foodstuffs. The ultimate handicraft heaven is the road to PCB (Pantai Cahaya Bulan), along which certain *kampung* are renowned for their particular handicrafts – grab a Tourism Malaysia brochure.

But for a wonderful variety of arts and crafts closer to town nothing beats the Bazaar Buluh, opposite the Central Market, where four floors of tiny shops display the best array of batiks in the peninsula. There's everything from hand-painted lengths of silk to hand-stamped sarongs, tablecloths, and cushion covers.

Kota Kinabalu

Kota Kinabalu is more orientated towards adventure and relaxation than shopping. Several air-conditioned plazas have an array of shops selling locally-made clothes and some international brands.

Some handicraft shops can be found in the Wisma Karamunsing and the Wisma Merdeka where Borneo Books and Iwase Bookshop (ground floor) have some of the best range of books on the country. Borneo Handicraft has plenty of handicrafts but purists will find that most come from Bali.

The Handicraft Market offers Filipino handicrafts, basketware and shell crafts. But beware of pickpockets; there have been reports of bag-snatching. Borneo Trading Post in The Waterfront complex has quality handicrafts and souvenirs.

Sport

The country's national sport is football (soccer), but favourites include badminton, basketball, hockey, netball, table-tennis, tennis, squash, *sepak takraw* (a local game), fishing, bowling, volleyball, martial arts and golf. In regional and international competitions, Malaysia has tended to shine in badminton and bowling, with squash being a rising star. Sports development falls under voluntary organisations, many affiliated to the Olympic Council of Malaysia.

Fishing

Malaysia offers good fishing but the sport is not regulated or organised. Boats range from bare basics to converted trawlers, and unless you go with a tour, you have to bring your own equipment. Shops stock the range, but do not rent. Malaysia is a manufacturer of rods and reels and is, in fact, a good and relatively cheap place to buy fishing equipment. Fishing tackle shops are plentiful in all major towns.

Freshwater Fishing

Malaysia's fast-flowing rivers offer good fishing upstream, with smaller fish, but a more pristine rainforest environment, usually accessible via four-wheel drive and some walking. Good spots include upper Sungai Endau in Johor, and the higher reaches of rivers that flow into Kenyir (Terengganu) and Temenggor (Perak). Here, you get the *kelah* (Malaysia Mahseer), a good fighter with which locals usually practise catch-and-release, and *tengas*, which also make fun fishing. Bigger-sized *kelah* are found in the middle river, as are *kaloi* (giant gouramey), *belida* (giant featherback) and the powerful *toman* (giant snakehead), the so-called shark of Malaysian freshwater fish.

Rivers in Sarawak and Sabah are excellent fishing grounds, particularly near the Kalimantan border, but the distances are great, and they are difficult to get to.

Besides artificial lures, live and dead bait are used for *toman* while fruits such as oil palm and rubber seeds are used as *kelah* bait.

Lakes and reservoirs are where the other big freshwater fishing opportunities are. Since Malaysia has few natural ponds, anglers head for dammed lakes such as Kenyir and Temenggor. However, these are relatively "young", in that the eco-system is still not developed. The best fishing is where the rivers flow into the lakes bringing *toman* and *seberau*. The natural lakes of Cini and Bera in Pahang are shallow, but good for *toman*.

Saltwater Fishing

There are plenty of boats for hire on the coast. Most are basic, but a handful offer reasonable facilities. Nonetheless, some anglers find this primitiveness an attraction. Minimum numbers are needed before a boat will set off.

Deep-sea bottom fishing is expensive, but compared to other countries in the region, relatively affordable. This involves going out with a rod and line with one or two hooks, using bait such as small fish and prawns, and fishing at depths of 50–100 metres (150–300 ft).

Some locations could be up to 4 hours away. A 2-day/1-night trip can be arranged, including boat, ice and bait. Meals can also be arranged.

Anywhere along the peninsula's west coast is good for fishing all year round, including Bagan Datoh and Pangkor (Perak), and Langkawi (Kedah). Table fish are the norm, including *kerapu* (grouper) and *ikan merah* (red snapper). Sarawakian locations include Miri and Tanjung Datu near Kuching.

The peninsula's east coast is good for blue-water game fishing. A popular centre is Mersing, the jumping-off point to the islands of

Aur, Dayang and Pemanggil. Here you get black marlin, mackerel, sailfish, baraccuda, and giant trevally. Redang is another good location. In Sarawak, Miri is a centre; in Sabah, Labuan is good for bill fish, and Semporna and Sipadan are the spots for yellow fin tuna, great fighters that go up to 100 kg (220 lb). The best times for this sport are March–September.

Angling operators providing full facilities:

Cherry Bird Travel & Tours
29 Jalan Barat off Jalan Imbi
Tel: 03-2141 1399
Fax: 03-2141 3610
e-mail: cherryb@streamyx.com
Fishing Masters
22 Jalan SS22/3, Damansara Jaya
Tel/fax: 03-7725 2551
e-mail:
fishingmasters_my@yahoo.co.uk
Hook, Line & Sinker
43 Jalan SBCI, Taman Sri Batu Caves
Tel: 03-6188 9390
Fax: 03-6188 9392
www.hook-line-sinker.net

Martial Arts

Silat is the Malay equivalent of *kungfu*. Its origin is accredited to the famous Hang Tuah of old Melaka, who did not hesitate to draw his sword, and even to strike to kill, for the sake of justice. Though mystical and requiring fasting and meditation, youths today regard it as exercise in an artistic form. Demonstrations at weddings and other feasts are given to the rhythmic beat of gongs and drums. It is also part of the school curriculum for boys.

Tai chi is widely practised among older Chinese as a form of exercise, and dawn sees entire fields of people doing various forms of the art. Young Chinese, and indeed, urban Malaysians, favour *tae kwon do* and *karate*, and competitions are held regularly. The Indian traditional martial art form is *silamban*, which sees the use of long sticks.

It's also worth checking out the *Malay Mail* and angling magazines. Remember to ask about group sizes and facilities.

Golf

The golf boom in the late 1980s has made Malaysia a golfer's paradise, especially on the peninsula's west and south coasts. The courses are designed to exploit the natural landscape and offer something for all levels of golfers, amateur or professional.

Generally, clubs are private. However, the so-called "resort clubs" are open to anyone, especially in holiday destinations, where the playing traffic is low. Courses are generally of international standard and are well-maintained; equal care is taken in the design and facilities of club houses. Equipment of every brand can be hired, and bought at affordable prices. Updated lists of golf clubs and resorts plus descriptions can be found in the monthly *Golf Times* magazine; www.golftimes.com.my; and www.geocities.com/Augusta/4411/

Peninsular Malaysia
Staffield Country Resort
Negeri Sembilan
Tel: 03-8766 6177/8/9
Regarded as one of the country's best, this 27-hole course sits on 136 hectares (335 acres) of transformed rubber estate, with 82 bunkers and seven lakes. The Tudor-style club house offers food and a wide range of sports facilities.
Damai Laut Golf and Country Club
Perak
Tel: 05-618 1020
This 18-holer is a challenging course on an isolated landscaped coast, designed by the golf course architect Ronald Fream. There is a club house, and a professional golf trainer is available. The club has links with the Swiss Garden Resort, across from Pulau Pangkor.
Datai Bay Golf Club
Langkawi
Tel: 04-959 2700
A scenic, but tight 18-hole course

Horse Racing

Races are held at the weekend and on Wednesday, rotating between Kuala Lumpur, Ipoh, Penang and Singapore. There are at least eight races a day between 1.30pm and 6pm. A minimum bet is RM5. A racing guide book can be purchased at the entrance of the race course. Off-course betting is also available, where you watch the horses on TV.

between the Andaman Sea and the lush rainforest of Gunung Matcincang. The course lies uphill and downhill with some flat terrain. There is a club house and watersports facilities.

Desaru Golf and Country Resort
Johor
Tel: 07-822 2333
Famous old 18-hole course designed by Robert Trent Jones Jr, sitting in 120 hectares (300 acres) of forest along the coast; lovely all-wood club house with good views. It is linked to the Desaru Golden Beach Hotel.

Awana Golf and Country Resort
Pahang
Tel: 09-211 3015
At a cool 1,000 metres (3,000 ft) up in the Genting Highlands, this scenic 18-hole course is fairly demanding but enjoyable. Bunkers, ponds and streams add to the challenge. There is a three-tiered driving range.

Sarawak
Kelab Golf Sarawak
Kuching
Tel: 082-440 966
This championship 18-hole course is situated on converted secondary forest and swampland in Kuching, with ponds, sand traps and water hazards around the course's total of 36 undulating holes. The club house's terrace bar has a fine view of the course.

Damai Golf Course
Santubong
Tel: 082-846 088
A popular and accessible course

with full facilities adjacent to Damai beach and the resort hotels.

Sabah
Sabah Golf and Country Club
Kota Kinabalu
Tel: 088-247 533
A tricky 18-hole course with wide fairways and fast greens. The wind makes play even more interesting, especially during the monsoon months. Facilities include a swimming pool, gymnasium and karaoke lounge. Panoramic views.

Kinabalu Golf Club
Kota Kinabalu
Tel: 088-817 396
The 18-hole course is set high on the slopes of Mt Kinabalu with magnificent views and the greater comfort of cooler air.

Borneo Golf and Country Club
Km 69 Papar Beaufort Highway
Tel: 087-861 888
The two Nicklaus-designed courses at Bongawan, an hour's drive from Kota Kinabalu, offer excellent golf.

Dalit Bay Golf and Country Club, near Shangri-La's Rasa Ria Resort, about 45 minutes' drive from Kota Kinabalu, and the **Sutera Harbour Golf and Country Club** both offer smooth greens, sea views and a luxurious clubhouse.

Adventure Sports

Sport Diving
Dive operators are divided into on-site operators and those which arrange scheduled trips.

BSAC is offered only by East Marine (tel/fax: 04-966 5805/226 3032; www.eastmarine.com.my) in Langkawi and Lang Tengah, a professionally-run outfit with multilingual dive masters and instructors.

Most operations are dive shops with dive masters and instructors; a few are certified dive centres offering the full range, from retail to rental and equipment servicing. Retail outlets are usually in the city rather than on the beach.

Peninsular Malaysia
Kembara Station
Tel: 03-5635 2015

e-mail: enquiries@kembarastation.com
Focuses on diving in West Malaysia.
Dive Connection
Tel: 03-2141 0031
e-mail: simrr@pd.jaring.my
Operates anywhere in Malaysia. It has a dive shop in Redang.
Pacific Dome
Tel: 03-2770 5771
Fax: 03-2166 9672
www.pacificdome.com.my
Reputable company that offers tours and dive instruction anywhere in Malaysia, including Mabul, and to Manado, Indonesia.

Sabah
Among operators for scheduled trips, including instruction, are:
Borneo Divers
Tel: 088-222 226
www.borneodivers.info
Dive pioneer specialising in Sipadan, nearby Pulau Mabul and the Labuan wrecks. It can also handle trips to the peninsula's east coast (including underwater photography trips).
Layang Layang Island Resort
Tel: 03-2162 2877
Fax: 03-2162 2980
e-mail: layang@pop.jaring.my
www.layanglayang.com
The sole resort on an island 1 hour's flight west of Kota Kinabalu. World-class diving and a luxurious resort.
Pulau Sipadan Resort and Tours
Tel: 089-765 200
Fax: 089-763 575
www.sipadan-resort.com
These resorts run their own excellent dive centres on Sipadan, Pulau Kalapai (close to Sipadan) and on beautiful Pulau Lankayan situated to the northwest of Sandakan.

Sarawak
Although diving is not a sport normally associated with Sarawak, there is interesting diving off the coast of Miri.
Seridan Mulu Tours and Travel
Parkcity Everly Hotel
Tel: 085-414 300
Fax: 085-416 066
e-mail: info@tropical-dives.com
www.seridanmulu.com
Seridan Mulu Tours and Travel, a

well-known tour operator, has a Scuba Diving Division offering dives on the reefs within an hour or less of Miri.

Mountain Biking

Mountain Biking is a popular new sport to hit both Sabah and Sarawak.

Sarawak

Trails around rural areas outside Kuching, and near Damai Beach, are increasingly popular with many locals. For inexpensive bicycle rental and off-road cycling, contact **Power Action Cycles**, 64 Jalan Carpenter, tel: 013-808 6820 and 013-894 5123.

Sabah

Popular trails include rural areas around Kota Kinabalu. A good route is to bike down from Park headquarters on Mt Kinabalu to Tamparuli, passing through magnificent verdant vistas and undiscovered villages. Contact **TYK Adventure Tours**, tel: 088-720 826; e-mail: tykadto@tm.net.my.

Rock-climbing
Peninsular Malaysia
Nomad Adventure
Tel: 03-8024 5152
www.nomadadventure.com
This indoor rock climbing gym at a shopping centre in Kuala Lumpur organises trips to popular sites, runs special classes for women, and offers equipment for rent and sale.
Tracks Outdoor
Tel: 03-777 8363
e-mail: Tracks@mol.net.my
This operator has a 12-metre (39-ft) featured wall at Kuala Kubu Bahru with a slight overhang, suitable for all levels. Abseiling is conducted from 20–40-metre (60–120 ft) cliffs around its whitewater centre. Equipment can be hired and mountain bike trips arranged, too.

Whitewater Rafting
Peninsular Malaysia
Minimum numbers are required for whitewater rafting trips. Some

companies also arrange transport from the city.
Nomad Adventure
Tel: 03-8024 5152
www.nomadadventure.com
Specialises in whitewater kayaking and rafting in Sungai Sungkai and Sungai Kampar, Perak.

Sabah

Sabah has some of the country's best white-water with trips available to the scenic Kiulu and wild Padas rivers. Contact **Riverbug**; tel: 088-260 501; e-mail: sales@traverstours.com; www.traversetours.com.

Aerial Sightseeing
Sabah
Sabah Air
Tel: 088-256 733/252 372
www.sabahair.com.my
View Mount Kinabalu, Sandakan or other Sabah tourist destinations from a helicopter in unique half-to-one hour aerial sightseeing tours. Aerial tours are also available over Kuala Lumpur.

Peninsular Malaysia
Aerial Sports
Experimental Aircraft Association of Malaysia, Nusajaya Flight Park
Tel: 07-387 7411, 012-799 2529
www.ultralight.bizland.com
Offers lessons in flying and recreational hire of four types of parachute and winged aircraft, the largest variety of recreational flying machines in Malaysia. Also offers hangar space rentals and maintenance as well as introductory flight lessons. You can solo in a powered paraglider or parachute aircraft in as little as 6 hours.

Language

General

Bahasa Malaysia or BM (Malay) is spoken by all Malaysians, and although dialects differ regionally, the basic structure is the same. Adjectives always follow the noun. *Rumah* (house) and *besar* (big) together as *rumah besar* means "a big house" and so on.

When constructing a sentence, the order is subject-verb-subject: *Dia* (he) *makan* (eats) *nasi* (rice) *goreng* (fried). *Dia makan nasi goreng* = He eats fried rice.

The traditional greeting is *Apa khabar*? – literally "What news?" but is the equivalent of "How are you?" to which the reply is *Khabar baik* – "I'm fine." Today, the ubiquitous "Hello!" or "Hi!" serve the same purpose. Here are some general pronunciation guidelines.

a as in c*a*r. *apa* – what; *makan* – eat

ai as in *ai*sle. *kedai* – shop; *sungai* – river

au as in h*ow*. *pulau* – island; *jauh* – far

c as in *ch*at. *capal* – sandal; *cinta* – love

e as in *ea*rly. *membeli* – to buy; *besar* – big

g as in *g*o, and not *g*em. *pergi* – go; *guru* – teacher

gg as in sin*g*le. *ringgit* – Malaysian dollar; *tetangga* – household

h as in *h*alt. *mahal* – expensive; *murah* – cheap

i as in f*ee*t. *minum* – to drink; *lagi* – again

j as in *j*udge. *jalan* – street; *juta* – million

ng as in sin*g*ing. *sangat* – very; *bunga* – flower

ny as in o*ni*on. *minyak* – petrol/oil; *banyak* – a lot

o as in h*o*p. *orang* – people; *tolong* – help
u as in p*oo*l. *ukiran* – carving; *minum* – to drink

Although nearly all syllables are given equal stress, sometimes the final syllable of a word is emphasised, especially the last word in an utterance. This has led to the widespread use of the appendage *-lah* to the important word, whose purpose is purely emphatic. However, *-lah* is also liberally used in English; for instance, you could get thrown a "*Cannot-lah!*", when you are trying to bargain.

Useful Phrases

Good morning *Selamat pagi*
Good afternoon *Selamat tengah hari*
Good evening *Selamat petang*
Good-bye *Selamat tinggal*
Yes *Ya*
No *Tidak*
Thank you *Terima kasih*
Please come in *Sila masuk*
Please sit down *Sila duduk*
Thank you very much *Terima kasih banyak-banyak*
You're welcome *Sama-sama*
Where do you come from? *Asal dari mana?*
I come from... *Saya datang dari...*
What is your name? *Siapa nama anda?*
My name is... *Nama saya...*
Can you speak Bahasa Malaysia? *Boleh anda bercakap Bahasa Malaysia?*
Only a little *Sedikit sahaja*
Do you like Malaysia? *Suka tak Malaysia?*
I like it here *Saya suka berada di sini*
Where are you going? *(Pergi) ke mana?*
I am going to... *Saya pergi ke...*
Turn right *Belok (ke) kanan*
Turn left *Belok (ke) kiri*
Go straight *Jalan terus*
Please stop here *Sila berhenti di sini*
How much? *Berapa harga?*
That's too expensive *Mahal sangat*

Can you reduce the price? *Boleh kurang?*
Wait a minute *Tunggu sekejap*
I would like to change money *Saya hendak tukar duit*
Excuse me *Maafkan saya/Maaf*
Could I make an enquiry? *Tumpang tanya?*
Where is the toilet? *Di mana tandas?*
In the back *Di belakang*
Over there *Di sana*
Over here *Di sini*
What time is it? *Jam berapa?*
One-thirty or half-one *Pukul satu setengah*
What time does the bus leave? *Pukul berapa bas bertolak?*

Useful words

Mr *Encik, Tuan*
Mrs *Puan*
Miss *Cik*
(When you address an older Malay man, you may call him *pakcik*, and a lady, *makcik*. Non-Malays may be addressed as "Uncle" and "Auntie" respectively. Someone obviously younger and children are addressed as *adik*)
I *saya*
you (to someone the same age or younger) *awak*, *anda* or *kita* (in Borneo Malaysia only)
you (formal) *encik*
he, she *dia*
we *kami* (excluding the speaker), *kita* (including the speaker)
they *mereka*
what? *apa?*
who? *siapa?*
where (place) *di mana?*
where (direction) *ke mana?*
when? *bila?*
how? *bagaimana?*
why? *mengapa?*
which? *yang mana?*

to eat *makan*
to drink *minum*
to sleep *tidur*
to bathe *mandi*
to come *datang*
to go *pergi*
to stop *berhenti*
to buy *beli* (*membeli*)
to sell *jual* (*menjual*)
road, walk *jalan*

airport *lapangan terbang*
post office *pejabat pos*
shop *kedai*
coffeeshop *kedai kopi*
money *wang, duit*
minute *minit*
hour *jam*
day *hari*
week *minggu*
Monday *Isnin*
Tuesday *Selasa*
Wednesday *Rabu*
Thursday *Khamis*
Friday *Jumaat*
Saturday *Sabtu*
Sunday *Ahad*

Numbers

1 *satu*
2 *dua*
3 *tiga*
4 *empat*
5 *lima*
6 *enam*
7 *tujuh*
8 *lapan*
9 *sembilan*
10 *sepuluh*
11 *sebelas*
12 *dua belas*
13 *tiga belas*
20 *dua puluh*
21 *dua puluh satu*
22 *dua puluh dua*

30 *tiga puluh*
40 *empat puluh*

100 *seratus*
263 *dua ratus enam puluh tiga*
1,000 *seribu*

Further Reading

Bookshops

The major book chains in Malaysia are Times, MPH and Popular, while specialist bookstores are found mainly in Kuala Lumpur.

A rich repository of Sarawakian, Borneon and Asian published work is the Sarawak Museum in Kuching. Another excellent bookshop sits within the Holiday Inn Kuching. Small but good collections of nature books, including specialist titles, can be bought at the Kuala Lumpur headquarters of the Malaysian Nature Society (MNS) (tel: 03-287 9422) and the World Wide Fund for Nature (WWF) Malaysia (tel: 03-703 3772).

There are decent maps of the country, including road maps, for sale in Kuala Lumpur; more detailed state maps can be found in the respective states.

Vision KL and *KL Lifestyle* are two monthly information magazines with useful "what's-happening" listings.

History/Political

A History of Malaya, by Barbara Watson Andaya and Leonard Andaya, Macmillan London (1982). Non-colonial objective interpretation of the country's development.

The Golden Chersonese: the Malayan Travels of Victorian Lady, by Isabella Bird, Oxford University Press Singapore (1883), reprinted. Lyrical 19th-century impressions of the experiences of this intrepid traveller.

Government and Society In Malaysia, by Harold Crouch, Allen & Unwin Australia (1996). An insider's view from an outsider on Malaysian politics, founding his analysis on the fact that Malaysian politics and society operates essentially on the basis of a "moving equilibrium".

The Malay Dilemma, by Mahathir Mohamad, Malaysia (1970). Important text that outlines the prime minister's thoughts on the country's racial politics and economics; recent books by him have been compilations of his speeches and policies.

Malaysia's Political Economy, by Edmund Terence Gomez & Jomo K.S., Cambridge University Press (1997). An insightful and accessible analysis of contemporary Malaysian business and politics, examining through detailed case studies political patronage on wealth accumulation, and policies and their consequences.

Malaysian Journey, by Rehman Rashid, Malaysia (1993). A witty, sharp treatise on contemporary Malaysia, though somewhat dogmatic.

Malay Society: Transformation and Democratisation, by Khoo Kay Kim, Malaysia (1992). The study of Malay society from the Melaka Sultanate to the 1990s, by one of the country's most prominent historians.

Paradoxes of Mahathirism: An Intellectual Biography of Mahathir Mohamad, by Khoo Boo Teik, Oxford University Press (1995). Like all books on the prime minister, this takes an academic approach to his ideas on nationalism, capitalism, Islam, populism, and authoritarianism – the core of Mahathirism.

General

The Crafts of Malaysia, Dato' Haji Sulaiman Othman, Yeoh Jin Leng, etc, Archipelago Press, Singapore (1994). A beautiful documentary of the development of the Malay arts in a changing society, with pictures of the best craft from museums and private collections.

Cuzinhia Cristang: A Malacca-Portuguese Cookbook, by Celine J. Marbeck, Tropical Press, Malaysia. A lovely collection of six centuries of the food of the Melaka-Portuguese Cristang people.

An Eastern Port and Other Stories: More Recollections of Singapore

and Malaya, by Julian Davison, Topographica (2004). A second collection of sketches and anecdotes drawn from the memory of an English expatriate who grew up in Singapore and Malaysia in the 1950s and 1960s.

The Encyclopedia of Malaysia, Editions Didier Millet, Malaysia (1998). A highly-illustrative topic-categorised presentation of Malaysiana from early history and architecture to plants, arts, literature and economics.

The Food of Malaysia, edited by Wendy Hutton, Periplus Editions, Singapore (1995). Handy-sized collection of local recipes with nice background information and lovely colour photographs.

Kuala Lumpur – A Sketchbook, by Chin Kon Yit, and Chen Voon Fee, Archipelago Press, Singapore (1998). Beautiful watercolour paintings of old Kuala Lumpur with suitably brief captions.

Lat, Malaysia, Times Publishing. Compilations of the work of the country's sharpest and funniest cartoonist; hilarious depictions of Malaysian life and psyche.

One for the Road and Other Stories: Recollections of Singapore and Malaya by Julian Davison, Topographica (2001). Autobiographical vignettes based on the life of an English child during the bygone era of Singapore and Malaysia in the 1950s and 1960s.

Rasa Malaysia, by Betty Yew, Times Publishing, Malaysia. A collection of Malaysia's best-loved recipes by a leading chef and writer of cookbooks.

Culture Shock! Malaysia, by Heidi Munan, Graphic Arts Center Pub Co. (1991). A witty and invaluable treatise on Malaysian customs, can-do's and absolutely-nots.

Natural History

Beaches of Malaysia, The Department of Irrigation and Drainage, Malaysia and Design Dimension Sdn Bhd, (1997). The first comprehensive photographic record of more than 168 beaches, illustrating their moods and beauty.

National Parks of Malaysia, by WWF Malaysia, New Holland,

Malaysia (1998). Pictorial, tourist-market coffee-table book, with an excellent bibliography.

Photographic Guide to the Birds of Peninsular Malaysia and Singapore, by M. Strange, and A. Jeyarajasingham, Malaysia (1993).

Pocket Guide to the Birds of Borneo, by Sabah Society with WWF Malaysia, Malaysia (1995).

A Diver's Guide to Underwater Malaysia Macrolife, by Andrea Ferrari and Antonella Ferrari, Nautilus (2003). This volume is illustrated with more than 800 colour photographs and describes in full detail 600 different Indo-Pacific marine species, focusing on those found in the South China, Sulu and Sulawesi seas.

Wild Malaysia: The Wildlife and Scenery of Peninsular Malaysia, Sarawak and Sabah, by Junaidi Payne, Gerald Cubitt (photographer), MIT Press (1990), World Wide Fund for Nature. A pictorial introduction containing 400 colour photographs of animals and habitats. The text, by a leading Malaysian environmentalist, examines conservation and development, as well as peoples and natural history.

Fiction/Biography

Lord Jim, by Joseph Conrad, Penguin, London (1900). The tale of an Englishman who abandons his ship and hides in Malaya eventually becoming a Lord. Conrad set many other stories in the Malay Archipelago, including *Victory: an Island Tale* and *The Rescue*.

Maugham's Malaysian Stories, by Somerset Maugham (1933, reprinted 1986). Masterful story-telling of British colonial life in the country.

Among the White Moon Faces: An Asian-American Memoir of Homelands (Cross-Cultural Memoir Series) by Shirley Geok-Lin Lim, Feminist Press (1996). A biographical recount of a Malaysian childhood and later life in the United States; the author has also published short stories.

Borneo

Travel

Into The Heart Of Borneo, by Redmond O' Hanlon, The Salamander Press (1984). A heartwarmingly and laugh-aloud treatise on O'Hanlon's hilarious expedition to Borneo, told with great sympathy and style.

Stranger In The Forest, by Eric Hanson (*out of print*). A gripping and sometimes chilling tale of one man's adventures as he learns the ways of the tribal folk during his solitary wander through the forest.

World Within, by Tom Harrisson, Oxford University Press Singapore (1986). A classic story by the man who later became curator of Sarawak Museum tells of Bario's Kelabit Highlands during the Japanese occupation years of World War II.

History/Culture

Sarawak Crafts – Methods and Motifs, by Heidi Munan, Oxford University Press (1989). Written by a Sarawak expert, this small book is filled with a wealth of information.

Sarawak Style, by Edric Ong, Times Editions Singapore (1996). Well-photographed book examining style in the Sarawak way.

Natural Man, by Charles Hose, Oxford University Press Singapore (1988). A reprint of a 1912 study by one of Sarawak's colonial administrators under Rajah Charles Brooke.

Enchanted Gardens of Kinabalu, by Susan M. Phillipps, Natural History Publications (Borneo), Malaysia (1995). A beautiful book of botanical paintings that include coral gardens, too.

The Malay Archipelago, by Alfred Russel Wallace (1869). A classic tale of a Victorian naturalist who spent several years wandering through the archipelago. He was also instrumental in assisting in the setting up of Sarawak Museum and his theories on evolution coincided with those of Darwin.

Online Information

For newsgroups, there's nothing like soc.culture.Malaysia, although you will have to wade through the usual diarrhoea. There are numerous discussion, news- and travel-sites on Malaysia. Try Malaysian search engine Malaysia Search: www.cari.com.my

Useful Websites

News: www.thestar.com.my
www.malaysiakini.com
www.freeanwar.com
Malaysiana: Malaysia Homepage, www.mymalaysia.net.my
Tourism Malaysia, www.tourism.gov.my
Sarawak Tourism: www.sarawaktourism.com
Sabah Tourism: www.sabahtourism.com

ART & PHOTO CREDITS

S.T. Amerasinghe 226
Amri/HBL Network 75
H. Berbar/HBL Network back cover
left top and bottom, 31, 37, 46,
85, 87, 89, 90/91, 110, 114, 150,
174, 215, 217L/R, 221, 223, 224,
225T, 299, 300, 306, 333
Dr Hans-Ulrich Bernard 267
S. Blanchet/HBL Network 149
David Bowden 71, 331
Marcus Brooke 143T, 173, 189,
236/237, 238, 242, 246, 249,
252, 258, 321
A. Buu/HBL Network 58
Frank Castle 24
C.L. Chan 326T
Wendy Chan 93, 279, 280, 283,
283T
Tommy Chang 335T
Alain Compost 52/53, 56, 167,
326
Robert Condrum 77
V. Couarraze/HBL 126/127
Alain Evrard 10/11, 57, 61, 66L,
142R, 200, 210/211
E. Fearn/HBL Network 14
K. Fletcher 270
Flyright Air-Sport 241
Jill Gocher front flap bottom, back
cover right bottom, spine bottom, 1,
2/3, 2B, 66R, 72/73, 104R, 111,
166, 180/181, 187, 192, 193,
194L, 205L, 217T, 255, 262, 268,
274, 281T, 282, 285, 286, 287,
288, 292, 293, 296, 297, 298,
298T, 301, 302, 304, 305L/R,
307, 315, 315T, 316, 317T, 318,
322T, 329, 332, 336, 338, 339,
341, 342, 343
Manfred Gottschalk 95, 135, 136,
171L, 197, 202
Grunau/HBL Network 244
Francisco Guerrero 231
Hans Hayden 228
HBL Network 48, 97, 141, 219T
Dallas & John Heaton 140, 190R
Hendrick/HBL Network 122
Hans Höfer 5B, 6/7, 21, 23, 27, 29,
30, 62/63, 69, 169, 172T, 178,
277, 281, 290, 320, 322, 324
Jack Hollingsworth 68, 78L/R,
329T

J. Houyvet/HBL Network 108/109
Wendy Hutton 319T
Jati/HBL Network 19, 50, 51
Ingo Jezierski 79, 88, 134T, 139T,
179T, 186T, 188T, 190T, 193T,
196T, 198T, 202T, 204T, 220,
221T, 222T, 225, 231T, 252T
Jungle War in Malaya 41, 42
Yap Piang Kian 120/121, 142L,
170, 203, 204
Anthea Lamb 162, 325
David Lane 255T
Max Lawrence 45, 152
Alan Lee 191
R. Lendrum 284
Philip Little 32R, 59, 185, 188,
190L, 194R, 205R, 229, 245, 313
Joseph Lynch 74, 76, 84,
100/101, 134, 156, 209T, 232,
253, 257, 266, 323
Malaysian Industrial Development
Authority 47
Malaysian Nature Society 235
R. Margaillan/HBL Network back
flap top, 60, 115, 243, 251, 335,
340
Richard Maschmeyer 247
Gloria Maschmeyer 105, 248
R. Mohd. Noh 4BR, 20, 22, 28, 81,
103, 106, 107L/R, 138, 143, 144,
144T, 146, 151, 163, 177T, 201,
207, 207T, 222, 230, 233, 249T,
264, 344
Reg Monison 96
Museu Militar, Lisbon 26
Muzium Negara, Malaysia 16/17,
18, 25, 34L/R, 35L, 38, 40, 43
National Archives, Singapore 33
Navaro/HBL Network 208, 263,
310, 337
Frank Newman 244T
Helen Newman 340T
R.C.A. Nichols 172
Private Archives 35R, 44

Photobank Singapore 32L, 55, 80,
92, 94, 214, 259
Picture Library/KL 64, 128, 147
G.P. Reichelt 8/9, 65, 70, 133, 291
David Ryan 148
D. Saulnier/HBL Network 160
Ruth Seitz 199
Hugh Sitton/Tony Stone Images
cover, 3B
S. Sreedharan 334
The Straits Times, Singapore 39
Morten Strange 269, 272/273,
289, 303
Larry Tackelt 330
Arthur Teng front flap top, back
cover right top, back cover centre
top, 4/5, 12/13, 49, 67, 82/83,
86, 102, 104L, 116/117,
118/119, 137, 139, 140T, 145,
153, 154/155, 161T, 164, 165,
170T, 175, 195, 196, 209, 212,
219, 227, 254, 278T, 291T,
308/309, 317, 319, 327
Albert Teo 304T
Trade Development Corp. of
Malaysia 159
Gorazd Vilhar 165T
Bill Wassman 132, 137T, 168,
171R, 250, 256
Westfries Museum, Hoorn 36
S.L. Wong back cover centre
bottom, 4BL, 113, 176, 177, 179,
198, 234, 235T, 258T, 265L/R,
268T, 271, 301T
Yeoh Thean Yeow 161
Joseph Yogerst 54
Chan Yuen-Li 112, 328

Picture Spreads

Pages **98/99** *All pictures by:*
R. Mohd. Noh.
Pages **182/183** *All pictures by:*
R. Mohd. Noh.
Pages **260/261** *All pictures by:*
R. Mohd. Noh.
Pages **294/295** *All pictures by:*
Jill Gocher.

Map Production Colourmap
Scanning Ltd
© 2005 Apa Publications GmbH & Co.
Verlag KG (Singapore branch)

INSIGHT GUIDE
Malaysia

Cartographic Editor **Zoë Goodwin**
Production **Caroline Low**
Design Consultants
Carlotta Junger, Graham Mitchener
Picture Research **Hilary Genin**

Index

Numbers in italics refer to photographs

INSIGHT GUIDES

The classic series that puts you in the picture

Alaska
Amazon Wildlife
American Southwest
Amsterdam
Argentina
Arizona & Grand Canyon
Asia's Best Hotels & Resorts
Asia, East
Asia, Southeast
Australia
Austria
Bahamas
Bali & Lombok
Baltic States
Bangkok
Barbados
Barcelona
Beijing
Belgium
Belize
Berlin
Bermuda
Boston
Brazil
Brittany
Bruges, Ghent & Antwerp
Brussels
Buenos Aires
Burgundy
Burma (Myanmar)
Cairo
California
California, Southern
Canada
Cape Town
Caribbean
Caribbean Cruises
Channel Islands
Chicago
Chile
China
Colorado
Continental Europe
Corsica
Costa Rica
Crete
Croatia
Cuba
Cyprus
Czech & Slovak Republic
Delhi, Jaipur & Agra
Denmark

Dominican Rep. & Haiti
Dublin
East African Wildlife
Eastern Europe
Ecuador
Edinburgh
Egypt
England
Finland
Florence
Florida
France
France, Southwest
French Riviera
Gambia & Senegal
Germany
Glasgow
Gran Canaria
Great Britain
Great Gardens of Britain
   & Ireland
Great Railway Journeys
   of Europe
Great River Cruises:
   Europe & the Nile
Greece
Greek Islands
Guatemala, Belize
   & Yucatán
Hawaii
Hong Kong
Hungary
Iceland
India
India, South
Indonesia
Ireland
Israel
Istanbul
Italy
Italy, Northern
Italy, Southern
Jamaica
Japan
Jerusalem
Jordan
Kenya
Korea
Laos & Cambodia
Las Vegas
Lisbon
London

Los Angeles
Madeira
Madrid
Malaysia
Mallorca & Ibiza
Malta
Mauritius Réunion
   & Seychelles
Mediterranean Cruises
Melbourne
Mexico
Miami
Montreal
Morocco
Moscow
Namibia
Nepal
Netherlands
New England
New Mexico
New Orleans
New York City
New York State
New Zealand
Nile
Normandy
North American &
   Alaskan Cruises
Norway
Oman & The UAE
Oxford
Pacific Northwest
Pakistan
Paris
Peru
Philadelphia
Philippines
Poland
Portugal
Prague
Provence
Puerto Rico
Rajasthan
Rio de Janeiro
Rome

Russia
St Petersburg
San Francisco
Sardinia
Scandinavia
Scotland
Seattle
Shanghai
Sicily
Singapore
South Africa
South America
Spain
Spain, Northern
Spain, Southern
Sri Lanka
Sweden
Switzerland
Sydney
Syria & Lebanon
Taipei
Taiwan
Tanzania & Zanzibar
Tenerife
Texas
Thailand
Tokyo
Toronto
Trinidad & Tobago
Tunisia
Turkey
Tuscany
Umbria
USA: The New South
USA: On The Road
USA: Western States
US National Parks: West
Utah
Venezuela
Venice
Vienna
Vietnam
Wales
Walt Disney World/Orlando
Washington, DC

INSIGHT GUIDES

The world's largest collection of visual travel guides & maps